7/24/89

To Miriam —
Friend and colleague — I hope you
enjoy reading the book

Herb

//
Librarians and the Awakening from Innocence

Librarians and the Awakening from Innocence

A Collection of Papers by
HERBERT S. WHITE

G.K. HALL & CO. • BOSTON, MASSACHUSETTS

Librarians and the Awakening from Innocence:
A Collection of Papers by Herbert S. White

Herbert White

Copyright 1989
by G.K. Hall & Co.
70 Lincoln Street
Boston, Massachusetts 02111

All rights reserved.

No part of this book may be reproduced without
the written permission of the publisher.

Library of Congress Cataloging-in-Publication Data

White, Herbert S.
   Librarians and the awakening from innocence : a collection of
papers / by Herbert S. White.
     p. cm.

(Professional Librarian Series)
    Includes index.
    ISBN 0-8161-1892-2
   1. Librarians. 2. Library science. 3. Information science.
  4. Information scientists. 5. Librarians—Professional ethics.
  6. Information scientists—Professional ethics. I. Title.
Z682.W645   1989
020'.92'2—dc19   88-32652
                                                                        CIP

Dedicated to My Wife, Virginia

Without whose constant support, encouragement, understanding, and wise counsel throughout a career marked by geographic and professional change, which is inevitably disruptive to home and family values, none of what follows would have been possible.

CONTENTS

Foreword by Beverly P. Lynch	ix
Introduction	xiii

Education and Training   1

Impact of the Increase in Library Doctorates (with Karen N. Momenee)	7
Accreditation and the Pursuit of Excellence	20
Defining Basic Competencies	31
Continuing Education: Myth and Reality	43
Employer Preferences and the Library Education Curriculum (with Marion Paris)	51
The Future of Library and Information Science Education	84
Generalization versus Specialization in the MLS	93
The Unity of the Library Profession	98

The Internal and External Political Process   103

Toward Professionalism	109
Organizational Placement of the Industrial Special Library: Its Relationship to Success and Survival	117
Management: A Strategy for Change	123
Special Libraries and the Corporate Political Process	145
Library Turf	154
Participative Management Is the Answer, but What Was the Question?	159
Respect for Librarians and Librarian Self-Respect	165

Public Libraries and the Political Process	171
The Trivialization of National Library Week	179
Catalogers—Yesterday, Today, Tomorrow	184
Entrepreneurship and the Library Profession	189
Oh, Where Have All the Leaders Gone?	207
How to Cope with an Incompetent Supervisor	213
Managing Libraries and the Societal Moral Good	222
Library Operations and the Library User	**227**
Growing User Information Dependence and Its Impact on the Library Field	233
Factors in the Decision by Individuals and Libraries to Place or Cancel Subscriptions to Scholarly and Research Journals	247
Ownership Is Not Always Availability: Borrowing May Not Satisfy Access Needs	270
The Use and Misuse of Library User Studies	281
The Other Barriers to Information Access	288
Interlibrary Loan: An Old Idea in a New Setting	293
The Several Faces of Librarianship	299
The Role of Information in the Modern Age	304
Economic Issues	**313**
Publishers, Libraries, and Costs of Journal Subscriptions in Times of Funding Retrenchment	319
Cost-Effectiveness and Cost-Benefit Determinations in Special Libraries	340
Why Don't We Get Paid More?	348
Differential Pricing	354
The Funding of Corporate Libraries: Old Myths and New Problems	358
Scholarly Publishers and Libraries: A Strained Marriage	367
What Price Salami? The Federal Process of Contracting Out Libraries	372
Index	377
About the Author	381

FOREWORD

Herbert S. White, Dean of the School of Library and Information Science, Indiana University, is a prolific and provocative author who has given much practical advice to American librarians. He has done more to shape consideration of the wide range of issues related to education for the profession and the management of libraries than anyone else writing today. Not afraid to speak his mind, White regularly provokes, nags, cajoles, and needles readers of his *Library Journal* column, "The White Papers," into thinking along the lines he proposes.

White describes himself as an educator who once was a practitioner rather than a practitioner who now is an educator. He does not think of himself as a researcher. Nevertheless, the findings of his numerous surveys are disquieting for the field both as it is practiced and as it is taught. The discussions of the results of his studies are remarkable for their insights into the future of librarianship.

Included in this book are several of White's important analyses of library education, education for librarianship having occupied much of his attention since his appointment to the faculty of Indiana University in 1975. The selections in this book also reflect his consuming interest in library management, his concern for the state of the profession as it is practiced, the interrelationship between education and practice, issues pertaining to library economics and costs, and how librarians view themselves as library managers.

The first paper in this book, "Impact of the Increase in Library Doctorates," reports the results of a survey of those receiving doctoral degrees in library science between 1930 and 1975. While the numbers of doctoral degrees granted have doubled in each decade since the 1950s, White found the majority of the jobs requiring the Ph.D. to be in library education, the trend in administrative posts in research libraries having moved away from the doctorate. A disquieting conclusion in this paper is that the increased numbers of doctorates have not resulted in an increase in the quantity or quality of library research. Further, nearly 25 percent of the respondents reported no interest in doing research unless required to do so. The results of this survey have influenced much of White's thinking about library science education, particularly in terms of the criteria used in accepting candidates into Ph.D. programs, the values that are stressed in those programs, and the requirements that are imposed.

The paper White published in 1975 with Marion Paris, "Employer Preferences and the Library Education Curriculum," offers evidence on the question of whether librarianship as it is practiced is an homogeneous profession. The results reported in the White and Paris paper demonstrate clearly that the type-of-library is a strong determinant—at least in the attitudes of the profession—about what should be taught in library school. White continues to pursue this theme in the paper, "The Unity of the Library Profession," in which he addresses the matter of the educational qualifications for school librarianship and the role of the National Council for Accreditation of Teacher Education (NCATE) in the accreditation for librarianship as practiced in school libraries. White remains firm in his resolve that regardless of the setting in which the librarian works, all fully qualified librarians must meet the educational standards designed in the professional accreditation process controlled by librarians. How the educational standards are translated into curriculum design or core course requirements are questions still before us.

White also is firm that librarianship as it is practiced must take the lead in the process of accreditation. The responsibility for accreditation has been assigned to the American Library Association (ALA), "primarily the society of practitioners," to quote White, not to the Association of Library and Information Science Education (ALISE), "the society of educators." Accreditation, says White, will mean something only if the practicing librarians care and pay attention to the standards for library education.

Each reader of "The White Papers" column will look for his or her favorite piece. Is it "Library Turf," one of the widely cited papers? or, "Oh, Where Have All the Leaders Gone?" or "Participative Management is the Answer, But What was the Question?" An example of the useful—and quotable—insights gained from reading White's work comes from one of the many papers not included here.

> One of the least attractive management styles, but one frequently practiced in bureaucratic environments, is called negation through the creation of impenetrable obstacles. The practitioner of this approach gains the advantage of never having to approve anything, while at the same time appearing to be positive and favorable. He simply keeps raising more questions and concerns until the subordinate ultimately gets discouraged and goes away. (Herbert S. White, "The Library Education Accreditation Process: A Retreat

From Insistence on Excellence." *Library Journal,* November 15, 1980, 2380)

White reads widely in the management literature and often quotes from the work of Peter Drucker, a long-time student of the management of public service organizations. Building on Drucker and adding insights of his own, White gives us valuable instruction in how to manage our libraries.

White does not hesitate to disagree with the conventional wisdom of the day. He says without hesitation, in the paper on "The Use and Misuse of Library User Studies," for example, that such studies are not worth much. A typical result of such studies, says White, is that "users ask for the services they get and get the library services for which they ask." Little improvement in service comes from such surveys. White's logic is persuasive.

To have in one volume selections from Herbert White's writings and investigations, provides a collection of thoughtful, penetrating, and disquieting papers on the important concerns before American librarianship. This book is a distinguished contribution to the literature of the profession.

Beverly P. Lynch
University Librarian
University of Illinois at Chicago

INTRODUCTION

Selecting and deselecting material for this volume from well over 100 research and exhortative articles allows me the opportunity to reflect on both the development of and changes in my philosophical approach to my profession. Unlike virtually all of the students with whom I now come into contact, I came to my own library education with no predispositions and no imprinting. I had been a user of both public and academic libraries as an undergraduate student, for pleasure in the first instance and as the result of class assignments in the second. I recall no interaction with professional librarians in either setting, although I do remember having to disguise my purpose to be allowed to use public library resources for my college work, something I occasionally sought to do because the college library was a ninety-minute subway ride from home. I do not even remember whether or not my high school had a library. My extracurricular activities meant that I never had a study hall period, and I gained the clear impression that "assignment" to the library was as a punishment, for slow students, or for those who had nothing better to do and needed to be occupied. I realize now that such a generalized perception is unfair, but it is nevertheless what I remember. My attraction to librarianship came from the realization in my undergraduate studies in chemistry that there appeared to be almost no basis for communication between librarians and chemists. All in the first group whom I encountered knew nothing about chemistry, and chemists had not the faintest idea of how to use a library. It occurred to me that there was a potential in bridging this gap, and Dean Wharton Miller at Syracuse encouraged me in pursuing that idea, and let me know gently somewhat later that I was not really the first to have thought of it.

My academic preparation as a librarian was followed by twenty-five years of increasingly responsible experience as a librarian, a library manager, and ultimately as an executive in governmental and corporate activities that were no longer called libraries but certainly looked like them to me. During that time I became active in professional societies and government advisory bodies at both the national and international level, and I began to write and speak about the issues that concerned me then, many of which still concern me today. Like most individuals with operational and administrative responsibilities that seemed to demand my days, evenings, and weekends, finding time to write was difficult.

In 1975 Dean Bernard Fry invited me to join the faculty of what was then the Graduate Library School at Indiana University as a professor, and I have remained at this institution. Since 1980, after the administrative retirement of Professor Fry, I have served as dean of what is now called, after the prevailing fashion, the School of Library and Information Science. This sudden and until then unexpected and unplanned career change opened new opportunities for me. It introduced me to an environment in which I could teach, and share ideas and attempt to stimulate students to a critical reevaluation of what we do and why we do it. I do the same thing through workshops and seminars for practicing librarians, whom we in academia call practitioners, but it has long been my conviction that our best opportunity for change comes through the new librarians we are now educating. Bernard Fry undoubtedly knew that when he thought I might be interested in making such a sudden and drastic professional career change. My academic post encourages me to write, and most of the material contained in this book was written since my assumption of academic duties. At the same time, I have been a practicing librarian, and particularly a special librarian, far too long to stop thinking like one.

The arrangement of the content of this volume into four separate sections serves as a reasonable convenience, but in truth the designations are not mutually exclusive and could even be considered arbitrary. All of my writings stem from a number of observations about my profession that are of long-standing. The first is that our success as librarians comes far more from what we are able to convince others to do in supporting our efforts than in what we are able to accomplish by "dedication," most specifically by working longer unpaid hours at lower salaries. The second is the conviction that it is we as professionals who must ultimately determine what good library service represents, and that we cannot simply respond to what users tell us they want. What they say they want is not necessarily what they ought to want, and may not even be close to what they need, when we remember that their expectations are preconditioned by prior experience and by our constant and shrill insistence that we are too poor and too busy to do more. I am convinced that users can perhaps differentiate between a large library and a small one, but not between a good one and a poor one. Ultimately, they will accept a poor library and even consider it good. Even when, as in academia, they demand a "good" library, they define good in terms of large quantities of material for self-service, and they are not certain of what role librarians play in the process except for the clerical routines they all recognize.

My profession's unwillingness to stake a claim to professional and unique expertise in a whole range of settings—in academic libraries in dealing with faculty, in corporate libraries in dealing with scientists and economists, in school libraries in dealing with teachers—continues to depress me. The results show up in a variety of ways, in the appointment of nonlibrarians to head major research libraries and in specifications for a White House Conference that insure that while we may instruct the participants as to the issues, it is they who will decide our priorities and directions.

All of this uncovers a number of traps that Peter Drucker, without once referring directly to librarianship, has described for us quite accurately. We are measured not by what we do but by how much we spend, and we accept the responsibility for doing whatever needs to be done whether or not there are funds. When even that fails, we pretend that it did not need to be done in the first place. We know that the essence of management communication is exception reporting, telling our nonlibrarian bosses not just what went well (it is human nature to report this) but what went badly, or what did not happen at all. It follows from this that our managers who control our funds must take responsibility for the funding decisions they made, and for the poor library service that may result. None of this happens very often in libraries, and a reading of annual reports will give little if any indication of festering problems with which higher level managers must deal. Instead, we rationalize that we cannot offer services for which we do not have committed funds on an ongoing basis, thereby assuring that we will never have the money. We even go so far as to excuse our funding bodies for their poor support of libraries and of librarian salaries by agreeing that this is all they can afford. When we say this we ignore Drucker's injunction that price is almost irrelevant in the creation of utility, and if we argue that this statement does not apply to us we only demonstrate how badly we have been brainwashed. The irony of all of this for us comes from the realization that as libraries and librarians have continued to suffer from benign neglect, terms such as information and information management have taken on new importance, often in the same organizations that claim that they cannot afford more support for their libraries.

The growth of information, the increase in its cost, and techniques for bibliographic and document resource sharing redefine for us the meaning of the word library. It is certainly not just material on the shelf on a given day, or things we can attempt to recall. The point has been made by others that the once proud American railroads failed because they failed to understand what business they were in. They thought they were in the railroad business, and forgot that they were in the transportation business. Had they remembered, various travel options that include train, bus, and airplane would now be among the range of services offered by a single transportation organization. Certainly they had the expertise to do this. Do some of us still think our business is books?

As I reviewed my writings I was struck by the near absence of material concerned with automation and the evaluation of computers, although much of my management career has been in large-scale sophisticated information facilities such as IBM and NASA, and although I served for six years as a member of the Board of the American Federation of Information Processing Societies. I conclude from this that I have not written about computerization because I do not consider it a major management issue. Here Drucker also has the last word. Automation, he reminds us, is not about machines. It is about how people work. The constantly expanding options of computer technology, none really developed for us but many clearly applicable to our problems, allow us to expand the vision of what it is we want to do, and how computers might help us do it. Computer specialists have expertise that we can buy or borrow for our needs. That interaction does not happen automatically, because individuals whose business is hardware and software tend to expand their horizons to include information delivery and, ultimately, information management. When that happens, a territorial clash is inevitable, and we could end up working for them. That is a disastrous scenario, because it has us report to individuals who do not understand the information process but think that they do, the most dangerous form of ignorance. It is an issue I see largely unaddressed in both corporations and academia, and more importantly it is a problem of authority and responsibility many librarians do not even seem to recognize.

The content of this book results from ideas and impressions I have acquired from countless thousands of individuals—teachers, colleagues, and students. Because the articles and chapters were written in different settings and for different audiences there is inevitably repetition. In teaching we call that reinforcement, and I hope that the reader will understand it is unavoidable for anyone who communicates with diverse audiences. Despite a pessimism about the risk avoidance and myopic tendencies I see in much of my profession, I am thrilled at the insights, innovation, courage, and leadership of some individual librarians. That they have survived and grown in an environment that does not usually reward the generally prized management values of innovation and marketing, but stresses collegiality and safe innocuous consensus, is remarkable. It gives me hope, and I am grateful to these colleagues. However, my greatest appreciation must be expressed to my wife, Virginia. She has served as a colleague, friend, sounding board, loyal and courageous supporter, and where appropriate as a very necessary incisive critic. It is to her that this work covering over thirty-five years of our partnership is dedicated.

EDUCATION AND TRAINING

There is no issue more crucial to the success of professional librarians than the question of how we prepare our new professionals and ensure the knowledge updating of those already in the field. The decision that librarians needed to be educated in institutions of higher learning, rather than simply trained in libraries, was made a long time ago, but that does not stop individuals from both inside and outside our field from questioning and trying to dilute the premise. Some of that arises from a genuine concern that we not implement arbitrary and unreasonable roadblocks for those seeking successful careers in our field, and valid equivalencies are a legitimate part of any job description process; but much of it simply results from the fact that education is expensive and must be rewarded in the first salary, and that continuing education is both expensive and never-ending. Organizations that recognize that they hired professionals accept that obligation and that cost. It does not surprise me that nonlibrarians would prefer cheap libraries even at the price of quality, and no pun is intended in that observation. After all, we already know that neither our managers nor our users can tell a good library from a bad library, only a big library from a little one and a costly one from a cheap one. The rationalization that all libraries are good libraries is followed closely by the second rationalization that anybody can run a library. "Anybody" is truly a range from well-meaning volunteers to clerks to distinguished professionals unfortunately educated in another field.

What does surprise me is that library managers would accept this scenario, because assumption of the premise that we run libraries cheaply as their primary characteristic only leads to the further suggestion that they be run even more cheaply. When we librarians accept the argument that the parent body cannot "afford" professional librarians, or cannot "afford" to pay them proper salaries, the shame is ours because the individuals who do this to us know what fools they make of us. We remember that school teachers used to be such fools, but they have learned. Without proper funds we are told that we do not have proper schools, and in some circumstances until there is proper funding there are no schools at all because the teachers refuse to work in them.

Library practitioners and library educators are part of the same continuum, and many individuals inhabit both communities. Our overall needs and strategies are the same because ultimately one group cannot succeed or be considered effective without the other. Our detailed priorities do not dovetail as neatly, however, primarily because we derive credit from different sets of management evaluations. Both groups report to nonlibrarians who understand very little about what we do, but library educators are evaluated in a framework that values scholarship even more than teaching, and is beginning to look at enrollment statistics and income in relationship to cost. Library managers are judged by individuals who all too frequently look at cost instead of substance, unless they can be forced to take responsibility for substance. In both instances we have nothing to gain by taking shortcuts in order to be cheap.

Our alliance should therefore be easy to forge. It must consist of a demand by practitioners that library education programs operate at sufficient quality, and that demand can be enforced through tougher accreditation standards. However, the emphasis must be on education, the understanding of issues and concepts and the development of skills and tools with which to deal with the specific problems that arise in libraries and that nobody can fully predict and anticipate. It should not emphasize training, the understanding of specific techniques for doing specific tasks, although library schools obviously do provide some training along the way. However, it is one of the characteristics of any recognized profession that first-time graduates are *not* ready to work productively until they receive lots of expensive and time-consuming further training. Continuing education also has both a cost and a time investment, and those are library costs and library time. Practitioners, whom I urge to insist on excellently educated graduates, must then keep their end of the bargain. Part of that consists in making the quality of the school and of the degree matter in the hiring process. Students who have gone to the trouble to obtain a higher quality educational experience deserve to be recognized. Part of it includes the payment of proper salaries for individuals who have completed a graduate professional degree, and there are statistics that show quite clearly what such a salary is. If we do not care to draw our data from MBA programs, at least we can check with Education, Public Administration, and Journalism. Finally, new librarians must be protected from irrelevant requirements, and these can be imposed either by librarians who believe (quite erroneously) that overqualified subordinates make them look better, or by users who feel comfortable with the premise that the librarians who serve them ought also to resemble them. That is part of the illogic of the suggestion that all academic librarians need to have doctorates. If that could be demonstrated by what they do, the argument could be accepted. However, asking for irrelevant degrees just to bolster the fragile egos of non-librarian faculty colleagues is a waste of money and of time, and when individuals are miseducated for what they are going to do failure is almost assured.

The issues are tough, but the stakes are crucial. Nobody promises it will be easy. Some of our predecessors, through their own weakness and vacillation, have now made it difficult for us. However, the effort is not only worth it, but success is essential to our professional identity.

IMPACT OF THE INCREASE IN LIBRARY DOCTORATES

A questionnaire was mailed to recipients of library doctoral degrees between 1930 and 1975 to determine the present and preferred areas of activity, evaluations of the doctoral degree as a factor in obtaining and performing present duties, and self-assessments of involvement in library research. Further, through an examination of position advertisements over a six-month period, the relative importance of a doctorate and other factors such as experience and special skills were weighed for positions in library education and academic library administration, and the dangers of potential fragmentation and compartmentalization based on these requirements are evaluated.

In 1970 Ray and Patricia Carpenter postulated an insufficient number of doctorates for the needs of librarianship.[1] They based this conclusion primarily on the number of faculty positions in existence (or about to come into existence) and assumed that such posts should be filled to a far greater extent by doctoral graduates.

The research reported in the present paper consists of two studies. The first is a survey of employment listings in library administration and education to test the Carpenter hypothesis and to determine how necessary the degree is as a credential for employment. The second is a survey of present holders of library doctorate degrees to determine how they perceive the importance of the degree to the performance of their tasks and to attempt a relationship between their academic credentials and their research scholarship.

Since the Carpenter study, which identified 249 earned doctorates through 1968, there has been a substantial acceleration in the production of terminal degrees in librarianship. While the availability of

---

This paper was written with Karen Momenee. Reprinted from *College and Research Libraries* 39 (May 1978):207–14.
Cowinner of the Best Research Paper Award, American Library Association Research Round Table.

federal support funds in the late 1960s and early 1970s served to provide considerable impetus for this program, the acceleration can now be expected to continue almost on its own momentum, if for no other reason than the fact that a large and growing number of accredited library schools are now involved in or committed to the establishment of library doctorate programs. They can be expected to recruit vigorously for students to keep their programs alive.

Although specific statistics vary, through the examination of the Eyman list of doctoral dissertations through 1972[2] and a specific screening of *Dissertation Abstracts,* we identified 280 such doctorates during the period in which the Carpenters reported 249. Similarly, Nancy Lane, in her 1975 doctoral dissertation,[3] located 289 library doctorates through 1969, while we were able to identify 308 during the same period. Since degrees granted in one year are sometimes not reported in *Dissertation Abstracts* until several years later, the discrepancy can be accounted for in this manner.

The growth of library doctoral degrees has been startling. We were able to identify 662 library doctorates granted by graduate library school programs at accredited library schools through 1975. (Since only those 1975 dissertations reported through August 1976 in *Dissertation Abstracts* are included, there may in fact be a few more.) Of these degrees, better than half have been granted since 1969 and better than one-quarter since 1972. There was a slight drop in 1974 but a resurgence in 1975. Even at present levels, which can be expected to increase as neophyte programs get into full swing, we will cross the 1,000 threshold by 1980. The 1930–50 cumulative total, which doubled in 1959, doubled again in 1967 and again in 1973. It will once again have doubled in 1980 or 1981.

ADVERTISEMENTS FOR POSITIONS

To determine what jobs specifically call for this new influx of doctoral degree holders, advertisements for professional librarians were checked over a six-month period, from June 1976 to December 1976, in *Chronicle of Higher Education, Library Journal, College & Research Libraries News, Wilson Library Bulletin, L.J. Hotline,* and a number of other publications.

Two kinds of positions were screened, those that requested candidates for library school teaching posts and those that offered head administrative posts in academic libraries. It was felt that these were the two kinds of positions for which the doctorate in librarianship would be most appealing, and spot checks of other kinds of positions bear out this assumption. The requirement of a doctorate, or its desirability, was not mentioned to any significant extent for any library post other than the two types mentioned above. During the period studied, forty-six library school faculty positions were advertised. Of these, ten were in schools whose programs were not accredited by the American Library Association, thirty-six in programs that are accredited by ALA. Of these thirty-six, there were seventeen in schools with active doctoral programs.

Thirty-nine of the forty-six advertisements categorically stated the requirement of a doctorate of some kind as a qualification for the position. Twenty-three specified a library doctorate, and sixteen indicated that a subject doctorate would be an acceptable alternative. There was little difference in the kind of school and the kind of program, although it might be expected that a school with an active Ph.D. training program might have a greater demonstrated need for this qualification than one that, for example, prepared largely school librarians in an unaccredited setting. Fifteen of the seventeen positions at doctorate-granting schools required a doctorate, although four were willing to accept subject degrees in lieu of library degrees. The other two advertisements indicated a strong preference for the library doctorate but did not absolutely demand it.

Of the nineteen positions at accredited library schools without doctoral programs, eighteen absolutely required the doctorate, although a surprisingly high number of twelve found a nonlibrary doctorate an acceptable alternative. The remaining school indicated its preference though not requirement for a subject rather than library doctorate. Of ten positions in unaccredited schools, six absolutely required the library doctorate, the other four preferred but did not insist on a doctorate and were equally divided in preference between library and subject specializations. Other skills, such as teaching ability and professional experience, were also required for twenty-two of these twenty-six positions, but in no case were these spelled out with any specificity.

For the twenty-five university and twenty-eight college head administrative positions advertised during this same period, the reverse tendency applied. Twenty-three of the university and twenty-seven of the college head administrative posts specified exact requirements of administrative experience (in years), specific skills in management, budgeting, automation, public relations, etc. Only five of the fifty-three absolutely required a doctorate, and for four of them it was a subject and not a library doctorate. Another twenty-one expressed the preference for a doctorate, with five preferring the library field, six a subject field, and eleven accepting either. The remaining twenty-seven job postings mentioned no doctorate at all.

The pattern appears to be clear. While the trend for library education posts has been toward the doctorate, the trend in administrative posts has been away from the doctorate and toward a demonstrated ability to manage. The most dramatic evidence for this comes in a study by Kaser, which reports that in 1960 90 percent of ARL (Association of Research Libraries) head librarians had achieved doctorates. In 1976 this had dropped to 15 percent of ARL library administrators.[4]

SURVEY OF DOCTORATES

We attempted to relate these findings to the self-perceptions of library degree holders. As stated, we identified 662 doctorates granted by library schools accredited by the American Library Association between the years 1930 and 1975. Of these, twenty-seven recipients were deceased. Another thirty-seven were foreign students who had returned to their native countries after receipt of their doctorates and were excluded because they represented special cases of no direct bearing to American librarianship. Finally, twenty-eight recipients could not be located, despite the excellent cooperation of alumni offices. Questionnaires were mailed to the remaining 570. Two of these individuals responded but disqualified themselves because they had been retired for some time, and they were dropped from the sample. Of the remaining 568 subjects, responses were received from 403. The response rate of 71 percent matches exactly the level of response achieved by the Carpenter study and provides ample evidence of the high degree of interest in and concern about this topic.

Further evidence of interest can be inferred from the fact that 31 percent of all respondents took the trouble to append specific comments to their questionnaires, some considerably elaborated. These comments ranged from cautions about overinterpretation of self-evaluative data to expressions of high interest in learning the results of the survey. Perhaps of greatest interest were lengthy explanations for self-perceived paucity of research, despite the fact that, in a totally anonymous survey such as this one, no conclusions about individuals could be drawn. A large number of respondents felt obliged to explain what to them was obviously an unsatisfactory record.

Areas of Specialization

Of 396 individuals responding to the question about areas of specialization, 33.8 percent categorized themselves as being in the field of library administration, 3.8 percent in library operations, 51.3 percent in library education, and 11.1 percent in library research, as distinct from any of the above. It is assumed that this last grouping includes individuals in government posts, in commercial firms having research contracts, and in academic institutions but without teaching responsibilities.

Respondents indicated a remarkably high degree of contentment with their present areas of activity, although, as pointed out above, the subjectivity of self-perception must be taken into account. Of doctorate library administrators, 76.1 percent in fact stated that they preferred administration to other areas, with education running a distant second at 10.9 percent. Of individuals in library operations, 53.3 percent preferred this activity, while 26.7 percent indicated that they would prefer administration, an assignment they probably view as a promotional opportunity.

Of the library educators who make up more than half the survey, a remarkably high 86.7 percent express a preference for their present area of activity, with only 7.1 percent indicating a preference for administrative posts. Along the same lines, 67.6 percent of the individuals calling themselves researchers expressed a preference for their present line of work.

While such statements indicate a high degree of job satisfaction or at least adjustment, they also suggest a high degree of compartmentalization and specialization. Individuals who choose to teach without prior operational or administrative experience are unlikely to acquire it at a later date. Even doctoral graduates who chose not to teach initially seem unlikely to do so in the future. As a result, insofar as it is considered desirable that library school faculty have operational experience in the areas in which they teach, it can be postulated that they must achieve it before they become doctoral candidates. If they enter faculty ranks upon receipt of their doctorates without prior operational or administrative experience, it does not appear from the survey data that they will be likely to acquire it later.

Evaluation of the Doctorate

Respondents were asked to evaluate the doctorate in obtaining and in performing their present duties by indicating whether they considered the degree essential, important, useful, or unimportant. With a weight factor of three for essential, two for important, one for useful, and zero for unimportant, respondents as a whole gave an average weight of 2.40 to the doctorate in obtaining their present posts and 1.99 in performing them. As might be expected, library educators gave the doctorate the highest rating, with 2.81 for obtaining their posts and 2.33 for performing them. Nevertheless, an average difference in rating of almost half a point from 196 library educators who responded to this question is not insignificant. Administrators ranked second, with a 2.06 rating for obtaining the position, 1.73 for performing it. As expected, personnel in library operations ranked the degree lowest, with a 1.20 rating for obtaining the position and a 1.07 rating for performing it.

Perhaps most surprising is the fact that self-professed researchers ranked the doctorate at an average of 1.86 in obtaining their posts and at 1.51 in performing them. (See table 1 for a summary of all responses.) Since this evaluation of what is fundamentally a research degree for the purpose of doing research ranks below that of administrators, as well as educators, it may be (although the survey did not seek to determine this) that a greater proportion of these researchers work in nonacademic settings where the value placed on the doctoral degree is not as automatic.

Survey respondents were asked whether they had taught and, if so, whether they had supervised the research of doctoral students. Of the respondents who answered this question, 136 had supervised doctoral students, 160 had not. The responses of this subgroup of individuals to the question that elicited their views concerning the importance of the doctorate in obtaining and in performing their tasks were then evaluated. Their responses differed somewhat from those of library educators as a whole, since some of the individuals who classified themselves as teachers were only teaching on a part-time basis and preferred to categorize themselves primarily as administrators or as researchers. Others have taught but were no longer doing so. Nevertheless, while the specific numerical values differ from those reported in table 1, the relationships remain closely consistent.

Those who as teachers were supervising or had supervised doctoral research rated the doctorate at a mean of 2.75 for obtaining their posts and at a mean of 2.33 for performing their duties. The same approximately .5 self-perceived overqualification differential noted earlier appears here as well. Those teachers who did not supervise doctoral

TABLE 1
IMPORTANCE OF DOCTORATE FOR OBTAINING AND PERFORMING PRESENT POST

Present Activity	N	(Mean) Obtaining Post	Performing Duties
(Essential = 3.00; Important = 2.00; Usefull = 1.00; Unimportant = 0.00)			
All Respondents	396	2.40	1.99
Administration	134	2.06	1.73
Operations	15	1.20	1.07
Education	203	2.81	2.33
Research	44	1.86	1.51
Have Taught and Supervised Doctoral Research	136	2.75	2.33
Have Taught but Not Supervised Doctoral Research	161	2.30	2.07

research rated the importance of the degree in obtaining their posts at 2.30, in performing them at 2.07.

Pre- and Postdoctoral Experience and Publications

The Lane study mentioned earlier indicated a correlation between predoctoral experience and postdoctoral publication and between predoctoral publication and postdoctoral publications. Individuals who had more experience before receiving their doctorates, according to Lane, published more after receiving it than those who had had less experience. Similarly, individuals with a record of publication prior to the receipt of their doctorate were more apt to publish afterwards than those who had none. As Lane points out, her statistics were drawn simply from author listings in *Library Literature* and made no attempt at evaluating the kind of literature being reported.

In our survey, correlations were drawn between predoctoral professional experience (both in and out of the library field) and published research prior to and after receipt of the doctorate. Even though the responses to these questions carry a bias in that the evaluation of what constitutes research is left to the authors (who are likely to be more charitable in evaluating their work as research than an outsider would be), both prior experience and prior research publication appear to bear no positive relation to postdoctoral research. In fact, there is even a slight negative correlation. (See table 2.)

Since almost all respondents answered this series of questions, it can be seen not only that the sheer quantity of professional experience brought to the doctorate has little impact on later research activity (as measured by a self-evaluated record of publication) but also that there is an average of less than one research publication per postdoctoral year. No attempt was made in this survey to determine the kind of professional experience prior to the doctorate. If any correlations on prediction

TABLE 2
Predoctoral Experience as Related to Postdoctoral Research Publication

No. of Years Predoctoral Professional Experience (N = 255)	Research Publications/Year Since Doctorate
Less than 1 year	1.06
1–3 years	0.87
4–6 years	0.65
7–10 years	0.69
11–15 years	0.93
More than 15 years	0.64

models are to be drawn, such an investigation would appear highly desirable.

The correlation of predegree research publication with postdegree research also seems to be insignificant (see table 3), although the number of annual publications since receipt of the degree for this group of respondents is consistently higher than that for the predoctoral reporting group. There was a difficulty in obtaining useful data for this group in that about half the survey respondents, while often willing to discuss predoctoral experience, were not willing or able to furnish data concerning their predegree research publications. No correlation with postdegree publication could be attempted.

The hypothesis can be advanced that individuals unable or unwilling to report predoctoral publications had little or nothing to report. While this might seem absurd in an anonymous survey, it has already been reported that a great many respondents felt constrained to explain what they considered to be an inadequate record even though no one knew who they were. Although we know that these reports of postdoctoral research are exaggerations because they would produce a greater volume of research publication than appears in print, it is clear that the patterns apparent in the Lane study, which measured only *publication* count, disappear when the authors are asked to count their own *research* publications.

Failure to Conduct Research

Individuals who, by their own assessment, had not performed or at least not published the results of postdoctoral research, were asked to explain

TABLE 3
PREDOCTORAL RESEARCH PUBLICATIONS AS RELATED TO
POSTDOCTORAL RESEARCH PUBLICATIONS

No. of Predoctoral Research Publications (N = 184)	Postdoctoral Research Publications/Year Since Doctorate
0	1.33
1	0.73
2	0.81
3	1.13
4	1.25
5	0.74
6	1.00
7	0.76
8 or more	0.87

TABLE 4

REASONS STATED FOR PAUCITY OF RESEARCH

Reason	Percent (N = 235)
Too busy	61.7%
Research not required	18.7%
Facilities lacking	7.2%
Too recent	6.4%
Not interested	6.0%

why. Their reasons are summarized in table 4. The explanation by 61.7 percent that failure to do more research was due to their being too busy matches the conclusions of Pauline Wilson in a recent article.[5] In it the author points out that there is increasing pressure on library school faculty for research and publication and suggests that, as a result of shifting priorities, teaching may have to be done less well and participation in professional activities may have to be curtailed. Wilson may be correct, but these authors view her conclusions with at least some skepticism.

Wilson does point out that some faculty do no research simply because they are not interested, and we would suggest that to the 6 percent in our survey who indicated no interest and the 18.7 percent who did no research because it was not required could be added a considerable portion of the 68.9 percent who blame somebody else (too heavy a teaching load, no support, etc.). This last argument can neither be attacked nor defended, because it is not possible to determine whether faculty producing no research are already working as hard as they could be or as hard as they ought to be. As Wilson points out, much of the test will come with increased requirements of library faculty research for promotion and tenure, but only if at the same time safeguards against the dilution of teaching quality are imposed.

The almost 25 percent who have no interest in doing research unless required are of particular interest. One wonders for what reason these individuals sought a research terminal degree.

Cynics might respond that the degree is merely required to obtain the "union card" to admit the successful candidate to a more desirable kind or level of employment and is unrelated to research. A number of respondents made this and similar points in their unsolicited comments. If this attitude does indeed exist to any appreciable degree, it would point to a regrettable laxness on the part of library school administrations in the acceptance criteria employed for candidates, in the values that are stressed and implanted, and in the requirements that are met.

Importance of the Doctorate

The importance of the earned doctorate for faculty in library schools in establishing and retaining status for the school within its own academic setting is recognized, cannot be ignored, and is probably behind much of the recent upgrading in educational requirements for faculty in library schools. In fact, schools that have recently undergone ALA accreditation visits recognize the stress placed by the accreditation teams on both the number and diversity of earned doctorates as an indication of faculty competence.

Nevertheless, it would appear that a balance must be struck, between the emphasis on the terminal degree and the emphasis on other qualifications, where all are not equally available. To require, for example, as one school has done, a doctorate to teach courses in special librarianship automatically eliminates by fiat almost all of the people qualified to deal with special librarianship from experience. Perhaps it is necessary for library schools to insist, as other professional schools have done, on diferent kinds of faculties for different courses. In schools of music, for example, there are differences in the background and requirements for teaching a course in music history and theory and for teaching performance classes.

To some extent library schools have attempted to offset these limitations by using adjunct and visiting faculty who do not possess other absolute requirements. However, such opportunities are usually limited to schools in or near large metropolitan centers and in any case tend to fail to provide continuity and stability of employment, participation of the individual in the governance decisions of the school, and a sequence of priorities in which course teaching becomes something more than a spare time avocation.

THE DOCTORATE AND RESEARCH

The substantial increase in library doctorates should reasonably be expected to cause a sharp upsurge in both the amount and quality of library research. To the extent to which this has not occurred, it may be because so many of the doctoral graduates are new (more than half, as indicated at the beginning of this article, have had their degrees less than five years); it may be because, as Wilson points out, opportunities for research are lacking; or it may be, as we suspect, that many library doctoral graduates (not unlike doctoral graduates in other fields) are not particularly interested in research and publication, at least not at the expense of other professional and personal activities.

The existence of doctoral graduates (in the library field as in others) who admit to having no interest in research—and it can be assumed that the real number is larger than the 24.7 percent in this survey who admit doing no research unless forced to—would appear to be a sharp indictment of the quality of present doctoral programs: in their selection criteria, in communicating to students the conditions and responsibilities of what the terminal degree means and requires, in the school's treatment of research, and in the acceptance of lesser standards in the undertaking of reserach leading to the dissertation.

The fact that only 22.6 percent of the survey respondents claimed any sort of even partially experimental approach in their dissertations, even in conjunction with other techniques, while more than 32 percent chose historical topics (see table 5) may suggest a paucity of innovation and initiative. Opportunities for Ph.D. students in other disciplines to learn research techniques are provided at two levels, explicitly within the curriculum as a course and implicitly through actual work as an apprentice on a professor's research project. The lack of enthusiasm for and commitment to research by many respondents to this survey may well curtail the amount of "laboratory" experience possible in a library school setting.

The most frequent justification stated in the survey responses for lack of research is that there is not sufficient time. If adequate instruction and learning experience in research techniques are not provided by the library schools themselves, then not only Ph.D. students but also post-doctoral faculty members now pressured to produce research wil be forced to find the time to develop these skills in addition to and before fulfilling the research requirements now increasingly imposed for promotion and tenure.

Other questions, which this investigation into the characteristics of our rapidly growing body of doctoral graduates suggests but must

TABLE 5
CHARACTERIZATION OF DISSERTATION TOPIC

(Mutually Exclusive)	Number	Percent
Historical	116	28.6%
Survey	136	33.5%
Experimental	83	20.4%
Other	44	10.8%
Historical-Survey	13	3.2%
Historical-Experimental	0	0
Historical-Other	2	0.5%
Survey-Experimental	7	1.7%
Survey-Other	1	0.3%
Experimental-Other	2	0.5%
No Answer	2	0.5%

leave to later investigations to answer, concern the changes in the perceptions of these graduates that the pursuit and attainment of the degree may or may not bring about. Does it, in any measurable way, change or sharpen their attitudes toward the profession, toward the role of the librarian, their own responsibilities, and the place, importance, or direction of research? Aside from the fact that it may enhance the status of librarianship in the academic setting, what difference will there be for the profession in 1980, when we have 1,000 doctoral graduates, as compared to 1972, when we had half as many, or 1966, when we had less than 250?

We assume that the identifying, undertaking, completing, and reporting of research needed by the profession (and certainly professions, unlike trades, have such needs), coupled with the training of still more future researchers, are the roles that our present and future library Ph.D.s are best and uniquely qualified to fill. Their acceptance of a research doctorate appears to embrace such a commitment. If it actually does, they can strengthen a bridge between library and information research and library and information operations, which is either in a serious state of disrepair or which has never even been completed. Evidence for assuming this bridging problem is the disdain practitioners express for the significance of the results of completed research, research they (rightly or wrongly) consider largely irrelevant.[6]

If library doctoral graduates do not accept a continuing commitment to research, and if they simply use the degree as a passport into the perceived safety and security of the library teaching profession (whether or not that safety and security are real), then an implication of this study is that the growth of doctoral programs could have the serious effect of widening the gap between those who teach and those who do not. This will almost certainly occur if perceptions of what makes an acceptable library teacher and an acceptable library administrator continue to move in opposite directions and if future doctoral graduates show the same tendencies to remain in their professional niches as the respondents to this survey have reported.

References

1. Ray L. Carpenter and Patricia A. Carpenter, "The Doctorate in Librarianship and an Assessment of Graduate Library Education," *Journal of Education for Librarianship* 11:3–45 (Summer 1970).

2. David H. Eyman, comp., *Doctoral Dissertations in Library Science: Titles Accepted by Accredited Library Schools 1930–72* (Ann Arbor, Mich.: Xerox University Microfilms, 1973).

3. Nancy D. Lane, "Characteristics Related to Productivity among Doctoral Graduates in Librarianship" (Ph.D. dissertation, Univ. of California, Berkeley, 1975).

4. David Kaser, "The Effect of the Revolution of 1969–1970 on University Library Administration," in Herbert Poole, ed., *Academic Libraries by the Year 2000: Essays Honoring Jerrold Orne* (New York: Bowker, 1977), p. 64–75.

5. Pauline Wilson, "Barriers to Research in Library Schools: A Framework for Analysis," *Journal of Education for Librarianship* 17:3–19 (Summer 1976).

6. American Society for Information Science, "An Investigation of Planning Requirements and Priorities of the Scientific and Technical Information Community." Report on research sponsored by the National Science Foundation, presented at the ASIS annual meeting in Boston, October 1975.

ACCREDITATION AND THE PURSUIT OF EXCELLENCE

Although library educators devote much of their rhetoric at professional meetings to the search for excellence, many of the real concerns deal with more fundamental issues, such as the maintenance of present levels and in some cases even survival. It is a problem which is not unique to library and information science education. As college bound populations decline in number over the next dozen years, and as federal and state support for higher education decreases, the commitment to excellence tends to be overshadowed by the commitment to avoiding elimination. Academic administrations face an almost impossible task as they seek to reallocate resources to those disciplines which need or deserve them most. Programs never volunteer to commit suicide, and the complexity of any major university prohibits intelligent evaluation of any school's importance or contribution by outsiders. Were it attempted, its findings would be challenged as being noninformed. Although this is true for all disciplines, it is particularly true for library and information science, which not only represents a tiny fraction of the campus enrollment and faculty size, but whose own graduates are not likely to rise in prominence in the campus power structure.

Given this lack of familiarity and lack of perceived urgency, it is not surprising that university administrators tend to measure library education programs with only two criteria: (1) some level of statewide, national, or international prestige they can see, understand, and incorporate into their own claim for institutional excellence, and (2) a protection of the historic relationship between income from student fees and the operational cost of the school. This second criterion becomes parti-

Paper presented at a meeting of the Association of American Library Schools, San Antonio, Texas, January 1983. Reprinted from *Journal of Education for Librarianship* 23 (Spring 1983):253–63.

cularly significant when it is recognized that probably the best scenario for funding from government agencies is continuation at present levels. Inflationary cost increases will have to be borne by students, either by more students, by the same students paying more, or by fewer students paying much more. This of course leads to still fewer students.

The question of quality is not really defined for library education on the campus except in terms of demonstrable perceptions. Most library school administrators and faculty would just as soon keep it that way. We prefer to evaluate ourselves, and not be judged by others whose appreciation of what we do we mistrust. Quality improvement, if it comes at all, does not appear to result from a conscious search for it. It comes from the things we do—the number of faculty members and what is expected of them, the number of students and the rigor of the educational experience. It comes from physical facilities, from library resources, and from equipment which keeps pace with technological applications in libraries. As measured against this expectation there is evidence that some educational programs are in serious difficulty, and that all are in at least potential difficulty.

Russell Bidlack has been collecting information for ALISE for quite a few years,[1] and even a cursory examination of these data is startling and disturbing. In the five year period since 1975–76, mean full-time enrollment at accredited institutions of library education decreased 37.5 percent, mean FTE enrollment 30.5 percent. In 1974, the then 53 accredited library schools in the United States produced 6,804 master's graduates. In 1981 the then 63 accredited schools produced 4,486, a decrease of 34 percent in graduates resulting from an increase of 19 percent of the schools producing them. All of this from schools generally acknowledged to be tiny by any general campus standards back in 1974. The statistics suggest that there is little doubt that there are too many library education programs. The movement toward reduction, triggered less by action of accrediting bodies than by specific and unrelated decisions on individual campuses, will presumably have at least that beneficial result. However, we are not certain that the schools which "deserve" elimination are the ones being targeted. Presumably these should be the weakest in terms of faculty competence and the quality of the educational program. No research on this question has as yet been done, but it would appear to even a casual observer that there is little if any relationship between quality of a library education program as judged by the American Library Association Committee on Accreditation standards and guidelines, and the threatened or accomplished demise of specific programs. A reading of the current professional journals would suggest that it is a political rather than a qualitative process, undertaken by campus administrators under pressure to eliminate something, often simply as a token of good effort. The elimination of library education programs appears to result from the belief that it can be accomplished without doing serious harm to the parent institution through a loss of prestige; and without the danger of inflaming influential alumni or legislators. Schools seeking to avoid the ax have quite correctly attempted to marshall their own forces. Political power is countered by political power. Qualitative evaluations have little or no bearing, in part because they are difficult to do and in part because they are disbelieved and ridiculed by those predisposed to disbelieve them. It has been suggested that academia has become almost too fragmented in its authority structure to permit any change, and there is evidence that this is true at least for change through agreement or consensus.

Successful or at least surviving library school administrators are not fools, and they recognize the need for dramatic and highly visible action, because they perceive the status quo as far too dangerous. The actions being taken ostensibly as proposed improvements in the program, but perhaps as much to present a picture of innovation and change, represent a range of activities. A large number of schools have changed their names to reflect information science or information management in the title, although the evidence of specific changes in curriculum is by no means as clear. Other schools have attempted to widen their base and their visibility through mergers with other programs, through the introduction of dual degree and interdisciplinary programs, through the expansion to off-campus sites, and through the introduction (in some cases a reintroduction) of an undergraduate curriculum. These changes are not necessarily bad, but they are also not necessarily motivated by the claimed objective of program improvement. To a large and perhaps predominant extent they are motivated by the need to seek protection and survival.

Despite all of this, if enrollment trends within library education in particular and in higher education in general continue to decline, and if government bodies continue to show the disinclination to heavy subsidization, the number of library education programs will decline, as probably it should. However, the method of effecting this change through the political process does not offer any suggestion that qualitative criteria will apply, and that the "better" schools will survive. Academic administration has few tools with which to tag. If the reduction is to follow some sort of logic or of survival of the fittest, then it is the library profession itself which must do it. It is not suggested that this be done through the development of arbitrary numerical expectations for numbers of institutions, but through the simple process of adhering to standards of quality. Such an adherence, which must inevitably have some quantitative connotations, would be automatically self-adjusting, at least to the extent to which quality demands some minimal level of resources. This is the role of the accreditation process, so assigned to the American Library Association and its Committee on Accreditation. The process of accreditation also at least suggests nonaccreditation and disaccreditation.

Does the accreditation process work? There is at least some argument that it does not, and that argument comes as strongly from fields outside library science, particularly in other professional disciplines. It has been suggested that accreditation does not lead, that it follows by adapting its standards to the reality of what exists. This is an inevitable risk in dealing with subjective standards, which are open to shifting personal definitions. It is a particular risk in a small and closely knit field such as ours, for which such decisions are immediately and directly personalized. The prescribed composition of the site visit team virtually insures that most if not all of the visitors will be personally known to at least some of the faculty, and in many cases we are talking about close friends, colleagues, and sympathetic fellow sufferers. There is no suggestion of a conscious bias. Rather it is a perfectly understandable human attempt to be compassionate, and particularly as we see in others problems we face ourselves. Understandable it may be, but acceptable it cannot be, because we function in a closed continuum, in which toleration of lower standards hurts those who achieve higher ones. The number of total students is largely independent of the number of schools, and determined primarily by factors such as perceptions of job opportunities, starting salaries, in addition to the overriding demographic pool of eligible bachelor graduates. The number of faculty members in library education will ultimately hinge on the number of students. Gresham's Law applies as surely to library education as it does to economics. In economics bad money drives out good money, and in library education poor programs will either drive out good ones or force them down to their own level. This is because bad programs, with little equipment and resources and with less qualified faculty, are cheaper. Unless there is a differentiation, the seeking of a lower common denominator is almost inevitable. Accreditation or the withholding of accreditation provides not only the best but the fairest approach to the search for and reward for quality.

However, the accreditation process for library education as for other education is flawed by self-adjusting subjectivity, by the desire to be compassionate, and by procedures which, in some twist of legal logic, consider applicants to be accreditable unless the evaluators can prove, and then defend, that the program is not up to standards which are fuzzily defined. Edward Holley, Dean of the School of Library Science at the University of North Carolina, has suggested quantitative standards[2] under which applicant programs would have to meet stated (and presumably inflation adjusted) minimums in financial support, as well as in numbers of faculty and in students. Well intentioned as this proposal is, it may nevertheless be simplistic, because an absence of size is not necessarily the over-riding concern. Size by itself does not insure quality. Three faculty members in a specialization, none of whom follows the literature, performs research, or provides professional leadership still does not add up to an adequate faculty in this area, despite its acceptable size. It might be fairer to impose quantitative guidelines, which would state levels of presumed expectation but permit the school to explain why its situation differs. The application of the Holley standards to the most recent perception study of library education programs[3] yields interesting conclusions. Not all large schools were highly perceived. Size is obviously not enough. However, all highly rated schools had doctoral programs, and it could be argued that this is essential to attract the research-oriented faculty which makes for high prestige. One school which fails two of the three Holley criteria nevertheless turns up as highly rated, and that school is the University of Chicago.

An exception? Perhaps, but the general reaction to all of these speculations is inevitably for each educator in terms of which conclusions fit his or her program. That is the root of the problem. Nothing is exact, nothing can be proven to the satisfaction of those to whom that proof is unpleasant, particularly if it serves to disaccredit their institution.

Are there some concerns which present C.O.A. procedures and emphases could address, aside from the imposing specter of arbitrary quantitative standards? Perhaps there are, although not all of them are presently possible under existing guidelines even if under the standards. However, guidelines and even standards can be changed, and at least a start can be made. The following are offered as unrefined suggestions, as a point of departure for further discussion.

1. C.O.A. should make its guidelines clearer and more specific, and use those to express both its expectations and an understanding of what will happen if those expectations are not met. It is perhaps one way to handle the question of critical mass for faculty, students, and financial support. If we expect certain things to happen, and normally they require at least certain quantitative minima, then this can be stated. The school still has the opportunity to explain why its situation presents an exception. Each year C.O.A. makes it quite clear in its letter review of annual reports that it is displeased with some of the schools for their lack of achievement in the area of faculty productive scholarship. But what of it? Is it a serious or perhaps final warning, or just an annoying goad? Perhaps more fundamentally, must a school meet minimum requirements (whatever they are) in all categories of the standards, or can a low productive faculty be offset by strong physical facilities? How many standards have to be met, anyway? All seven, or six out of seven for an A minus, five out of seven for a B plus?

2. The composition of C.O.A. needs to be broadened, and perhaps expanded in size, to enlarge the role of practitioners, of students,

and of other academic professional disciplines to add consistency and perspective. This runs contrary to the suggestion which has been made to have library educators take greater or full responsibility for the accreditation process. It will not work, and not because library educators are devious or Machiavelian. They certainly want all schools, particularly their own schools, to be as good as they can make them. But most of all, the process makes pragmatists of them, and the first objective is survival. It is the observation of this writer, after careers in both business and academia, that there is virtually no difference in the ultimate decision processes. Income, sales, and cash flow have other names, but they are just as important. Only prestige and recognition are added to the formula.

    3. C.O.A. should be a monitoring and evaluative body, and quit worrying so much about improving the quality of specific programs through helpful advice and suggestions. This is a change from present C.O.A. priorities and thinking, but it is a necessary reorientation of emphasis. In principle there is nothing wrong with trying to be helpful as well as evaluative, as we try to be in the classroom. However, this concern, compounded by the close camaraderie of a small profession, tends to make us more apologists than evaluators. Basketball referees do not call fouls more strictly on teams which lead by 50 points, or more leniently on teams which trail by 50. At least they are not supposed to. C.O.A. should concentrate on evaluation and grading, and leave advice to others. Schools can always get help, although they might have to pay for it. There is no shortage in the availability of deans and former C.O.A. members to serve as consultants. Evaluation can and should lead to improvement, but it can undermine the first to make them part of the same process.

    4. C.O.A. must redefine its relationships with its own teams of site visitors, even if this requires some clarification of ground rules. Presumably, C.O.A. has site visitors because the committee members cannot make all the trips, but the site visit team is, or at least ought to be, an adjunct to C.O.A. itself, and responsible to that body. It is important that the site team's factual report be reviewed by the school being visited. An evaluation based on a factual error is bound to be flawed. However, the evaluation section of the site visit team's report is really the essence of the document. Factors not discussed in the evaluation cannot be brought up in the recommendations, and making only that last recommendation section a proprietary document seems a bit pointless. Anyone who can read an evaluative report can tell pretty well where it leads, and this means that the site visit team, and not C.O.A., is really making the basic decisions. At least, it is difficult for C.O.A. to change the drift, or to correct the inadequacies, of a report the school has already seen. Evaluative reports should be submitted by the site visitors

as draft documents to C.O.A., and be released by C.O.A. with the recommendations to which they are inevitably tied. This has at least two advantages. C.O.A., which may have a much better historical perspective about this school and certainly about the overall process, can question inclusions or omissions, and make whatever changes it deems appropriate. Secondly, the site visitors can be freed to comment on anything which strikes them, without worrying about whether or not it legitimately fits the ground rules for accreditation. C.O.A. can make that decision. There is also the question of the school's right to remove proposed site visitors from the team. For specific cause (bias or conflict of interest) certainly, but the principle of the peremptory challenge as granted to the defense in a court of law is also made available to the prosecutor. Who is the prosecutor here?

5. The evaluation of a school's program follows from the claims which it stakes out for itself in its goals and objectives, and most experienced administrators have known for some time that they get into the greatest trouble if they make claims and then do not deliver. It is therefore better to make fewer claims. Schools are not required to claim that they prepare academic, school, public, and special librarians, and as long as they do not claim it, they cannot be faulted for not doing it. They are only required to prepare students at a level which stresses principles common to all types of libraries, and it is true that C.O.A. has interpreted that small phrase a little more rigorously than in the past. However, how practical is the caveat, when it is known both that students apply for jobs where they can find them, and that the C.O.A. list of accredited schools provides no clues for the prospective employer as to what special strengths were or were not claimed?

There is a continuing argument in library education as to whether we should emphasize special types of libraries at all, or simply concentrate on principles common to all of them. However, the one side of that argument has little support from students and even less from employers, who understand full well that their libraries have different characteristics and different needs, and expect us to meet them. Research, public, special, medical. The fragmentation is endless, and each group insists that we do not prepare students adequately for entry level positions in their libraries.

Perhaps library schools should not have to claim an adequate preparation for special librarianship. Perhaps four or five schools really concentrating on turning out medical librarians would be preferable to 69 schools. There is neither such a great need, nor that many competent faculty members.

However, if we do this, how do we inform the employers from which five schools they should hire? And how do we inform prospective students of the five schools they should consider. As a minimum, it would greatly complicate the accreditation procedure. Schools not claiming a competency in preparing academic librarians would not be judged against these requirements, but then also would not appear on the new C.O.A. list of schools which have claimed and validated a competency for academic librarianship. And, of course, there would have to be simliar lists for other types of libraries. Reservations and restrictions now appear as footnotes in miniscule type, legible only to those with uncorrected 20–10 vision. Implementation of such a concept would necessitate separate lists of accredited schools by type of library, perhaps a half dozen or more of them. This in turn implies partial accreditations. Claimed competency in one area is accredited, in another area it is not. And as though all of this were not bad enough, there is more. It follows further that the school not claiming to educate students for certain types of libraries must clearly inform its prospective students, at least through its bulletin, that this is a school they might want to consider not attending.

It is far too cumbersome, and because of this, C.O.A. had best eliminate the shelter of the non-claimed preparation area, unless it can find a way to assure keeping graduates out of types of jobs for which they are not prepared. Right now graduates of all accredited schools (and of course non-accredited schools) take jobs where they can find them—in academic, public, school, and special libraries, and who can blame them? Accreditation provides a level of approval of which the employer may or may not avail himself, but that is all C.O.A. reports. It seems only fair that accreditation standards must relate to what is reported to employers, which is that these graduates are ready for their libraries. There is a large and growing body of literature in which special libraries are developing the specific characteristics of their profession, and special librarians have the right to insist that all accredited schools have faculties able to convey and interpret these developments to their students. School librarians, public librarians, and research librarians have that same right. The fact that the school does not claim this expertise is, under present accreditation procedures, irrelevant. The claim is implicit in the approved charter for any type of library employment which accreditation confers, and is confirmed by the absence of any sort of disclaimer in school bulletins and catalogs. Under this approach, critical mass numbers for faculty size and professional competencies become much more plausible, and the minimum of ten faculty members suggested by Holley begins to look conservative.

6. C.O.A. should stop worrying so much about whether or not the school meets its own institution's criteria and determine whether or not it meets those of the library school accreditation process. At present, acceptable levels in many areas are geared only to the insistence that the program meet the overall standards of the institution in which it is housed. To put it sarcastically, it may be all right to have a non-rigorous

program as long as the rest of the institution is also not rigorous in its expectations and standards. If the institution tenures individuals without what C.O.A. guidelines would consider adequate productive scholarship for the faculty as a whole, then what difference should that make to library education accreditors? If the entire faculty is already tenured and faculty productivity is inadequate, then the required step is to add what would otherwise be surplus faculty until the problem can be resolved through resignation or retirement. Those who consider this solution too far fetched may have been ground down by the process. The fundamental question is whether or not accreditation is worth having, and that question can ultimately only be answered by the campus administration, and not by C.O.A. How they will answer it will depend in large part on how they have been prepared to answer it by their library school.

C.O.A. policies as this article envisages them are not intended to be threatening or frightening, nor designed to entrap. They should be clear, consistent, and unbending. If a school is surprised by the loss of accreditation or by failure to achieve it something is wrong, just as something is wrong in the communications process when a student who has seen all of his or her test grades is still surprised that he or she received a B minus rather than the expected A plus. The alternative ultimately posed to university administrators with programs in library education, "improve your program to meet required standards or perhaps consider closing it entirely," is not an unreasonable set of choices.

The problem is not now, nor has it every really been, one of money. University administrators have budget difficulties, but the level of library school expenditure is trivial and not the cause of that difficulty, nor will cutting or eliminating the program solve their problems. They know that. If they threaten to cut or eliminate, it is not because of a need to preserve money. It is because of the need to make a political gesture, and the perception that cutting or eliminating library programs is an acceptable sacrificial action, either because it is assumed that nobody will care, or because the university will be little affected, or both of these.

The pursuit of excellence in library education is of course not totally addressed through money and resources, because adequate resources do not insure quality, but quality without resources is difficult to achieve. At a time when all of our enrollment and support are being challenged, we also face the need for larger and more diversified faculties as the subject scope of what we teach becomes more complex. We need increasing quantities of laboratory facilities, computer equipment, data base access, field trips, and guest speakers. To a great extent quality costs money, although that does not assure quality. None of this should surprise academic administrators. They hear this from all of their other academic programs, too.

Is this a bad time to ask for additional support or for additional resources? Well, it is not a great time, but then there has never been a good time during which administrators volunteer largesse. Even in these times of constriction two basic management truths continue to assert themselves. First—in the absence of money there is always money for something which is really worth doing. Second—it is usually easier to get a lot of money than a little bit of money. Whether or not we get it, of course, depends on what we promise in return. As noted earlier, an administration which understands very little in detail about this or any other academic program looks for what it can understand and compare. It looks for protection of enrollment income and a presumed or perceived quality it can brag about.

The accreditation process provides us the opportunity to insist on the maintenance of quality standards—and it goes almost without saying that as library education complexity increases the interpretation of those qualitative standards must rise with it. Tomorrow's schools must be better than today's, because if they are only as good they are effectively worse. The accreditation process provides this opportunity because it can be consistent, it can be fair, it can be highly visible, and the implications can be easily understood by everyone. Obviously the university does not have to opt for accreditation. It can close the program or it can proceed without accreditation. Either of those is perfectly acceptable. However, if it chooses the latter, and particularly if quite a few schools do, then it obviously also becomes important for C.O.A., A.L.A., and the accredited schools to stress to their prospective publics what accreditation means, and what the lack of it implies, as the Underwriters Laboratory and Good Housekeeping do.

The alternative is not really very attractive. Unless library educators and the rest of the profession keep their sights high, and keep them unaffected by the economic pressures and the so-called "realities" which constantly swirl around them, they will be as surely affected by Gresham's Law as is international monetary policy. In any open and uncontrolled environment, in which qualitative standards are not perceived, stressed, or enforced, the activities of lower quality will inevitably drive out those of higher quality. Because they are cheaper. Academic campus administrators, like international bankers, will head straight for that option if they can—not because they are vicious or vindictive, but because, like everyone else, they are looking to survive.

The search for excellence or the identification and protection of quality through the accreditation process will certainly not be easy. It requires a certain amount of pragmatic realism which some might label ruthlessness. It is never painless, and it is particularly difficult in a small profession which holds humanitarian values to be important. However, it offers what may be the only opportunity to provide an objective and professional control for a process which, if we abdicate our responsibilities, will take place without us. The results of such an abdication would be far worse for library education and for the library profession.

References

1. Association of American Library Schools, *1982 Library Education Statistical Report.* AALS, State College, PA, July 1982.
2. Holley, E.: Remarks at the Open Session of the American Library Association Committee on Accreditation. January 1982. (Available from the author.)
3. White, H.S.: Perceptions by Educators and Administrators of the Ranking of Library School Programs. *College & Research Libraries,* 49:191–202, May 1981.

DEFINING BASIC COMPETENCIES

PART 1: IMPROVING LIBRARY SCHOOLS—THE KEY IS TO DISTINGUISH EDUCATION FROM TRAINING

About three years ago, Anthony Debons and some coworkers at the University of Pittsburgh and King Research identified a group of 1.6 million individuals as United States information professionals.[1] Although I served as a member of the review committee for this National Science Foundation-funded study and generally concurred with its approach and methodology, I nevertheless found its conclusions, particularly its identification of such a large body of professionals, to be too sweeping.

Although the study placed the largest body of professionals in the computer field, over a quarter of a million people were identified as professionals in the fields of library and information services. I have thought often about who these people were and where they were hiding, and I have concluded that some of the categorizations used in the study may have been a little too generous, at least for purposes of planning.

The NASA scientific and technical information facility I directed in the 1960s had about 100 "professional" employees. A cursory sampling of them in the 1980s indicates that perhaps 75 percent had no particular commitment to information work, but were simply passing through assignments as systems analysts, programmers, and scientific specialists on their way to something else. Similar questions of definition arise when the 1983 mid-year meeting of the American Society for Information Science is told that there are at present 100,000 professional online searchers, but membership in ASIS, which most directly claims to represent this activity, is less than 5,000.

Interesting as some of these conjectures may be, they are rela-

From *American Libraries* 14 (September 1983):519–25.

tively harmless, except perhaps for those planning publications or educational programs aimed at "information professionals." A potentially more dangerous exercise comes through the attempt to define membership of the library and information profession by identifying minimum or basic "competencies," with the inevitable conclusion that anyone who has these "skills" is a professional, no matter how they got that way.

Attempts to define professions through minimum competencies are increasingly popular with a variety of federal and state agencies and even have supporters among fully credentialed professionals. Defining minimum competencies means that jobs can be filled more cheaply, as the Office of Personnel Management has already discovered. They provide upward mobility to long-term employees, a feature that is particularly attractive when employees in otherwise dead-end positions are members of minority groups. Credentialing based on skills frequently provides the most direct and perhaps the only opportunity to meet affirmative action goals, and librarians are perhaps more sensitive to the achievement of overall societal objectives than some other groups. I certainly have not heard it suggested that either contract law or brain surgery qualifications could be achieved through competency testing, although the results might be as attractive.

I am not suggesting that competencies could not be acquired outside formal educational channels in our field, only that the method of identifying these basic skills needs to be carefully defined. In particular, I am concerned about self-fulfilling prophecies and the automatic downward validation of the profession that may occur if basic skills are determined by asking professional librarians what they do. To a large extent, what they do is clerical work, but not because they want it that way. Professional librarians and information specialists perform clerical duties because they are not assigned enough clerical support, and because in the organizational setting of today's library, clerical duties take precedence over professional duties.

"What needs to be done?"

The question, "What do you do?" as a basis for determining competencies is an exercise that in engineering is called retrofitting, and in research means fitting facts to conclusions already reached. The more appropriate questions are: What should you be doing? or, What needs to be done? The last question opens up all sorts of vistas because few of us have had the luxury of thinking about what needs to be done.

If practitioners cannot be asked simply what they do as the basis for determining needed competencies, then it is equally true that educators cannot answer that question arbitrarily, either. As Peter Drucker has pointed out,[2] educators in almost any discipline will seek to complicate and prolong the educational process. Competencies are almost always cheaper to acquire on the job rather than through the educational process, particularly if their acquisition is considered automatic after a certain number of years' experience. This does happen, in some cases, if the suggestion that volunteers in public libraries acquire valuable "professional" experience is to be taken seriously. Hospitals use lots of volunteers, but none of them can claim experience in anything but the mundane if necessary tasks they are permitted to perform. Certainly, none of them are called professionals, and will not be even after 40 years of volunteering. Nurses, who go through a formal educational process, have troubles of their own in achieving professional recognition.

"Educationandtraining"

It is clear to me that part of our difficulty comes from our failure to differentiate between education and training. The distinction between them is so blurred that often they are pronounced as one word—"educationandtraining," bringing to mind that other famous compound word, "libraryandinformationscience," identified by Michael Buckland of the University of California at Berkeley.

There is a vast difference between education and training. In most fields education precedes training and can be acquired in a limited number of ways. Training, we are told from textbook definitions, occurs most frequently on the job and through seminars, workshops, and specific courses, but rarely through formal degree programs. In other words, education prepares you to accept a professional job, not to perform it. The latter is the role of training, a distinction that has been understood from the very beginning in the fields of medicine and law that I cite so fondly. After receiving M.D. degrees, graduates are put through rigid and lengthy programs of at first closely supervised and then less supervised training, before they are allowed to function "professionally." The law degree usually qualifies its recipients to become law clerks, and then to be trained as lawyers.

Medicine and law are not the only fields in which such a distinction is made. From my consulting activities I know that chemical firms hire chemistry graduates and then spend a year training them to be chemists in that particular company. For part of that year they are negatively productive because they require fully qualified professionals to train them.

In librarianship, however, we somehow expect to hire people at 9 A.M., send them through personnel indoctrination, and turn them loose on the backlog at 10 A.M. If that is what we all want, then basic competencies are relatively easily acquired. However, we may then be dealing with not a profession but a trade, even if a skilled trade.

Educator and Practitioner Values Differ

Part of the reason for continuing friction and misunderstanding between practitioners and educators is that we are talking about different values. You practitioners don't necessarily want us educators to educate your new hires, you want us to train them. In large part we comply and teach "skills" you could as easily teach or teach better. We comply because your hiring practices would discriminate against our graduates not so prepared. But for some of us our hearts aren't in it.

When I hear that the vast majority of online searchers are trained in specific search strategies by database vendors, not library schools,[3] I am far from chagrined. I am pleased. Given the limits of the library school program in time and credit hours, there is no reason for us to spend time doing something that others can do so effectively. I would prefer our courses to deal with the intellectual and philosophical questions of why and how we approach information needs and problems through the application of new technology. If such questions are important (and I am not certain practitioners agree they are), I suspect that their educational component cannot be learned on the job, at least on most jobs.

The classic debate between practitioners and educators is hardly limited to librarianship, but I can recall it for at least the 33 years I have been professionally active. In fact, for the first 25 years I was on the other side of the debate, which is international in scope.[4]

"Plenty wrong" with Library Education

Complaints about library education are not without basis, because there is plenty wrong with it. However, complaints rarely address the real problems, and even teachers know that if you ask the wrong questions you are likely to receive the wrong answers. An artificial barrier exists between educators and practitioners; we need an easier interchange between the two groups. However, agreeing with that statement doesn't make it happen. The value systems of educators and those of practitioners don't match—I doubt that any ARL library would give me a crack at directorship for one year. We may interchange—and the Council on Library Resources is to be commended for furthering this activity—but we don't necessarily give each other meaningful things to do.

There are too many small and weak library schools, a topic I have addressed in other writings.[5,6] There are certainly too many library schools for the number of graduates—perhaps twice as many as are needed—but you and the students like geographic convenience. You argue, sometimes quite correctly, that much of library school research is esoteric and of little practical value, but when a study with practical implications is reported at ALA meetings, the audience invariably consists of other researchers.[7]

While practitioners argue that library schools have not been responsive enough to their needs, I would argue that we have probably been too responsive in offering the specific courses you have demanded. You have demanded (and the students have concurred because they know you want to see it on the resumé) more practical work experience before the first professional job—perhaps so that we can start the 10 A.M. backlog attack at 9:30 instead. I have no objection to work experience, but I would prefer to see it acquired in part-time jobs for pay rather than for educational credit; particularly if we are not sure the professional supervising a practicum is up-to-date and interested, and not reinforcing bad habits or unsubstantiated tradition.

At the most recent ASIS meeting, library schools—Indiana certainly among them—vied with each other to show how much experience in online searching and microcomputers they provide. However, the continuing (and seemingly endless) growth in number of courses being added to existing curricula only causes students to substitute the new courses for others. The fact that nearly all students now take a course in online searching means they don't take something else. Intellectual Freedom? Introduction to Research? Government Documents? Literature of the Humanities? If I kept on, I'd ultimately find a course you care about.

Indiana's curriculum for the MLS is fairly standard, at least among larger and more complex library schools. Students must take 12 courses to graduate; they rarely take more voluntarily. Of these, five are required, the other seven are electives from among 40 to 50 offered during an academic year. When online searching becomes a required course or is taken by most students as an elective, their open electives are reduced from seven to six.

Our problem is not only that we need to teach more skills, as is frequently suggested. We also need practitioner help in identifying courses that are not needed (although I am skeptical about that possibility). More to the point, there may be skills we should not include in education because the employer should include them in training. Other skills may belong in continuing education and/or continuing training, providing we can assure that either one takes place. I teach a course in personnel management that I would prefer to offer after two or three years of post-MLS experience. However, I don't expect to see most of these students again so I teach the course while they are here.

Grievances about library education are myriad and to some extent contradictory. Michael Koenig argues persuasively[8] that library education does not stress the values of special librarianship. That complaint is echoed by large academic, small academic, large public, small public, and school libraries, with each group suspicious that we are training our students for work elsewhere. And the issue of training, of course, is really the point. I don't believe we should be training our students. We should be educating them, and perhaps education is the more generic. Training is quite specific, but it occurs later, and it takes time and money. Self-respecting professions know and accept that.

The list of suggestions furnished by helpful practitioners are usually confusing, sometimes contradictory, and invariably more than can be accomplished in a one-year program. They contain few thoughts on which courses should be eliminated. They frequently contain contrasting emphases between specific skills (training?) and basic values (education?).

There are other contradictions. While special librarians argue for more management preparation, half of the public librarians in one survey considered it a waste of time.[9] This is puzzling to me, because I would argue as a former special librarian that while it is just possible, although not desirable, for many special librarians to get by without management skills in environments in which they are tolerated but barely noticed, public librarians are constantly in the grip of bureaucratic stresses.

The Alternatives

The problems appear almost endless. There are alternatives, but they pose problems, too.

1) We need to monitor the quality of library education programs, at least of accredited programs. Because Gresham's Law works. And the toleration of lower standards will reduce the quality of programs that are better.

2) We could develop special schools or programs that concentrate on some parts of library education and ignore others, or that point students interested in being academic, public, medical, or school librarians toward other educational institutions. Library education has been weighing this alternative for some time, but it presents significant problems. It would, of course, completely change present accreditation criteria, which demand that basic education must be sufficient for any first

professional position. It might create more scattering and schools with even smaller enrollments. It would pose severe political problems for state institutions, which would be forced to suggest that residents get their degrees elsewhere. Finally, not all students know what specialization interests them at the time they enroll. Some decide after a particularly exciting course, some after meeting a dynamic teacher, some after surveying the job market. What happens to students who find themselves halfway through a program in the wrong school?

3) We could increase the one-year degree to two years, perhaps more. Library educators have also discussed this alternative. The two-year program is common among Canadian schools, but is used by a small number of U.S. schools. In that scattering of approaches is also the root of some of the difficulty with two-year programs. While Peter Drucker may be correct in suggesting that educators lengthen and complicate the educational process if given the opportunity, Commissions of Higher Education and Boards of Trustees sometimes feel otherwise. Offering an accredited, two-year degree program becomes difficult to justify when a nearby institution offers an equally accredited one-year program. Canadian schools overcame this problem through concerted action, but no consensus is apparent in the United States. Finally, some of us feel uneasy about increasing course requirements to qualify for jobs that sometimes pay as little as $10,000 per year.

4) Probably the most attractive alternative would involve expansion of continuing education and training programs. Continuing training through workshops and seminars and continuing education through advanced degree and certification programs would be included. Academic institutions could then participate in the training process without penalty to the education process. Continuing education and training are heavily used in many other professions. It is unfortunate that they don't work well in ours. Experience shows that priority lists for continuing education courses frequently fail to materialize into registrants when it is determined that a course will be offered next fall rather than in the indefinite future, that it will be on Tuesday night, and that it will cost between $150 and $300.

Successful continuing education and training courses require a combination of "carrot" and "stick" approaches. In the carrot approach, the employer accepts responsibility for supporting such courses by paying tuition, granting administrative leave, and recognizing the employee's accomplishment at the time of salary increases and promotions. The stick approach involves the insistence—not uncommon in other fields—that continuing education and training are necessary not just to advance, but to keep the present job.

None of the alternatives is particularly attractive. As funding problems continue and perhaps intensify, there will be pressures for short-cuts, i.e., to adapt standards to people who are already in libraries but who cannot meet higher standards. We usually accomplish this by ridiculing earlier standards as idealistic or unrealistic. Many of these pressures come from outside management, as well as from the federal Office of Personnel Management. We can frequently deal with outside pressures and we can always fight them.

Far more insidious pressures for short-cutting come from within—from the desire to avoid confrontation, advance worthy employees, or recognize marginal candidates, and from the hope that we can continue to do everything even when deprived of staff and of dollars. Such pressures lead to the identification of so-called "practical" competencies. These are the competencies that cause concern because they are indeed fairly easily acquired, and therefore provide opportunities to cut budgets or provide upward mobility without the price of an educational program.

PART 2: IDENTIFYING BASIC COMPETENCIES: A RIGHT WAY AND A WRONG WAY

These easy and attractive alliances are worrisome as we face the identification of basic competencies called for in a contract awarded by the Department of Education to King Research, Inc. Unless precautions are taken, the contractor could end up with a list of "needed" basic skills that represents neither a professional approach nor a philosophy, and addresses only today's crises, not tomorrow's needs and hopes. I am concerned about a pragmatism that lives only from day to day, and I have reasons and suspicions for that concern.

I served on the panel to develop a library research agenda for the 1980s, a process I have described briefly.[10] In developing the agenda, we had little time for discussion or consensus. Instead, balloting was required—a dangerous approach to intellectual issues in which really innovative ideas will be, at least initially, threatening and unpopular. The heavy hand of pragmatism and of solving today's monumental problems ruled even this agenda, and what emerged was recognition of the need for more effective management justifications and analyses and concern for the application of technologies. The concern was not with future technologies, as might be expected in an agenda charged to look ahead 10 years, but with implementation of present shelf technology, even though the time frame extended past 1990. Despite continuing complaints about the educational process, only the educators on the panel supported research in this area.

Problems of "Myopic Pragmatism"

There will be problems enough in the long term from this myopic pragmatism. But there is an immediate danger in the quick-fix mentality of "tackle the backlog after an hour of orientation," if that is what is represented in identifying basic competencies. If responses are drawn from a population of pressured, frenzied, survive-at-all-costs individuals whose approach to professional shortages is to shift duties to clerks and volunteers, then basic competencies could become sufficiently pliant to not only prove the Office of Personnel Management correct, but perhaps lead to the elimination of professional qualifications. Because Gresham's Law works. In a free and uncontrolled environment, the ill-prepared and less competent will always drive out the competent: the less competent are more plentiful and cheaper.

In today's libraries, perhaps at times because those who are only trained and not educated to basics don't ask so many embarrassing questions, potential and intellectual abilities are not often held in high regard. Individuals who have immediately useful skills are preferred. Applicants with two years of experience in which they have shown beyond all doubt that they will always be mediocre are usually preferred to bright, innovative graduates who don't have experience and therefore have to be taught. The payoff from these individuals is ever so much greater, but it is a longer term payoff, and there's no time to wait. As a dean, I keep hearing from library directors that they are looking for bright and innovative graduates. I suggest to them that in some cases the supervisors who do the actual hiring prefer docile drones who have basic skills, don't need to be taught, and don't ask philosophical questions for which supervisors have no answers.

What We Must Do

I am not an apologist for academia. I hope that my 25 years of management experience allows me a balanced approach. There is plenty wrong with library education. However, the present pressures for so-called improvement found in surveys and articles from a whole range of practitioners do not provide solutions. We must begin to talk about the difference between education and training, between what is brought to the first job, what is learned on that first job, and what *must* be (not just *can* be) learned later through formal and informal job and educational experiences. If we do this, I suspect we will emerge with a list of beginning competencies entirely different from most of those I have seen to date. It will be a demanding list, and there will be few opportunities for acquiring the skills on it by hanging around a library for 20 years.

In a sense that's unfortunate, because we like to provide as many options as possible. However, most self-respecting professions provide few if any shortcuts to established educational criteria. I doubt I would get much consideration for the posts of attorney general or surgeon general of the United States, but for library posts we not only accept other qualifications, we sometimes seem to prefer them. We do indeed need to develop basic competencies and differentiate as to whether they should be acquired by education or training.

Once we have established that crucial difference, the question that plagues all wage and salary analysts—the relationship between education and training—falls into place. Some things can be learned on the job; some things can be learned only on the job. Some can be learned only in an academic setting away from production pressures, even if there are supervisors who have the time and inclination to train. Some things don't come with time at all, and many cannot be acquired automatically. As one case study points out, seven years of experience is not the same thing as one year of experience repeated seven times. The distinction is clear enough, but is often ignored in the search for career ladders. We are not dealing with spawning salmon. Professionals need and are entitled to help and advice, but by and large they must build their own ladders.

It may be necessary to develop several different sets of competencies differentiated by type of library, type of function, or type of process. However, before we fragment the educational process even further we must determine if we can put at least a portion of it into the realm of training, into the approximately one year after graduation in which professionals are not expected to be very productive. Alternatively, and particularly for people in small libraries who have little opportunity for training, we must ask if part of library education belongs in post-degree periods of planned, demanded, and assured continuing education, continuing training, or both.

SUMMARY

In summary, I see the identification of basic competencies as useful, but only to the extent that it addresses each of the following questions:

1) What parts of initial basic competence are normally acquired through education? Can they be acquired through alternatives to education on the job, or through home study? If so, which alternatives, and how? Who determines whether skills really have been learned? Certainly not just employees' supervisors, because we all adapt what we find to conclusions we have already reached and to realities we encoun-

ter. If we can't find someone to promote who is promotable, we usually promote someone who is not promotable.

2) What parts of initial basic competence are best acquired after education, or perhaps before education? Presumably these are best acquired on the job, but are there alternatives? How can such competence be measured or evaluated and by whom? Probably the judgment of the immediate supervisor is most appropriate in this case, though not exclusively so.

3) Assuming we can indeed identify an initial competence, no matter how acquired, how do we factor in the need for continued growth as complexity grows? In other words, what does one have to keep doing not to qualify for the next job, but to keep this one? If they do nothing, the qualified presumably become unqualified. Basic competencies accurately described today are only a snapshot of today's conditions. They will have changed five years from now.

4) What are the characteristics of the next rung up the ladder, and how does one get there? Are there specific components of getting to that rung achievable only by progressive experience and job growth? Are there specific components achievable only by formal coursework, or seminars and workshops?

Our colleagues in primary and secondary education, through their union contracts, may define these components too simplistically. To get ahead, to get promoted, teachers need further formal education. Almost any sort of education. Five pounds of courses equals a $3,000 raise. I don't care for this approach. However, the other extreme, which equates experience with education, usually through a formula counting two years of experience as one year of education, is equally simplistic. Experience counts only if it demonstrates growth. One year of experience repeated seven times counts as one year of experience.

I do not know whether the Department of Education, which contracted for the current study of competencies without really consulting anyone, has a hidden agenda. I don't know whether they have already decided that librarianship can be downgraded and are only looking for proof. I know that our profession doesn't have much support or understanding in the present administration. We have seen this already in the posture of the Office of Personnel Management—a posture that ignores all facts for the sake of bureaucratically and economically based prior decisions.

Regardless of whether the DOE already has a conclusion, we can turn this study to our advantage. The government must get information from this profession, and the profession will have ample opportunity to respond to the conclusions once they are presented. More important, we will sustain our responses by what we do, not by what we say. If we hold fast to our own ideals and standards, even if funding authorities don't allow us to reach them, we will be all right. If we temporize and rationalize in order to do as much as we can with the funds allowed us, there is no reason those funds can't be cut more.

Our colleagues in the medical profession, who understand quite clearly what a paramedic can be allowed to do, and control that job description, understand the professional/paraprofessional distinction quite well. In hospitals, paramedical and volunteer duties do not expand if there is a shortage of medical staff. The shortage is magnified and spotlighted. Perhaps one hospital even closes, but the point has been made. Drawing up my own will or arguing my own case in court may be within my capacities, but will never bring me acceptance as a lawyer. It may be time to learn some of the confrontational skills used by our colleagues. It may be time to stress to our public not how free we are, but how worthwhile we are, and to realize that insistence on institutional standards may be preferable to survival at all costs.

References

1. Debons, Anthony, et al. *The Information Professional. Survey of an Emerging Field.* Dekker, New York, 1981.

2. Drucker, Peter F. "Managing the Public Service Institution." *College and Research Libraries* 37:4–14, Jan. 1976.

3. Bourne, Charles P. "Issues and Challenges for the Online Industry." Keynote address presented at the 12th Mid-Year Meeting of the American Society for Information Science, Lexington, May 23, 1983.

4. Cronin, Blaise. *The Education of Library-Information Professionals: A Conflict of Objectives?* ASLIB Occasional Publication No. 28, 1982.

5. White, Herbert S. "Critical Mass for Library Education." *American Libraries* 10:468–70 and 479–81, Sept. 1979.

6. White, Herbert S. "The Library Education Accreditation Process: A Retreat from Insistence on Excellence." *Library Journal* 105:2377–2382, Nov. 15, 1980.

7. White, Herbert S. "ALA Conference Raises Questions on the Purposes of Research." *American Libraries* 12:568–69, Oct. 1981.

8. Koenig, Michael E. D. "Education for Special Librarianship." *Special Libraries* 74:182–196, April 1983.

9. Bakewell, Ken. "The Library/Library School Interface." *Information and Library Manager* 2:73–75, Dec. 1982.

10. White, Herbert S. "The Research Agenda: No Panacea, But a First Step." *American Libraries* 13:270, April 1982.

Continuing Education: Myth and Reality

I will assume that nobody in this room needs to be convinced of the desirability of continuing education programs. Continuing education has assumed the mantle of being self-evidently good and wholesome.

The risk in our readiness to embrace the virtue of continuing education is that we will convince ourselves that we really have such a program in the library profession. In a talk at the 1983 ALA conference in Los Angeles, one speaker indicated that our pretense to having a continuing education activity was really a fraud. I won't go quite that far, because fraud implies an attempt to deceive, and self-deception is rarely malicious. I prefer to label continuing education in the library profession as a mirage.

I will have more to say a little later about why C.E., as we practice it, doesn't work very well. I will state at this point only that C.E. does not work because it is left totally to individual options and individual initiative. You do it, if you do it, because you are self-motivated to that decision to learn and improve, and not because of anything you will either receive in return or because of any real or implied threat. There are some, including some of my faculty colleagues, who would argue that this self-motivation is the best and most valid of all motivations, and I would not disagree. However, the number of individuals willing to give up a Thursday night when IU is playing (or even if Purdue is playing), drive twenty miles, stay up until midnight, do homework on the weekend, and pay for the privilege will be small in this profession, as in any other, if the only reward is self-gratification.

We have built some incentives into the obtaining of the MLS, and particularly the accredited MLS. Most specifically, many jobs are simply

From *Indiana Libraries* (1984):138–45.

foreclosed to those who don't have it. We have had students, particularly older students, who took their MLS degree quite resentfully, convinced at least initially that there was nothing we could possibly teach them that they didn't already know. I would hope that we were able to convince them to the contrary, but the point is that they came even though they didn't want to come.

The MLS, like many professional degrees, is frequently labeled as a terminal degree. Not because you die from it, but because it is the only education you will ever be required to have, for the next 40 or 50 years if you work that long. The degree is called a union card, because that is exactly what it has become.

I doubt that I need to spend a great deal of time telling this audience why continuing education is essential to any professional, and certainly to a library professional. Education, no matter how well provided, is fixed in time. Teachers in the 1960s could hardly lecture about AACR-II and shared bibliographic utilities, microcomputers or file downloading, because there were no such things. Education is fixed in time, but technology changes, systems approaches change, and needs change. Students sometimes insist that they don't really need to learn about budgeting. Sometimes, after two years they still insist that this information is irrelevant. After five years, when they have achieved their first management post, they complain that we didn't tell them enough. The obvious answer would have been for them to come back for that piece of education as it began to loom important. Why they didn't is the crux of what we need to discuss.

The problem is not with the provision of educational opportunities. There are plenty, and if there were demand for more, there would be more. The problem is that there is hardly any demand for what is offered. Is that because librarians are more close-minded than others? I don't think so.

We offer a post-masters specialist degree program which allows a remarkable versatility to structure an interdisciplinary curriculum specifically suited to the student's interests. I am pleased to note that one of the graduates of this program is on this panel, but it is still nevertheless true that we have never had more than four or five graduates of the specialist degree program in any one year. It can hardly be argued that the Specialist Degree meets a major professional need. Our experience is not unique, other library schools report the same experience. All but two of the continuing education courses scheduled for last fall's MFLA meeting had to be cancelled. That's two classes, with perhaps a total of 40 attendees is that many, for the librarians of a multi-state area. ACRL, which has a major program of course offerings with regard to both ALA and bi-annual ACRL meetings, reaches perhaps 5 percent, probably fewer, of the academic librarians whom it might seek to reach, and that only with one program each. The perhaps most aggressive and successful of the professional associations in this area, the Special Libraries Association, held 24 courses for its 1983 annual conference. At an average attendance of 20, they enrolled 480 students assuming each took one course. Related to the membership of the Special Libraries Association, it means that less than 4 percent of the members took one course, 96 percent got nothing at all at least through this mechanism.

In the spring of 1983 Professor Daniel Callison of our faculty, who is a recognized expert in the field of media programming, developed a workshop on this topic, because we had been told that this was an area of great need and importance. We planned two sessions, because he felt that 20 enrollees were as many as he could handle in any one group. The charge was $80, including the cost of materials, equipment, film, processing and recording tape, for 20 contact hours. That's $4/hour. Try getting a plumber for that. We ended up with one class, with 7 students. We really should have cancelled the program, but I felt a commitment both to the students and to Professor Callison, who had developed the material. That's enough examples. Continuing education? What continuing education?

There are a variety of ways in which continuing education can be provided. In a survey which doctoral student Marion Paris and I have just completed, we examined not only library administrator reactions to the present curriculum, but also to the various options for education and training outside the MLS degree program. There are at least five techniques for continuing education which we identified: 1) Education or training on the job, as provided possibly by more senior members of the library staff or at least in the library and on library time. 2) Education and training provided by vendors and other commercial services. Vendor training is frequently free or unnaturally cheap, but it is obviously also specifically directed at what they want to teach you. They are not likely to disclose competitor options. 3) Opportunities provided by professional societies and associations, at the national, state, and local level. 4) Education and training provided by and through government agencies. 5) Services provided by educational institutions, either with or without academic credit.

Our survey response, from close to 400 library administrators, was not aimed at continuing education except as part of the overall strategy spectrum. However, it disclosed some interesting answers. There was a professed willingness, particularly among larger libraries, to assume a greater responsibility for in-house training, but no clear understanding of what they were prepared and capable to teach. There was very little enthusiasm for education as provided by vendors or by government agency programs. The preference was for approaches as provided through professional societies and associations (and I think that would include such structures as the ALSAs) and as offered by educational institutions.

Two problems in the implementation immediately emerged, and it is these problems with which we must deal if we are to have meaningful continuing education programs. The first is the question of willingness to pay for such programs. Answers to what one professional 8-hour long program might be worth ranged from $10 to $500, but half of the respondents positioned themselves at the $50 level or below it. That means that anyone offering a full day program and charging $50 will automatically miss half of the potential audience, and that is a grave risk in a small profession. The Special Libraries Association charges $75 for a 6-hour course, and of course they miss people. However, their courses are designed to recover costs, including payment for the instructor and administrative costs of the program, and they meet that objective. A reluctance to pay more than $30, or even $10, is understandable, but it is totally unrealistic in the framework of a continuing education program. Continuing education has a cost, and we will not be able to decide what to do about that cost until we accept the fact that an 8 hour program including lunch for $10 has to be subsidized by somebody, even if ultimately the presenter.

It is not difficult to understand why someone earning $13,000 per year might be reluctant to invest $50 of her own money, on her own time, on a continuing education experience for which she got no credit from her management or her Board. And this brings me to the second problem.

Programs for continuing education lack a motivational basis, except for the self-motivation to learn simply for the sake of learning. That will spur some, but relatively few. As part of our survey of library administrators, Marion Paris and I sought reactions, in addition to the financial judgment already mentioned, with regard to continuing education. We found a great deal of what I have to call passive support. Managers are pleased to see their subordinates engage in continuing education, many of them encourage it through release time, some even pay partial or complete travel expenses and conference fees. Not all, by a long shot. But even this, I would argue, is not enough. Continuing education takes work and effort, from individuals who already put in a full day on the job, who have home responsibilities, and who also have outside interests. What is missing is what I would call the carrot and stick approach. The carrot means that if you participate in continuing education, something good will happen as a result of it. The stick means that unless you participate in continuing education, something bad will happen.

Allow me to share with you responses to our questionnaire designed specifically to elicit reactions in this area. In response to the question: "Would completion of additional academic programs or courses lead to a promotion or raise?" the positive responses ranged from a high of 22 percent for middle-sized academic libraries down to 8 percent for larger and middle-sized public libraries. The response to the question of whether or not a commitment to continuing education was required to qualify for further promotion, the positive responses ranged from a high of 13 percent to a low of 3 percent, the high again for medium sized academic libraries. Finally, for what I consider the most interesting stick-type question: "Would your library insist that professionals engage in continuing education to keep their present jobs," responses ranged from an academic library high of 7 percent (probably tied to the tenure process) all the way down to a flat zero.

This is not true in all fields. In primary and secondary education, for example, the completion of continuing education is tied directly to salary increases, and those of us at Indiana University are used to seeing the horde of school teachers back in the summer for more courses. I am certain that at least some of them would come anyway, even without incentives, but how many? Even in our present plans for continuing education activities at SLIS, we find a sharp differentiation in attitudes. Some potential students are simply interested in learning the material, some will not attend unless they can receive IU academic credit, even though this process invariably increases the price. In librarianship we dutifully grant CE units, but I am not sure what the going value of a CE unit is. For continuing education to work, first of all somebody has to pay for it. We have exhibited a strange unwillingness to even want to find out, because we might not like the answers we get. However, it is not that difficult to approximate.

Professional societies such as SLA, MLA, ACRL, and ASIS, have pretty well determined that a one day 6- to 8-hour course or seminar must bring in about $2000. That's $50 each if you have 40 registrants, more if you have fewer. Probably $75 or $80 is a safer figure, because then you can break even with 25 registrants, and might not have to cancel if you have only 20. If you think that's expensive, check out the course fees for the American Medical Association or the American Management Association. And yet we know that the great majority of our responding library managers thought that $75 was too much (although some thought $500 was OK). The range is tremendous, and finding a common denominator is difficult if not impossible. And remember, we weren't even asking them what they considered a reasonable cost from their own checkbooks.

It seems clear to me that continuing education isn't going to work very well unless we provide either incentives or threat (and certainly incentives are better) and some sort of realistic financial base. Expecting continuing education to work by simply preying on the good nature of desired instructors is too narrow a ground, and provides no real philosophical planning base. It provides only targets of opportunity. So and so is going to be in town. Let's grab him. In addition to being too narrow, such an approach is unfair and unprofessional. It also seems clear to me that expecting librarians to pay for continuing education, when their salaries are low and when, unlike teachers, they get nothing in return, is also impractical. That leaves two sources—employers and government agencies. Both, I think, are appropriate.

Continuing education for professional staff members should be a normal part of any library's budget. That it is not, and there really has never been a concerted effort to try in so many libraries, surprises me. Certainly the doctors, lawyers, and other professionals who comprise many of the public library boards know this is a reasonable cost of having professionals in their own fields. The fact that it doesn't happen in libraries may in fact help them to wonder whether librarianship is a profession after all. There are basically two approaches, and only two. The employer can pay for continuing education either as a fringe or as an investment, and corporations do this on a routine basis. If not this, then the employee can pay, and be rewarded with a clearly and contractually defined promotion or pay increase when he or she is through. That is the educational model.

Alternatively, government can underwrite part or all of the cost. It is a logical extension, particularly at the state level. Government pays for all of primary and secondary education, and about 60 percent of the cost of a public university education. Is that the place to stop? Not if we know anything about the continuing nature of the educational process. Some states, such as Wisconsin, have a long history of support for alternative and continuing education. Some, such as Indiana, have virtually none.

In addition to payment for the continuing experience, we must look for ways to implement the carrot and the stick, because they are realistically part of the same motivation. Academia has the tenure process, which tends to work pretty well as a motivator for at least the first seven years. The academic educational literature is full of articles which discuss the dilemma of how to continue to motivate people who already have tenure, and who therefore don't really have to do anything.

In librarianship we have almost nothing beyond the demand for the MLS, particularly the accredited MLS, and as you know, even that is under constant attack. The Medical Library Association, in what I consider a courageous and forward looking step, has imposed its own review of certification for medical librarians on the heretofore automatic union card, but it remains to be seen whether or not the employers of medical librarians will be prepared, legally or morally, to fire people who haven't kept up with their professional society's injunctions.

In the public library sector which many Indiana librarians represent, we know that only stringent enforcement of ground rules describing educational qualifications for those holding posts in certain classes of libraries has protected us at all. This is a battle we have not always won, as in the needed qualifications for school librarians, and I think it is unfortunate for the state that school librarian qualifications are largely determined by educators who have never understood very much about libraries, and who suffer from the additional handicap of being deluded into thinking that they do. Without state-wide rules, many library boards would hire or promote individuals without library degrees—in part because it is simpler, in part because it is cheaper, and in part because they can't really see what difference it makes to the operation to the library. And, of course, that difference is not automatic. Some librarians function as clerks, and some clerks operate on professional levels. We know that, and it is a continuing problem we need to address. But it is certainly not a reason for us to abdicate our insistence on professional education for professional posts.

What I am suggesting, then, is that to strengthen the continuing educational process we must insist on it, and place it on a realistic platform of professional expectation, cost recognition, and financial reward for its participants. There is no doubt that the provision of continuing educational opportunities will follow the development of such models, and we must then devise mechanisms for a qualitative assessment of what is being offered. However, first things first. It appears to me the wrong priority to concentrate on structure of monitoring when we have so little to monitor, and so little cohesiveness.

My suggestions place a heavy responsibility on all Indiana professional librarians to safeguard and enhance their profession, but probably most directly on the State Library. After all, I am suggesting both that the State Library take the initiative in demanding state funds for continuing education, and that it also seek to implement standards of professional certification for continuing education.

Is this a good time for such initiatives? An understanding of management communications tells us that resources are never offered, and that the excuse of poverty is always made, whether or not it is reasonable. In other words, during times of largesse, normal funding, or of disastrous financial constraints, we will always be told that there is no money. It is the job of the subordinate to sift the truth from the rhetoric, to demand what he or she really needs, and to point out what will happen if this doesn't occur. Former Governor Otis Bowen, writing to the State Library Conference which preceded the White House conference, gave us some very good advice, but I am not sure we were listening. He told us that we had been ineffective in rallying political support, because politicians reacted to promises of reward and threats of retribution, in terms of their own political hopes and expectations. We have not really been successful in doing either, and for this reason have not been able to share in the largesse which has suddenly befallen this state.

Is this a good time to get money in the state of Indiana? It is a superb time, and its like may not come again for many years. There are two reasons. First of all, this state has a surplus and projected further surplus so large as to be embarrassing. One alternative is of course to return it as a tax cut, and that possibility exists. However, that is not the preferred approach, because tax cuts followed by tax increases followed by further cuts and increases tend to anger the electorate. They have already accepted the tax increase, it is better to find innovative ways for spending the money.

The second reason is the groundwork which our colleagues in the field of education have already laid for us. They have succeeded in convincing a basically conservative administrative leadership that spending more state money to upgrade the quality of education—to upgrade the preparation of teachers—is both good sense and good politics. Politicians have not made the connection between upgrading the quality of teachers and upgrading the quality of librarians, and the educators have not made the connection for us. Why should they? However, we should be able to make that connection ourselves, and get some money while there still is some.

I begin with the assumption that continuing education is crucial to our profession, and I assume that you agree with that. There is always some question as to what constitutes education and what constitutes training, and how much should be acquired in school, how much on the job, and how much later. These are serious and complex questions, which defy easy and simplistic answers, but they don't have to stop our progress. What I am suggesting is that if we believe in continuing education we had better approach it pragmatically and realistically, and develop a game plan which meets the needs of all the participants. I think that up to now we have not only failed to do this, but also refused to acknowledge the need for this step. That acknowledgment is only the first basic small step, but that is how we must begin.

Employer Preferences and the Library Education Curriculum

Directors of academic, public, and special libraries were asked to relate the curricula of master's degree programs in library and information science at accredited library schools to their own perceived needs and preferences in the hiring of junior professionals. They were also asked to examine and rank options for alternatives to education and training outside the traditional one-year degree setting. These options include an expansion of the present curricula, movement of courses from the degree program to job training and continuing education, and the elimination of material from course content. Specifically with regard to continuing education, they were asked to rank various options and to relate these to the various techniques of professional and economic motivation. Responses are presented and tabulated both by type and size of library. Tentative conclusions and directions for further research and discussion are identified.

BACKGROUND

Discussion of the appropriateness of the library education process has been continuous and often acrimonious. As early as 1923 C. C. Williamson issued his report on training competencies for the Carnegie Corporation.[1] Some forty-seven years later Ralph Conant attempted to update those issues in a report that received scant praise and consider-

This article was written with Marion Paris. Reprinted from *Library Quarterly* 55 no. 1 (January 1985):71–133.

able criticism, particularly from library educators.[2] Concerns about the adequacy of library education have not been reserved to any type or size of institution, however. There have been many professional society meetings devoted to this topic, together with articles, special journal issues, and conference proceedings.[3-13] Practitioners representing academic, public, school, and special libraries have all tended to agree that there is much wrong with library education; educators, too, have engaged in considerable self-examination and self-criticism. The noisy consensus that change is indeed necessary has hidden the fact that there is little agreement on what those changes should be. Finally, the Department of Education, in recognition of this major concern, contracted with King Research, Inc., for a report outlining suggested new directions in library and information science education.[14]

For some time it has been strikingly clear that many of the statements about library education are simply expressions of opinion and preference. Where practitioners are asked to express their feelings about what the library education program should encompass, they are never asked to fashion these comments within any framework of either the present or some specific future alternative educational program. To a great extent, the King Research approach repeats this technique.

Such methods provide much useful background information but, at the same time, fail to deal either with alternatives for implementation or with the reality of the existing curricula. It is, after all, not likely that present educational programs will simply be eradicated and new programs built from the ground up. It is far more likely that whatever changes are made will be implemented within a framework of existing degree programs. It was decided, therefore, that an approach that asked for proposed modification as applied to existing curricula would form a far more useful basis for later discussion and evaluation.

Moreover, the present master's degree program, which forms the basis for most educational preparation, is constrained in length. With only a few exceptions in the United States, the M.L.S. program is considered a one-year master's degree, with a curriculum which normally ranges from twenty-seven to forty-five credit hours, or from nine to fifteen courses. To the extent to which changes in this curriculum are desirable, they can be put into effect by altering the content of existing courses, by removing present courses and substituting others, by shifting courses to other programs, or by lengthening the program to include more courses. Furthermore, the educational or training experiences offered in the present M.L.S. degree programs (the words "education" and "training" mean different things and must be carefully defined) must be considered in concert with other opportunities to learn—before entering library school, through practice or internship experiences while a student, through on-the-job training after graduation and employment, and through a whole range of postdegree educational and training opportunities, some as formal as advanced degree programs and others considerably less rigid.

A review of earlier writings, as well as of specific discussions with individual library administrators, also led to the disturbing conclusion that there is little consistency in what individuals deem important. It might be assumed that special, academic, public, and school librarians would emphasize different competencies, and two of the overriding questions are whether all of these requirements can be met within a "reasonable" degree program and whether there is enough of a common denominator to identify a consistent core curriculum for all types of libraries. Such a basic educational preparation, whether offered through a core or other educational opportunities, is assumed by the standards and guidelines of the ALA Committee on Accreditation (COA).

Beyond the expected divergence between what librarians working in different types of institutional settings expect, there also seems to be some inconsistency in the type of educational preparation being demanded. While some writers call for a concentration on the development of overall intellectual abilities in such broad areas as liberal arts, communications skills, and the ability to deal with societal issues and concepts, others stress a general preparation in the fundamentals of the library profession, with the learning of specific skills to follow, largely through on-the-job training. Still others—perhaps primarily the supervisors entrusted with this training—express a preference for individuals already trained to the specific requirements of the job in question, even if necessary at the cost of other more general qualifications.

In summary, the many opinions and surveys reported in the literature and at professional meetings provide a great deal of information, much of it contradictory and little of it useful for consideration within the framework of existing library education programs. Merely asking individuals what they would like to see happen—without making them take responsibility for the ramifications of their decisions—is tempting but perhaps too simple. (Some astute respondents to earlier questionnaires indeed commented that offering criticisms in such an unstructured environment was probably enjoyable but too easy.)

Library education does operate within a number of finite constraints, and some of these will be discussed in the analytical section of this paper. To identify only one, length of preparation for professional status cannot be separated completely from the rewards offered (particularly salary) at the completion of the process. Nancy Van House, in a paper presented at the January 1984 ALISE meeting, pointed out clearly that it was probably unrealistic to expect to recruit bright and innovative candidates to the profession in large numbers when these people are also bright enough to recognize that they can earn a lot more in other fields.[15] One of the obvious concerns in considering an enlargement of the educational process is that, if this is accomplished without financial adjustment, it can result in an improvement of the curriculum and a decline in the quality of students.

PROCEDURES

In undertaking this study, it was determined to ask managers responsible for the operation of academic, public, and special libraries, and ultimately responsible for the selection of newly prepared M.L.S. graduates, to react to a list of specific courses presently offered at the master's level and to indicate how important these courses are as a prerequisite for anyone they would consider hiring for an entry-level position, or for anyone they would consider hiring for certain specific beginning positions. The list of courses, which totaled eighty-seven, was drawn from the bulletins of the largest library education programs in the United States and Canada. Because many schools may teach what is essentially the same course under different titles, some editorial modification was required. Respondents were invited to add further needed courses not already on the list. However, the list compiled was apparently comprehensive. Few courses were added at all by respondents and none with any consistency. In fact, some respondents commented on the exhaustiveness of the list and on the difficulty of choosing. That, of course, had been the intent and represents much of the problem. After completing their selection of a potential curriculum, respondents were asked to choose among a variety of options for alternative and continuing education, particularly to the extent to which their "requirements" might exceed the confines of a traditional one-year master's degree. These responses, and the conclusions drawn from them, are presented in great detail in later sections of this paper.

Eight subject groups were identified (see table 1), and each group was mailed the questionnaire, color coded so that respondent groups, but not individual respondents, could be identified.

With the aid of a computer-generated list of random numbers, libraries were selected at random from the *American Library Directory*, accepting that reference work both for the identification of type of library and for the size of professional staff reported. The survey was mailed directly to the individual listed in *ALD* as chief administrative officer, with the request that it be completed in person and not delegated to other staff members.

A pretest was mailed to two libraries in each of the eight sample groups. Following return of these responses, modifications in the instrument were made.

TABLE 1

THE POPULATION

Respondent Groups and Size of Their Professional Staff	Responding (N)	Surveyed (N)	Response Rate (%)
A. Large academic libraries (60 or more)	34	43	79.1
B. Medium academic libraries (20–59)	58	69	84.1
C. Small academic libraries (4–19)	50	68	73.5
D. Large public libraries (60 or more)	34	54	63.0
E. Medium public libraries (20–59)	49	80	61.3
F. Small public libraries (4–19)	48	70	68.6
G. Large special libraries (8 or more)*	56	69	81.2
H. Medium special libraries (3–7)	52	74	70.3
Total	382	527	72.4

*Staff sizes for special libraries are different because it is known, from reports of professional societies, that large special libraries are extremely rare.

LIMITATIONS

Several gaps in the survey population immediately became apparent. Academic libraries with fewer than four professional employees are excluded; many such libraries exist. Public libraries of the same size are also excluded, and we know that the great majority of public libraries is small. The same is known for special libraries, the majority of which have only one or two professional staff members. Finally, school librarians and media specialists are completely excluded from the survey, and that omission is obviously significant for any consideration of curriculum. In undertaking this survey, the choice was made to elicit the preferences of managers who hire librarians, and who in all probability are themselves librarians. Professional librarians in small public and special libraries, and in school systems, are hired primarily by nonlibrarians who may engage in little or no consultation with professional librarians regarding appropriate expectations. What these nonlibrarians are looking for when they hire an entry-level librarian constitutes an important research question of considerably greater complexity. We were merely taking the first and certainly easier step, an attempt to determine the preferences of librarians who are involved in selecting other librarians.

In developing respondent libraries through the random sampling techniques already mentioned, we desired to receive approximately fifty returns in each of the response categories, and sample sizes were designed with this objective in mind. In two categories this was not possible. According to the *American Library Directory,* only forty-five academic and fifty-six public libraries have professional staffs of sixty and above. With two responses already used in the pretest, questionnaires in these two size categories were sent to all libraries listed in the *ALD,* and responses in these two groups, not surprisingly, fell well below the level of fifty. However, response rates for these groups as well as for others were strong. Statistical consultants have provided assurance that the response levels are certainly more than adequate to claim statistical significance.

One additional finding may be of general interest. Because of the random sampling approach used, members of the survey population were asked to let us know if, for any reason, they were unable or unwilling to complete the questionnaire and should be replaced through an additional randomly drawn respondent. Relatively few library directors availed themselves of this option. Most, as already noted, did complete the questionnaire. Some others failed to respond at all or responded too late to be included in the sample population. However, one particular group of responses is worthy of note because it was not anticipated. Eight "large" special libraries, listed in the *ALD* as having professional staffs of eight or more, responded that they felt obliged to exclude themselves from the sample population. While they did indeed have the indicated professional staff size, most of those professionals were not librarians.

SURVEY RESULTS

Curriculum

The list of eighty-seven courses identified through library school bulletins as customarily constituting master's degree programs was presented in such a manner as to force respondents' choices concerning the importance of each course. A seven-part scale was constructed and values assigned as follows; 1 = essential for anyone we would consider hiring; 2 = essential for certain hires but not all; 3 = desirable as part of the master's program; 4 = useful but not a major factor in a decision to hire; 5 = should be learned on the job; 6 = can be acquired through continuing education; and 7 = unimportant for hiring of professionals in this library. For each of the eighty-seven courses, medians and modes were computed for each of the eight respondent groups—large, medium, and small academic libraries; large, medium, and small public libraries; and large and medium special libraries. Since the scale is not continuous and at best the values are measured at the ordinal level, the mean would have been an unreliable, even meaningless, measure of central tendency and thus was not computed.*

*An appendix containing the results, by type and size of library, is available from the authors.

This critically important segment of the study rests on two assumptions: first, that among library educators and practitioners alike there is a high degree of consistency in course identification; that is, that accredited master's degree programs tend to feature courses with the same or similar titles. While it is known what the courses tend to be called, their exact content and their instructors' expectations are not known. Thus when it is reported, for example, that 100 percent of the respondents indicated that basic reference is an essential part of the preparation of all junior professionals hired, it can be said only that what each respondent thinks of as the basic reference course is essential. The second assumption is that students enrolled in those courses master the subject matter taught at a level that enables them to use what they have learned in the first professional placement.

Recommended Courses

The criterion score selected for a course's inclusion on the roster of "recommended courses" was a median of 2.5 or below on the seven-point scale. Recommended courses, then are those that more than half of the respondents deem essential for the preparation of some entry-level professional in their organizations. The respondents would appear to be recommending that those courses be available to every student enrolled in a master's program. Table 2 lists the courses recommended by each of the eight respondent groups.

Noteworthy is the number of courses which the respondents recommended. Across all eight groups these total forty-one. With the addition of school library/media center courses which would presumably be highly ranked by such a group of respondents, the number of recommended courses would be even higher.

Although the lists of recommended courses manifest little variability within type of library group (percentage of overlap calculations exceeds 70 percent in most comparisons), there is far more variability between types of library groups. Simply stated, the respondents would appear to have identified, in addition to common basic courses, one curriculum for potential academic librarians emphasizing courses in academic libraries, subject bibliography, both Dewey and Library of Congress classification as well as advanced cataloging and classification, library automation, and specific technical services, for example, serials; another curriculum for the preparation of public librarians emphasizing public libraries, children's/young adult/adult services and materials courses, and Dewey classification; and a third curriculum for special librarians emphasizing literature of science and technology, advanced cataloging and classification, and system-specific online searching.

TABLE 2
Recommended Courses (Medians of 2.5 or below) by Respondent Groups

Large Academic Libraries (N = 34) (60 or More Professional Staff)	Medium Academic Libraries (N = 58) (20–59 Professional Staff)
Basic reference	Basic reference
Advanced reference	Advanced reference
Government publications	Government publications
Music bibliography	Music bibliography
Health sciences bibliography	Health sciences bibliography
Business bibliography	Collection development
Collection development	Literature of the humanities
Advanced collection development	Literature of the social sciences
Literature of the Humanities	Database selection
Literature of the social sciences	Archives and manuscripts
Literature of science and technology	Rare books
Library management	Academic libraries
General online searching	Library management
Library automation	Personnel and human relations
Advanced cataloging and classification	Introduction to information science
General technical services	General online searching
	System-specific online searching
	Library automation
	Organization of materials—Dewey
	Second course in materials organization—LC
	General technical services
	Specific technical services
	Cataloging of nonbook materials
	Rare bookmanship

Small Academic Libraries (N = 50) (4–19 Professional Staff)	Large Public Libraries (N = 34) (60 or More Professional Staff)	Medium Public Libraries (N = 49) (20–59 Professional Staff)
Basic reference	Basic reference	Basic reference
Advanced reference	Advanced reference	Advanced reference
Audiovisual materials	Children's services	Children's services
Collection development	Adult services	Young adult services
Literature of the humanities	Storytelling	Adult services
Literature of the social sciences	Collection development	Collection development
Literature of science and technology	Materials for adults	Advanced collection development
Academic libraries	Materials for children	Materials for adults
Introduction to information science	Materials for young adults	Materials for children
General online searching	Public libraries	Public libraries
Library automation	Introduction to information science	Library management

(continued)	(continued)	(continued)
Organization of materials—Dewey	Organization of materials—Dewey	Personnel and human relations
Second course in materials organization—LC	General technical services	Introduction to information science
General technical services		Organization of materials—Dewey
Specific technical services		Advanced cataloging and classification
Cataloging of nonbook materials		General technical services
		Cataloging of nonbook materials

Small Public Libraries (N = 49) (4–19 Professional Staff)	Large Special Libraries (N = 56) (8 or More Professional Staff)	Medium Special Libraries (N = 52) (3–7 Professional Staff)
Basic reference	Basic reference	Basic reference
Advanced reference	Advanced reference	Advanced reference
Children's services	General online searching	Collection development
Young adult services	System-specific online searching	Literature of science and technology
Adult services	Advanced cataloging and classification	Database selection
Storytelling	Cataloging of nonbook materials	Special libraries
Collection development		Introduction to information science
Materials for adults		General online searching
Materials for children		Organization of materials—Dewey
Materials for young adults		Advanced cataloging and classification
Public libraries		General technical services
Library management		
Personnel and human relations		
Library finance		
Organization of materials—Dewey		
General technical services		

It is also important to notice how many courses each group recommended; numbers range from highs of twenty-six and eighteen for medium academic and medium public libraries, respectively, to a low of six for large special libraries. It might be hypothesized in the case of the large special libraries that, since those organizations often are quite subject-field-oriented and those subjects vary so widely, little consensus as to what preparation is necessary for entry-level positions could be reached. Postulating a reason for the medium-sized academic and public library groups' many course recommendations is more difficult. Possibly however, the managers of the medium-sized academic and public libraries have a greater need—whether mandated in reality by mission statements or not—to do more, to be more things for more people, so to speak; to be both research institution and provider of specially tailored student or client services. It may be that medium-sized public and academic libraries, and in the latter case the institutions that house them, feel a need or a pressure to grow. Larger libraries and universities may sense that they have more nearly arrived at where they hope to be.

Curriculum Tracks

Next an attempt was made to find agreement within the three major respondent groups—academic, public, and special libraries. It became apparent immediately, as was indicated above, that special libraries are indeed special: their managers named significantly fewer courses (χ^2 significant at $P < .05$); and from those recommended courses, curriculum tracks could not be identified, due in large measure to the specialization of the special libraries in the survey population. Thus, tracks were determined for the academic and public library groups only.

Criterion for a course's inclusion in a "curriculum track" was established as a median score of 2.5 or below in at least two out of three academic and at least two out of three public library groups. Table 3 gives the tracks. The percentage of overlap between academic and public library tracks is only 46 percent. Those courses the two groups list in common are basic and advanced reference, collection development, library management, introduction to information science, Dewey classification, general technical services, and cataloging of nonbook materials. Divergence occurs when the academic library track emphasizes subject bibliography and automation, while the public library track features adult/children's/young adult services courses as well as personnel management.

These findings would appear to have serious implications for what library educators have endeavored for years to do: to provide a broad, general course of study that would prepare holders of the mas-

TABLE 3
CURRICULUM TRACKS FOR ACADEMIC AND PUBLIC LIBRARIES

Academic Libraries (N = 142)	Public Libraries (N = 132)
Basic reference	Basic reference
Advanced reference	Advanced reference
Government publications	Children's services
Music bibliography	Collection development
Health sciences bibliography	Materials for adults
Business bibliography	Materials for children
Collection development	Materials for young adults
Literature of the humanities	Public libraries
Literature of the social sciences	Personnel management
Literature of science and technology	Introduction to information science
Academic libraries	Organization of materials—Dewey
Library management	General technical services
Introduction to information science	Cataloging of nonbook materials
General online searching	
Library automation	
Organization of materials—Dewey	
Organization of materials—LC	
Advanced cataloging and classification	
General technical services	
Specific technical services	
Cataloging of nonbook materials	

Note—These are courses with medians of 2.5 or below by at least two-thirds of academic and public library respondent groups.

ter's degree for most, if not all, entry-level positions they might secure. What the academic and public library managers seem to be asking for, though, are two substantially different tracks for the education of their junior professionals.

Core Curricula

Somewhat greater agreement was found when the investigators went about identifying core curricula (see table 4). Criterion for a course's inclusion in the core was a mode of one on the seven-point scale; that is, the majority of respondents in a group indicated that the course is "essential for anyone we would consider hiring." Those courses, then, are the ones the respondents suggested should be required for all graduates of master's degree programs. Core curricula number fewer courses than the tracks, but in two instances contain as many as eight courses (out of the average of twelve courses that constitute the typical one-year master's program) that the respondents believed should be required of everyone.

Table 5 lists the core curricula for academic libraries (six courses) and public libraries (four courses), as determined by mode one responses from at least two out of the three academic library groups and at

TABLE 4
Core Curricula (Courses Given Modes of One) by Respondent Groups

Large Academic Libraries (N = 34) (60 or More Professional Staff)	Medium Academic Libraries (N = 58) (20–59 Professional Staff)	Small Academic Libraries (N = 50) (4–19 Professional Staff)
Basic reference Collection development Personnel and human relations	Basic reference Collection development Academic libraries Research libraries Library management Personnel and human relations Introduction to information science Organization of materials—Dewey	Basic reference Collection Development Literature of the humanities Literature of the social sciences Literature of science and technology Academic libraries Introduction to information science Organization of materials—Dewey
Large Public Libraries (N = 34) (60 or More Professional Staff)	**Medium Public Libraries (N = 49) (20–59 Professional Staff)**	**Small Public Libraries (N = 49) (4–19 Professional Staff)**
Basic reference Collection development Public libraries Introduction to information science Organization of materials—Dewey General technical services	Basic reference Collection development Public libraries Introduction to information science	Basic reference Collection development Public libraries

TABLE 5
Core Curricula

Academic Libraries (N = 142)	Public Libraries (N = 132)
Basic reference	Basic reference
Collection development	Collection development
Academic libraries	Public libraries
Personnel and human relations	Introduction to information science
Introduction to information science	
Organization of materials—Dewey	

Note—These are courses given modes of one by at least two of three academic and public library groups.

least two out of the three public library groups. Once again scant evidence was found of the existence of a real core for special libraries.

Courses that were not recommended either for tracks or cores are as notable as courses that were. Conspicuously absent, for example, is the practicum, or one-term fieldwork experience. Within every group the practicum received a mode of 3, or "desirable as part of the master's program." Other courses which were rated overall as less desirable or totally unimportant include area studies bibliography courses; library history; courses like intellectual freedom, copyright and legal issues, and information theory; and quantitative courses like bibliometrics and introduction to research. It must be emphasized that the respondents do not oppose such courses; they merely rate others as more important for the preparation of entry-level professionals. Another surprising omission is a course in microcomputers, which had modes of four, or "not a major factor in a decision to hire," in two of the eight groups and modes of three, or "desirable" (but not essential for anyone), in the remaining six groups. Practitioners' evident lack of support for both the practicum and a course in microcomputer applications would appear to contradict at least part of what today's students so vocally desire in their preparation for their first jobs. In fact, the question, Whither the practicum? might well be asked yet once more. And indeed, the dichotomy between what this study reveals about practitioners' valuation of a practicum and the fieldwork experience that students seem to demand underscores the critical need to plan, in a constructive, reasoned manner, for the future of education in library and information science.

On-the-Job Training and Continuing Education

Values five and six on the seven-point scale represent course content which "should be learned on the job" and "can be acquired through continuing education," respectively. It must be noted with emphasis that not a single course rated a mode of five or six. That is, there would appear to be no consensus that anything in particular should be learned on the job or acquired through continuing education, leaving, by implication, the education of entry-level professionals entirely in the hands of library educators.

Options

The second part of the study was intended to elicit suggestions for—if not possible solutions to—what was perceived a priori to be a desire on the part of some practitioners for an enlarged master's degree program. Five options were presented in a closed-end format, and respondents were asked to rank them in numerical order from one (first choice) to five (last choice) (see table 6). First choice of all eight respondent groups was to increase the content of existing courses. Increasing the duration of the master's program beyond the present one year was the second choice overall; two groups—large academic libraries and large special libraries—ranked this option fourth, however. Tied for third were moving courses to postmaster's study and removing courses from the curriculum entirely, although very few individual respondents nominated any courses for this treatment. In fact, some of the courses suggested for removal by some respondents were considered important by others. Ranked fifth was the option to leave more material for on-the-job training—notably automation and online searching.

Increasing the content of existing courses—the respondents' first choice and probably the easiest answer—thrusts the problem back to library schools. Moreover, by listing on-the-job training as clearly the last choice, respondents confirm the unwillingness to teach on the job that was demonstrated in the first part of the study by a total absence of modes of five, or "can be learned on the job."

Hiring Consideration and Salary Improvement for Graduates of Two-Year Programs

One of the concerns about the two-year master's program voiced by both educators and practitioners has been and continues to be whether two-year graduates would be given hiring preference over one-year graduates and whether the former group would be compensated at a higher level initially. The question was posed as follows: "If more

TABLE 6
Options

Option	Respondent Group								Overall Rank
	A	B	C	D	E	F	G	H	
Increase the program beyond one year	4	2	2	2	2	2	2	4	2
Increase the content of existing courses	1	1	1	1	1	1	1	1	1
Move courses to post-master's study	5	4T	3	3	3T	3	3T	3	3T
Remove courses from curriculum entirely	2	4T	4	4	4	4	3T	2	3T
Leave more material for on-the-job training	3	3	5	5	3T	5	3T	5	4

Note—Responses are to the question, If expressed curricular needs cannot be met through the traditional one-year master's program, what should be done? Options are listed by groups in rank order. T indicates tied ranks.

schools were to enlarge their programs, would the graduates of such programs receive greater hiring consideration than graduates of shorter programs?" Two hundred sixty-five or 64 percent of the respondents replied in the negative, and 117 or 30.6 percent in the affirmative. Table 7 depicts the responses by groups. In answer to whether graduates of two-year programs would be offered substantially higher salaries, 325 or 85 percent of the respondents said no, while only fifty-seven or 15 percent said they would pay two-year graduates more money. Those who answered that question in the affirmative were asked how much. Minimum and maximum figures for each group are given in table 7; they range from a minimum annual salary difference of $400 (medium special libraries) to a maximum salary difference of $5,000 (large and medium special libraries). The combined median salary difference for all eight respondent groups is $1,860. Ideally, median differences between and within groups would be examined statistically with the median test, an extension of the χ^2. Since so few respondents provided dollar amounts, however, the sample size was so small as to preclude the performance of a reliable test of significance. Nevertheless, it must be emphasized that at least half of the already small group of respondents who suggested salary differences deem $2,000 too high an amount for compensating individuals who would spend an additional year earning a master's degree.

Postmaster's Study

The next part of the study addresses the issue of postmaster's degree education and training. The question was posed as follows: "If there were to be greater emphasis on education and training after graduation with the master's degree, rank the options listed below (1 = first choice, 2 = second choice, etc.)"; on-the-job training; in-service training (workshops held in the library); training by systems vendors; government workshops and seminars; workshops and seminars conducted under the auspices of professional associations; individual graduate courses; and graduate degree programs. On-the-job training was ranked first by all of the eight respondent groups, which is surprising because on-the-job training received so little support in earlier questions. Ranked second was individual graduate courses. Respondents ranked professional association workshops and in-service training third and fourth, respectively, while training by systems vendors and graduate degree programs were tied for fifth place. In last place was government workshops and seminars. Table 8 gives detailed results by respondent groups.

TABLE 7
Consideration and Salary Improvement

Respondent Group	Greater Hiring Consideration		Higher Salaries		Amount of Increase ($)		
	Yes	No	Yes	No	Minimum	Maximum	Group Medians*
A	9	25	4	30	700	2,000	1,375
B	23	35	16	42	750	3,000	1,750
C	20	50	10	40	1,000	3,500	1,625
D	5	29	1	33	1,500	1,500	1,500
E	5	44	4	45	1,500	3,000	3,000
F	17	32	4	45	1,500	3,000	2,250
G	21	35	12	44	1,000	5,000	2,500
H	17	35	6	46	400	5,000	5,000
Total	117	285	57	325			

*Overall median, all groups, is $1,860.

TABLE 8
POSTMASTER'S STUDY

| | Respondent Group | | | | | | | | |
Option	A	B	C	D	E	F	G	H	Overall Rank
On-the-job training	1	1	1	1	1	1	1	1	1
In-service training	4	4	4	4	4	2	6T	5	4
Vendor training	6	5T	7	6	7	6	5	4	5T
Government workshops	7	5T	6	5	5	5	6T	7	6
Association workshops	3	3	3	3	3	3	2	3	3
Individual graduate courses	2	2	2	2	2	4	3	2	2
Graduate degree programs	5	5T	5	7	6	7	4	6	5T

Note—Choices are in rank order; T indicates tied ranks.

Continuing Education Seminars: How Much Are Managers Willing to Pay?

The question of the level of funding library managers are willing to commit to continuing education concerns those organizations and individuals who would offer them as well as those librarians who would enroll in them. For this reason the question was asked, "What do you consider an appropriate ceiling charge per attendee for a one-day seminar or workshop?" The low figure of ten dollars was proposed by respondents from medium and small academic libraries, small public libraries, and medium special libraries, and the high, $500, by a respondent from a medium-sized public library. Table 9 depicts the range of responses—including medians and modes—for all eight groups. It is noteworthy (perhaps even astonishing) that the combined median for all eight groups is sixty-nine dollars. That is, over half the respondents regard seventy-five dollars as too high a fee for a day's worth of continuing education. Such response might indicate either that library managers expect subsidies for continuing education from outside agencies or that they simply are unprepared or consider themselves unable to pay more than seventy-five dollars per seminar to keep their employees up-to-date in this time of rapid, turbulent technological, organizational, and societal change.

Types of Support for Continuing Education

In the final part of the study, we sought to ascertain, first, whether the respondents as managers give tangible support to continuing education and, second, what types of support they provide. In answer to the first part of the question to which respondents were asked to reply yes or no, an overall total of 353 or 92.4 percent of the respondents indicated that their libraries do support continuing education in some fashion. Only twenty-one or 5.4 percent do not, while eight of the respondents failed

TABLE 9
THE COST OF CONTINUING EDUCATION ($)

	Respondent Group							
	A	B	C	D	E	F	G	H
High	300	250	350	150	500	200	300	250
Low	35	10	10	15	15	10	25	10
Median	79	64	50	65	74	47	100	74
Mode	50	100	50	50	50	50	100	75

Note—Overall median is $69.

to provide either a yes or a no. A list of six common types of support was presented, and respondents who replied in the affirmative to the first part of the question were asked to indicate the type or types of support their organizations provide. That list appears in table 10, together with the results for each respondent group.

It would appear that, across all eight respondent groups, support for continuing education is provided largely in the form of tuition, travel or lodging, and released time (time off with pay); 79 percent of the respondents say that their organizations underwrite at least part of tuition costs; 80 percent pay full or partial expenses for travel or lodging; and 86 percent make released time available. Where professional support and professional expectation are concerned, however, affirmative answers are substantially fewer. Only 6 percent insist on continuing education for retention of the present job, 19 percent insist on it for promotion, and a surprisingly low 30 percent offer raises or promotions on completion of continuing education. The support that has been shown to exist is passive and reactive. Whereas other professions are grappling with issues of quality control, and some are even insisting on completion of specified continuing education units for renewal of certification, it would appear that there is little or no professional insistence on continuing education in library and information science and a correspondingly low professional expectation of it. It may be supported and applauded; however, there is little reward for it and even less insistence on it. The initiative must come from the individual. The Medical Library Association's recent efforts to tie continuing education to continuing certification is an exception, but as of this writing no other sectors of the profession have moved to follow this example.

IMPLICATIONS

The results of this study can be compared with and contrasted to some of the options that have been suggested for dealing with practitioner concerns with regard to library education. It is quickly apparent from the results of this study that no simple, obvious approach emerges. If the study confirms any earlier perception, it is that problems with library education as a preparation for professional activity defy simplistic solutions and cannot be addressed simply by asking individuals what they think somebody else should be doing. The more rapidly we can dispose of these narrow, quick-fix approaches, the more directly we can deal with the issues. Personnel management theory tells us that the manager's greatest responsibility is to deal with problems for which there is no simple and apparent solution and for which none of the available

TABLE 10
TYPES OF SUPPORT FOR CONTINUING EDUCATION

Type of Support	Respondent Group								Total	Overall %
	A	B	C	D	E	F	G	H		
Tuition (full or partial)	32	40	34	31	41	37	46	40	301	79
Travel or lodging (full or partial)	30	50	39	28	39	35	45	39	305	80
Promotion or raise on completion of graduate degree	9	23	16	8	11	15	18	15	115	30
Released time (with pay)	28	54	41	29	42	43	48	42	327	86
Insistence on continuing education for promotion	3	14	12	7	14	10	8	6	74	19
Insistence on continuing education for retention	1	7	7	0	5	3	2	3	28	8

alternatives appears totally attractive. It is precisely this sort of dilemma that we appear to be confronting.

Suggested approaches for "correcting" the problems of the library school curriculum are many, and the following are not exhaustive. However, it may be useful to review some of these recommendations, particularly in light of the data generated by the study reported.

Solutions That Comprise Slogans Rather than Approaches

1. *Increase the content of the curriculum.*—This option, which was posed to the respondents somewhat as a test and which a large group immediately embraced, must fall into the "somebody must do something" category. To the extent it is suggested that some curricular components be removed and other components substituted, such recommendations provide reasonable alternatives. However, the respondents suggested few components for removal or for transfer to later continuing education or on-the-job training. The option for increasing the content of existing courses, thereby requiring students to work harder or longer, cannot be dismissed cavalierly. Probably many of us already surmise that the academic program in such fields as law and medicine requires greater rigor and more work on the part of the student. Indeed, some students complain that the library school program presently lacks sufficient content, while of course others complain that it is too demanding. The situation undoubtedly varies from school to school, and probably ought to be addressed through the standards and guidelines of the accreditation process if it needs to be addressed at all. However, if this question is to be broached, it must be articulated in some detail, even one course at a time. It must also be recognized that any increase in intellectual content has its price chiefly because it may disqualify some of the students presently admitted, perhaps including groups of disadvantaged students presently considered marginal or probationary.

2. *Increasing the quality of students admitted.*—The complaint is voiced frequently at practitioner gatherings that the quality of graduates of library educational programs is not what it should be or even what it used to be "in the good old days." That argument has a reverse side because sometimes graduates complain that their work assignments underutilize both their intellectual and professional preparation. The arguments tend to be circular and in any case not to the point. By and large library schools do not recruit their students. Rather, they distribute publicity about the school and about career opportunities, aimed particularly at students with specialized subject backgrounds in the physical sciences or at minority students. Most students who attend library school, however, recruit themselves either from a background of prepro-

fessional or student work experience in a library or according to a perception of how libraries operate. Most important in recruitment are library practitioners, who influence potential students for better or worse. Schools do, of course, have the option of rejecting applicants, but they do so with two very real constraints. First, their rejection must be based on tangible or demonstrable grounds to meet legal requirements. It is no longer permissible, and it undoubtedly was never appropriate, to reject students because it was felt "they would not fit." It is from such totally subjective judgments that biases emerge. Second, library schools operate their admissions processes with an understanding of approximately how many students they need. In general, the willingness to reject is based at least in part on the luxury of having more applicants than are needed. The concern that there may be too many library schools has already been addressed in detail by many writers. If this is in fact a problem, then the problem of admissions quality must be seen as secondary. The problem of applicant quality is yet a further problem. That concern, if it is indeed a concern, can be addressed only by the role models provided by professional leaders and mentors, the attractiveness of employment opportunities, and entry-level salary offers.

3. *Adjust the emphasis of the curriculum.*—It is fairly clear from earlier surveys and conference papers, as well as from the reactions of respondents to our survey, that many library administrators feel the curriculum emphasis is not particularly well suited to the needs of their libraries. An interest in certain types of courses for certain types of libraries might be expected and was indeed found. Academic, public, and special libraries might be expected to have a greater interest in curriculum offerings that matched the activities of their own institutions, and this was the case. Moreover, one would expect public libraries to have a greater interest than their academic and special counterparts in courses dealing with the literature and reading interests of children. However, such differentiation also reaches into other areas. Some practitioners would prefer an emphasis on library skills, while others would prefer more courses in human relations skills, writing, public relations, and speaking. The emphasis may be on the training of generalists, to the exclusion or at least to the detriment of specialized instruction, or the reverse emphasis may be chosen. This is especially noteworthy in respondents' reactions to courses in cataloging or other forms of analysis. Traditionally, many if not most library schools have considered at least one such course essential for any professional librarian, regardless of future job specialization. Our respondents, who generally failed to list such courses as essential for any of their new hires, apparently do not share this judgment. Finally, there is the balance between library science courses and subject courses. Traditionally library educators have preferred a broad liberal arts undergraduate background. Some libraries,

particularly academic libraries, have added the further requirement of a subject master's degree to the professional degree. Other practitioners, perhaps confronted by the reality that starting salaries cannot justify a subject master's, might prefer specialized undergraduate preparation, even at the expense of a broader education. The alternatives, by no means clear, will be discussed in greater detail as other possible approaches are examined. At this juncture it will suffice merely to point out that "adjusted emphasis" is a loaded phrase that means different things to different people.

Potential Approaches with at Least a Degree of Plausibility

1. *An undergraduate library and information science curriculum.—* This approach is, of course, not new. Prior to the establishment of master's degree programs and their accreditation by the American Library Association, library education took place at the bachelor's level, frequently as a second bachelor's degree, or in lieu of a subject or general liberal arts degree. Over the past twenty years many graduate library educators have indicated an aversion to those undergraduate degree programs as preparation for graduate education by considering them deficient in liberal arts. Nevertheless, undergraduate programs have persisted. What is new is the resurgence of such programs in major universities with accredited graduate programs; for example, the University of Pittsburgh and Drexel University. Although each school has developed a rationale for its program and claims that it is heavily enrolled, it is not totally clear what positions these graduates will apply and be hired for. If the newly developing undergraduate programs at major universities provide an undergraduate preparation on which a more sophisticated graduate curriculum can be superimposed, then there is clearly potential benefit. If, on the other hand, these are terminal degrees and these individuals become cheaper replacements for graduate librarians and information scientists, professional qualifications and emphasis could be downgraded. There is an unfortunate tendency for job qualifications to adapt to the capabilities of the individual holding the position rather than the reverse.

2. *The inclusion of library science courses in the undergraduate curriculum to provide greater flexibility in the graduate curriculum.—*The suggestion that some basic courses now offered as part of the master's program become undergraduate prerequisite courses is in one sense nothing more than an extension of the program beyond its present traditional one-year limitation: the extension is added to the front rather than to the back. This may be more politically palatable to students, boards of trustees, and state legislatures than increasing the length of the one-year master's program. It also would allow students who make an early commitment to library education to be able to incorporate such courses

as free electives in their undergraduate curricula, provided they attend institutions at which such courses are available.

Other students would presumably be admitted to the graduate program with the requirement that they remedy these undergraduate deficiencies. It is difficult to assess the impact of such an action without determining the number of courses to be moved from the graduate to the undergraduate curriculum, but the transfer of even three or four courses would significantly increase the number of course options in the one-year graduate degree program. Ultimately, this change, though perhaps more acceptable from a legal or even marketing standpoint, would be perceived correctly as an increase in the length of the graduate program, particularly for those who have not completed these courses as undergraduates. It should be recognized, however, that a considerable number of students do not move directly from undergraduate education to their graduate library degree programs. As would be the case with a more direct extension of the graduate library degree program beyond the present one year (or roughly thirty-six credit hours), acceptance would depend on consistency of implementation among institutions, support by the Committee on Accreditation, and the willingness of employers to take such additional experience into account when establishing starting salaries and other opportunities. In addition, a substantial infusion of library science courses into the undergraduate curriculum might defeat our expectation that new students have a broad liberal arts education.

3. *Expansion of the graduate degree beyond its traditional one year.*—The study sought reactions to this alternative. In general, expansion of the present degree program was neither ardently supported nor opposed. Of greater significance, however, is the fact that it failed to elicit any significant support for higher starting salaries, better employment opportunities, or career advantages. At present in the United States, only a small number of accredited library school programs offer what is called the two-year master's degree, although it should be noted that these terms are not exact. The "one-year" degree program frequently takes more than a year to complete, and the "two-year" program is sometimes only six months longer. Nevertheless, the implications for the student in terms of time and tuition cost are not inconsequential. The schools in the United States which have moved to the so-called two-year program share the characteristics of lower-than-average tuition and a lack of pressure from the university administration to maintain or increase student enrollment. These two conditions are related because it is usually when students contribute a substantial portion of their own instructional cost that academic administrators become particularly concerned about numbers of students.

When a student enrolls in a longer program without gaining in either employment opportunities or starting salary, the future employer may benefit considerably by acquiring a librarian who has completed more of the courses that this survey indicates as desirable or even demanded. It may even benefit the library school. As a simplistic example, if students are required to stay twice as long, only half as many are needed to produce the same enrollment income. However, such a situation would be decidedly unsatisfactory for the student, who would be expected to invest time and money for little if any tangible reward. It is therefore unlikely that, when longer and shorter programs are equally accreditable and therefore carry the same "official" status, many students who have a choice will select the longer program. It seems likely that, if an enlargement of the present master's degree program were indeed desirable (and there is not as yet any consensus that it is), then the impetus for such a shift must come primarily through the criteria established by the Committee on Accreditation. Furthermore, compliance would continue to depend on both a school's and a student's perception of what an accredited degree is worth. It is possible that present attacks on the library degree in general and the accredited degree in particular will continue and perhaps succeed, or that schools of library education may look at other alternatives than accreditation for the validation of their programs.

4. *The use of degree specialization tracks in the present M.L.S. program.*—Some schools already specify that certain courses must be taken as students opt for degree tracks within the master's program. Other schools implement such a requirement for dual master's degree candidates but prefer the process of persuasion and counseling in urging, but not requiring, students to take certain courses in keeping with their professed interests. The study leaves little doubt that specialized tracks are attractive to the respondents. Beyond this, there are specialized requirements for specific jobs in those libraries. Based on these preferences, it would appear desirable to elicit from each student at the time of admission to the program a career preference oriented not only to type of library but also to specialization within that type of library. Such specializations as bibliographic searcher in a science-technology special library, children's material specialist in a large urban public library system, or Western European languages humanities monographic cataloger in a major research library all come to mind. In all probability, at least, the largest of the presently accredited library schoools could develop such specialization tracks and perhaps enforce them for their students. There would appear to be, nevertheless, a number of attendant problems. Many of the advanced and specialized courses in library school curricula are offered only once annually. A student completing an accelerated program, or devising a class schedule to accommodate full- or part-time work, must sometimes make compromises between courses that are desirable and those that are conveniently available. Further-

more, the specialization interests of many students remain largely undeveloped until they are fairly far along in the master's program. Still others may have specialized interests but would prefer to consider themselves generalists available for a range of positions in any type of library; this is particularly common where there are overriding geographic or personal limitations that affect mobility. It could be argued that library school students will simply have to accept such restrictions and become accustomed to tracks in the interests of better, more specialized education. After all, it can be pointed out that engineering students are forced into such choices very early in their professional education. Nevertheless, many library educators would be sorry to see such a limitation rigidly enforced. Some library school students never understand the range of opportunities in special librarianship, for example, until they have been in school a semester or more. Furthermore, present standards and guidelines for accreditation concentrate on general qualifications common to all types of libraries. Those standards do not discourage specialization but, rather, insist that specialization supplement general education, not substitute for it. If specialized career tracks were carried to the extreme of, for example, not teaching cataloging at all to those who disavow an interest in being catalogers, accreditation guidelines would probably require modification.

5. *Special schools handling only certain career track specializations and ignoring others.*—This proposed approach is a variant of the one described above and proceeds from the premise that the resources of individual schools of library education are too slim to permit all schools to develop specializations in all areas. That observation, made most recently by Jane Anne Hannigan in a paper prepared for the Department of Education,[16] is probably accurate. Moreover, as proponents of this viewpoint argue, the need for some specializations is so sparse that perhaps one or two schools could meet the entire need on a national basis. The national requirement for newly educated rare book librarians, or newspaper librarians, presumably, could be met by only one or two schools that would concentrate their resources on only a few areas and direct would-be students interested in other specializations to other programs. This proposal has the attractions of simplicity and fairness, but it shares some of the same problems mentioned earlier. It would require students to make early, nearly irrevocable career specialization decisions, and it would require substantial modification in the way library education programs are presently accredited. However, there are yet further problems. The proposal assumes student mobility to an extent not previously encountered or expected, although it is certainly true that such mobility is demanded and achieved in some other fields. In addition, however, the proposal raises questions about the role of state and municipally supported educational institutions and their ability to reject

students within their own constituencies. At minimum, given the substantial difference in tuition charged to students from within and without the political service area (usually the state), satisfactory implementation of such a proposal would require a considerable expansion of the policy of fee courtesy exchange. At present, such implementation is normally not at the discretion of the library school or even the educational institution itself but is part of the political process.

6. *The movement of more curricular material into internships and practice work assignments.*—There has, over the past decade, been a considerable upsurge in interest in the development of internships and practice work assignments to introduce students to the "real world." One of the surprising results of this investigation is the relatively low rating of this option. While many and probably most respondents found such opportunities useful, few considered them essential as part of the educational process, and it may be that first-level supervisors might rate this option more highly than the library directors who constitute the survey population. In any case, a number of questions need to be raised. The first and most obvious is whether these experiences are to be offered for academic credit or outside the curriculum, and whether the students are to be paid. If practice assignments were to be undertaken for academic credit, then this approach would only complicate and worsen the pressures under which the one-year master's program already operates. Practice work frequently supplants another course. Additionally, if practice work assignments were to carry academic credit, then the supervisors for those experiences must not only be chosen carefully but must also be trained, which would assure a broader range of experiences for the student, exposure to new ideas and technologies, and the opportunity to secure answers to that most common and most important of all student questions, Why do we do it this way? There is at least one additional concern with regard to the presumed obvious desirability of practice work experience: many if not most library school students come from long and continuous backgrounds of library work experience, as students, volunteers, and clerical staff members. Many others continue to work in libraries on a part-time or even full-time basis while pursuing their master's degrees. It would appear that practice work assignments might be redundant for them, and that other courses might appropriately be substituted. There are two classes of students, though, for whom practice work assignments might indeed be desirable. The first includes individuals who have no experience working in libraries and who might want to be exposed to such opportunities before they seek professional job placement. The second group includes students seeking experience in specialized library settings such as a rare books collection, a corporate information center, or a social service agency. Even in these instances, however, it is by no means a given that such experience should be

carried under the umbrella of the master's program instead of simply being an outside part-time job.

7. *The movement of more curricular material into postdegree on-the-job training.*—In their responses, the library directors who constituted the respondent population generally declared themselves willing to consider the transfer of certain topics or issues from what might otherwise be an overburdened and cluttered curriculum to on-the-job training. However, when they were asked to suggest specific courses or topics amenable to such treatment, very few recommendations emerged, and no consensus was apparent. The most frequently mentioned suggestion concerned training in the online searching of specific databases (as contrasted to a general course in online searching, which was generally considered important as part of the curriculum). While such training may be offered by the supervisor, it may also be obtained from vendors through workshops and in-house training. Positive response was sufficiently rare to suggest the necessity of caution when considering an increase in on-the-job training. It is of course possible that the first-level supervisors who must manage backlogs, and would be charged with the responsibility of carrying out on-the-job training, would have responded even more negatively. However, there is yet another issue. This survey, as already noted, was not addressed to the small libraries that constitute the bulk of our profession. There are no responses from libraries with fewer than three professional staff members, and we know that a great many public, special, school, and even small college libraries fall below this level. Who is to carry out on-the-job training if the individual being hired is assumed to possess the highest level of professional expertise within the organization?

8. *The movement of more material into post-M.L.S. continuing education.*—So much has been written on this topic that it is unnecessary to expound here the presumed virtues of the continuing education process, for this field or for others. Continuing education is assumed to be good and useful, and support for this belief comes from practitioners, educators, professional societies, and government agencies. This positive reaction was confirmed by the respondents. They support continuing education, and they encourage staff members to participate in the process. In many instances they attempt to make that support tangible by providing released time or paying full or partial tuition. However, their responses register all but no incentive in the form of either financial or promotional rewards on the completion of continuing education units or degrees or insistence that continuing education be undertaken to safeguard the present job. Continuing education for librarians, therefore, continues to be an option, selected by an individual primarily because of personal desire to learn, without either the significant encouragement or threat that employers in some professions

provide. Given this narrow approach to continuing education, it is highly doubtful that continuing activities will affect a significant portion of the library profession, thereby providing an effective alternative or addition to the master's degree. Indeed, reports from professional societies, state agencies, and individual libraries document a level of participation which touches at best only a small part of the profession and then only haphazardly. Moreover, respondents' indications of what they consider reasonable fees for continuing education programs reveal not only a wide variance of opinion but also an unrealistically low midpoint level, above which most respondents consider continuing education courses too expensive. Without subsidization by the provider or by a government program, and without strong inducement or threat from employers, it is unlikely that continuing education activities will grow substantially. It should also be noted that the respondents to this survey represent an elite of directors of larger libraries, managers of librarians who are in large part themselves librarians. It is doubtful that representatives of smaller institutions, or nonlibrarians responsible for funding the continuing education of librarians, would respond more positively. The development of continuing education units has established a form of coinage or premium, but it remains to be seen what value these acquired units will have for librarians. The Medical Library Association has developed a continuing education program that carries with it the threat of decertification for those who do not participate. However, it is simply too early to determine the effectiveness of that presumed threat. The idea has, in any case, not yet spread to other professional library segments in this country. Given all of these concerns and restraints, it is likely that continuing education will continue to be an important part of the strategy for imparting new knowledge, and it may expand to some degree. It is extremely doubtful, however, that it will provide a significant alternative to and extension of the one-time educational experience of the master's program. Sad as such a thought is to contemplate in a professional environment, it is still probably true that for many, perhaps a majority, the education received while earning the master's degree may be the only significant professional education received.

SUMMARY AND CONCLUSIONS

This study was begun with the belief that the issues were complex and defied simple solutions. Certainly nothing in the results suggests anything else. There is no one practitioner approach to library education, any more than there is a consensus among library educators. The respondents approached the priorities of the curriculum in terms of the specific needs of their libraries. It is not an unreasonable approach. However, in addition to the expected differences of emphasis among the broad types of libraries, there are other differences—some by size of the institution, some by institutional objectives, and still others based on the personal viewpoint of the individual making the choice.

It may be possible, for example, through a series of progressively refined discussions and surveys, to find a curricular strategy involving education, training, and continuing postdegree activity on which all public librarians might agree. It would be far more difficult to develop a strategy on which public, special, academic, and school librarians, as well as the representatives of the information industry who also hire library school graduates, might agree. Even that would not be enough, though. What is ultimately required is an overall strategy on which practitioners and educators all agree. As Boyd Rayward has already noted, the academic educational system has values of its own, and educational administrators who ignore these in order to follow the mercurial pleasure of self-appointed practitioner spokespersons do their schools a great disservice and will ultimately be forced from the scene.[17] It is possible that no single overall strategy can be devised and that it will be necessary to fragment our profession into a series of subprofessions, at least into a series of educational specializations. That would be unfortunately, but it might be necessary.

What this continuing debate does not need is a further series of articles or conference programs roughly titled, "What Is Wrong with Library Education?" Such practitioner activities would be no more useful than academic seminars on the topic, "What Is Wrong with Public Library Directors?" which mercifully no one has yet suggested. There are indeed things "wrong" with library education, as there are with public library administration. However, the changes may not have been as much for the worse as some might imagine. There is a general tendency to romanticize the past at the expense of the present. All of this is beside the point. Whether there is a lot, a little, or even nothing presently wrong with library education, library education must change as the profession changes.

It may be of some consolation, although little is found here, to recognize that shopping lists do not work in other disciplines, either. They do not work because they are too easy to articulate and because they fail to exact a commitment from the individual making the decision.

This survey sought to enforce at least some level of responsibility by making respondents deal with the consequences of their decisions and their preferences. To some extent they did so unwillingly and, in large part, inconsistently. This was not unexpected. Some found the questionnaire difficult to answer and indicated this in their responses. It was difficult precisely because it required them to deal with alternatives.

Decisions and preferences have their prices in the real world; lists of professed competency requirements do not. It is to the credit of the survey group that so many did take the trouble to respond as well as they could.

What is needed is a series of opportunities for interchange in which the various protagonists have an opportunity to explore, in an open and nonaccusative environment, the options that present themselves. As with most options, perhaps none will be totally attractive. All will have their drawbacks and their costs. But, just perhaps, some closure is possible.

The Association of Research Libraries and the Council on Library Resources are to be commended for their attempts to create such a discussion environment through the recently announced founding of a research institute to expose educators to research library issues and to allow them to comment in return. The University of Michigan Libraries* are also well in the vanguard of the development of post-M.L.S. internships on which the primary emphasis is further learning rather than volume of work produced. These are first steps, and many more are needed. Some parts of the library profession are almost totally untouched by meaningful dialogue concerning these issues; a start must be made. Professional societies and interested organizations such as CLR would appear to be the logical conveners of these activities, since library educators are also librarians. It is in professional societies that these groups intersect.

Finally, it seems almost inevitable that the upgrading of professional qualifications will have a price. That price will be one of time, effort, and financial cost. If that price is to be assessed and paid, then rewards for those willing to do so must also be available, be they employers, new professionals, or library schools. The rules for this game must be devised by the professional associations and, particularly, by those groups charged with accreditation.

References

1. Williamson, Charles C. *Training for Library Service: A Report Prepared for the Carnegie Corporation of New York.* New York: D. B. Updike, 1923.

2. Conant, Ralph W. *The Conant Report: A Study of the Education of Librarians.* Cambridge, Mass.: MIT Press, 1980.

3. Battin, Patricia M. "Developing University and Research Library Professionals: A Director's Perspective." *American Libraries* 14 (January 1983): 2–25.

*The University of Michigan Libraries offer such post-M.L.S. training opportunities specifically aimed at recent graduates.

4. Clough, M. Evalyn, and Galvin, Thomas J. "Educating Special Librarians." *Special Libraries* 75 (January 1984): 1–8.

5. Cronin, Blaise. *The Education of Library-Information Professionals: A Conflict of Objectives?* ASLIB Occasional Publication no. 28. London, 1982.

6. Debons, Anthony, et al. *The Information Professional: Survey of an Emerging Field.* New York: Marcel Dekker, 1981.

7. De Gennaro, Richard. "Theory vs. Practice in Library Management." *Library Journal* 108 (July 1983): 1318–21.

8. Dougherty, Richard M. "Library Education—Quo Vadis?" *Journal of Academic Librarianship* 5 (November 1979): 251.

9. Eshelman, William R. "The Erosion of Library Education." *Library Journal* 108 (July 1983): 1309–12.

10. Koenig, Michael E. D. "Education for Special Librarianship." *Special Libraries* 74 (April 1983): 182–96.

11. Marchant, Maurice P., and Smith, Nathan M. "The Research Library Director's View of Library Education." *College & Research Libraries* 43 (November 1982): 437–39.

12. Marchant, Maurice P., and Smith, Nathan M. "The Public Library Director's View of Library Education." Paper presented at the January 7, 1984 meeting of the Association of Library and Information Science Education, Washington, D.C.

13. White, Herbert S. "Defining Basic Competencies." *American Librarians* 14 (September 1983): 519–25.

14. King Research, Inc. "New Directions for Library and Information Science Education." Contract report to be submitted to the Department of Education, 1984.

15. Van House, Nancy. "The Return of the Investment in Library Education." Paper presented at the January 7, 1984, meeting of the Association of Library and Information Science Education, Washington, D.C.

16. Hannigan, Jane Anne. "Vision to Purpose to Power: A Quest for Excellence in the Education of Library and Information Science Professionals." Paper presented at the January 7, 1984, meeting of the Association of Library and Information Science Education, Washington, D.C.

17. Rayward, W. Boyd. "Conflict, Interdependence, Mediocrity: Librarians and Library Educators." *Library Journal* 108 (July 1983): 1313–17.

The Future of Library and Information Science Education

> It is difficult to forecast the direction of specific change in library and information science education, because that process is impacted by pressures from practitioners, the larger academic community, and the general public, all of which are at least potentially dangerous to quality improvement and maintenance. A number of alternative responses to these political pressures are examined, and all are found largely unattractive. Instead, a scenario which can only be implemented through assertiveness and the close cooperation of educator and practitioner communities is proposed.

Predictors of the future always operate at their own peril, and that danger increases when their projections are intended to cover the short term—the period of the next five to ten years. People have an annoying tendency to remember, and to remind the writer of his fallibility. This author clearly recalls, as an aerospace technical librarian, finding a report written by the individual who later had become chief engineer, which stated with confidence that jet propulsion would never be practical for commercial aviation.

History tells us that forecasters invariably overstate the changes which will occur within the next few months or the next year, and understate change in the more distant future. This is because, try as we will, predictions of change are still set within a framework which assumes the eternal continuity of basic premises. The answers turn out to be wrong, because it is difficult to predict that the questions also change.

In addition to all of these general dangers, the predictor of the future of library and information science education also encounters several other risks. Library education is difficult to forecast because it is impacted by a number of forces almost totally outside the control of those who administer the educational process. Unfortunately for library educaion, the thrust of the great majority of these potential impacts is negative. The writer is reminded of the comment attributed to the late Robert R. Neyland, football coach at the University of Tennessee, who stated that when teams passed the ball only three possible things could happen, and two of them were bad. In the same sense, almost anything which might happen to change library education is at least potentially troublesome. However, we also know that we cannot isolate our programs from these impacts. They include:

1. *Pressure from the professional community of what, for the lack of a more inclusive term, we will continue to call librarians.* These pressures have always existed as in other areas of professional education, but in recent years they have become more insistent and more pronounced. They center, for each of the professional communities represented, on the concern that graduates are not as prepared as they "should be." Expressions of that concern include the belief that graduates are not adequately prepared to deal with issues of management, public relations, communications, and the political process. Other writers have stressed their concern that graduates are not able to "function" on the first professional job. Finally, there has been a rather sweeping indictment that students are not of the high caliber they ought to be, or perceived as they once were in the "good old days." Many of these arguments are contradictory (such as the emphasis on basic concepts and the garnering of specific skills), and the library profession's tradition of airing in public all of its own uncertainties and insecurities has opened the door to others such as the Office of Personnel Management, to state their conclusions and then seek a rationale for those conclusions. The turmoil and insecurity which now surrounds the library education process risks its trivialization through the application of catch phrases such as "basic competencies," which become distracting in the absence of definitions of whether such competencies address the conceptual preparation commonly found in a profession (if it does, equivalency through experience would be difficult to obtain), or the working tools acquired by a skilled artisan.

Whatever we think of this process, it will continue and probably increase in intensity, and it can only be hoped that this intensity will be channeled to the energy form of light rather than heat. Broadening of the accreditation and evaluation process to include other and previously neglected segments of the professional community is a healthy activity, but only if expectations for the first professional degree can be defined. At least one survey[1] concludes that, despite all of the verbiage, many practitioners are looking for graduates with the skills to tackle specific backlogs in the shortest possible time. This is an understandable reaction to pressures caused by increasing workloads and decreasing resources, a political problem for which practitioners have found no effective answers. Not surprisingly, educators have reacted to what has been perceived as unwarranted interference in the professional education process.[2] While that reaction has centered initially on other professional programs, its extension to librarianship is inevitable. Clearly, one of the major imponderables for the future of library and information science education is the way in which the always differing agendas and priorities are addressed by the educator and practitioner communities. If we agree on common objectives and mutually acceptable strategies, we can make a strong case for a strengthened and vibrant educational program, because the field continues to have promise and excitement. If we do not, we can be easily picked off by outside snipers.

2. *Pressures from the academic community in which library education programs are housed.* Some of these pressures are economic, and this can be expected to increase as public institutions of higher education are challenged to approach the level of funding self-sufficiency which private institutions have endured all along. These financial pressures are most simply expressed in accounting terminology—income and expenditures. Income comes primarily from student tuition—more students, students who pay more per course, or students who take more courses. Where income is not forthcoming expenses can be cut, by attritioning faculty vacancies or firing untenured incumbents, or by the withholding of funds for equipment, supplies, and travel. This financial process has no natural limits of reasonableness, and library schools are particularly vulnerable because they are small to begin with, and are perceived to have little political clout through their alumni. Once this process begins it resembles a death spiral, and closing the school can be the greatest mercy of all. Library school administrators must respond to these economic realities and have learned that they ignore them at their gravest peril, even when their own faculties lack interest. Academic programs which educate only graduate students without an undergraduate component are both unusual and expensive, and there can be no doubt that one of the attractive characteristics of the recent startup of library undergraduate programs is their financial viability. Undergraduates cost less to educate.

Other academic pressures that buffet the library education program come from the expectation of achievements in scholarship and research, and these pressures are usually greatest in the major institutions which house the library education programs most highly regarded in all recent perception studies. Here the dichotomy between education as at least endorsed by major library educators and first job training as espoused by at least some practitioners comes most sharply into focus. It is indeed our job to create what may appear to be obstreperous subordinates—individuals who will want to know why certain practices are followed, and why alternatives are not considered. Library education programs also suffer in the academic community from the low esteem in which our profession is held. Quite aside from whether library educators are capable of performing meaningful research, it appears both that other academicians have no expectation of a research component from their view of librarianship, and that library practitioners have no interest and sometimes a genuine aversion to research which might question what they do and how they do it. If this were not true, then the obvious alliance between academic librarians and library educators to use the university library as a research laboratory, and through this perfectly acceptable academic device to wrest control over decision processes and priorities from the faculty—would have occurred long ago. This too is a problem for which library educators must find a solution, if their programs are to have prestige, acceptance, and support. The success of such an endeavor is by no means certain.

3. *Pressures from the public sector.* This pressure most frequently takes the form of low prestige and low salaries for the graduates of library education programs. They are also evidenced in continuing attempts to bypass the educational requirement in favor of the cheaper and politically more expedient alternative of promoting staff members who are already on the premises. These individuals lack the educational qualifications and may even lack "experience" unless this term is simply defined to mean time on the job without evidence of learning something new on the job. These pressures also come into play in the lack of recognition for funding continuing education programs for librarian incumbents, and it is this lack when combined with an absence of professional insistence that tends to make whatever education is achieved a one-shot lifetime process.

Educator responses to the very real political problems engendered by this combination of circumstances have been varied. The list which follows is only a partial roster of alternatives. Not only are other choices possible and being considered, but it is also conceivable that some of these alternatives can be implemented in parallel or in tandem:

1. Lengthen the professional degree requirement beyond its present one year.
2. Add front end prerequisite requirements to the present degree, in effect lengthening the program in a more politically acceptable environment. These prerequisites may represent undergraduate courses taught within the library school, or courses co-opted from other disciplines. They can be taken as part of the undergraduate curriculum by those planning all

along to become librarians, or required of new students during the first semester of their enrollment as deficiencies to be removed.
3. Implement an undergraduate degree program as a prerequisite to graduate study.
4. Implement an undergraduate degree program as a career option, leading to specific jobs for which the M.L.S. degree is not required or is not appropriate. Options 3 and 4 are not mutually exclusive, at least in principle. However, in practice schools will probably quickly have to decide on one approach or the other.
5. Specialize the present one year degree program to prepare graduates to work in one or more specific settings. Schools would specify which of these options they claimed, and the accreditation process would take cognizance of evaluating these claims. Students would have to make a pre-admission career choice by specialization (as they now do in engineering), and the process would also require some sort of monitoring to assure that, for example, public librarians do not somehow end up in the academic or special libraries for which their education does not qualify them.
6. Abandon all controls, including accreditation. Move to a free market-place environment, in which ultimately the surviving schools will attract those students interested in the courses in which employers are interested. Major academic institutions might not be interested in hosting such programs particularly at the graduate level, but this writer suspects that such a *laissez faire* approach would ultimately result in a heavy emphasis on undergraduate courses for work in what is roughly defined as the information industry.

The author does not look at most of these alternatives with a great deal of enthusiasm. All have drawbacks, and most have been discussed extensively in the literature. The lengthening of educational programs which already exceed in cost the financial rewards which they promise on completion[3] only increase the threat that we might improve curriculum but decrease the quality of students attracted to our program. This writer also has a suspicion about the co-existence of undergraduate and graduate programs in the same environment, without some clear definition of what the completion of an undergraduate degree program does *not* represent and does *not* permit. It has already been stated that library education is particularly vulnerable to applications of Gresham's Law, in which the weak and cheap drive out the strong and more expensive.[4] This is because the public which utilizes the services of librarians in academic, public, special, and school settings has not been trained by us to a high level of expectation. It is unfortunately true, as confirmed in almost countless so-called user studies, that not only are expectations for library service largely clerical in emphasis, but that users quickly adapt to and rationalize poor library service and call it adequate.

The alternative to a doomsday scenario would require the implementation of strong professional standards and criteria, through the combined efforts (they could even be called the conspiratorial efforts) of a library practitioner and library educator community insistent on high standards. The writer is as uncomfortable with this suggestion as he supposes the reader to be. He shares in large part Peter Drucker's suspicion[5] that educational programs, left to their own resources, will continue to increase the length and complexity of the educational process beyond that which is necessary or reasonable. However, such empire building tendencies cannot realistically be attributed to librarians, be they educators or practitioners. The risk is that the reverse will happen—that librarians will adapt to rather than combat the general public apathy which allows salaries to remain low, which requires that librarians accept objectives which cannot be altered despite declining resources, and which considers it reasonable that professional library positions be filled by individuals for whom no equivalent qualification is even suggested, be they clerks or historians.

This article began with the premise that the direction of future library and information science education could not be predicted with any degree of accuracy. There are too many outside variables, and our profession has shown neither the inclination nor fortitude to control any of these. The writer will therefore allow himself the luxury of developing the scenario he would prefer to see implemented, in the recognition that the achievement of this state is neither easy nor impossible to achieve:

1. Have strong(er) standards of educational accreditation, but make them worth something more than they are even at present, by clarifying what accreditation means and what its absence means.
2. Maintain the master's degree as the basic professional education preparation.
a. Lengthen the degree requirement beyond its present one year only to the extent to which rewards systems for new graduates warrant such a change. A $15,000/year starting salary for a fifth-year degree is already pitifully low, and we know both that some employers expect more education and that others pay less (and some do both). Practitioners generally acknowledge this problem, but plead that its solution will require "time." The writer rejects this argument, and suggests

that the problem can be solved rather quickly with some assertiveness and will power, unless there are those who seriously believe that low salaries are caused by an inability to afford higher ones. For any such readers, the author has a bridge in Brooklyn he would like to propose for sale.

b. Look at undergraduate courses and curricula in this field with care and with caution. In particular, we must make sure that undergraduate courses and programs support and not supplant the graduate programs we have labored so hard (and certainly without public demand) to implement. We must determine whether it is indeed true that an undergraduate curriculum is appropriate for certain jobs not related to graduate preparation, or whether we are simply taking an economically easy approach to supplying what employers prefer to hire. If we have failed to consummate the dialogue with employers to show what our graduates can or could do, then it is past time that we began. Let us, under no circumstance, simply respond blindly to what the marketplace asks us to provide. Surely we must have learned by now that in this field employers must be educated as well as served.

3. Keep the graduate degree as a qualification for entry into a profession, not as a so-called basic competency for working on a job. This is a crucial concern, and it requires an understanding with practitioners of what constitutes education, training, continuing education, and continuing training. It also requires a clearly spelled out commitment to a continuing process of professional preparation, for which educational institutions, employers, professional societies, and individuals all must take their share of responsibility. The price is high, because it requires a more realistic assessment of what can be accomplished with what resources, the establishment of priorities for what happens in professional environments, and the transfer of responsibility (and guilt) to those who make resource allocations in a political environment. The cost in money is probably high, but the writer is comforted by the recognition that it is *only* money. In most settings, money is generally available to those who can make a case for it, and considerable sums are usually easier to justify in the political process than small ones. By contrast, we should know by now that spending very little money is no protection against either further cuts or perhaps even total elimination. We must also know by now that those who fund us will never volunteer money, or even admit they have any.

Implementation of the concept described above has

two immediate and direct benefits, in helping us cope with problems which presently plague our field:

a. It puts the issue of equivalency into a proper framework. No recent writer has suggested that in our profession the graduate degree is the *only* possible approach to professional status. However, when professionalism derives not from time on the job or specific skills required but on conceptual knowledge, disputes will be easier to adjudicate. Organizations with a commitment to affirmative action might well find that the most effective approach lies in scholarships to support individuals in their pursuit of the appropriate educational qualification, rather than unwarranted promotion.

b. It permits a general qualification of professional librarians, with the recognition that some and perhaps most of the preparation necessary to qualify special, academic, research, public, and school librarians—to prepare government documents librarians, rare books curators, and systems development specialists—comes through a later and continuing process of education and training—a process both supported and demanded.

Will all or any of this occur? The writer cannot pretend to know, because he cannot really assess professional determination, assertiveness, or political astuteness. It is much easier to predict that change will take place than to forecast what that change will be. The occurrence of change in library and information science education, and in the profession itself, is a foregone conclusion. If educators and practitioners do not find a basis for agreement as the independent equals into which our roles and responsibilities inevitably thrust us, our profession will be dramatically changed for us. Not by our enemies. We have no clearly definable opponents, perhaps because we control no real power base. However, there are tasks and skills which are part of the information process which are ours both by historic tradition and professional qualification which others will gladly and eagerly wrest away from us. They include the "nontraditional" activities of information analysis, information intermediation, and problem solving, and they are not in any other profession's sphere of activity because they are too newly evolved to fit earlier definitions. That will not deter them, and it should not deter us. If we lose the vision and the will to fight for our share of this spectrum what will remain to us will be a set of clerical and housekeeping functions increasingly prescribed by national and international standards. If that were to occur, both librarianship as a profession and its graduate educational component would become increasingly irrelevant, and it is not certain that anyone would care or notice.

References

1. White, H.S., and Paris, M: Employer Preferences and the Library Education Curriculum. *Library Quarterly,* 55:1–33, Jan. 1985.

2. The Committee on Institutional Cooperation. *Accreditation: A Statement of Principles.* Evanston, IL, March 14, 1984.

3. Van House, N.:*The Return of the Investment in Library Education.* Paper Presented at the January 7, 1984, Meeting of the Association for Library and Information Science Education, Washington, DC.

4. White, H.S.: Defining Basic Competencies. *American Libraries,* 14:519–525, Sept. 1983.

5. Drucker, P.F.: Managing the Public Service Institution. *College and Research Libraries,* 37:4–14, Jan. 1976.

GENERALIZATION VERSUS SPECIALIZATION IN THE MLS

There is no logical pattern to the distribution of accredited library education programs, nor do we really have any reason to expect that there will be. Library schools are established (and more recently closed) as decisions of specific universities. The Committee on Accreditation (COA) evaluates these programs to determine whether or not they meet standards for approval, but only when and if it is asked. Furthermore, we know that accreditation will not protect a school from being closed by its parent institution. Conversely, some library education programs that have never sought accreditation seem to live in perfect harmony within the larger body, and other programs that have lost or failed to achieve accreditation have not necessarily shriveled up and blown away.

As a result, the geographic distribution of accredited programs has never made a great deal of sense. Out of the 53 in the United States as of this writing, there are eight in New York State, with five of them in the New York City metropolitan area, but only three in the much more populous and geographically dispersed state of California. There are none in Virginia but three in North Carolina, none in the Northwest between Madison, Wisconsin and Seattle, but two in Denton, Texas. The situation in Canada is not much different.

FOREGOING THE DEGREE

What happens to prospective students when the only accredited library education program in the area closes? There is some evidence that they simply forego the library degree, or at least the accredited degree. At Indiana we have developed strong programs of offering courses in other

From *Library Journal* 113 (15 February 1988):148–49

cities throughout the state because Bloomington is a residential campus not convenient to centers of population and many students attend part-time or not at all. We also know that the large majority of our students still come from within the state of Indiana despite a national and international reputation and a healthy program of financial support and incentives to out-of-state students.

Colleagues in other universities report similar situations. It must be concluded from all of this that geographic convenience, rather than specializations in the curriculum, is still the primary motivator in the decision of many students of which school to attend. As we have suspected all along, it is also the primary motivator for employers in deciding whom to hire, except for academic libraries required by the search and screen process to do a national search.

BUILDING SPECIALIZATIONS

What does all of this mean in the development of accredited and accreditable library education programs? First and foremost, it means that the process of building specializations in only a few specified library schools will not work very well, because neither the students nor the employers are willing to abide by the limitations. COA recognized this some time ago when it insisted that programs claiming a specialization in such an area as school media do so in addition to and not instead of general preparation for any first professional job, including work in academic, public, and special libraries.

Until that clarification was made, small programs could claim that their absence of faculty expertise in areas of public or special libraries was acceptable because it was not their intention to prepare graduates for those types of libraries. However, the evidence clearly pointed out that many of the graduates of "media only" programs were working in academic, public, and special libraries. COA closed that loophole, and saved itself a lot of trouble because of the immediate decrease in self-studies in the hope of accreditation with programs with three, four, or five faculty members all with one specialization. Surely nobody can blame students for taking a job if one is offered whether or not they are qualified, certainly not if we accept the premise of nonlibrarians directing major research libraries.

Certainly from the standpoint of students the preference is for an accredited MLS that allows them the opportunity to apply for a range of beginning jobs. Many of our students are part-time, some with geographic constraints caused by family responsibilities. Others are returning to the work force and are trying to match experience already gained in earlier years to the program of the library school in the local state that offers the lowest, and in some cases the only affordable, tuition.

EMPLOYERS PREFER FLEXIBILITY

What about the preferences of the employer? Here there is clear evidence that there is a preference for the same kind of geographic flexibility preferred by students, and particularly for an ability to hire from the nearest library school. Part of this is a matter of economics, part a matter of timing. Corporate libraries frequently fill positions from advertisements placed in the local Sunday newspaper. The individuals likely to respond to these ads are students in a local library school, or those who happen to be in town. Small public and school libraries also tend to fill positions from a local pool, in part because they lack funds for either interview expenses or for relocation.

Even large municipal public libraries, with professional staffs that can exceed 200, frequently fill their positions from either a regional market or from individuals willing to pay their own interview expenses. A large number of directors of major public libraries indicate an inability to rank library education programs on the basis of their own experience, because for them the hiring process is not a national one. Academic libraries, and university and research libraries in particular, appear to be the only group that truly hires from a national pool.

The last few years have seen an upsurge of interest by the specialized professional associations in what is taught in library schools. These groups are concerned that sole control of accreditation in the hands of the American Library Association disenfranchises them, and deprives them of a voice in evaluating and critiquing the curriculum and its results.

At least at this point there appears to be general agreement that it is the schools themselves that must determine the curriculum, although input to the process would be desired and would usually be encouraged if offered in the form of advice. ALA has welcomed this increased interest on the part of other library associations, and although formal mechanisms may yet founder on the issue of allocating costs for the accreditation process, there appears a likelihood that other organizations of librarians and information scientists will have a greater voice in shaping accreditation standards and in carrying out accreditation evaluations.

NEW DIRECTIONS FOR SOCIETIES

There appear to be at least two directions this increased interest can take. One is for specific societies to establish criteria, objectives, faculty competency, requirements, or even specific curriculum that they consider necessary to achieve a level of approbation or commendation above and beyond the level of basic accreditation. This is a claimed and validated specialization above and beyond the level of the generally accreditable MLS, and it is an option even under present standards although only one or two programs have ever claimed it. If professional societies were to attempt to develop their own approved list as an adjunct to accreditation, it is possible that some or perhaps a great many programs would attempt to meet these special requirements.

I can only speculate on this as possible in part because much would depend on how stringent and how expensive the requirements, beyond what some of the major schools are already doing. The other question is whether or not such an approbation would be worth having, because it would clearly imply that in return for doing the necessary work the schools in question would secure for their graduates appropriately prepared a distinct advantage, or perhaps even an exclusive qualification, in applying for certain jobs. This in turn would require either a voluntary or mandatory policing process within that society for its members, to insure that the promulgated requirements are indeed used as hiring criteria.

Whether or not this would happen is at best conjectural, because it would impose on the members and their parent organizations greater requirements of cost, time delay, and perhaps even legal ramifications that would have to be clarified. At the same time, if library schools are to invest in advanced specialized programs beyond the requirements of accreditation, and even more importantly if students are to commit to a program of narrowing and specialization, that is the quid pro quo. I find this scenario less than likely, at least at this time.

A MORE PRACTICAL APPROACH

The other possible approach, and perhaps the more practical one, is for specialized societies to clamor for an input into the basic standards for accreditation. For example, the Medical Library Association could attempt to insist that any accreditable program had to offer at least a certain level of educational preparation and exposure, including at least one or more elective courses dealing with the specific concerns of medical librarians. The rationale for such an insistence would be the fact that, given local hiring patterns, the graduates of any accredited program might end up in hospital libraries and should at least be afforded the opportunity to enroll in such courses.

Whether or not this becomes important to the employer as a hiring criterion is difficult to predict, because it depends primarily on the willingness to insist on standards even in the face of cost and inconvenience.

THE SPECIALISTS OF TOMORROW

If the representatives of special constituencies within the library and information profession adopt the second course of demanding that regular accreditation requires exposure to specialized curricula on the premise that the presumed generalists of today often become the specialists of tomorrow, then accreditation will require of candidate schools a far greater commitment in effort and resources than many are presently willing to make.

An earlier survey (with Marion Paris, "Employer Preferences and the Library Education Curriculum," *Library Quarterly,* Jan. 1985, p. 1–33) indicated at least 50 courses that some group within our profession considers essential for at least some of the positions for which they hire junior professionals. If we stay with local and regional hiring patterns, it follows that all accreditable programs must offer this level of education at least as an option to their students. The question that follows for library educators is whether or not accreditation is worth having even if it costs the school more to meet the requirements; the answer depends directly on what an accredited degree is worth, and what level of exclusivity it will command in the marketplace.

THE COST OF QUALITY

Quality costs more than the absence of quality, and unless we reward it in educational programs as in employee performance evaluations we will inevitably fall victim to Gresham's Law of Economics: the bad will drive out the good in the absence of other intervening factors. Because we know that many library school graduates will accept the first reasonable offer rather than keep searching for the ideal job, and because we also know that many nonacademic libraries will hire the first reasonable candidate who meets the salary criteria, concentrating on the general educational quality of our programs seems more useful even for those employers looking for specialist.

If, on the other hand, employers are going to insist that qualified candidates must have taken certain specific courses to be considered, then it becomes their part of the bargain to library schools and students to give true preference to these qualifications, even if it means importing interview candidates from across the continent.

The first scenario appears more likely, and because of this an insistence on excellence in the education of our junior professionals, including the ones who are not going to work in our kinds of libraries, seems our best bet. We will continue to be judged as one profession, and the word librarian will still mean something—for good or bad.

THE UNITY OF THE LIBRARY PROFESSION

While I have written prolifically in a number of general library publications such as *Library Journal,* and while I assume that at least some of what I write reaches some school librarians and media specialist, I have never attempted to address this audience directly. There is good reason for my hesitancy. As a special librarian who has now attained some familiarity with academic libraries through my stint as an educator and academic library user, I will readily admit there is probably no branch of librarianship with which I am less familiar than school librarianship. It is precisely because I recognize my own shortcomings in this and other parts of the library profession (I know little about rare books, also), that I try to surround myself with colleagues who do.

And yet, despite the increasing fragmentation of our profession into distinct and often non-communicating specializations, the reality has grown for me that librarianship possesses a uniqueness that transcends where we work and whom we serve. Moreover, unless we preserve that uniqueness across institutional boundaries, we become homeless nomads who are considered junior accessories to whatever the other professionals with whom we work happen to do. This is as true for school librarians in their relationship with teachers as for academic librarians in their relationship with faculty, and corporate librarians in

From *California Media and Library Education Journal* 11, no. 2 (Spring 1988):8–10.

their relationship to other organizational professionals. We may be teachers, or professors, or organization men and women, but we must be much more than that or we are nothing at all, or at least nothing of significance.

In *LJ* columns I have written about the importance of turf, a concept well understood by street gangs. Turf is that which is uniquely yours and which nobody else can claim, and street gangs understand well enough that even without wealth and other resources, the ability to control something, even one square city block, is worth something. The turf we must control is the library, through our unique knowledge of what the library can do and should do, and through our development of programs and strategies to make the library (or media center or technical information center or resource materials center—the phrases are almost interchangeable) an effective tool for helping to establish and meet the parent organization's mission. Simply doing what the users (be they teachers or administrators or even students) tell you they want done does not accomplish this. It is, of course, bad for our professional status, but more importantly it is bad for the organizations we serve. The ignorance of our users with regard to the potential we represent is excusable, but what is inexcusable is their failure to acknowledge that they don't know. What would be unforgivable would be the shedding of our responsibility to point out their ignorance and our expertise.

The determination that school librarians must be school teachers was made a long time ago, and it was not made by librarians. It was made by teachers, who have established a stranglehold political control over the entire institution, including its library, and who feel at least more comfortable dealing with "fellow" teachers. The situation is not unique. Corporate users of scientific and technical libraries frequently insist that the librarians who serve them match them in educational qualifications with degrees in physics or chemistry. Whether this is simply because of a preference for collegial comfort or because of a specialized need they truly recognize is difficult to generalize. As often as not, probably a little of both. At least I make that assertion about science librarians, about whom I know something. Just to test your endurance with one more example from yet another part of librarianship: academic librarians spend a great deal of time and effort attempting to emulate teaching faculty members, because they believe that this will impress them. Unfortunately, it does not. Academic librarians are only considered second-rate professors, and more significantly, what they uniquely can contribute as librarians may not be recognized at all. You probably begin to recognize the pattern.

One thing that is clear to me is that librarians, regardless of what else their employers require them to be, must be first of all librarians, and in that sense I consider the minimum level of education for librarians not dilutable. We all do the same things, we just do them in different settings and with different emphases and different added responsibilities. The statement in *LJ* that caught some school librarians' eyes read, in part, "When school librarians are prepared in 'media only' library education programs, they may be well *trained* for what their bosses want them to know. They are not, however, nearly as likely to have been exposed to the rich heritage and the complexities of the library profession more likely to be available in diversified library schools." It is a statement in which I believe and behind which I stand.

There is certainly room for argument about what constitutes an acceptable level of library education, whether present standards of ALA accreditation are too high or too low, or even whether or not ours is a profession even requiring education at the graduate level. It is a discussion in which I am happy to participate at any time, but this article is not the setting. Here I will simply posit that whatever that level of appropriate education turns out to be, it is the correct level for all of us.

I am certainly not unaware of the reality that it is precisely in the education or training of school librarians that we permit the substitutions and shortcuts that we have by and large foreclosed in academic, public, and even corporate settings. Why is this? Is it because school librarians don't need to know as much as other librarians, because their libraries don't serve as significant a need or as complex a requirement? I certainly do not agree, and I would hope that you do not agree. If anything, the reverse is true. If it is important that school librarians must be teachers as well as librarians, then they are teachers of teachers as well as of students. It then follows that they are more important than "mere" teachers, because they know this and more. It is exactly the *more* we emphasize for true professional status.

The villain in this process for us is the educational establishment, and our failure to make our case with this constituency will continue to affect all of us as long as federal library programs are considered a subset of what teachers do. There is perhaps no professional community with a collectively lower opinion of the importance of librarians than that of education (medicine perhaps runs a close second, but doctors tend to discount all other fields). This is not because educators are inherently evil or power crazy. Heaven knows they have enough troubles of their own. It is rather because, unlike some other professionals who don't know what libraries and librarians can do and are willing to admit that ignorance, teachers think that they do know. Unfortunately, they are wrong. If librarians in the school system, just as librarians in the university and in the corporation, are to achieve acceptance as professionals in their own right, it will be because as full librarians as well as teachers they are unique. It will not be as pale replicas of some other profession. Surely California school librarians need not be reminded that in times of stress there is a tendency toward paranoia. As Proposition 13 gripped your state, classroom teachers defended their own precarious hold by bad-mouthing everyone in the educational system who wasn't a "real" teacher like themselves. It could happen again, unless school librarians make the point that they are full-fledged members of two professions, with no shortcuts. It is an important political argument, because you will not be treated as equals if you are perceived "only" as teachers who don't "really" teach. How many school librarians become principals, with authority over other teachers? However, beyond the political implications, the insistence on full undiluted librarianship as well as teacher qualification makes sense, because only fully prepared librarians can serve their clienteles anywhere without shortchanging something or somebody. As noted earlier, emphases shift throughout our profession, but the basic values and concepts are the same in a school library and in a corporate technical information center.

I am of course aware of the recent ALA controversy concerning the desire of AASL, to participate in the National Council for Accreditation of Teacher Education (NCATE) process of legitimatizing library education programs that do not meet ALA standards for accreditation, diluted as at least some of us think those standards are now. The issue is, of course, fraught with emotion, and understandably so. It brings out intensely personal reactions. Whatever our level of educational preparation for the positions we now hold, we must insist that those qualifications are adequate or we brand ourselves as illegitimate. Not only are we unwilling to do this to ourselves, such generalizations are also unfair. There are always exceptional examples of individuals who are self-learners and who beat the system, as there are individuals with graduate degrees from prestigious library schools who appear to have learned, or at least remembered, nothing. We deal with generalizations and we deal with averages, and yet those averages mean something. Students not exposed to the diversity of a more complex curriculum, to faculty with genuine research as well as teaching credentials, or to other students with different backgrounds and value systems, lose something in the process. Of that I am certain, although no individual quantification is possible. A colleague who works closely with school librarians and media specialists tells me that, at least on the average, these individuals are less prepared for concepts of resource sharing and computer networking at the very time these initiatives become essential for school librarians. Perhaps it may be because nobody taught them.

As the dean of one of the largest and most highly rated accredited graduate library education programs, a program that prepares many students for school librarianship and wishes it could reach more, I would be a hypocrite if I did not truly feel that ours is the better way to educate librarians—any professional librarian, and most certainly including school librarians. As I look at the AASL/NCATE initiative so emotionally pushed through the ALA Council meeting in San Francisco, I have mixed feelings. I can certainly understand the demand for recognized legitimacy from a large group of ALA members. Beyond that, I see both dangers and potential. If AASL participation in NCATE accreditation only acquiesces in what educators ignorantly believe to be proper standards for the preparation of school librarians, then we will have done nothing more than legitimize that ignorance. Sitting at the accreditation table might make participating school librarians feel better, but only if they have become impervious to the slights all around them.

However, if opening the NCATE process to AASL allows for education (what could be more appropriate than educating educators), and for the introduction of new vistas and standards through explaining to NCATE accreditors what good libraries really are all about, then I see a potential for great promise. After all, it is we who must tell them what good libraries and good librarians are and do, because they do not know and will not find out by themselves. For me, there is no logical end to this growing and learning process short of a set of requirements that includes both what educators consider uniquely important in the preparation of school librarians, and the full accreditation requirements specified by the ALA Committee on Accreditation for all librarians. That committee determined a long time ago, while I was its member, that specialization could not be a substitute for generalized library educational values common to the entire profession. It supplemented it. That determination must ultimately become the bottom line for all of us. If school librarians must be teachers and technical librarians must also be chemists, then so be it. But they must all be fully qualified librarians, meeting whatever standards are deemed appropriate in a professional accreditation process controlled by librarians, and not by either the American Chemical Society or NCATE. These bodies can appropriately evaluate chemists and teachers, and some of us are chemists or teachers. However, we are also librarians, and that is something they can't evaluate.

THE INTERNAL AND EXTERNAL POLITICAL PROCESS

In this section of articles I have combined those that deal with the issue of management within the library with those that address management concerns in dealing with the nonlibrarians who ultimately control our ability to succeed. This is by intent, because I consider management as a continuous process, changing only in detail but not in concept. The relationship between the head of circulation and a circulation clerk is exactly the same as that between the president of a multinational conglomerate corporation and the vice-president for international marketing.

The job of managers is to decide as well as to control, and they frequently control a lot better than they decide. It they do not decide personally, then they must see to it that decisions are made, either by upward or downward delegation, assignment, or abdication. The various management styles—autocratic, consultative, participatory, abdicative—are really subsidiary to the question of whether or not the process takes place, and how well it works. All have at least a potential place in certain scenarios, and certainly the worst approach is one management style masquerading as another, such as autocracy under the guise of a participatory style. Good managers know that they should interfere as little as possible, and the problems of dealing with octopus managers has been amusingly described by Loren Belker in his book *The First-Time Manager*. However, managers must never forget that they are responsible for both control and decisions, and of the two the second is far more important. Control can now be accomplished with some success through computer programmed accounting mechanisms, and may not require a manager at all. Decisions still require people.

Occasionally, although rarely, individuals go to their management for advice. More frequently it is for permission and for authority. Ultimately, what our management has to a greater extent than the rest of us is authority, and it is this that we reach for. Librarians, in any setting, have ultimate access to authority *if* they can get managers to do their jobs, because the management chain involving the librarian may be long but it is unbroken and it reaches all the way to the top.

Authority is rarely freely granted in sufficient quantity to be able to function, and experienced librarians understand that they have to acquire whatever authority they need, because they will ultimately be blamed for not doing what nobody allowed them to do. Responsibility, by contrast, is gladly distributed to subordinates, and it is usually (everything must be qualified because no two individuals react the same way despite the generalizations in the management literature) gladly received. However, responsibility without authority becomes frustration.

Nonlibrarians above the level of the library frequently distribute responsibility (run a good library that will please everyone or at least shield me from complaints) without a willingness to distribute authority, most often in terms of staff and dollars. They hide that absurdity in such pious nonsense as "I have confidence in your ability to figure out a way" or "Do the best you can." They reach instinctively for what Peter Drucker has described as the acceptance of the "moral imperative" by service professionals, that somehow with or without funds or staff we have to do everything or it is our fault. The process is continuous when librarians then pass the same nonsense on to their staffs, using the same phrases and adding such other gems as "because our budget has been cut we have to do more and work harder." A brave subordinate (and there are only a few) might ask why he should work harder because you have failed in your job of securing adequate resources.

Ultimately, every manager within this chain is responsible for assuring that his or her subordinates know what they are supposed to do, and that there is a plan that recognizes that it can be done with the resources and within the time frame provided. If we fail to do this, if individuals have no sense that they can "win" no matter how hard they try, then morale sinks, apathy increases, and a sense of team unity unravels. It is hard to play baseball without balls and bats.

Here again Peter Drucker has sage advice for us, although he is not talking to librarians, and his advice is equally germane to librarians as managers and librarians as subordinates, because ultimately we are both. Writing in the *Wall Street Journal,* Drucker made the case for managing our own bosses as our primary responsibility in seeking success for our own endeavors, and noted that the primary responsibility of any manager was the making of decisions, because it is only through decisions that resources are dispensed. Drucker notes that favorable decisions are based on trust, and he suggests a regular conversation centering around the question of whether or not we are trusted, and if not what it would take to earn trust because we must have trust. He also argues that we must align our bosses to our own objectives, by asking them if they agree, and once they agree asking what they are planning to do to make it happen. Finally, and in stressing the contractual relationship that really exists between any employee and his or her boss, Drucker states that it is important that we inform our management of what we are planning to do, but that it is far more important that we inform management of what we are *not* planning to do; either because we do not think it is important, or because it is important but the resources have not been provided. Therefore, the decision (that word again) of whether to agree that this will not happen and take responsibility for that result, or alternatively to provide the resources is for our boss to make.

It is a scenario that applies throughout the management chain, and I hope that we do not allow style and rhetoric to blind us to the reality that management is a hierarchical chain. It is perhaps ironic that the blurring of that chain is often urged as a tactic within the library, but never as a style in dealing with corporate, university, and municipal officials above us in authority. Management is tough, and management is not for everyone, but incompetent or unwilling managers are something none of us can afford. Management is, as Thomas Galvin noted, a contact sport.

TOWARD PROFESSIONALISM

In the broad consideration of the Special Libraries Association and its future, it is appropriate to think in terms of the outlook for special librarianship itself. Much of our energy is devoted to a consideration of the pros and cons of professional standards, or membership requirements, and of the place or absence of a place for library technicians. All such considerations occur without any clear discussion or definition of what it really takes to be a special librarian—except for the general assumption that you certainly cannot go wrong with a library degree.

We are much preoccupied with the shortage of librarians in general and of special librarians in particular. Our own staff vacancies give ample evidence that the shortage is real. At the same time some of us are nagged by the suspicion that the shortage might not be as great if we did not squander professional talent on non-professional tasks; and that the problem is really more one of logistics, of moving available professionals into professional assignments.

Librarianship, and special librarianship in particular, is a profession in transition. There is no profession more dynamically involved in change; and the end results will depend on us. This is challenging and exciting.

The road of special librarianship is branching, and we must look down both forks of the road. Our dilemma arises from the fact that, quite suddenly, we have competition in the information business. Until quite recently, the acquisition, storage, analysis, and dissemination of information were our business; and our customers were stuck with us whether they liked our approach or not. We made the rules, and we enforced them. Information service has become a big business and a lucrative one. In part this has occurred because expanding technology places a high premium on complete, timely, up-to-date information; in part because

From *Special Libraries* 60 (February 1969):69–73.
Inaugural Address as President, Special Libraries Association.

scientific management is supposed to be based on facts rather than intuition; and in part because new sophisticated pieces of hardware make so much of this increased manipulation and sophistication feasible.

SERVICE OR SELF-SERVICE

There has always been something of a conflict between the two functions of a library: as a part of the educational process and as a service institution. At least part of our problem comes from the fact that library service—as special library customers have a right to expect it—really conflicts with the emphasis on librarianship as an educational adjunct, which still dominates our profession. In school librarianship and in much of public librarianship, the emphasis is on teaching the client how to help himself. We tend to make value judgments about our customers on the basis of their understanding of bibliographic tools and their ability to serve themselves; and we strive to improve that understanding and that ability. It is difficult to realize that, in a special library setting, this standard may have no meaning. For a particular customer, his ideal library service may be one in which he need know nothing (or do nothing) about the way in which we handle material or secure answers. He has a problem, he needs a solution—and no moral judgments, please. (You will notice that I insist on using the word, *customer*, although many may find it more irritating than patron.)

There are many indications that we do not function as well in the service area as we should or, perhaps, as we think we do. Traditionally, the responsibilities of the librarian have been directed toward a strong program in acquisitions, a professional effort in making materials ready and available through their preparation for use, the preparation of tools to assist in their location, and finally in assistance to the user in finding the information he needed. *Assistance* to the user? Yes, but the responsibility was still basically that of the customer. In fact, the "morality standards" of the library profession were and still are largely based on the assumption that knowledgeable, educated, cultured, worthwhile people are the ones who know how to use a library. We have, in various shadings, all of the subtle little devices for showing disapproval of those who do not measure up to our expectations, from outright shock to friendly paternalistic condescension. "Oh, you mean you've never used *Engineering Index?* Well, come, let me show you how it's arranged." Such an approach hurts only the librarian. If the would-be user now feels foolish and inadequate, he will find reasons not to use the library at all. It then follows that "Since I never use the library anyway, why does it need such a big budget? We need to cut expenses!"

Glib generalizations may be very unfair on an individual basis to many, or most, of us. Nevertheless, part of our problems of importance, status, and recognition has come from an insistence on providing service on our own terms; by giving the user what we feel he ought to get, and by making him do for himself what we think he ought to do himself—with no concern as to his opinion on the subject.

This sort of an attitude cannot succeed in a service organization. The special library—whether it be in an industrial, nonprofit, government or university environment—does not produce or market a product. The library will have difficulty proving its impact on sales volume or production costs. What can be easily established from the accounting ledgers is that the library is a not insignificant overhead expense, and that it therefore dilutes the operating profit. It is a perfectly natural and understandable reaction on the part of operating managers to question and challenge the validity of the library operation in terms of their own needs. As executive director of Leasco's NASA Facility, I have operated a direct contract project with profit objectives, and have supported, from my operating profit, the corporate library. Even though I am a librarian, I have also questioned its costs and the cost impact in terms of the services it provides to our operation.

Our problems in this area are caused largely by our own stubborn refusal to admit that, to any appreciable extent, we are a service and not only an educational organization, and by our insistence on providing information services as we think the customer ought to be receiving them. When I emphasize the necessity for providing information services as the customer needs them, I am not saying that they should be provided as *he says* he needs them. I am emphatically not stating that the internal techniques for information manipulation can be directed by the user. The librarian has management responsibilities which he cannot delegate to his customers.

Some libraries have developed well in such an environment while others have just continued to exist. Nevertheless, these conditions might have continued indefinitely, with the library supervisor finding his own place in the organization by his ability to manipulate and maneuver, but for one rather recent innovation: the development of information centers. Many of our libraries have simply become information centers, and the library managers are now managers of these information centers. There is nothing particularly wrong with this, unless you feel an attachment to the historic nomenclature. The manager of the information center (formerly the librarian) can probably command a new job description with a comparably higher salary.

Our areas of deep concern come in situations in which an existing special library has been *supplemented* by the formation of a new information center with no connection to the existing library organization. Inevitably such information centers have been formed to provide information to the users in easy-to-digest, packaged forms—frequently, though not always, through the use of computerized equipment. What such information centers—with their computerized search, their SDI services, their annotated bibliographies, and their competitive product evaluations—are providing, or promising to provide, is *information*, not materials and not procedures for obtaining materials.

PIONEERING TECHNIQUES

There is irony in this development. Much if not most of the early experimentation with such information techniques as SDI service was pioneered by librarians, frequently through the necessity of overcoming reluctance and apathy of management. It is sad, indeed, to find that our own tools have been turned to use by others, while much of the library profession has hidden behind the endless refrain: "We know machines are coming, and we know they will have applications in the library, but nobody has proven their usefulness yet." Apparently others do not agree.

It now becomes fairly obvious that the reason for the instant success of these programs is the fact that they provide or promise to provide a kind of service which the customer has wanted all along and for which, despite the protestations of corporate poverty, he would gladly have been willing to pay.

There is no service performed by an "in-addition-to-the-library" information center which should not legitimately be performed by the library. If our concerns are information and all of the intermediate processes necessary for the full, proper and successful utilization of this information, then the business of the information center is part of the business of the library. I cannot visualize the continued co-existence of the two concepts as separates in the same organization, without eventually relegating the library to the status of a high level stock room.

STAFF SERVICES

Without doubt the special library staff will need the assistance of subject specialists, of translators, of systems analysts, of programmers, and of budget analysts. These individuals, however, must provide staff services to the special librarian. When full-time assistance is required, these subject specialists, analysts and programmers must be members of the library's staff, reporting to the special librarian.

All librarianship, but particularly special librarianship, must change to meet expanding desires and interests of the user community, or be relegated to a supply room function. Certainly the advent of computer processing, with greater and more rapid access to large information stores, rapid large-scale printing, and reprographic processes, has had considerable impact on the philosophy of information service. Our customers simply cannot keep up with the developments in their fields—scientific and humanistic alike—without assistance.

An additional area of significant change with impact on the library profession is directly related to computer technology, and, through it, to the interchange of information between library locations.

When I speak of the developing application of computer technology to library operations, I am not talking about its pertinence to library housekeeping functions, to such tasks as ordering, check-in, routing, circulation control, etc. Machine applications here have been feasible and practicable for at least a half-dozen years, despite the never-ending pleas for more study and for more time. Such library functions are very like similar tasks in insurance companies, banks, mail order firms, and warehousing operations. Techniques and principles long established fit our needs quite nicely with only minor adaptation. I am addressing myself to the far more significant and far more difficult questions involved in computer assistance to the library in the performance of intellectual functions within the library

The NASA Information Program has been distributing computer tapes to NASA Centers and selected major contractors for over five years. The National Library of Medicine has been active in the program for about four years, and the Library of Congress and the Defense Documentation Center also have programs in being or in preparation for the distribution of machine readable information. These programs of centralized processing, as they affect libraries, are being tremendously accelerated through the development both of remote access consoles for input and output to computers at distant locations, and through the feasibility and practical economic necessity for computer time sharing. To a greater extent, today's computers have excess processing capacity. They can handle more manipulations within a time span than any one input device can demand. It therefore becomes both economically and technically practical to make one central computer location *the* information reference store for a large number of libraries, with each of these libraries querying the information store in what to the machine is sequential but to the user appears to be a simultaneous manner. This development, accompanied in turn by greater sophistication in microstorage and blowback and by cathode ray tube projections of computer information, changes all of the economics of computer storage of library information.

It also changes all of the ground rules for the library itself. It simultaneously multiplies the reference resources of the participating organizations and places greater emphasis on the use of this material through professional reference work, through bibliographic search and through selective dissemination, while at the same time considerably de-emphasizing the local requirement for technical processing. Because, in this kind of cooperative organization, processing can only be done once within the system, and that processing must be accepted by all of the other members. I doubt that we will have difficulty adapting to this, once we realize its inevitabililty.

INTRAPROFESSIONAL RELATIONS

We worry about our relationship to other professional associations which seem, in large part, interested in the same kinds of programs and ideals in which we are interested. A quick glance at the American Society for Information Science membership roster discloses the names of some of the most active members of SLA. The American Library Association has now established a formal division for systems studies and mechanization, an area we tended to consider our private domain. But such concerns are an inversion of the real problem. People will affiliate with groups which best satisfy their needs and interests, regardless of what those groups or associations are called. SLA's decision—whether to be completely independent, to cooperate closely, or eventually to merge—will follow as a natural result of which path we choose as a profession, and how well this Association, or any other, responds to meet the needs which are generated.

Our concerns with recruitment, our concerns with professional standards, and our concerns with the continuing questions about what kind of people we ought to permit to become members of the Special Libraries Association are valid and topical, and I am not suggesting that they be side-tracked. I have already expressed my own personal opinion, in other forums, that I consider the library degree by far the most suitable training for work in special librarianship and information science, but that I consider the degree as neither an exclusive qualification nor an automatic one.

What I am suggesting is that the question of formal educational qualifications becomes secondary when compared to the total need for all special librarians to continue their education and preparation—no matter what their original training. Those of you who attended library school a decade or two ago, as I did, know how ill prepared you would be for coping with the operational problems you face today if you had to rely exclusively on that training. It is safe to say that this year's graduates, if they put their minds into the deep freeze, will be just as unqualified and ill prepared ten years from now.

This is not the fault of the educational institutions, much as we like to blame them for many of our problems. A library school, or any other school, can only prepare its students with the information available at that time, no matter how well it orients its curriculum to special library needs. A physician who attended medical school twenty years ago and who has learned nothing since graduation is not someone I would like to have treat my illness. A special librarian who has learned nothing since graduation twenty years ago is a poor bet to run a special library.

There is no one single simple solution to the problem of continued updating, and it is certainly not unique to us. Technical obsolescence or, to be genteel, technical erosion affects many professions. Some of the solutions can and must come from our educational institutions, and some library schools are aware of their responsibilities. Others, of course, are still turning out masses of graduates with cookie cutter uniformity.

However, not all of the activity in this area can come from the library schools, and even when it does, it will require your support and assistance. It is the exponents and developers of new ideas and new technologies who must teach about them. Much of the activity must come through your own participation and initiative; much of this activity should be channeled through the framework of your professional association.

Special librarianship will not be a profession for the faint of heart, for those lacking in intellectual stimulation, for those unwilling to commit themselves to continued self-education and improvement, and for those looking for a nice quiet place to retire immediately upon graduation.

We need not do it. We can quietly step aside and let the ranks be filled by the scientific informationalists, logicians, behavioralists, philosophical empiricists, empirical philosophers, and the thousand-and-one others, who can see the expanding frontier and who want their piece of real estate. Even these people, in their projected scheme of things, have a place for us. They need somebody to run their information stock room.

THE ANSWERS ARE CRUCIAL

Our consideration of these questions is not just germane but it is crucial for the future and growth of librarianship, specifically special librarianship, and even more specifically the Special Libraries Association.

The task of information analysis, information dissemination, and information packaging will be performed, whether we do it or not. We still have the option of being the ones to do this. We have the head start in the fact that we are the incumbents, and that we have the education and training for the handling of information. But we rapidly throw that advantage away when we refuse to recognize all the signs which indicate what management and the customer really want—when we insist on talking about back-orders, filing backlogs, lack of cooperation in returning overdue material, crises in binding because of missing issues, by insisting on talking to our management about tools and mechanics in which nobody but us is remotely interested, and by failing to translate our needs into the concepts which management does understand.

We can fight to retain what was ours by default at a time when it was too mundane to interest others, and has now become a challenge of tremendous scope which has attracted many outsiders—some earnest and qualified, some quacks and charlatans. We can fight to demonstrate to others what we so clearly know, that the management of information services is properly ours by training, experience and attitude. Or we can nestle securely in our fortress, ordering material only on demand, indicating its location in the system once it arrives—through an intricate cabala of symbols—and keeping accurate records of who borrowed what. This is a job even our newly arrived competitors in the information business are willing to concede to us. After all, who wants to spend his life running a stock room?

We still have the opportunity to do something about it. But it must be soon.

Organizational Placement of the Industrial Special Library: Its Relationship to Success and Survival

> *Because of the researcher's greater appreciation for library services, it has been generally assumed that special libraries operate more effectively reporting through research than through management. Experiences during the recent wave of industrial retrenchments make re-examination of this assumption appropriate.*

A substantial percentage of special libraries and information centers serve industrial corporations with an emphasis on science and technology. Scientific and engineering firms were among the first business organizations to recognize the value of formal information collections staffed by trained professionals.

Many of these special libraries and information centers, while oriented toward technical and scientific needs, in fact represent the only formal library collection within the company. This is so because of the appreciation of formal information needs by management and non-technical personnel is a relatively recent development.

Graduate programs in management spend little time worrying about the optimum placement of the library within the organization, and as a result libraries have ended up reporting either where some management body was anxious to have them, or where it appeared a convenient place to lump or dump the administrative responsibility. Because of this, most such special libraries have reported either within the research and development wing of the organization—sometimes

From *Special Libraries* 64 (March 1973):141–44.

directly to the Vice President or Director of Research—or they have reported within an administrative center to someone with a title such as Director of Administrative Services, and pooled with such functions as the mail room, office services, the print shop, and engineering drawings and specifications.

RESEARCH AND DEVELOPMENT/ADMINISTRATIVE SERVICES

Most special librarians consider themselves fortunate to be able to report within the research and development structure. The reason is not difficult to understand. In this environment the library operates in a close relationship to people who use information and appreciate its value, who possess intellectual qualifications and enjoy intellectual pursuits, and who treat the library as an important tool in their own work. The Vice President for Research can usually be relied upon to understand and endorse the library's needs for funds and materials, and to use the library himself.

On the other hand, the Manager of Administrative Services may often be either a generalist administrator or an up-from-the-ranks veteran employee, who treats the library as simply one of a number of centralized services to be performed in a static-free manner, and who makes no pretense of understanding library problems or complexities, or for that matter of using the library.

It is therefore not surprising that libraries under the shelter of the research and development organization have, during periods of corporate growth and expansion, benefited in terms of support and status, as compared to those centered in administrative areas.

It should be noted that, while this has historically been true, it need not necessarily have been the case. Managers of administrative service areas usually have as must desire for personal growth and advancement as anyone else, but the areas they supervise present little opportunity in terms of startling innovation or corporate impact. The library can, in fact, provide such an opportunity, whether or not this concept is grasped either by the library supervisor or his boss. In most cases it has not been grasped, and the potential symbiotic relationship of a librarian in search of a stronger library and an administrative manager in search of prestige and glory has gone unnoticed.

The test of many a library's support strength and vulnerability has come during the wave and cutbacks and retrenchments which rocked the industrial community, particularly during 1970 and 1971. While no complete account of the impact of this economy wave on industrial libraries may ever be possible, we do know that some libraries escaped completely or almost unscathed, while others suffered severe decimation and even extinction. Among the libraries most severely hit were many which had assumed themselves to be in virtually ideal environments—large and respected organizations reporting to Vice Presidents of Research and Development. These had every reason to believe that they provided excellent and appreciated service, and had never even had much difficulty in securing additional funds for materials, furniture, services, or even staff, let alone faced cutbacks or terminations.

ACCOUNTING CONSIDERATIONS

To understand what happened it is necessary to understand something about the accounting treatment of library expenses. Virtually all companies which try to determine profitability on a product or product line basis—and that includes almost all companies—classify costs as either direct or allocated. Direct costs are those specifically concerned in the production and marketing of a revenue-producing product. Allocated costs, labelled either as overhead or G&A, are applied as expenses on a distributed basis after the determination of a gross profit, with a resultant final net profit. When this net profit turns to a net loss, a frantic and sometimes brutal scramble begins to turn the red ink black again.

Most attention is concentrated on the distributed and allocated costs. This is true because obviously any hopes of a turn-around must be based on the continuing manufacture of a product and its aggressive marketing. It is at times such as this that indirect cost, overhead, or G&A tends to become suspect as potential "frill."

Almost without exception, industrial libraries, whether they report within R&D or administrative services, are part of this distributed package, and so are the larger organizations to which the library belongs. When huge and frontal attacks on the G&A structure occur, they impact administrative services and research alike, and neither the Vice President for Research nor the Manager for Administrative Services is of much help. All of his organization is under fire. This can be a traumatic shock to the librarian who has always had appreciation and compassion from his boss. To understand his attitude one must remember that in asking him to exempt the library in whole or in part from the cruel edict, one is in fact asking him alternatively to take an even larger slice out of another program, perhaps a research program in which he fervently believes. Librarians who report to administrative services managers do not necessarily fare any better, but they tend to react with less shock because they have less expectation of loyalty and support, and because they have probably been through some of this, on a lesser scale, before.

It can be argued, with great persuasiveness and probably irrefutable logic, that times of corporate depression are the worst times in which to curtail funding for research programs and for library activities. These arguments are essentially useless, because they assume a willingness to endure a short-time disaster for the long-term rainbow, and this ignores the fact that corporations are owned by public stockholders who have a great concern with earnings per share and market valuation *now*. If the company sustains a loss now, something must be done about it now. Six months from now the stockholder may have sold the stock.

Librarians must realize that the injunction to cut budget, to cut service, and to cut staff, is rarely based on any sort of personal dislike for the library or librarian. Cuts in allocated budgets are usually edicted on a dispassionate across-the-board basis, because that is the easiest and sometimes the only practicable way in which to perform such an onerous chore. For the most part, the library is treated like every other organization with similar credentials.

LIBRARY RESILIENCY

The author is therefore led to the conclusion that the success of the library in withstanding cuts in overhead and G&A funds caused by poor profitability has little to do with where the library is placed administratively. If anything, in times of trouble, placement within the research and development organization may be a disservice—in part because the library manager may have become lulled into a false sense of security, in part because reporting to R&D will frequently monopolize all of the library's time and attention, and in part because in times of stress and difficulty your very best users are too powerless and too preoccupied to help you. They have problems of their own.

Any library can grow and expand as the organization it serves is growing and expanding through years of profitability. The resiliency of the library organization in time of trouble is based on its ability to escape the general dictum, with the ax falling on someone else instead. This ability is based on someone's saying at the high level meetings at which such decisions are rather randomly and casually made: "We have to exempt the library; let's take a larger slice out of organization Y," instead of saying nothing, or of saying, "We have to exempt organization Y. Instead, let's take a larger slice out of the library."

At times like this, and confronted by pressure on his own little backroom experiments which he hopes will win him the Nobel prize some day, the Vice President for Research becomes very much of a fair weather friend. He is probably measuring in his mind the relative problems of recouping what has been lost when things get better, and he thinks that this is probably easier with the library than with a research problem on which he thinks others are also working. He may even be right.

The effective support for the library at such a terrible time can come only from two sources—corporate management, which does not really care from where the cuts come—and operating profit center management, which either does not care either, or which may (wonder of wonders) be willing to carry a higher allocated cost because it feels your operation is worth keeping.

If the librarian can count on one thing, it is that the people who will ultimately make these major decisions (and this group includes neither the head of administrative service nor the director of research) will act selfishly. They will vote in favor or dispensing with services they do not use, and keeping services they do use.

The library's strategy, in terms of self-protection and survival, must be geared to making itself indispensable to these people—whether or not they ever ask for information (and they probably do not), whether or not they take an interest, and whether or not you are even chartered to serve them. If you are the only library in the place, you must serve everybody, and you must resist the tendency of the R&D people to monopolize all of your time—even though they like you, appreciate you, and ask you interesting questions. The time to start this program of ingratiated irreplaceability is now—when trouble starts it is too late.

Ingratiated irreplaceability does not mean justifying the library service in terms of a dollar and cents profit impact. It would be very nice if this could be done, but, as Kramer inferred,[1] it is doubtful that this can be done with any success, certainly not with any consistent success. This author agrees with Kramer and with Holm[2] that the major advantage of an information function is that it can find the answers for the inquirer more rapidly than he could himself. To this might be added that it can also provide answers which the inquirer needs but has not thought to request.

This problem of top management justification was posed to a class in the management of special libraries and information centers. None of these students had operating experience in special libraries, and their approaches were perhaps naive and unworkable, but nevertheless interesting. One student offered to host with his own funds a cocktail party for all of the executive secretaries, which he would use to enlist them in his campaign not only to channel all of their bosses' information needs to the library, but also to keep him informed of what particular problems and frustrations were being encountered.

Another student suggested making a secret alliance with the company union leadership, under which the library could serve as a resource for the reading and training interests and needs of the membership, and in return for which the union would insist on the maintenance of an adequate library as a contract negotiating condition.

Naively humorous as these suggestions may be, they at least point to a recognition and a concern. The library retrenchment and cutback program may be at an end, as some economists tell us the recession is at an end. The problems faced by industrial libraries in 1970 and 1971 may not come again for a while, but in the cyclical economic pattern it appears inevitable that they will come some day. If and when this happens, I believe that the success of the library organization in riding out the storm will be far less dependent on its size, its budget, and its location within the management structure, than on the simple question of how its curtailment or demise would personally affect the people confronted with the decision of where to apply the ax.

References

1. Kramer, J. / How to Survive in Industry—Cost Justifying Library Services. *Special Libraries* 62: 487–489 (Nov 1971).
2. Holm, B. E. / How to Manage Your Information. New York. Reinhold Book Corp., 1968.

MANAGEMENT: A STRATEGY FOR CHANGE

I distinctly recall an International Federation of Library Associations meeting I attended six years ago in Budapest. The program at one of the sessions was one of the earlier discussions of budget justification in libraries. One distinguished and senior academic library administrator, who could finally stand it no longer, rose to his feet and approached a floor microphone. In a voice heavy with emotion, he said: "I deeply and bitterly resent this entire discussion. Libraries are not products to be packaged and merchandised, like soap flakes or breakfast cereal. Libraries are self-evidently good."

Nobody responded to him. None of us had the heart to tell him that the world had played a trick on him, and changed the value system of his profession without the grace of allowing him to complete his distinguished and scholarly career.

The world has played a trick on many a library administrator. Librarians are most often humanists, rarely scientists or engineers. They are drawn into the field because of their love of books, their love of knowledge, and their idealistic desire to contribute to the making of a better society. With a quaint impractical streak we still treasure in some fields (such as archaeology or the study of 14th century German minnesingers), they chose the field because it promised scholarship, reflection, and an absence of competitive pressures. They did not seek power or wealth, and they have been quite successful in not achieving either.

Their approach to management is at best wary, at worst openly hostile. I still find this predisposition in many if not most of today's library students. Management, they instinctively feel, is a conspiracy to

Paper presented at the first plenary session at CLA's 1978 conference in Edmonton.
Reprinted from *Canadian Library Journal* (October 1978).
Distributed by Conference Organizers to All Delegates, U.S. White House Conference on Libraries and Information Services.

keep people from doing what they want to do and to make them do what somebody else wants. It is repressive, it is devious, it is undemocratic. "When I get to be a librarian I'm not going to be like that. I'm going to allow people to make their own decisions and do what they want to do, because we all have the interests of the library and of society at heart."

It is an attractive concept, and it still has adherents. They are frequently found outside the library, among academic faculties. Feeling themselves increasingly isolated and besieged, they have circled their wagons, wallowed in self-pity, and blamed politicians, the business community, and the general public for a materialistic and self-centered attitude under which the finer and nobler values are no longer appreciated.

That's a comfortable thesis—self-proclaimed martyrdom is always spiritually uplifting. But it is not that simple. This hard core resistance to management values also has its adherents in the library profession, and because their arguments have become more forceful and shriller, they may even appear to some to be gaining in strength.

One of the central battlegrounds in the public library field concerns the continued provision of "free" library service, and the insistence that if it can't be provided on those terms to everyone it shouldn't be provided at all. The argument has appeal and merit—deprivation of information because of an inability to pay is as unacceptable as deprivation of food. But the argument, as far as it goes, is simplistic.

The view presently embraced by some that only services available to all without fee or strings should be provided—without the assurance that this does happen without curtailment—leads nowhere except to the continual erosion of library services, and to the replacement of the library as the service institution by some other mechanism. Library service may be price-less, but it is not cost-less. If you want to provide it without charge, it increases your management responsibility to assure that outside support is sufficient to allow you to do so.

"INFORMATION" MAGIC WORD

The weakening of support for library services is not tied to a weakening of support for the provision of information services. Information, in fact, is the magic word of the late 1970s and the coming early 1980s. Various estimates now tell us that we spend more on information services than on goods, and Daniel Bell's view of the post-industrial society gives us an indication of the directions in which we are heading.

If you need yet another barometer of emerging value systems, let me offer one that has been a good predictor in the past. IBM, you may have noticed, has stopped calling itself a computer manufacturer. IBM is in the information technology business. Libraries ought to find the information dissemination and retrieval business a good combination. Why isn't it?

"SELF-EVIDENT GOOD"

For at least part of the answer let me return to our anguished colleague at the IFLA meeting. Libraries are self-evidently good, he said. Not a bad ploy if you can get away with it. If things are self-evident, they don't need to be explained or justified. In fact, anyone who has the audacity to suggest that they are not self-evident only indicts him- or herself in the process as ignorant, uncultured, insensitive, or any combination of the above.

One of the world's most eloquent and frequently quoted political documents gets right at the heart of this approach after only the briefest preamble "We hold these truths to be self-evident." A very effective tactic by Thomas Jefferson, which neatly cut off all discussion of the premise, and led 18th-century readers immediately into the implementation of these premises. However, "that all men are created equal" was hardly self-evident in the 18th century, unless you were prepared to define what you meant by "men." We would have considerably less difficulty in the world if some of these "truths" were in fact self-evident in the 20th century.

This has been the precise tactic in support of library services throughout the late 19th and this part of the 20th century. We hold this truth to be self-evident: that library service is good, that more library service is better, and that most library service is best. We have largely gotten away with this view because we were able to maneuver our opponents or would-be opponents into playing Philistines. Consider the phrase, "the purpose of the library is to provide improved and enhanced cultural and information services to the community." It is a beautiful phrase, with all the right buzz words—improved, enhanced, culture, information, service, community. It is unassailable. It is also unquantifiable, unmeasurable, and uncompletable. In other words, it is a perfect campaign platform. But recognize that as a meaningful justification and as a management plan, it is pure gibberish.

Our Russian colleagues do it still better. Their libraries serve the cause of culture, humanism, and peace. To be against what libraries want is, by extension, to be for war.

Before I examine why this doesn't work any more I also want to stress that this level of acceptance was always a mixed blessing, and never worked very well. Support as a self-evident good may be assured, but it is not very enthusiastic, as most constrained support is unenthusiastic. Products and services perceived to be of tangible value and benefit have fared better in the allocation of resources. Truckers and longshoremen, whom nobody has ever called dedicated public servants, have done far better economically in recent years than educators and librarians, although we are presumably held in higher esteem and toil nobly in the cause of human betterment.

The need for justification of library budgets and indeed of library existence, the period into which we are entering, is a danger, but it is also an opportunity. We can indeed do worse than the automatic low-level funding increments we have won for ourselves. On the other hand, we can do much better. Funding at the self-evident good level has never been satisfactory to begin with.

The questioning of intrinsic values and the requirements for justification have come as a great shock to a large number of library heads—I am loath to call them library administrators because they haven't been that. Many have not survived the change. Perhaps the most dramatic indication in the shift in value systems and priorities comes from a study of Association of Research Libraries (ARL) directors undertaken by Professor David Kaser at Indiana University.

ARL libraries are the slightly more than 100 largest academic and research libraries in Canada and the United States. According to Kaser's findings, in 1960 90 per cent of ARL directors had earned doctorates, although not normally in librarianship. The library doctorate was not that prevalent. It can be assumed that they held their posts because they were recognized and respected as scholars and academicians. While management skills were not objected to, they were not really part of the job description.

By 1976, only 16 years later, there had been a multiple turnover in virtually all these posts. Only 15 per cent of the 1976 directors had doctorates, despite the far more ready availability of the library doctorate.

STRONGER LIBRARY MANAGERS

It is not hard to determine what has changed. Job descriptions in *American Libraries, Canadian Library Journal,* and the *Chronicle of Higher Education* confirm it constantly. Academic administrators have discovered that the university library is more than an expensive toy. It is a valuable and costly resource, which can be administered for good or ill. Management of libraries is no longer something scholars do in their spare time, and the search is for library administrators who understand something about productivity, cost effectiveness, evaluation and monitoring, and even program budgeting.

It is interesting that this shift toward stronger library managers comes at the same time as a growing surge toward participative management and library staff self-management, perhaps more in Canada than in the United States. Weak managers are not necessarily benevolent or staff-involved administrators, and many studies from fields outside the library tell us that the absence of leadership and direction is far more destructive of morale than demanding toughness, providing that demand is reasonable and consistent.

Demands for greater self-autonomy on the part of the staff arise, at least in part, from the same non-leadership vacuum that upper administrators to which the library reports now recognize and find objectionable. I am not sure how this will end, but I am quite certain that decision processes that do not specifically identify responsibility and accountability will not be acceptable alternatives. Staff council decisions have the attractiveness that nobody can be held responsible, and nobody can be fired, but that is also their weakness. The premise that staff decisions represent a higher level of virtue and responsiveness to user needs is as self-serving and suspect as the "self-evident" ploy.

In the long run, I suspect the dichotomy is nowhere as great as may be assumed. The opening of factory management to representation of the workers in Scandinavia has actually changed little in the value system. Responsible professional workers and responsible administrators fundamentally want the same things—effective and productive organizations. Incompetence, laziness, and willful disregard are their common enemies, and this will be the case in the library as well.

Libraries will have to be effectively administered by someone, as the price for convincing upper management that what we do is important. If it's important, then it is necessary that it be done well. The historic lack of higher management concern was never an expression of trust, but rather an assessment of triviality. In the future, not even that option will be open to us. Accountants have come to notice that libraries are expensive beasts to feed, and that they have insatiable appetites.

LOST MYSTIQUE

What has changed us, in upper management's eyes, from an accepted if under-supported self-evident good to a topic of more considerable concern and interest is due to a number of factors. First of all, librarianship has lost some of its mystique. Through most of the 19th century, before library service to the public became fashionable, librarians were guardians of their collections, as well as scholarly collectors. If you wanted to use the library, you made an appointment to see the library director, and petitioned for permission to use it. You explained and defended your worthy scholarly purpose, and if you were fortunate, you were allowed limited access to some part of the collection. And you were both impressed and grateful. I am not suggesting that this was effective library service, but at least it had snob appeal. Our clientele was small, but it was selective and influential; we helped select it, and it was grateful.

There is a perverse streak in people that causes them to cherish what they cannot get or what is at least difficult to get, and to disdain what is freely and readily available. Probably the worst public relations mistake librarians have made is to label their libraries as "free" libraries, some even to the extent of chiseling the words over the entrance. First of all, as I have already indicated, library service is hardly free of cost. More importantly, however, any advertising or marketing expert will tell you that labeling something as free as its primary quality immediately suggests that the other qualities aren't worth much.

People are suspicious of things that are given away—in some cases they won't even take them. Even as we intend for library services to continue to be offered without payment or charge, it is the wrong value to stress. Far better to stress its usefulness, its importance, its relevance to today's society. Some public libraries are now trying to do that, but not many, and it is late in the game.

USER SELF-SERVICE

We have not only removed the sense of grandeur and importance that comes from closed stacks and chained catalogues, we have insisted that people learn to use the library for themselves. This, of course, is part of the thinking that includes libraries as part of the educational process, and packages libraries into the overall educational value system. It narrows our options considerably, and frequently can prevent us from providing desired service, because that service would contravene the educational process.

Consider, for example, the request for book reviews to assist in the preparation of a book report. If the request came from a prominent adult citizen, we might honour it. If it came from a high school student, we would probably angrily reject it, as a sneaky way to circumvent the educational process. You are supposed to read a book, and report on that.

There is some concern in my mind about the desirability of allowing ourselves to be relegated as the supply branch of the education army, because there is considerable evidence that even during the good days of education funding, we were treated by our "fellow" educators as shabby second cousins at best. With the competition for funds on the increase, there is evidence on both sides of the border that even this tolerant alliance was a fair-weather friendship. Confronted with problems of allocating scarce resources, educators find that their other and more direct priorities outrank libraries, and librarians suddenly find that they have little voice in how the pie is carved up.

In the United States, when the Office of Education decided about five years ago that it had to curtail the number of its Educational Resources Information Center (ERIC) clearinghouses, it asked the educational community which of the 20 or so clearinghouses was most expendable. The educators decided, not surprisingly, that it was the clearinghouse on library and information science—and that activity was then submerged at Stanford University under a program on educational technology, from where it has only recently emerged.

Insistence on user self-service for the user's own good has perhaps diminished the quality of information service—the quality of the answer obtained. We can't really tell. We have no way of measuring or evaluating quality, only quantity—the number of things people carry in and out. I could argue, if I wanted to be perverse, that quantity could be an inverse measurement of quality. The less directly any one source answers my need, the more sources I need to take home with me.

In any case, our general withdrawal from information gatekeeping to self-service has focused attention on the least attractive and least professional aspect of library service, the circulation desk. I have never attempted to study the question formally, but I am convinced from enough random casual conversations that much of the general public thinks of librarianship as stamping due dates in books, sending out reminders, and collecting fines. They cannot conceive of these as professional, stimulating, intellectual, or important activities, and they are genuinely puzzled as to why a master's degree (or for that matter a college education) is required to perform them.

PROFESSIONAL ACTIVITIES HIDDEN

We have taken elaborate care to ensure that our professional activities, those which can be argued to require education and experience, are carried out where nobody can bother us, and also where no one can see us. It is only a slight exaggeration to argue that most patron contact in libraries is at the clerical level, while the professionals congregate (or hide) out of sight.

Hide is perhaps not as unfair as it sounds. Despite the fact that librarianship calls itself a service profession, I can sense from the applications of many of the master's degree applicants, at least at our own institution, that what attracts them to our field is the promise of being able to deal with books and other inanimate objects, and not having to deal with people. This must stop. We must interact with our clients on a level that is not only visible, but recognizable as professional.

LIBRARIES LOSE MONOPOLY

At least our processing operations still provide some semblance of mystique for what this is worth. The intricate details that appear on many of our catalogue cards, the arbitrariness of some of our classification assignments, the difficulty of finding things in particularly our larger and more complex libraries, combined with our gentle chiding of those who have difficulty in operating effectively in our environment—all of this at least creates an aura of complexity that can be assumed to demand considerable wisdom and training.

Unfortunately, we are about to lose even this last semblance of mystery. The rapid development of on-line data bases, accessible from any place with an electric outlet, will, in my judgment, create great changes in libraries. It bypasses entirely our monopoly on information announcement. With built-in training programs for the uninitiated (because the data base developers want you to use their files—that's how they get paid), home and office terminals may become easier to use than card catalogues, and threaten to bypass the library as a source of bibliographic access. This is not just for magazine articles, but also for books which have been received and processed in one national or source library.

Such direct bibliographic access will still require the user's contact with the library to get a copy of the desired document, as the development of information centres and information analysis centres began to do in the 1950s and 1960s. Some librarians, those who count only circulation as the measurement of their performance, might even welcome such simple fulfilment business as an enhancement of their service. However, the supply of specifically requested items is nothing more than a stockroom activity. It may be a well-stocked or rapidly responsive operation, but it is a stockroom nonetheless, and stockroom managers are rarely considered professional or treated as such.

There is, however, an additional problem for our technical processing people in direct bibliographic access. Up until now users have not known about materials received in the library, or even available somewhere in the world, until we were ready to tell them. With direct bibliographic access that bypasses the local library, users may be pleased to learn that the desired book has indeed been received. They will find it difficult to understand why it is going to take another five weeks or five months to get it ready for use.

CHOICES NECESSARY

The second significant reason, probably more tangible than the loss of status and mystique, is the simple phenomenon that funding bodies no longer have enough money to pay for all the things it is agreed are worth doing, even the support of libraries. This is a development of the last 10 years, in both Canada and the United States. Until that time we stubbornly clung to the insistence that we could somehow afford to do all the things worth doing, and government programs attacked education, poverty, hunger, environment, employment—all frontally and simultaneously.

Even the most optimistic of government planners now accept that goals and objectives must be toned down to the pragmatically possible, and more significantly, that choices between self-evident goods must be made. The choice between library support and enhanced police protection, or between library support and more efficient street repair, is an uncomfortable one for librarians, and we have no training in how to win such a debate. Libraries have never figured out how to get funds in competition. Our money was traditionally earmarked for us, and we only had to fight against apathy or ignorance to get it. We now find that firefighters, garbage collectors, and even teachers are articulate and persuasive opponents.

GROWTH ONLY MEASURE

Linked with this problem are two other concerns. One is the emergence of the "small is beautiful" movement, a conscious turning away from an automatic dedication to growth, and from quantitative criteria. This is indeed a disastrous development for a profession which has had, historically, no way to measure its progress except quantitatively. To get better you must get bigger—for academic libraries in size of collection, for public libraries in circulation. Most of us know in truth that these are not effective yardsticks, but we have not had anything better.

Coupled with this concern is the general suspicion with which education is now viewed, and as I have already indicated, we are tightly bound, in the public view, to the educational process and educational value system. Education is now suffering some of the disenchantment of having been an oversold commodity. For 20 years following World War II we were told that education was the solution for society's problems with human understanding, unemployment, and a more meaningful life style. We invested heavily during those years in the educational solution to society's problems, and those problems are still with us. Many have intensified. Coupled with declining birth rates and decreasing numbers of people ready to enter our educational establishments, we also now hear questioning of the premise that everyone should get as much education as possible. We now have people dropping out of the educational process, for a while or for good. We have the promulgation of the suggestion that perhaps for some, 12 years of formal education, or perhaps 10, are enough, and we have a return to more pragmatic training programs—for jobs rather than for life.

There is, of course, a significant role that libraries could play in helping to implement these changed goals; in fact it can be argued that the role of the library in this environment is even more fundamental. However, chained to formal and traditional educational values, it has been and continues to be difficult for us to adopt the flexibility that is so much needed. This is particularly true for school and academic libraries, which if you think about it, have always been totally captive of their faculties—their tool if you want to be charitable, their toy if not.

The result is that we are dealing with a much narrowed constituency. It has never been all that large. Public libraries dependent on citizen support from actual library users would be in difficulty at once. Fortunately, libraries have had the tolerant endorsement and financial support of those who, although they did not use libraries themselves, thought libraries were good, that others should use them, and that in any case they should be around for those who wanted to.

It has been one of the tragedies of librarianship that we can deal effectively and usefully with children (the education process)—despite the inroads of television—but that we lose them when the formal education process stops, because we have no information process with which to replace it. In the context of management, this becomes a particular problem when we realize that today's managers are largely yesterday's children who have escaped us.

LIBRARIES EXPENSIVE

Some might argue that this generalization does not hold for academia, that here indeed there is an appreciation for libraries. True, but only up to a point. The academic value system does rate the university, and through it the department and the individual faculty member, in terms of the library—but that concern only involves the library as a collection, and does not extend to its staff. In fact, most academicians are unsure about what they expect librarians to do except acquire materials. It is perhaps poetic justice. Having stressed collection size rather than any concepts of service, we are now being hung by our own noose, by faculties that won't let us forget the priority of collection building.

All the foregoing gloom and doom might yet be acceptable, and the self-evident truth of the goodness of libraries prevail, if libraries indeed were, as they were historically assumed to be, trivial expenditures. However, this is not the case, and suppliers of funds have become increasingly aware that the maintenance of libraries, let alone their improvement, requires the expenditure of more and more funds.

There are a number of reasons for this. First of all, libraries are labour-intensive institutions. Our studies at the Indiana University Graduate Library School Research Center show that labour costs approach or exceed 60 per cent of total expenditures for academic and special libraries, and 75 per cent for public libraries. Moreover, this labour intensity is increasing, not abating. Our survey shows that, in many instances, libraries are forced by salary increase commitments not necessarily of their own making to support increments that, on a percentage basis, exceed the growth of their total funds. This, in turn, necessitates shifting funds from other budgets, particularly the materials budget. Our studies indicate that, in the years since 1969, the percentage of the academic library's budget allocated for labour costs has increased, at a steady and almost inexorable one-half per cent per year.

The process does not appear to be reversible. A number of library administrators have informed us that although materials dollars can be shifted to pay salaries, the reduction of salary increase percentages to purchase materials is not permissible, because of administrative fiat and union contracts, but primarily because of the rising cost of living.

Depending on the type of library collection involved, materials costs have risen anywhere from 10 to 16 per cent per year, with particular problems encountered in the renewal of serials, most specifically continental European published serials, against which both Canadian and American currencies weakened substantially in the past six years. However, a library that simply renews existing titles or purchases at existing rates is not a static library, but a deteriorating library. Maintaining a constant place requires at least a pro-rated growth in acquisitions, pro-rated to the growth of the literature itself. This has been estimated at a number of levels from zero to eight per cent annual net growth, without much substantiation for any number, but an assumption of three or four per cent is not unreasonable.

Libraries have, up to now, resisted attempts at cost reduction. They have mechanized, they have joined networks and cooperative cataloguing projects, but none of these steps have freed funds for reassignment, and the best that our survey has been able to project is a decrease in the increased pressure for funds. That's like saying things are getting better on the crime front because the rate at which murders are increasing is decreasing. Say it fast and it almost sounds good.

NOT BEING PICKED ON

It may surprise some of you to learn that we have uncovered no evidence that libraries are being picked on. Somewhat given to paranoia, we like to imagine a giant conspiracy out there of people trying to get us. It simply isn't true, either because we are still held as a self-evident good or because we're so innocent we don't attract enemies. We find that library budgets, in the academic and public sectors, don't grow any less rapidly than those of education as a whole. If it is any consolation to us, all the occupants of the same leaky boat are shipping water at the same rate.

However, even a cursory examination of the significance of some of the numbers I cited earlier will suffice to convince any upper administrator of the impossibility of sating the avaricious appetite of the library monster. Supporting library materials budgets at a four per cent increase in quantity level, when added to price increases, when added to increases in salary and benefit costs, and at least some slight increase in staffing to deal with increased material, would require an annual budget increase of between 17 and 20 per cent. That's a doubling every four years—and that's just to stay even. We're not talking about improvements in the collection, acquisition of special collections, or building of expertise in new areas of study and research.

"BOTTOMLESS PITS"

The reaction of a manager at a level above the library who is told that a budget increase of 17 to 20 per cent is required for the library to stay even is likely to be frustration, annoyance, anger, and ultimately disinclination to bother. An article by Robert Munn published in *College and Research Libraries* as far back as 1968 is indicative by its title alone. It is called "The Bottomless Pit: Or the Academic Library as Viewed from the Administration Building."

Libraries can indeed begin to look like bottomless pits; the more you fill them up, the emptier they get. Requests to legislative bodies for funding support are not accompanied by the promise of any finite accomplishment, only that the granting of this request will move us somewhat closer to meeting our responsibilities to improve library services for all the people. Administrators, be they appointed or elected, must deal in shortrange realities. They must be able to point to accomplishments during their tenures of office that are quantifiable and measurable, which can be shown to make a difference. Asking an administrator to allocate you some of his or her scarce resources to make things slightly less rotten is not an effective communication technique.

The characteristics that differentiate managers from the rest of us will obviously differ depending on the environment in which the manager functions. A manager in the academic setting will probably share many characteristics of the group he or she manages, simply because academic search and screen committees tend to demand research credentials even from their administrative appointees. Managers in the public sector, particularly elected officials, tend to have far different characteristics. Finally, managers in the private sector, particularly the for-profit sector, must show at least some dedication to or understanding of what is called "the bottom line" if they are to survive.

In his 1973 book *Information Systems,* our British colleague Brian Vickery differentitated three kinds of information needs based on work activity. He characterized the scientist's role of producing knowledge, and indicated the information needs this generates. He indicated that the technician's role is to create functional designs, and that the manager's information need is for the generation of decisions. Each implies a need for different types of information and involves different search strategies and information needs.

MANAGEMENT ATTITUDES

The manager's task, then, at least according to Vickery, is primarily the making of decisions, and this implies the need for timely, succinct, and specifically directed information, as opposed to the kind of large quantities of generalized information libraries tend to generate for the user's own analysis and evaluation. Library systems are not generally designed with the needs of the manager in mind, although some special libraries and some information centres have been able to make that adaptation. Library systems are primarily geared to what Vickery called the scientist, although his definition would certainly also include humanists and other scholars.

I am not sure where librarians fit into this scheme of things. Some of us, particularly those in the academic setting, would like to consider ourselves scientists. Many are in posts that at least demand that they ought to be managers. Most, however, I suspect, operate in the role of technicians.

The background the manager brings to the task will also vary with the kind of management environment, but managers do not tend to come from groups that are heavy users or appreciaters of libraries and their benefits. Scholars and researchers are, for a lot of reasons and with relatively few exceptions, badly suited to management and its value system. They tend to see things not in black and white, but in shades of gray, and they tend to be careful and demand complete information before reaching a decision. Management, however, frequently requires decisions reached in a time frame that may allow for little gathering or evaluation of information, and may even prefer a wrong decision to a slow one.

Managers in the public sector tend heavily to come from backgrounds in law, as law is considered the traditional path to political appointment or election. The backgrounds of most managers in the industrial sector come, by my observation, from three areas—law, accounting, and marketing. Accountants deal largely with numerical and analytical data libraries tend not to contain. Lawyers, while heavily dependent on information, work in a narrow field not given to interdisciplinary interchange, and in any case quickly palm off library research to their junior associates. Their approach to the value of libraries is also not geared to a professional acceptance of librarian colleagues.

Managers with marketing backgrounds frequently espouse value systems that are actually anti-library in nature, although not consciously so. Entrepreneurs and wild ducks, they not only brag about being able to make decisions instinctively in the absence of information, but even pride themselves on their ability to make seat-of-the-pants decisions which fly in the face of all information. These non-information decision-makers are, of course, the survivors of a much larger group, most of whom fell by the wayside; even they probably also make a lot of wrong decisions, but like the gamblers at Las Vegas and Monte Carlo, they remember only the winnings, not the losses.

Managers tend to share one additional characteristic. They consider themselves important people (humility is not their strong suit). They expect to be served and are used to being served. The egalitarian self-service concept of library use is something they tend to find both humbling and embarrassing, since use of the library must start with the admission that there is something you don't know, and so these individuals tend to stay away from libraries entirely.

Many librarians, who much prefer to serve clients who appreciate them, have shed no tears over being ignored by this group, but they pay a heavy price for this. Dr. George Shapiro, a professor in communications theory at the University of Minnesota, has spoken on this topic at two meetings of the Special Libraries Association, and he is well worth listening to.

NON-LIBRARIAN MANAGERS

The inability of libraries to enlist managers in general, and their own managers in particular, in interest in the work of the library is based in part on the fact that librarians, somewhere up the management chain, work for non-librarians. That's not necessarily true of sales personnel, accountants, lawyers, and doctors, who can frequently depend on being able to go a long way up the decision ladder dealing with individuals of similar training. Librarians quickly run into non-librarians who not only do not share our value system but don't even understand what we are talking about. They insist, perhaps not unreasonably, that we learn to speak their language.

Since managers are geared to the making of decisions, they are also geared to the facts that can fuel these decisions. They are geared to innovation and change, in part because they feel that although not all change involves progress, all progress involves change. They also work in a short time frame in which to get things done. Elected officials have perhaps two or four years to create a tangible reason for re-election, or all the long-range plans become only so many empty words. Industrial managers must validate themselves continually. In the musical "How to Succeed in Business Without Really Trying," president J.P. Bigley says to Pierpont Finch, his newly appointed vice-president of advertising, "You've been vice-president in charge of advertising for 30 minutes now, and, quite frankly, up to this point I am very dissatisfied with your work."

NO SPECIFIC GOALS

Librarian approaches to these managers and their value system seems almost designed to ensure negative reactions and failure. What do we bring them? First, more of the same. We need more books, more subscriptions, more staff, more space, more equipment. Why? To do more of what we are doing. There is no attempt at qualitative justification, and in fact the justifications tend to be circuitous. More acquisitions will require more staff, and both will require more space, at which point we start over. And what are the limits of these needs? We don't really know, nor are we willing to allow ourselves to be pinned down to specifics. What librarian is willing to answer the question: at what point will you have enough materials and people to do all the things you want or think you ultimately ought to do?

When we do develop what we call goals and objectives, they tend to be an ambitious and amorphous mass that cannot be quantified or realized. When we do quantify some of our targets, as with the development of standards, we make sure that these are so idealized that they are unachievable. Quite aside from the fact that these standards, sometimes for circulation or for holdings, are never really explained or justified as not being as arbitrary as they appear, we seem to feel that our objectives, to be at all valid, must be akin to Don Quixote's "impossible dream." We wish to improve the quality of life. For the pragmatic and decision-oriented manager, our goals point down an endless road, which in terms of the manager's own limited and finite stewardship, leads nowhere.

We demonstrate an insatiable desire to start new programs, but no willingness to evaluate and discard old ones. Fundamentally, we develop little that can be described as innovative. Our definition of change is accretion. As with a forest, sometimes a library can be strengthened by lopping off trees and branches that only draw strength from the main purpose, and accomplish little or nothing. Doing this not only strengthens the library, but also gives management the appearance of another manager in action.

Because of these factors, some of our management doesn't care, or just goes through the motions of pretending to care. However, even where there is some management concern, communications tend to be frustrating and frustrated.

I know of one special library situation in which I have done consulting in which the librarian complains bitterly about managment unconcern, and points to reams of recommendations and requests that have gone unheeded. He is convinced management just doesn't give a damn. My discussion with the vice-president for research shows a different side to the problem: "Yes, I get all of these requests and I know the librarian is very unhappy with me, but frankly, I have the responsibility of determining whether requested expenditures will assist us in meeting our own overall goals—which after all, are not the development of the library, but rather the development of new products and the improvement of profitability—and from the library's requests I simply can't tell." These two are really not that hard to reconcile, but first the librarian must make some attempt to understand his management and its decision process.

LIBRARY NOT END IN ITSELF

The information that libraries report to a non-librarian management could hardly have surprised you. Why then, do we persist in reporting information, particularly statistics, that have no significance whatsoever for anyone but another librarian? Statistics on the number of books purchased or in the collection may have some significance in the academic setting, which is as used to counting the same statistics as we are, but it has no meaning anywhere else.

I can almost predict the non-librarian manager's response to the librarian's stated need to increase the book collection. Why do we need more books when we have all these books on the shelf that nobody is reading? It is an irrelevant answer to be sure, but to the extent to which the request was based on sheer collection numbers without any indication of purpose of the planned additions, the response is just as valid—or invalid.

When we talk about the need for additional staff to reduce backlog, we tend to forget that the reduction of library backlogs is not in itself a concern of the parent organization. It only becomes a concern when it can be shown that this increased backlog causes things to happen, or not to happen, which are of concern to the parent organization.

We must stop thinking of the library as an end in itself, and think of what the library is supposed to be doing. What will happen with a library that won't happen without one, and why does this matter? What will happen with a better collection and more responsive service that won't happen otherwise? In theory, we do this all along. The library is, after all, a service institution, and its justification is in the service it provides. However, when we lose sight of that and begin to adopt the rationale of justification as a self-evident good, we run into difficulty. There just isn't enough money for all the self-evident goods.

Justification of library requests in pragmatic terms is not easy. We don't cure cancer or foil bank robberies, and payout on a dollar-for-dollar basis is really not possible. But nobody has asked us to do that. Much of our carry-over good will remains. We are only asked for plausible reasons that make sense, and that can be presented to others as making sense. We are asked for some tangible evidence, not even proof, of what difference additional support makes. Finally, we are asked to develop plans and programs under which even the less than idealized but perhaps achievable support that can be provided does make a difference, so that management can at least get some credit. If in response to doing what they think is their best they will get called names, get no credit, and still retain an image of anti-intellectual pikers, why bother?

BECOMES SHELL GAME

Managers share the problems of shifting resources among disparate needs. These needs are hard to rank, and hard to relate to one another. The manager may know more about some of these programs than others, but he or she is not sufficiently expert to cut and slash, or to rank with confidence. And always, even in the best of times, the total of request far exceeds the available resources.

It becomes, then, something of a shell game, and a continuing problem of sifting substance from shadow. The game is played imperfectly, and many times, capriciously. But it is not played with a malicious feeling toward the library, only one of resignation, and sometimes, as I have indicated, frustration at the librarian's stubborn unwillingness to understand management's problems and to help it. The most popular tendency on the part of managers is to allocate increases in resources across the board on a pro-rated basis. Because of the inadequacy of the available resources this obviously doesn't solve library problems, but I know many librarians who would happily settle for getting their share.

The difficulty is that the rules of the game, and perhaps their own honest evaluation of their own plight, requires your competitors to ask for more than their share. If the average available is six per cent, and some group demands and gets eight per cent, then somebody has to get less than six per cent, and that somebody could well be the library. The competition for funds is never direct and frontal, but it is real all the same, and this is why being good and appreciated is not enough. You are competing not primarily against the provincial or local governmental structure or corporate management. You are competing against other noble and worthy causes, which you would not think to disparage.

Ultimately managers, who on the whole are neither better nor worse than the rest of us, will decide, as we would decide, selfishly, on what they perceive to be best for them. And what they perceive best for them is what will help accomplish their other, larger cherished goals, will get them re-elected or promoted, will get them credit for having accomplished something.

This need have nothing to do with a personal use of the resource, although it helps if it does. I am personally well acquainted with a situation in a large city in which a much-needed new library building was approved and built—and a magnificent library building it is—under the administration and with the support of a mayor who prided himself on his populist background and self-made image of success without "book learning." He made that library happen in part because he believed that a proud major city needed a strong library to claim that it was a cultural centre and thereby attract business and industry—and in perhaps larger part because that library building will now stand for decades as a monument to his term as mayor. Understanding the people you must deal with and their wants, aspirations, and motivations, is half the battle.

I don't mean to sound glib. I know that library funding support encounters monstrous problems because of antiquated regressive funding mechanisms in addition to all our other problems. And yet, some librarians succeed, at least relatively, while others fail. Your own Canada Institute for Scientific and Technical Information is a magnificent example, in an allied field, of what can be accomplished. Those who fail can always find a host of causes to blame. That may be comforting, but it's not much help.

UNDERSTAND PEOPLE, PRIORITIES

What should be our tactical approach to our dealing with management? Tactics will differ with types of libraries and specific political settings, but some generalizations are, I think, possible.

Understand the personality of the person or persons to whom you report. Try to help them address their own information problems if you can. At least try to understand what they need from you; you know what you need from them. They are probably totally unaware that there is anything you can do to help them.

Have the political astuteness to understand the priorities of the larger organization in which you are housed. What are important or sensitive or political issues? What does the management with which you deal really want? Who are the power brokers who really make decisions? Sometimes they are not the people shown in the organization chart. Whose support is crucial, whose enmity must be avoided? If these comments offend any of you, then I am afraid I must offend those of you some more. Get out of library administration, and into an area of specialized skill, such as subject bibliography. An administrator is a political creature, and if you can't effectively protect and represent your library politically, then you can't perform effectively in your job.

UNDERSTAND FUNDING

Understand the realities of funding. One fact of life in any administrative setting is that you will not be told the truth about fund availability. If funds are tight you will be told funds are tight. If funds are normally available you will be told funds are tight. If funds are in fact plentiful you will be told funds are tight. This is true in any sector—academic, public, societal, industrial. It is an essential defense mechanism on the part of the administrator. Any contrary admission will lead to a deluge of requests, an upsurge of expectations, and chaos. Learn to differentiate between meaning and verbiage.

SET PRIORITIES

Develop your own plans and your own priorities. It is remarkable how many libraries have neither, except to try to get bigger and to provide more service. What programs that you are espousing are essential, as opposed to just beneficial or even peripheral? What would you be willing to give up to get approval of critical programs? There are always trade-offs and alternatives in any organization. Cost-effectiveness is not only possible, but necessary in any organization, and cost benefits, although difficult to demonstrate for library activities as they affect things outside the library, are certainly applicable to a comparison of programs inside the library.

Allow me just one example. Quality of cataloguing, or acceptable error rate in cataloguing, is not a stand-alone ideal. It affects and relates to size of backlog, and perhaps to funds for materials and staff. As your non-librarian manager shifts scarce resources above the library organization, so must you inside it. Don't simply react and complain; develop operational plans for various levels of activity.

One academic library administrator responded to our question concerning the development of library management philosophy in the face of decreased materials purchasing power by stating that the philosophy and strategy were quite simple. We spend the money til it's gone and then we beg for more. The response may have been facetious, or the tactic may even work to some extent, but it won't get you much credibility, and it's not a tactic for the future.

SELL PROGRAMS

Gear your own plans and programs to the implementation of bigger plans and programs outside the library, preferably those to which there is already a commitment. Sell your support programs, first conceptually, then in detail, and only then develop the costing of an implementation plan for a program already approved in principle. It won't always work, but it will work a lot better than starting the other way, with level of funding. Whoever heard of a car salesman who started his sales pitch with the cost of the car? First he sells you the model, then all the marvelous options, and finally at the very end he lets you in on the bad news of what you have selected costs. That's plain, commonsense selling practice.

For libraries and other administrative organizations it has a fancier name: program budgeting. Some of you are now required to do program budgeting. You're lucky—at least potentially lucky, if you have programs to budget. Sell the program and let the program sell the budget. Program budgets are harder to do than line-item budgets, of course. But line-item budgets lead nowhere except to five per cent budget increases in the face of 12 per cent cost increases.

In doing program budgeting, remember the need for innovation and change. A static organism is a dying organism, and is of no value to a politically sensitive management. You will need the ideas for new programs, and you should have some ideas of programs which should be modified, curtailed, or eliminated. Your credibility as a manager will improve considerably, if in the process of trying to get three new things, you suggest disbanding one old one that is not worth the cost.

PLAN REALISTIC GOALS

Develop specific implementation plans. You will need long-range goals, but even more you need objectives that are specific, short-range (not exceeding your management's span of attention or office), quantifiable, measurable, and most important, achievable.

Don't propose to do things you know you can't accomplish. You only destroy your own credibility, with your staff and with your management. On the other hand, if you feel tasks can be accomplished, then you must convince your staff and your management of that reality, and you must not allow yourself to be dissuaded or distracted from that accomplishment. If management has approved your implementation of the plan or program, then provide feedback, in management terminology, and so arranged that your boss can get some credit when things go well.

GET SUPPORT, ATTENTION

Organize support. Nobody is against libraries, but nobody is exactly for them, either, except in general terms, and that becomes shaky support when pitted against something else.

Make noise. Your library needs positive publicity and attention, from the newspapers and the media and from users and voters. You may not be able to instigate petitions and attendance at government meetings, but you don't have to discourage them either. Your management needs publicity repayment of its support when you get support, and criticism when you don't.

Demand attention. Many librarians allow themselves to be sloughed off with a pat on the head and the general approbation, "I'm sure you're doing a fine job." That's not enough. Your management has a responsibility, too. Ask for specific acceptance or rejection of your programs, and once they're accepted, ask what management is going to do to help them come about. There is an old management ground rule which equates attention with importance. A hard-pressed manager appreciates subordinates who never demand attention or resources, but he or she also instinctively feels they're not very important. Good subordinate programs demand a lot of attention, but they're worth it.

WORK WITH MANAGEMENT

Many of these tactics can be described as common sense. There are no magic tricks in management, or in dealing with a higher level management. Individual styles and personalities differ, but the relationships are fairly fundamental. Except for the devious or malicious, who would be a problem in any environment, your managers are trying to make decisions, survive, and progress in a situation in which there is never enough time, never enough information, and never enough money. The same problem confronts the director of the library, in his or her own smaller environment.

Dealing successfully with your management requires an understanding of this process, and working within it. You cannot change or ignore it, and at least part of our historic problem has come from an unwillingness to adapt to a management evaluation and decision process, an unwillingness to deign to seek support, publicity, and a power base, and in many instances an outright unwillingness to manage at all—a contentment with the process of drift and complaint.

As we develop new library managers who really want to manage, this situation will improve, but we must also work to accelerate the change. Time counts, and wasted time hurts us, individually and collectively.

SPECIAL LIBRARIES AND THE CORPORATE POLITICAL PROCESS

Webster defines politics as the art of science of government and as the science dealing with the regulation and control of men living in society. Artemus Ward, a hero of the American Revolutionary War, was perhaps less given to sexist terminology and more within the mainstream of common perception when he observed, "I am not a politician, and my other habits are also good." Whatever the reasons, political adroitness is frequently equated with sneakiness if not outright dishonesty. Librarians, no less than other professionals, find discussions of political strategy disquieting or unpleasant. The literature is full of suggestions for improving the quality of library service but it states little about the tactics needed to improve the appearance of quality library service.

This is not intended to suggest that quality and the appearance of high quality are contradictory. Ideally, virtue becomes its own reward, and there is no reason why the competent librarian and omnipotent administrator should not exist in an atmosphere of mutual respect and appreciation. Indeed, there are special libraries in which this occurs. However, the achievement of such a status by itself is certainly not automatic, probably not likely, and it cannot be left to chance.

Any complex organization, and certainly a corporation, is subject to political forces as long as the available resources and the assignable power are not adequate to fulfill the expectations and hopes of the participants, and this writer knows of no organizations in which this does occur. Individuals who speak piously of the hope for cooperation usually define the term as having others do things their way. If this seems cynical, it is a cynicism born of many years of experience in a

---

This paper is adapted from a talk presented at a meeting of the Petroleum and Energy Resources Division at the 1983 SLA Conference in New Orleans. Reprinted from *Special Libraries* 75 (April 1984):81–86.
H.W. Wilson Award as SLA Best Paper for 1984.

variety of settings—corporate, governmental and academic. The nomenclature changes but the process remains the same.

Librarians are usually not participants in the corporate political arena but, like innocent bystanders at a bank holdup, they sometimes get shot in the process. Despite our frequently expressed paranoia, librarians do not have enemies in the corporate decision battles. They have no power base and, lacking this, they are not considered important enough to attract enemies. They are the victims who do not control and, largely, do not even understand.

Before we examine the corporate, political decision process and the way it affects libraries, it is important to understand why libraries are often taken for granted. Cuts in library service may be regretted but the organization may not consider them to be serious problems. The personnel department's assignment of corporate misfits to the library staff is usually considered preferable to an assignment to another department where it is thought they might really do some harm. There are a number of apparent reasons for such attitudes of which the following are but a sample.

1. Users do not know what good library service is and, therefore, are not in a position to know when they do not receive it. Despite his years as a special librarian and as a consultant, this writer is still amazed at the wide range of library services in organizations of similar size and orientation. No comparisons of library services are ever made by corporate management; if they were, management would probably be pleased to find that its library services are less expensive than other's, instead of feeling concern that the services may be inferior or inadequate. When new hires arrive with higher levels of expectation nurtured by a previous experience, they are quickly put into their place, sometimes directly by the librarian. "Unreasonable" requestors, unless they are vice presidents, are quickly forced into line by peer example, especially if they are new and insecure.

2. Users will accept bad service. They may patronize a weak librarian, and accept excuses or make allowances for problems to an extent which would be unthinkable if the service really mattered to them. Librarians pay a terrible price for such toleration, which is really a benign indifference.

3. One reason users exhibit toleration for poor service is that they have alternatives to using the library to solve their information needs. Studies carried out by a wide range of organizations, including the RAND Corporation and Auerbach Associates, discovered that corporate users prefer to consult their own files, visit down the hall, call a colleague across the country, and attend conferences to gather information rather than submit a request to the library. Many professional users have additional means of accessing information within the organization

which allows them to circumvent the library. For example, they can purchase their own books and periodicals, subscribe to alerting and reprint services, or develop their own terminal access to databases. Some short-sighted libraries not only tolerate but encourage such independent behavior because it frees the library from work.

4. In a corporate environment, particularly one in which the ultimate purpose is the manufacture of products to be sold on the marketplace, information is not an end in itself but a means to an end. The importance of that means depends largely on the alternatives. Based on the tradition of the self-service library, which stresses the educational value of learning to use the system over the importance of finding the answer, much library service is poorly suited to the needs, preferences and priorities of the corporate information user. Herbert R. Brinberg clearly distinguishes between the information needs of researchers, engineers and managers.[1] Basic researchers, he argues, are looking for quantities of relevant or potentially relevant materials which can serve as the springboard for their own analyses and conclusions. Time is clearly of less importance than the completeness and accuracy of the information. In contrast, engineers, as well as marketing and production managers, seek specific answers to specific questions and usually do so only at the last minute. For this reason, they care less where the answer is found, and paradoxically, whether it is correct. It is more important that the answer fit into the scenario which has been constructed to house it, be it a report with conclusions already written or a presentation already on viewgraphs. Finally, managers, according to Brinberg, need to know what alternatives are available. Potential solutions for which there is neither time nor sufficient resources are not useful; they become particularly frustrating when it is suggested that unimplementable solutions are the only plausible solutions.

Owing to the preferences of their staffs and the academic experiences of their users, many corporate libraries treat all users as though they were basic researchers. While there is undoubtedly some basic research going on in corporations, it is probably a limited amount. Ladd and Lipseth suggest that little basic research occurs even in universities, and that most researchers are working on grants and contracts to find proofs for conclusions already reached.[2] These are, at best, applied researchers whose real preference is not large quantities of materials but supporting documentation. If they do indeed continue to ask for large quantities, it may be that they do not realize the library is capable of supplying more specific material, or they may be convinced that this is what they are expected to do.

4. Provision of accurate information services will never come at the expense of time or cost schedules. Librarians must bear in mind that a report due on Monday morning will be delivered Monday morning,

with or without library input; the user will simply proceed as if all available information has indeed been located.

5. Even the best of special libraries serve only a small portion of the corporate population. In an earlier article in *Special Libraries*,[3] The author examined the usual reporting relationship for special libraries and argued that, in times of financial stress, neither reporting within the research and development department nor reporting within a large administrative services group provided an automatic safety net. Decisions which affect library support are usually made by corporate officials who are not instinctive library users. These include officers in production, marketing and accounting whose support, or lack of it, is based largely on their own personal reactions and experiences. Special libraries do not share one of the luxuries generally enjoyed by academic and public libraries—support by non-users. In a corporate environment there is a tendency to support what is used. While this does not imply a disdain for services which are not used, the political process and the overall shortage of available resources force such a conclusion. Matarazzo's study on the closing of corporate libraries[4] indicates a lack of broad corporate support. The libraries' users may have been supportive, but there just were not enough of them.

THE LIBRARY'S ROLE IN CORPORATE FINANCIAL CALCULATIONS

The library, together with other general support services, is part of the overhead cost allocation, sometimes called an indirect cost allocation. The word allocation is important because overhead budgets are rarely viewed as dollar sums. Rather, they are percentages of "direct" and, by implication, more important numbers. Overhead may be computed as a percentage of sales income, of direct cost or of gross profit.

Corporate management and stockholders will resist pressures to increase overhead expenditures, because the accounting statement shows them as the difference between the hefty gross profit and the much skimpier net profit. If that net profit becomes a net loss, the pressures redouble. It does little good to argue that in times of poor sales, research efforts should be redoubled, unless that research will lead to guaranteed profits. Sadly, the library can never offer such assurances.

The determination of overhead is a corporate decision, normally expressed in percentages; a 10% increase is certainly better than a 2% increase, and this in turn is preferable to a 5% reduction. The larger unit in which the library is housed is also a recipient and not a dispenser of the largesse or frugality, and is not in a position to help. The fundamental and simplistic assumption made by corporate managment is that a 5% increase in overhead becomes a 5% increase for all affected units, including the library. That assumption quickly disappears in the political process when it is argued that exceptions must be made and that certain units must be given larger increases or spared the effect of traumatic cuts. The movers and shakers in the corporate structure do not really care about such infighting, as long as the totals remain unchanged.

Library budgets benefit when the library has a champion in the corporate meeting, but that is rare, particularly if no real attempt has been made to insure administrative dependence on the library as an information resource. More frequently, the library budget is cut, sometimes even further than originally planned, because another project must be protected. Although it is a highly political process, it proceeds without rancor or recrimination toward the library. This phenomenon is perhaps better understood by public librarians who commonly face budget cuts to accommodate police salary increases or other public expenditures. Yet, the same principle holds true in corporations; during a budget crunch, only those who can promise fast results tend to have influence. It is also important to recognize that librarians are perceived to play certain roles within the organization. Some of these perceptions are based on stereotype and bias or on earlier experiences with librarians in corporations, universities or public libraries. Librarians will not be blamed or challenged if they match expectations, but they will not get much done, either. In contrast, any attempt to change set perceptions or stereotypes involves probable risk. Individuals must decide whether they are willing to face the risk of appearing to be "different" from what was expected.

PRESUMED CHARACTERISTICS

These following characteristics are generalizations and undoubtedly unfair in some specific cases. Nevertheless, they tend to hold more often than not. Librarians are expected to be neat and orderly and to be concerned more with rules than results. They are informed about corporate plans and strategies infrequently because it is assumed librarians are not interested. For some, this is true. Every stereotype is unfair in the specific, but if there were not some kernel of recognition in either the present or the past, it would not persist.

Librarians are not considered to be risk takers or innovators. Risk takers start a project with the expectation that, if it is worthwhile, someone will help them continue it. They recognize the general management truth that in the absence of available funds there is always money for things which someone in authority really wants to do. With regard to innovation, Peter Drucker has stated that managers get credit only for two areas of accomplishment: innovation and marketing. Continuing to do the same satisfactory job may be safe, but it will earn no credit because it commits that greatest of corporate crimes—it is boring.

Innovation may require value ranking judgments and the elimination of some older projects to fund exciting new ones. More importantly, innovators recognize the second great management truth—that it is usually easier to get a lot of money than a little money, provided that the funds are used for a highly visible activity which will generate credit for the individual providing the funds. It may be possible to receive generous funding to start a competition evaluation report for corporate management, but the library will have a difficult time getting the small amount of money needed to hire a clerk to help reduce the cataloging backlog, because no one except the librarian cares.

3. Perhaps even worse than being insulted and ignored, librarians are patronized. This may be a result of historic bias toward women in professional positions. Librarians will not be taken seriously until they take themselves seriously and insist that they be treated as professionals. It is a serious risk, particularly for women, but one which ultimately must be faced if anything is to be accomplished. Such a risk also requires a willingness to make decisions and accept responsibility—indeed, the insistence that this happen.

The erosion of a political power base is a subtle and insidious process. Matarazzo's studies[4] clearly indicate that some of the librarians who were fired and whose libraries were closed had no inkling of what was about to happen. The following situations may indicate trouble for a library which is not serving its constituency or attracting other potential users.

Situation A: Corporate administration is not served at all, or whole blocks of users (engineering, production, marketing, public relations, accounting, legal) are not served. Even if the facility is officially designated the R&D library, the key question concerns whether there are other libraries in the organization. If there are none, then the library must function as the corporate information center. If money is a concern, reasonable funding allocation mechanisms can be proposed. Even if these fail to produce immediate results, the library should attempt to reach nonusers and encourage them to become dependent on its services.

Situation B: The library's contact with users is defined by the interpretation of rules, most particularly the return of overdue material. This is not only a level of contact which most users will consider irritating and trivial, it is also a fight you cannot win, and it serves to confirm the stereotype that librarians are preoccupied with rules. If you are told the material is still being used and can not be spared, you are not going to get it back. It is better to establish a corporate policy under which unreturned library material will be repurchased and billed to the department which has the library's copy. The recalcitrant borrower will not care because the expense is trivial, and the accounting department can be convinced that it is a reasonable policy. It is essential that libraries maintain control over their purchased collections and not allow the materials to dissipate into individuals' offices as academic libraries have done. Books which remain in offices for two years are not being used; they are being maintained in an unauthorized branch library. The argument that the material is only of interest to that one person is erroneous because more and more activities are interdisciplinary. It is important to have current, up-to-date materials in the library, and not just in the catalog, to make the library a worthwhile place to visit and to instill in users confidence that useful information is available to them. If the shelves are already crowded, the library may need more, or it may be time to discard obsolete materials which are of interest to no one.

In a similar vein, if user departments must be charged for library services such as interlibrary loan and photocopying, it is preferable to allocate a portion of the library budget based not on actual use but on assumed use (i.e., the organization with 20% of the professionals gets charged 20% of the cost). This step encourages rather than discourages use and accountants will accept this kind of procedure as willingly as any other.

Situation C: New units have arisen within the organization to undertake activities which more properly are the function of the library. This situation is harmful to both the library and the organization. Newly created information centers, information evaluation centers or corporate alerting services, despite their grandiose names, rarely accomplish more than the competent corporate library. If they arise, it is an indication that a vacuum exists. The library should hasten to fill this vacuum by providing new services, even if funds have never been specifically allocated for this purpose.

Some library managers tolerate or even encourage other departments to purchase books, periodicals or online databases through an outside service in order to relieve the library of budgetary pressures. This policy is unwise because it erodes the library's uniqueness. One of the characteristics of a valued operation is that it provides services not available elsewhere. If the library does not have the funds necessary to pay for these services, but other departments obviously do, the wise manager will approach management with the following argument: If the company cannot allocate library funds for these expenditures, no other units in the organization should be able to afford them either . . . but since they apparently can, available funds should be transferred to the library.

Situation D: The library's clerical support is understaffed. Almost all corporations tend to understaff their clerical functions, particularly in overhead areas. Furthermore, most organizations operate with head-count ceilings and consider it foolish to "waste" an authorized position on a clerk. For libraries this poses particular problems because clerical routine takes precedence over professional duties. Professional tasks only get done when there is enough time; in the absence of enough clerks, the professionals become clerks. It is an easy trap and one which serves to confirm management suspicions of the low level of library work. Some nonconfrontational alternatives may apply. When appropriate, the use of temporary workers or those supplied by staffing agencies, the contracting out of clerical functions and the use of computerization, all provide options.

Some options are by necessity confrontational; for example, bring the need for additional clerical assistance to management's attention, and then provide the foretold disaster if the request is not met. Such options are clearly not for everyone. The minimum staff for any library that is expected to operate professionally is two—one professional and one clerk. If the staffing level is one, that individual should probably be a clerk.

The problems and the solutions presented here are admittedly simplistic and, at best, approximations. Personnel management theory holds that nothing works all the time. It is hoped that individual librarians will find better strategies appropriate to their situations. In a corporate environment, as long as the political process involves people who are all different, theoretical approaches will work only as well as these individuals resemble their models. Management theory will never take the place of common sense.

Dispassionate and unemotional mechanisms must be developed in each library to evaluate the state of political safety or risk. This is not easy to do. Sometimes it requires the help of outsiders. If a problem or area of risk is uncovered, a strategy must be developed for dealing with it. Ignored management problems, like untended lawns, never get better. They only get worse.

References

1. Brinberg, Herbert R./"The Contribution of Information to Economic Growth and Development." Theme Paper at the 40th Congress of the International Federation for Documentation, Copenhagen, Denmark. Aug. 18, 1980.

2. Ladd, Everett C./"The Work Experience of American College Professors: Some Data and an Argument." Paper presented at the Annual Conference of the American Association for Higher Education, Washington, D.C., April 16–19, 1979. ERIC Document ED 184406.

3. White, Herbert S./Organizational Placement of the Special Library and Its Relationship to Success and Survival. *Special Libraries* 64:144–44, March 1973.

4. Matarazzo, James M./*Closing the Corporate Library: Case Studies on the Decision-Making Process.* Special Libraries Association, N.Y. 1981.

LIBRARY TURF

Turf as it is defined in the political context certainly needs little explanation to managers on the Washington political scene. It is instinctively understood by members of street gangs, such as those described by Leonard Bernstein in *West Side Story*. Turf, in that context, is an area of responsibility or a physical piece of property which is exclusively yours. What you may or may not do with your turf is not a significant question. The point is that nobody else can use it at all. Turf is jealously guarded, sometimes because it is really needed for actions contemplated at a later date, but as often simply because of the prestige and importance which its ownership conveys. It represents real and potential power.

By nature, librarians are not acquirers and guardians of turf. We seek only what we need, and we will gladly cede turf we already own if we believe that others can accomplish what we find ourselves unable to do. We are sometimes pragmatists in seeking solutions to problems, but we are not often political strategists in pressing for our specific solutions or authority, or opposing other solutions.

CEDING TURF

There are several immediate problems which can occur when the library cedes its responsibilities to those who are willing and perhaps better financially or politically endowed to carry them out. 1) Those who take over our unfulfilled duties may not do the job as well. They may lack understanding, perspective, or educational preparation. 2) They may do the job at greater cost, or at least with less cost effectiveness. Both of these points should seem obvious, but librarians are generally unwilling to claim an exclusive knowledge for themselves while other professions assume this as a matter of obvious knowledge. 3) When we cede what

From *Library Journal* 110 (15 April 1985):54–55.

we find ourselves unable to cultivate, we frequently end up giving away not what we want to transfer, but what others find interesting and desirable.

It is this last point, and the naïveté with which we often approach it, which give this writer the greatest concern. Libraries run ultimately on clerical routine. Even if nothing else happens, clerical routines must be performed. These tasks are ours in part because of the nature of the library activity flow, in part because nobody else would want them. The professional duties hardest to schedule during times of budgetary curtailment are also, and not surprisingly, those in which outsiders are most interested.

We are, and have been for the last decade, in a period of declining resources for the library profession. This decline, as measured both in such initiatives as Proposition 13 and the zero funding proposals for library programs at the national level, are not maliciously aimed at us.

We have no real enemies, at least in part because we don't control enough of a power base to attract enemies. Our greatest danger comes from indifference, and from a lack of understanding of what we could accomplish. It is precisely because the political process of declining public support is not aimed at libraries that we are probably powerless to reverse the general trend.

We may be able to alter things in specific instances, and certainly individual battles will still be gloriously won. However, the general philosophical trend toward less government, which may have had its strongest articulation in conservative Republican philosophy, now transcends the major political parties. The question for us concerns what to do about it.

MANAGING DECLINE

Little was written about the management of declining resources until the last few years. What has now appeared would indicate that library strategies adapt badly to this new scenario. The development of strategic alternatives would suggest that declining resources cannot be ignored, and that their impact cannot be absorbed.

The all too common library stratagem of attempting to absorb budget cuts and staff attritions through greater "dedication," through harder work by all members of the staff, has several pitfalls.

First, it does not work as a management plan. Staff members may accept on the surface, but will most certainly reject in their own response strategies, the suggestion that they can do more by working harder, because this implies a self-indictment of previous indolence.

Second, an emphasis on doing more with less puts the emphasis on quantitative rather than qualitative measures. We may do more, but we may also do the wrong thing.

Finally, any success achieved in the process of work absorption only leads to a further round of budget cuts, since no administrator above the level of the library knows except by trial and error what can be cut without producing dire consequences.

Libraries face a particular problem, not uniquely ours, but that we have approached quite badly. Those who fund, and even those who use libraries, have no particular ability to distinguish a good library from a bad library. They can tell a large one from a small one. They can certainly distinguish one that is open from one that is shut.

While users can be trained to appreciate and even expect a high quality of professional library service, they are also easily sidetracked into an acceptance of the rationalization that what is happening is "the best that can be afforded," as though there were a figment of truth to that statement.

PROFESSIONAL WORK GOES FIRST

When library budgets are cut, it is the professional activities that suffer most directly, because it is these that are least expected and most readily rationalized away. Of course, when the library's inability to act is replaced by another mechanism which accepts these tasks, hardly anyone notices at all. That is the point of this essay.

Librarians have become so good at absorbing and minimizing the impact of budget cuts that hardly anyone notices. Where even this has failed they have permitted and in some cases even encouraged others to take on the responsibility for what we are no longer able to do, although often funded by the same source. What these others take over from us is not necessarily what we would like to abdicate. It is rather what appears most interesting to them. It is poor turf management. Both the Jets and the Sharks of *West Side Story* would be disappointed in us.

A PUBLIC, CONTINUING DECLINE

The overriding principle of the management of declining resources is that with fewer resources fewer things are accomplished, although in the trade-offs that go with any management decision, more of some things may ultimately be done than before. The net result of declining funds, however, is declining activity. It is a decline that is publicly acknowledged and visible for which those who caused it must be held accountable. Moreover, it must be a continuing decline until we are given the resources with which to alleviate it. That pressure and that gap continue without surcease, and they are never shifted or transferred.

The principle of turf oriented management argues: "It we don't get to do it, nobody else does it either. Certainly not with funds from the same primary source."

Librarians are not often instinctively good political managers, although a few have become very proficient at it. We are, by nature, not the direct descendants of Madame de Pompadour, whose *"Après nous, le déluge!"* was probably stated with as much self-satisfaction as conviction. A number of years ago this writer sat in on a meeting at a library school in which students unceremoniously told a representative of a "Friends of the Library" organization that they had no interest in providing free support service for a system whose municipal government had seen fit to cut back on staffing because of another of a series of real or imagined funding crises (crises which never affect the level of police and fire protection).

The students concluded that a municipality not prepared to support library service should close its library and suffer the consequences. It was a harsh statement which left the community representative shocked and bewildered. It is a most untypical response from the library community. Yet a case can be made for confrontation as a strategic option, an option that might work in certain communities and with certain officials. Our other strategies have not worked particularly well.

FALLOW TURF

Budgetary cutbacks have resulted not only in a reduction of services, but in a reduction of turf. They have also caused us to fail to seek new turf which should be ours. In some cases, the ground has remained fallow.

When online searches are not provided by a public library for its clients, they are generally not provided by anyone else, except for the elite few who can afford an information vendor. This is unfortunate. It is particularly short-sighted when that failure to provide service is hidden by a rationalization that is isn't really the library's mission to provide reference service except through traditional means.

It would be more honest to continue to publicize the gap as an unmet and unfunded need, and to make that statement in annual reports and news releases to the media. Public libraries should provide online searches for their patrons. When they fail to provide them because they prefer not to charge and have not been supported to provide them without a price, their decision may or may not be correct. The point is arguable, but the decision not to provide the service is no solution, it is expediency. The searches are still needed, and the problem has not disappeared.

The ceding of turf in special and academic libraries has much worse consequences. Here it isn't a question of saving money at all, at least for the parent institution. It is only a question of the appearance of an economy, in special library settings by tranferring the cost of materials and database acquisitions to specific departments.

In academic libraries, the most recent gambit is to deny a responsibility for online reference work as outside the scope of the library mission (some academic libraries would just as happily deny responsibility for any sort of reference work) and shift that cost to other departments, usually funded from the same source. In abdicating responsibility for the search process and transferring both the cost and work to other academic units, the libraries turn their backs on what is probably the greatest opportunity to achieve professional status and visibility. Of course, that abdication serves nothing. It only transfers and hides the cost in other budgets, and inevitably costs the university more dollars. The cost to the academic library is far more than dollars.

THE LIBRARY OR NOBODY

The turf conscious manager's insistence that services and activities properly in the library's mission be funded for performance in the library or not performed at all may seem strange to many librarians. It is hardly strange in other fields. We had better begin to think in such terms. We can argue convincingly that this is the most cost effective approach both for our users and for our parent organizations.

There is probably some level of library service which even the most obstinate budget cutters and turf grabbers will allow to survive. We can only guess at its scope, but we can be certain that its emphasis will be on responsive ordering of specifically requested material, and on keeping track of what happened to it. That is a clerical function performed in any stock room or warehouse. I certainly want no part of it as a scope note for my profession. To the extent to which they will listen to me, neither will my students.

Participative Management Is the Answer, but What Was the Question?

One of the most popular quiz shows is based on the premise of supplying contestants with answers, and then requiring the formulation of an appropriate question. The approach is considered entertaining because there is probably some underlying recognition that this is in fact the way most of us operate in our everyday affairs. We reach conclusions, and then decide why they were valid conclusions. There is more than a little evidence that academic research proceeds along the same lines.

All of this leads to the consideration of participative management, as urged on us in increasingly shrill tones in both the general management and the specific library literature. It has been proposed to us as an "obviously" good thing, although we should probably be suspicious of anything being obvious in a field as dependent on the diversity of individual objectives and personalities as management. Nevertheless, it has been argued that greater participation has such clear benefits, and it is assumed that those benefits will most certainly turn out to be tangible and financial, although no direct proofs have as yet been offered.

A whole series of articles could be written about "assumed" management truths that are considered too obvious to require proof and so no proof is offered—that happy people work harder, that "flexitime" decreases absenteeism, etc. For all of these this writer argues with a great deal of courage—"that depends."

There has been some recognition in the management literature that supervisors are sometimes unwilling to involve themselves in the participative management process, and it is suggested that the reasons

From *Library Journal* 110 (August 1985):62–63.

range from a lack of understanding to a reluctance to give up power. Nobody has yet suggested a participative seminar for managers to let them decide whether to delegate to a more participative model. Nor is there much mention in the literature of a phenomenon that most of us have recognized: that some subordinates fail to leap at the opportunity to have greater involvement in management decisions, for reasons which range from fear to indifference to the belief that managers should do what they are paid to do and leave subordinates free to do their work. However, this article does not oppose participative management, and it certainly favors a greater involvement by more individuals in the management decision process.

PARTICIPATIVE VS. CONSULTATIVE

It is important here to differentiate between *participative* management (presumably the allocation of the decision together with the responsibility for the correctness of that decision, although this is rarely the case—committees tend not to be accountable for their decisions which makes the process so attractive to those inclined to avoid risk), and *consultative* management (a participative input to a management decision to be made at a higher level). Consultative management is not new, it has been practiced by good managers for a long time, and of course bad managers have tended to avoid this like any other communication process.

In general, participative management is at best a delegative process, at worst an abdicative process. Authority is consciously yielded, and at least in the specific instance, that yielding is not reversible. The decision made by the group cannot now be overruled by the manager because it was the "wrong" decision. Within the constraints of what has been earmarked for participation as opposed to consultation, there are no wrong decisions.

It makes sense in those instances in which any decision made by the group is acceptable, and the most proper settings are the two extremes in which either the issue is emotional but not substantive (there are a lot of those in libraries—procedures for use of the staff lounge, site of the annual picnic), or where the issues are so complex that a group approach is essential to understanding the questions.

Where participative management works, it works superbly, however, there are clearly risks. For one, it must be recognized that the process works slowly, and to the extent to which meetings are held on library time, expensively. The group decision process tends to result in a search for common denominators, and while these solutions are usually safe, they are frequently unimaginative. Innovation does not come from groups, it comes from iconoclastic individuals who are well ahead of the group and frequently unpopular. Managers must protect these people *from* the group.

Managers who use participative management must spell out in advance the range of acceptable alternatives, because usually there are limitations of dollars, staff, space, and often, of time.

Consultative management also, like any good management communication, requires a spelling out of ground rules in advance. (It will be noted later that people *like* rules, *if* those rules make sense.) In this case, it must be clearly understood that what is being sought is advice, and not a decision. That advice must be risk-free to the giver; there can be no wrong suggestions. For this reason, it is essential here as well as with participative management, that the ground rules be spelled out in advance to avoid misunderstandings.

The consultative manager owes his staff one additional important courtesy: an explanation for the decision reached, particularly if that decision contradicted advice solicited. That explanation does not need to convince, it need only explain that there was a reason which made sense to the manager. In my experience I have encountered few autocratic managers. Librarians don't tend to come from that background. I have seen many managers who appear autocratic because they don't explain their decisions. However, I find that appearance often to be deceptive. They appear aloof and despotic because they don't know how to explain why they decided as they did. They don't know themselves.

EMPLOYEE HAPPINESS

The question of whether participative or consultative management is more appropriate depends in large part on the question to be decided. There is not a moral issue at stake here, and that is why the urging of participative management as a separate "good" is both simplistic and potentially dangerous. It is particularly dangerous when delegation to a committee is done for the wrong reason by a manager who sees the clear opportunity of avoiding the risk of making a decision while at the same time getting credit for being "democratic." As these managers know, committee decisions are safe decisions. One can't fire a committee.

Participative management in its purest and nonmanipulative form works some of the time, and at other times its application is inappropriate. It is not an end in itself. The end is the effective functioning of the library, and lest this seem callous and insensitive it must quickly be added that organizations don't function effectively unless people function effectively, and people don't function effectively unless they are at least clear about and reconciled to their own responsibilities and roles. Reconciled and acceptive—not necessarily happy. Employee happiness is not really an appropriate organizational goal, and can even be a deterrent to performance. "Happy" people who stand around all day exchanging snapshots and planning engagement showers and bowling parties don't get much done.

What makes people productive and acceptive? It is a difficult question about which to generalize because no two individuals in the work place are alike. To use only the most obvious example, some individuals center all of their aspirations on their work, while others work only so that they can afford to do the things that really matter to them. Either group can include effective performers as well as troublesome ones, but it takes no great genius to figure out that the second employee is going to be less enthused about serving on a committee that meets on Saturday morning.

What is it that almost all people do want? It is not necessarily participative management as it has come to be defined as a voice in making policy decisions. Some do want this, some abhor it and wish their bosses would make the decisions they are presumably so well paid to make. What just about everybody wants has been clear for some time, and can be spelled out in five short sentences: 1) They want to know what is expected of them; 2) They want to be left alone to do their own work in their own way as long as this does not interfere with the accomplishment of expected results; 3) They want to be helped if they ask for help without feeling diminished by the request; 4) They want to be told how they did, and be permitted an open, nonthreatening discussion about improvement and future growth; and 5) They want to be rewarded in accordance with the performance that has just been evaluated.

That is a great deal, but none of it is unreasonable. Nor is it confrontational. And yet, on a very personal basis, they need two things more. They need to understand the significance of their own work in terms of the organizational whole. They also need to believe that if they do a good rather than a poor job, that not only will the boss notice and appreciate it, but the organizational objectives will be one step closer to achievement. In other words, they need to believe that what they do will make a difference if they do it well.

LESSONS FROM THE JAPANESE

It is this that the Japanese management structure has understood all along, and it is this part of their value system that is worth emulating. The Japanese do not have anything remotely resembling participative management. Management decisions are far more autocratically developed than most of us would find acceptable, and the greater qualifications and knowledge of higher level managers are assumed and accepted. What the Japanese worker has and cherishes is some control (often through a group process which is participatory) over how he works to accomplish what management has told him to accomplish. That management also stresses why working well is important to the overall success of the organization. When that organization succeeds, the Japanese worker is made to feel a genuine part of that success.

There is a time to work, and there is a time to celebrate accomplishments. Without that opportunity to celebrate achievements, working harder or with greater dedication has no particular significance. What difference does it make whether I am here or not, whether I work hard or not, whether or not I make mistakes, whether or not I make suggestions? Who will care and who will notice? Without a positive answer, morale suffers regardless of management style, because it is quickly replaced by defeatism and indifference. These are the great demoralizers caused by the belief that no matter how hard we try, success is not possible.

It is this issue rather than participation in the greater overall decision process that probably poses the greatest amount of challenge and opportunity for library managers. We must provide an environment in which individuals can reconcile their personal objectives (diverse as these are) to organizational objectives. Most subordinates are willing to meet us more than halfway, because they accept the premise that in order to be paid they and their co-workers ought to do something productive.

Organizational objectives, unlike goals, we are reminded, are finite targets of a short-range duration. They must be important, and *they must be accomplishable*. If that accomplishment requires resources of money, staff, space, time, and equipment, and those resources are not available, then the objectives must be adjusted to reflect what can be done. If not, hypocrisy reigns, and employees have no difficulty in spotting that sort of environment.

Libraries, to a greater extent than other political units, embrace or allow themselves to be coerced into accepting objectives for which there are no resources, no plan, and no hope of success. We tell our staff members to "do the best they can," thereby clearly absolving them of responsibility but also depriving them of any hope of success and of ultimate celebration. In other words, the objectives are gibberish, and nothing really matters.

The most important thing we can provide for our staff members is not necessarily a participative structure. That is certainly appropriate where it fits, but a consultative structure with genuine feedback can work as well in some instances, and better in others. That isn't the main problem and the main source of disaffection, anyway. What we owe our subordinates is a chance to work as they feel comfortable working as long as the outcomes (as opposed to specific methods) are acceptable, and an opportunity to individualize their jobs for both accomplishment and the feeling of accomplishment.

They look to us quite properly to give them a chance to succeed at their jobs by either providing them with tools and resources that fit the game or games that fit the resources. Nobody likes to lose all of the time, and if library workers perceive that they never had a chance in the first place, they will quite understandably quit caring and trying. Let's concentrate on these issues before we form still another committee.

Respect for Librarians and Librarian Self-Respect

You can't attend any professional meeting of librarians without hearing laments about how little we are appreciated. The complaint usually emerges by the second or third drink at the hotel bar or vendor cocktail party. I have been hearing it ever since I graduated from library school. A more recent, and more provocative, topic is the possibility that we don't appreciate ourselves, that we lack regard for our own profession and its importance. The two thoughts are related. Obviously, to convince others of the pivotal role that librarians can and should play we must believe that what we do is important.

Why do we do such a poor job of "selling" librarianship as a profession? Whether we do a good job of promoting libraries or not, we certainly do a better job promoting our institutions than ourselves. By contrast, educators make it quite clear that good schools depend on good teachers, and that means happy, respected, and well-paid teachers.

There are obvious examples. National Library Week, our major promotional tool, sells libraries but doesn't feature or even mention librarians.

Many library users think of librarianship as the stamping of due dates into books because this is still the most visible activity in many libraries. The distinction between professional librarianship and what anyone who works in a library does has never been clearly understood by our public or emphasized by us. The public assumes, out of an ignorance we have never corrected, that anyone who works in a library is a librarian.

Public libraries are probably not our worst culprits in this scenario. Major academic libraries have large professional staffs, but most of them work behind the scenes. The clerks and students are most visible.

From *Library Journal* 111 (1 February 1986):58–59.

The most obvious example of promoting the institution and not the profession comes in the rank ordering of priorities for academic library expenditures. We have heard so often from academic faculty that the quality of the library is in the collection that we have even come to believe it.

The quality of a library, or of any service institution, is in what is *done* with the collection, and that observation applies to just about any field. The "doing," of course, is the responsibility of librarians. My academic nonlibrarian colleagues have no reason to be knowledgeable about issues of library service. Their personal approach to it is inevitably conservative, unimaginative, and passive. That is not their fault. There is no particular reason for them to know. It is our fault if we allow them to continue to think that they know.

The problem becomes more serious when you realize that faculty appetites (and sometimes librarian appetites) for collection accretion are insatiable. This priority will effectively shut out all others. More important, the suggestion that the quality of the library is in the collection clearly suggests that professional librarians are not a particularly important part of the process—that it is possible to have good libraries without good librarians (perhaps without any, or at least with fewer).

Any turf-conscious profession would move directly and forcibly to correct that faculty misconception and misstatement. From our own profession there is largely silence. Possibly there is even some agreement, but even honest agreement must be reevaluated in the face of recent developments in resource sharing and document delivery. Our clients do not know most of this. It is not important that they understand it. It *is* important that they understand that they don't know, and that they are not qualified to decide issues about which they are ignorant.

INFORMATION INTERMEDIATION

The public perception of libraries is narrow and focuses on our role in education. This role is important and it is important that we do it well, but it is not all we do or should do, most particularly in universities. Our potential role in information intermediation meets a crucial need, and promises greater recognition and visibility.

I have no quarrels with programs in bibliographic instruction, but I sometimes wonder if the intent of teaching self-service to users is ultimately to avoid having to do any reference or bibliographic work ourselves. Certainly total self-service leaves little professional room for us. Many special librarians approach this issue quite differently. Rather than educate users to do their own work, they tell them what the library can do for them, and they urge them to be as "unreasonable" as they like in initiating requests for assistance. That, of course, is the staking and managing of turf.

We could learn how to go about upgrading a professional image from our colleagues in education.

The first step is to insist on professional pay for professional work. National education leaders now talk brashly about a minimum starting salary of $24,000 for teachers. They won't get all of that, but they will get some of it, they will gain public awareness of a perceived problem, and generate a good deal of guilt and apology about the shortfall. Do teachers merit higher starting pay than librarians? Are the excuses about the inability to pay more heard less often for the one profession than for the other, and are they not equally nonsensical for both? Society affords what it wants to afford. It finds ways to finance what it considers worth doing, yet *LJ* still runs letters begging understanding for public libraries which cannot "afford" professionals.

Without pretending to be complete or that research has validated the list, I think of three areas in which true professions which demand recognition and respect have established clearly visible ground rules:

CREDENTIALS

It is important that the many issues surrounding credentials in our profession be carried out internally—within the profession, and without involving uninformed outsiders. Only librarians would invite representatives of the federal Office of Personnel Management, already predisposed to lowering professional requirements and salaries, to a meeting at which we air our own concerns and uncertainties.

Such concerns are real in any profession, and periodic reassessment is certainly necessary, but it is an internal process the results of which are then divulged to the outside world. "This is what *we* have decided, and *you* can now react accordingly." Self-criticism is a family matter.

Perhaps we need the sort of fanatical self-devotion I experienced growing up in Brooklyn as a die-hard Dodger fan (Rumor has it that there is another team with the same name now). When they played badly we could call them "bums," but no fan of any other team had better dare. It was a family dispute. Our profession should act something like that. Let it be known that we can criticize ourselves, but we won't tolerate misinformed criticism from others.

Doctors and lawyers react that way to attacks on their professional image, and nurses and teachers are heavily involved in creating a professional area of expertise. I see very little turf protection in our field. Nonlibrarians get top library management posts, to cite an obvious example. In another highly visible manifestation of the phenomenon, the President appoints new members to our National Commission on Library and Information Science. Don't we have any feelings about qualification for service on the commission? Is there a proper ratio or mix of people from our own profession and others for NCLIS? What kind of expertise are outsiders expected to bring? Have we articulated our views to members of the White House staff? Were we really satisfied with the delegate mix of professionals and the general public at the first White House Conference or the state conferences which preceded it? Are we so anxious to have another conference that we will take it on any terms? More important than my views on these questions is the fact that as a profession we haven't even begun to discuss the questions of what we want.

When we do discuss credentials in determining our needs, I hope we will not let ourselves become part of the trivialization that would result from talking about skills rather that perceptions and attitudes, about "training" instead of educational frameworks.

PROFESSION TO TRADE

Obviously, if we decide to turn the description of what librarians do from professional educational preparation for training to a list of specific job skills, we'll need no help in turning librarianship from a profession into a trade.

The determination of what professionals should bring to the first job is central to the questions of whether and why an accredited degree is important and what equivalency means. Our desire to be "fair" here really borders on the suicidal. Fair to whom? Certainly not to those who endured the rigor, time, and expense to obtain what they thought was a meaningful educational experience.

RESEARCH

Professions recognize the importance of research as an integral balance to practice. I sympathize with those who argue that current research has little relevance, but I never see their list of alternative concerns and priorities. The Department of Education-funded project to develop a research agenda for the 1980s produced nothing but the desire for better strategies for coping with existing or coming technology, or with management ploys designed to force us to operate with declining resources.

These are important concerns, but at most, they are applications issues, not research questions. Are we so certain that what we believe and do is correct that we can brook no inquiry? Are we so certain that Mortimer Taube was wrong when he suggested, more than 20 years ago, that the advent of technology warranted a complete reexamination of how and why we do subject analysis? We might not need research if we had no professional problems. . . .

CONTINUING EDUCATION

Any self-respecting profession recognizes that learning must be continuous. Just as a profession is changed through research, its practitioners become obsolete and irrelevant without continuing education. Few of us want to be treated by a doctor who has no knowledge of new developments in medicine in the last 25 years. I would not want to be served by such a librarian, either. Some time ago both lawyers and doctors began the process of assuring, through peer judgment and pressure, that education continues after the terminal degree.

Our cousins in education also recognize this necessity. Most teacher contracts provide specific financial rewards for additional academic degrees or the completion of credit hours. As librarians we are so committed to the idea of continuing education that we lose sight of how little there really is, and of how few practitioners are touched in any significant way.

For us continuing education is a totally voluntary process carrying neither salary benefits nor promotion, nor the danger of being fired if we don't participate. There is neither carrot not stick.

Continuing education can really only succeed with two possible strategies. We can recognize—as doctors, lawyers, and business executives (the very people who serve on public library boards) recognize so clearly in their own fields—that continuing education is a legitimate organizational expense that belongs in the operating budget. Alternatively, we can follow the example of the field of education, which largely makes educational expense the responsibility of the individual, and then also provides clear rewards for completion and dangers for avoidance.

In librarianship, we have generally done neither. We applaud continuing education. We even provide support of sorts in release time and even in tuition payments, but this only helps to mitigate the inconvenience. The carrot and stick are still absent. It is a mistake, despite our genuine affection for continuing education, to believe that we really have programs that work.

BEGIN WITH SELF-REGARD

To have any hope of convincing others, we must begin with a regard for ourselves and the importance of what we do. Longfellow said, "He that respects himself is safe from others; he wears a coat of mail that none can pierce." That may be simplistic for librarians, but it is on the right track.

The outside world won't change our profession for us. People like librarians and libraries just fine the way they see them. The willingness of users to accept poor library service is almost limitless. That has been confirmed for me through much observation and work as a consultant. Guidance counselors will continue to send us the wrong recruits, individuals who lack assertiveness and interpersonal communication skills but who are neat, orderly, and love to read.

If librarianship is to change its outside perceptions it must first change its self-perceptions. This does not mean a wholesale process of purges and firings (although there are certainly incompetent librarians who are hardly ever fired). It suggests a process of evaluation which recognizes, encourages, and promotes to library leadership those restless and dissatisfied risk-takers who espouse the values and characteristics which any self-respecting profession demands of itself.

PUBLIC LIBRARIES AND THE POLITICAL PROCESS

I am not a public librarian. Let that be noted immediately, before some of my friends in public libraries hasten to make the point. I am, however, a student of the management process, and I find myself fascinated with the way in which librarians function (or fail to function) as part of the political process.

Let us make no mistake, public libraries are very much part of a political decision process in which decisions are made less on the basis of the worthiness of the claim than on the rewards and punishments perceived by the decider. This is a relatively new revelation for librarians (I first addressed it in a 1978 talk to the Canadian Library Association).

SELF-EVIDENTLY GOOD

Library strategy has been, and to a large extent still is, based on the premise that libraries are self-evidently good, and that therefore justifications are too obvious to be necessary. It was, at best, a dubious strategy even during the affluent (at least for libraries) 1960s. It obtained for us some funding, but never at the levels achieved by some of our more politically astute colleagues in other disciplines. In the 1980s the appeal to self-evidence is a bankrupt strategy. There is nothing on the political horizon that makes me think that the future will be any brighter.

Whether we like it or not, the Reagan administration has been able to reverse the directions of public political thinking as only the Roosevelt administration had been able to do 50 years ago. For the foreseeable future, suspicion of large government "give-away" programs will know no political party. Many of the more astute Democratic politi-

From *Library Journal* 111 (15 June 1986):49–51.

cians are trying to free themselves of the "big spender" label and to reclaim the center of the political spectrum that they have lost.

If we accept the premise that library support cannot be justified simply on the premise that we deserve it, it becomes necessary to understand how politicians make their decisions. I noted in an earlier column that the decision process usually involves reaching a conclusion and then "proving" that it was the correct one. Invariably this involves deciding what is best for the decider, and then quite comfortably concluding that coincidentally this is also best for the larger organizations. Librarians do this too, but nobody is better at it than elected politicians.

UNINTENDED TARGETS

Libraries have not fared as well as other agencies in the political arena. This failure has nothing to do with need. In fact, we do such a good and persistent job of pleading our poverty that we run the risk of annoying even our friends. Nobody likes a nag. Our failure deals rather with the power we are unable to generate, the fear we are unable to inspire, and the rewards we are unable to deliver.

The proponents of Proposition 13 (the well-known California Tax-cutting initiative) and similar measures did not particularly have libraries in their gunsights. They will admit this if pressed. Their targets were what they perceived as a bloated bureaucracy and a whole range of "give-away" programs.

It is irrelevant whether or not we agree with them in whole or in part. They have been successful in cutting budgets where their initiatives have been adopted. They have not been particularly successful in reaching their targets, because to a great extent these were too solidly entrenched and, in some cases, legally protected. So, instead, the proponents of Proposition 13 wreaked havoc with library programs, even though these were not their targets. Some of them even express some degree of regret. Others just shrug off any responsibility for what they see as our political ineptness. All of this becomes particularly ironic when we recall that libraries really have few if any enemies, in a public, academic, school, or corporate setting. What they lack is powerful friends who will fight and risk for them.

ALL WE CAN AFFORD

In my seminars on management communication I stress that bad news is frequently sugar-coated because most of us prefer to be nice. That makes it necessary to sift the verbiage from the reality. For public libraries the bad news is usually phrased in the argument that whatever is being provided is all that the village or town or city or state can afford. This is total nonsense, and those who tell us surely know it.

We afford what we want to afford, and we can certainly afford libraries. A thriving market for video games was carved from an economy that, we were assured, had absolutely no elasticity. Where do the dollars for music videos come from? In part from the people who can't afford taxes for libraries. Or the funds for suddenly needed toxic cleanups? Or to halt a "sick-out" by fire fighters? The total of public spending may have remained the same, but priorities shift, and funds move from one sector of the economy and of the budget to another. They have been moving from libraries to other expenditure categories, but there is no fundamental reason that this trend could not be reversed.

For public libraries the true financial status obviously varies from one community to the next, and some are undoubtedly really unable to do very much for any group, including libraries. However, we must be able to separate fact from fiction. The claim of poverty will be made whether there is a lot of money, a modicum of it, or none at all. One of our obvious strategic errors is that we ask for too little.

WITH FRIENDS LIKE YOU . . .

It may seem strange that libraries fare so badly in the political arena, because we really have no enemies. However, a lack of enemies is not enough in a competitive environment. Peter Drucker noted that in a political setting there are no neutrals. People are for you or they are against you, because if they are not for you they are for something or someone else who wants the same money you want.

We do not ally ourselves with powerful friends. Public library programs are largely aimed at service to children and to the aging. Those are goals with which everyone concurs, but which few find particularly urgent. If we are forced by "lack of funds" to stretch them out, is there really any demonstrated harm?

People are far more likely now than 20 years ago to support those services without which they would be personally inconvenienced. Service to children and to the aging are still self-evidently good, and nobody in his or her right mind would dream of attacking either. At the same time, they are recognized as old problems with imperfect solutions, and if we don't deal with them today we can still deal with them tomorrow. Politicians also recognize that these are elastic problems without finite solutions, and in the absence of finite solutions there is no credit to be had within the very finite time span of the next campaign for public office.

We must not make the mistake of assuming that the local urgency which is expressed when the school system is in danger is transferrable to libraries. Schools serve as baby sitters for families which, to an evergrowing extent, have something else to do as soon as the kids are packed off to school. Libraries can pose no such threat to the personal convenience system that governs individual decisions.

There is far more public awareness of urgency when citizens consider school service to children than when they consider public library service to children, although of course library service to this constituency is still "good."

To these two self-evident priorities, we are in danger of adding a third, the most politically dangerous priority of all because it can easily swallow all the resources it can claim without making a ripple, let alone a splash. I am referring to the issue of adult illiteracy.

LITERACY: NOT OUR PROBLEM

Despite years of efforts and billions of dollars spent in virtually every country, society has yet to focus on what it really wants to accomplish. As Kenneth Levine (*Harvard Educational Review*, August 1982) points out, we haven't even agreed on *why* we want to teach people how to read. Is it to enable them to obtain a better job? To understand an eviction notice or a warning label? To enjoy the classics? Each of those purposes involves very different issues. Ultimately it depends on whether or not people want not just to learn how to read, but to read, a problem now correctly separated and labeled as "aliteracy."

A skill that is learned but not used quickly atrophies, a fact easily proven when I now try to use the French I was taught in high school. Motivation is apparently as great a problem as mechanics. That means getting people to want to put the effort into learning to read because reading is something they want to do, and not just a skill we think they should learn.

I am not uncaring about the concern, which is very real. However, I don't think it is basically a problem for which we can accept a primary responsibility. It is one of the failures of the educational process, and perhaps even of larger societal values. Slowly and even with reluctance these issues are being faced in the educational community. Educators have always had far greater access to resources than librarians. If they want librarians to help (and they should), then they must provide *additional* funds, on a contract or grant basis.

I am not suggesting that libraries give up any of our present programs. By nature, I am not inclined to cede turf. I do not seek to discount the importance of a population that can read, wants to read, and does read as part of the process of developing a strong and democratic society.

MAKING LIBRARIES INDISPENSABLE

What I do stress is that the library must find a more pluralistic role. It must broaden its constituency. It must find a way to make itself and its activities indispensable to the work and life habits of a wider constituency, particularly of those who make the decisions which control our resources. "Ingratiated irreplaceability" is the name I gave the concept in an article addressed to corporate special librarians who live or die based on whether or not they succeed at it.

Where do we find these constituencies and these supporters? It takes no genius to recognize that the emphasis of municipal and state government concern these days is on economic growth, sometimes seen as economic survival.

Depending on the locality, this concern may concentrate on a shift from heavy industry to sophisticated technology or from an agrarian to a non-smokestack-manufacturing economy as is the current emphasis in my own state. Every locality has its own urgent economic agenda.

Librarians and their public libraries are superbly qualified to contribute to this effort. That they don't make this contribution is due in large part to the fact that bankers, corporate leaders, chamber of commerce officers, and municipal officials don't know what information is lacking but attainable for their deliberations. They don't even know they don't know, yet they are natural enough clients, because they are information users who place a value on information. They just don't get it from libraries.

W. Randall Wilson, in his "Partners in Economic Development" (*LJ*, March 15, p. 32–34), describes the involvement of the Canton Public Library, Illinois, in that community's economic development programs. It is an excellent description of what public libraries can and should do. The fact that Wilson's article is unique reminds us that few, if any, other public libraries are doing similar things.

There seems to be something short-sighted in our strategies. Not in our praise-worthy desire to concentrate on individuals who cannot read and do not read. Such a goal is not only appropriate as a national priority, it helps extend our visibility and our importance because we really can help. The inconsistency appears when we concentrate on these constituencies to the exclusion of those who can and do use information.

Recently a great point has been made of the fact that libraries serve largely the better educated and more interested. While that is correct, the prevailing notion that librarians should feel some guilt about the phenomenon is spurious. The condition of use by a particular constituency is not restricted to libraries. Divided superhighways are built for the benefit of those who drive cars. Surveys tell us that educational TV programs are watched primarily by children and even adults who least need them, and for whom they weren't produced.

GROWTH MEANS SURVIVAL

For our own survival we must expand and grow. Theories of economic tension tell us that survival requires growth, because remaining the same equates to getting smaller in a growing universe. We must create a perceived imbalance in the public mind between what we do and what we should do. We must generate a demand for services we cannot now provide. We must then direct the clamorers for most of this service to those who have power. Because they want to keep their power they will fear that they are making important enemies.

In his message to the state conference which preceded the 1979 White House Conference on Libraries, the governor of Indiana (at the time) gave us some very practical advice. He noted that librarians, at least in his state, had been largely ineffective in the political environment because they had not figured out ways to reward their friends and punish their enemies.

For a special librarian like me, there is a certain irony in this entire discussion. The Special Libraries Association was formed in 1909. Public librarians were heavily represented among the founders. John Cotton Dana, the acknowledged founder of SLA and its first president, is also remembered for developing business information services at the Newark Public Library, New Jersey. The public librarians founded SLA, at least in part because of frustration with existing public library value systems as represented in ALA discussions and policies. They were concerned that service to this clientele was not accorded proper recognition in public library and professional structures.

Now, 75 years later, we again hear the suggestion that public library service to business is not as important as other services. Many assert that for-profit organizations (which help pay for public libraries through their taxes) should pay additional fees for services that are traditionally provided free of charge to everyone else. It should not surprise us if the business community sometimes feels unloved and unwelcome in the public library. We have no right to feel chagrined because we perceive that, in turn, they don't love us as much as we think they should. Our responsibility to provide information to tenants appears clear. Is our responsibility to provide information to landlords equally clear to us?

SACRIFICIAL LAMBS

Library costs in the overall budgetary context are truly trivial. No community ever faced or survived bankruptcy because of what it did or did not do on behalf of its library. New York City's financial mess of the 1970s was largely of its own making, but it did not result from largesse heaped on its public library systems, any more than universities can solve their money problems by closing their tiny library schools.

It is the appearance of economy rather than actual economy that dominates political thinking, and when C. Northcote Parkinson told us that the amount of time and energy spent on an issue is inversely proportional to its importance, he was telling us what we have all seen and experienced. Libraries make good sacrificial lambs because they don't wiggle as much when their heads are on the chopping block.

Politicians perceive that the credit for cutting expenses captures more votes than cutting library budgets loses. The former governor of Indiana instinctively knew that, probably without giving the matter much thought. We, who think about the problem constantly, should certainly know it as well.

MARKETING POLITICS

For some the word "marketing" has a sleazy connotation, at least in the pages of *LJ*, but I think it is shortsighted to give the term that connotation. Marketing is designed to get people to want something they don't have. While it may induce them to want something they don't really need, that does't have to be the case. If we can't convince ourselves that marketing libraries is marketing for the public good, that individuals really need what we don't now provide for them, we certainly aren't going to be able to convince anyone else. "Politics" is another word with a negative connotation, as I recognize when I try to convince new, idealistic students that their chosen career demands political skills.

All academic, special, school, and public libraries operate in the political arena, because politics is the process of making decisions, of allocating resources that are always insufficient to meet the expressed demand. Good politicians get resources, poor politicians get apologies and vague promises about "maybe next year," promises which we should recognize have no substance.

Peter Drucker, with his Churchillian gift for short and memorable phrases, said it all a long time ago. Managers (and of course librarians who control resources are managers) only get credit for two things, innovation and marketing, because successful continuation of the status quo is assumed, and earns no credit. Even more to the point, it is boring. In politics, "boring" is a synonym for "fatal."

THE TRIVIALIZATION OF NATIONAL LIBRARY WEEK

I look forward to the annual spring rite of National Library Week with a mixture of annoyance and uneasiness. NLW is a lost opportunity. Lately I have begun to suspect that others may share my feelings.

The general public does not know what librarians do, or often what they think they know is wrong. The impression is of individuals who paste pockets and stamp dates into the backs of books, and then recall those books after they become overdue. These are activities which tend to be annoying and are in any case clerical. Few people I encounter understand why a master's degree is necessary for our profession.

To counter that public misperception we have the opportunity of National Library Week, or as I would prefer, National Librarians Week. Do we use this opportunity to stress what professional librarians do, or, more important, what people could expect if only there were a professional librarian? We do not. Instead, we urge people to READ, and we bolster that simplistic campaign with pictures of boxers and their lovable children, lovable old comics, ballet dancers, and, for me at least, not-so-lovable rock singers with strangely colored hair, all holding, reading, or hugging books. Reading is the thing to do, the pictures and text urge. What should people read? Anything at all, because the very process of reading is ennobling.

Where does one find things to read? Why, in the library, of course. And that, of course, defines the word library. It is the place with the books. What sort of library—good, bad, or indifferent, passive or interactive, professional or clerical? We don't say. Practically anything with four walls and eight books is a "library," and the person who is found there, with or without pay, with or without education and training, and presumably from the age of eight on up, is the "librarian."

From *Library Journal* 111 (1 October 1986):66–67.

National Library Week attempts no distinction between what libraries do and what they could and should do. It makes no attempt to describe the role of professionals in that process. The NLW approach activates our own version of Gresham's Law of Economics. If we can't or won't differentiate between a good library and a bad library, a library and a pseudolibrary or reading room, then the bad will replace the good because it is cheaper.

I once worked closely with one of the founders of National Secretaries Week. Initially that movement wanted to differentiate between true "professional" secretaries and others who falsely (in the eyes of the founders) laid claim to the title. National Secretaries Week failed in its original intent because it was taken over by florists and candy manufacturers, but at least it concentrates on the individual, not on the presumed activity. No NSW publicity suggests that to celebrate we should sit down and type something.

It is irritating when the work of librarians is trivialized and when we become the butt of ridicule based on our presumed characteristics. When we contribute to that image by our failure to outline even the most fundamental role for professional librarians, it becomes stupid and suicidal. We need to come to grips with the question of what constitutes professional library service, what constitutes some lower-level alternative (with a different name to avoid confusion), and what we believe should be offered at certain community levels.

Others have done so. The words "doctor" and "hospital" are not available to anyone who wants to use them. We may never have the clout of medicine and law, but we don't have to acquiesce in our own downgrading. The National Library Week campaign, spiced up with the sale of cookies or surplus books we don't want and shouldn't foist on others to raise funds to bolster our inadequate budget, is a step toward professional self-abasement.

The timing of John Berry's May 1 *LJ* editorial was ironic. He pointed out, correctly, that the newly perceived shortage of professional librarians is raising the level of starting salaries for individuals with master's degrees higher than some library boards wish to pay. Rather than pay those salaries (for some, anything above $12,000 is exorbitant), some boards may return to the practice of hiring bachelor's degree graduates. Even that is also only a temporary solution. As bachelor's degree holders develop pay expectations comparable to those with other college degrees, they'll return to that last refuge of those who "think cheap," the loyal volunteers. They perform wonderful supportive services in libraries as in hospitals, but when the price for that service is our professional title, it is too great. What volunteers run can't be libraries, or what we run must be called something else and operated at some higher level of service interaction. National Librarians Week should articulate that difference. So should a White House Conference. If we can't accomplish these things as a minimum, we may not survive as a profession. If we don't care enough to try, we don't deserve to.

That May 1 *LJ* carries a letter to the editor in which the author claims he is "running" nine libraries with a professional staff of just himself. If all nine units use the same generic name, it is no wonder clients are confused about what is and isn't a library.

I would be glad to examine the financial records of any community that claims it can't afford to pay an appropriate librarian's salary to identify items of greater importance upon which it spends money. Individuals and communities can afford what they must or want to afford. When money is needed, it is found.

It is ironic that the retreat from graduate to undergraduate librarians as salary expectations rise, coincides with major efforts by educators to demand graduate degrees of all would-be teachers. In suggesting that teachers carry graduate degrees superimposed on subject bachelor's degrees, educators advocate educational preparation librarians have had for some time. How sad if our descending elevator passes their rising one. The demand for higher-level educational preparation is made in the name of quality schools. It is stated as given that this higher quality requires higher salaries. States and municipalities are expected to pay those salaries, and they appear to recognize that they must and will.

The higher price of what is presumed to be a better-quality education will be paid by the same states and municipalities that now argue that if they can't get a graduate librarian for $12,000 they'll have to hire what they can get for $12,000.

Are we professional librarians so suicidal that we are unwilling to address the question of a minimum level below which there is no real library, only a pretend library? If we won't fight for ourselves, we should at least fight for those who will never know what an adequate library is unless we tell them. They'll never learn the difference from our NLW publicity.

Here are some off-the-top-of-the-head suggestions, alternative approaches for our public posture throughout the year, but particularly during National Librarians Week (they aren't meant to be inclusive):

1. The week of————we celebrate and recognize the efforts of professional librarians. Librarians manage libraries, and everyone has a personal understanding of libraries with which they are already familiar. They may not know about the libraries that they could have, or the libraries to which they are entitled. Libraries serve their users at many levels, including developing interest in reading in a child, providing recreational reading for retirees, continued development for people of all ages, and access to information needed for personal, business, and governmental decisions. For these reasons libraries, or as they are some-

times called, learning resource centers or information centers, exist in many different settings, including communities, schools, colleges and universities, government agencies, corporations, and many others. You are entitled to access to an adequate library. Adequacy is determined by what you want and need, not by what somebody is willing to give you. This is true because the absence of needed information is, in the long run, much more expensive than having information in the first place. Do you have access to adequate libraries?

2. Libraries may be large or small, and their collections may concentrate on books in public libraries, on books and periodicals in university libraries, or on government reports and pamphlets in other settings. They may be highly automated with computers, or they may appear little changed from the libraries of 25 to 50 years ago. Their size has nothing to do with the information that libraries can obtain for you if you need or want it, and their appearance is deceptive. All libraries, regardless of size or location, now have potential access to information sources through computer terminals to let users know what is available, and can deliver it to you through rapid mail and even electronic delivery services within a matter of days, if necessary, even hours. All of this costs money, but what of value doesn't? It is, however, an integral part of library service, and those who fund the library should fund its access to services. What the library doesn't have it will get for you, and if the library budget provides you with what it already has, it should also provide you with what it doesn't have but can get. You are entitled to it, from the funds you already pay to support the structure of library service. Good libraries cost more and they are worth it.

3. The key to providing quality library service is the librarian. Librarians have been educated in graduate university programs in which they achieve master's degrees to prepare them for professional work in libraries. They should be paid like other professionals with similar qualifications, such as accountants, engineers, and teachers. There are exceptions, remarkable individuals who have taught themselves, often by attending many workshops and seminars, to work as professionals without the specific educational qualifications. These exceptions are rare. One does not become a librarian by simply working in a library any more than one becomes a doctor by working in a hospital. There is room for many nonprofessionals and volunteers to contribute in libraries, and their labors are often crucial to the success of the library, just as hospitals also rely on volunteers and nonprofessionals. However, these individuals are not professional librarians, and if the person in charge is not a professional, then what you have is not really a library. Maybe a reading room. It also goes almost without saying that if you put professionals in charge you let them run the place. Library boards and committees in the public, university, school, government, or corporate setting are impor-

tant for providing an overall context and liaison for the work of the librarian, but it is librarians that make the professional decisions about what happens in libraries. That makes sense, doen't it?

4. Can your community afford a properly run library? The real point is that it can't afford not to have one. Libraries are real bargains. In the absence of adequate libraries two things can happen, and they are both bad. Individuals either do without information they need and deserve, or they spend much more money to get it elsewhere. That is foolish and unfair. Not everyone has the money. Communities seeking to attract new businesses to create new jobs have found that employers look for more than tax breaks. They want a healthy climate of life for their executives and employees. They want good schools, good municipal facilities, and good libraries. A qualified professional librarian can work effectively with the Chamber of Commerce to develop growth and prosperity. And you thought that libraries were only for children and senior citizens! Of course they are, but they do so much more!

5. Do you have access to the kind of library service that has just been described? Do you get professional help with your information problems, whether that involves choosing something light to read this summer or an important decision affecting your career or style of life? If not, don't accept it, you are being short-changed.

6. For further information, and suggestions of what you can do to improve the library service you get, contact the Committee for National Librarians Week at the address or toll-free number listed.

Many professions do no less in support of their own work status, and many do much more.

CATALOGERS—YESTERDAY, TODAY, TOMORROW

In an earlier column devoted to salaries and staff shortages (*LJ*, March 1, 1986, p. 70–71), I made the observation that to a great extent today's library school students opt not to become catalogers not because of any faculty plot to divert them to other areas of the profession, but because students have the opportunity to see how cataloging is done in the libraries in which they work and have worked, and to a large extent they don't like what they see.

The statement was not intended to be provocative, but only to report on what I could see quite clearly as a library education administrator. The comment nevertheless drew some heated rebuttals, and I find that discussion of what I wrote continues among catalogers even today. With the fearless if reckless bravado that readers of this column already recognize, let me try to examine that issue in greater specificity.

IN DEFENSE OF CATALOGERS

Heated defense of cataloging from what may be perceived as attacks from outsiders does not really surprise me. In a talk in 1983 to an audience totally composed of New England technical services librarians, I suggested that catalogers had turned long ago to inward and closed-loop value and recognition systems because they had not been allowed a stake in the larger framework of objectives achievement from which any professional draws his or her satisfaction.

As noted in earlier columns, libraries are generally quite good at articulating idealistic goals, but poor at turning these into specific objectives tied in implementation to adequate resources. If the resources are

From *Library Journal* 112 (1 April 1987);48–148.

inadequate, management literature tells us, then the objectives are curtailed, and the higer-level managers ultimately responsible for that decision are also held accountable for the paucity in service. This is a theme to which I will certainly return in the future.

However, catalogers have been deprived even of a share of what little can be celebrated as day-to-day triumphs. Reference librarians occasionally experience the pleasure of encountering a satisfied patron or of receiving a note of thanks. In fact, reference work provides such direct gratification that I fail to understand why academic librarians don't insist on doing more of it.

Catalogers, however, are deprived of this pleasure. Patrons and reference librarians are not likely to write them gushing notes about the elegance of added entries; communications, if any, are more likely to be carping criticisms pointing out real or imagined picayune errors. Administrators in and above the level of the library are also unlikely to take note of what catalogers do, except perhaps in a quantitative context, and here again almost inevitably critically.

By and large, catalogers work out of sight and out of mind, moving material from the truck on the left side of their desk to the truck on the right side, and the left truck is never empty. It is little wonder that catalogers have developed their own value systems to produce the evaluations and recognitions that every employee needs and deserves.

THE ADVENT OF THE COMPUTER

What has suddenly changed all this (20 years is sudden in this profession) is the advent of computerization, most directly applicable to technical services operations. I need not take the space in this brief column to elaborate on these changes, except to note with some regret that we have tended to concentrate on mechanizing existing protocols of descriptive analysis rather than look at opportunities to reexamine the premises initially developed to fit manual techniques and the limitation of the 3 x 5 card.

However, even without major changes in philosophy, there have been sweeping alterations in procedure. Interinstitutional agreements more often than not center on areas of technical service cooperation, and, once they are signed by library directors, it is up to catalogers to implement them and make them work. This, in turn, requires an orientation toward interactions with people perhaps even beyond that required of the reference librarians we expect to be "people people."

Inevitably, it also requires a strong understanding of technology as it is applied to libraries. We see this most directly in library schools. Faculty members with the dual capability to teach cataloging and information science courses are no longer rare, in fact they are becoming quite commonplace.

MORE THAN THE CATALOG

Computer networks have also made information outside the holdings of the card catalog accessible to library users, and our backlogs are no longer "safe" because others now have access to bibliographic information we have not yet divulged.

The card catalog is no longer the only source, and it may not be for long even the primary one. Its primacy has been in the humanities and some of the social sciences, because users of the physical science collection concentrate on the journal and report literature to which our cataloging procedures have never adopted—something we first learned through the hundreds of thousands of technical reports generated by World War II, which classic library cataloging procedures didn't know how to handle, and which catalogers didn't want to handle.

In many scientific corporate libraries, book cataloging today is done by clerks. The professionals do subject analysis in depth. The fundamental question posed many years ago—Should we concentrate our efforts on document analysis (even for documents that will never be retrieved) to simplify the retrieval process, or do we simplify analysis and concentrate on more sophisticated retrieval techniques?—has never been examined in libraries.

We choose the former approach because we assume that we are creating a self-service environment in which untrained users are expected to be able to find things. That is one approach, but it is certainly not the only one. A system geared to skilled intermediate searchers could make other assumptions.

PART OF THE LIBRARY STRATEGY

Other changes are far more certain. Cataloging can no longer be a self-contained process performed to standards never considered as part of the whole library operation. Issues of cataloging quality, acceptable error rate, cost of cataloging, rapidity of access, and backlogs are all interrelated questions that must be answered as part of an overall library strategy.

Libraries learned this fact of life when directors noted that new access to OCLC online was slowing rather than speeding up the cataloging process, because it was providing yet another advisory input to an in-house decision. That was fixed quickly enough and, at least in some libraries, what is called copy cataloging insures that input moves directly from paraprofessionals to the file, without review by professionals who might "correct" it.

Lest anyone misunderstand my meaning, I perceive the new role of cataloging and technical services as crucial to the organizational mission. A few libraries have changed to organic structures in which cataloging is decentralized and the input/output functions are combined in settings close to the ultimate user.

However, most libraries still maintain the classic dichotomy of technical and public services, and probably will for some time to come. When this occurs, communication and decision patterns must break out of traditional boxes. Cataloging policy decisions become too important to be left exclusively to the preference of catalogers, but it is equally true that catalogers must be involved and consulted in all major organizational decisions. For the first time, catalogers can become part of the larger decision structure, and they can trade their internal games for larger contests in which they can actually win some of the time.

STEREOTYPING THROUGH OBSERVATION?

Many of the most dynamic and innovative librarians of the last 20 years have chosen technical services as the area of their professional contribution, and these are individuals who combine an understanding of specific rules with an understanding of technology, an appreciation for organizational structure and decision patterns, and the enjoyment of interacting with others in settings that range from the participatory and democratic to the consultative and autocratic, with a further understanding of the appropriate place of each. It is probably these individuals who most object that the characterizations in my earlier article are stereotypical and unfair.

Stereotypes are inevitably unfair in the specific, but if they were not recognizable they would not exist at all. While there are bright and dynamic young technical services librarians (young as a state of mind and not of chronological age—there are librarians aged 25 who are very old), there are also still fuddy-duddies who run cataloging departments as they have always run them, to standards that are totally oriented to their own unexplained and unexplainable whims.

That such individuals have been allowed to remain in positions of power must ultimately result from the inertia or cowardice of library directors, but students see these people *because they are there,* and students are also desperately afraid that this is the kind of person to whom they will report. And they might be right.

We are not far enough removed from stereotypes so that a proposal for a doctoral dissertation was submitted only five years ago based on the assumption that all public services librarians were outgoing, articulate, and interested in people, while all technical services librarians were shy and withdrawn, loners, impractical, fascinated by detail, and perfectionists in the extreme. The proposal was discouraged, the study did not materialize, and the generalization is of course grossly unfair, but where did the student come up with these ideas except through observation?

COMPETING FOR THE BEST

If you who are the new breed of technical service professionals want our best and our brightest then you must compete for them, because others want them, too. Part of that competition is financial, but much of it comes from informing students that their preconceptions could be wrong.

Come to our classrooms and tell them, but then also make your statement a greater reality by insisting that library directors do their own jobs and clean house. Having done that, be prepared for one last phenomenon. The best and the brightest are also the least docile, and they are the ones who demand explanations and justifications of why certain procedures are followed. Such questions are rarely welcome when nobody knows the answer or wants to think about it. Sometimes these questions are naïve, sometimes they are very insightful. However, they should always be welcome, and this is an assurance you should be able to give to our best students.

ENTREPRENEURSHIP AND THE LIBRARY PROFESSION

The management literature, along with numerous biographies and autobiographies, serves to describe the entrepreneur for us quite accurately. The dictionary definition of an individual who starts and conducts an enterprise does not really begin to scratch the surface. Entrepreneurs are perceived to be risk taking innovators, individualistic, believers in themselves and in their own competence regardless of the views of others, and as often as not stubborn, selfish, insensitive to the concerns of others at least when those concerns get in their way, and sometimes arrogant and ruthless. We know from statistics put out by the Department of Commerce and other government agencies that most individual entrepreneurs fail, and yet we have a tremendous admiration for those who succeed. Somehow their perseverance and courage in the face of overwhelming odds, negative research findings and the advice of friends, colleagues, and "experts" strikes a responsive chord, and the careers of Howard Hughes and Ted Turner fascinate us, perhaps because these individuals have dared to do and say what most of us know we would never have the courage to attempt.

Entrepreneurs of the "old breed" may also command our awe because we recognize them as a dying breed, killed off by changes in the organizational decision process. Entrepreneurs, as already noted, are rugged individualists, who will ignore the admonitions of others because they believe so firmly in their own judgments. Entrepreneurs are not only thought to be too often wrong to be tolerated by the organizational structure, but perhaps more importantly we believe that organizational decision making now tends toward committee approaches, consensus, participation, and consultation. In part this is because of the perception that this leads to better decisions, but to a greater extent

From *Journal of Library Administration* 8 (Spring 1987):11–27.

because it leads to acceptable decisions. Entrepreneurs frequently rub people the wrong way, in part because of their own low level of patience or tolerance for disagreement. The development of management theories that urge a greater level of involvement and decision sharing are largely based on the argument that this not only improves the quality of decisions but also enhances morale and commitment in the office, factory, or laboratory. At the same time, there are other and less glorious reasons. Participation and the use of committees can be seen as an escape hatch for managers who wish to avoid making decisions at all costs, and who would prefer to distribute them to a committee decision process which is risk free simply because that many people can not be fired or even punished. Management writers have therefore noted, in describing the growth of formal decision-making structures, what has been called the end of an era. Not in totality, of course. The Ross Perots do occasionally surface, but the greater trend is evidenced by the risk avoidance strategy of the leveraged buyout, or the stock market tactic of not building an organization but of acquiring wealth through infiltrating one through the process of borrowing on its own equity, or of threatening to do so to receive a bribe which, under the nomenclature of "greenmail," is perfectly legal even if ethically odious.

The less we now seek to emulate entrepreneurs in the business community, the more we have come to look upon them as heroic larger than life figures. We recognize, at the same time, that entrepreneurs, even successful entrepreneurs, have their failings as executives. Most significantly, they are usually done in by the very success of the organization they have created. As organizations prosper and grow as the result of the drive, innovation, and ingenuity of its entrepreneur founder, they take on characteristics of the more standard bureaucratic model and exceed the ability of that individual to make all decisions. Entrepreneurially started organizations which have succeeded have done so because that success has then been transformed into a more traditionally structured mechanism or they have failed because of their success and growth. Either the span of decision making exceeded the ability of the one key individual unwilling to delegate to others or other fundamental problems such as unchecked growth leading to cash flow imbalances do the organization in. It is an interesting study to note that IBM was totally restructured to diffuse both authority and responsibility by Thomas Watson, Jr. after the death of his entrepreneurial father who founded the company. Entrepreneur founders often insist on making all decisions even when the sheer size of the company makes bad decisions inevitable and no decisions even more likely. Management analysts suggest that this happened just in time, not because IBM would have perished (at least not yet) but because it could not have continued to grow. A library example can be drawn from the administration of Librarian of Congress

Archibald MacLeish. His greatest contribution perhaps was a restructuring of the decision process to circumvent policies established by his predecessor, a great entrepreneurial builder who failed to recognize that his unwillingness to delegate was now strangling decisions. Entrepreneurs are generally seen as unwilling to adapt and as resistant to the sage advice of others who presumably know better. The willingness to make decisions is their strength and the insistence on making all decisions is also their weakness. They can start organizations but they do not often manage mature ones.

In recognition of this trait, it is generally acknowledged that entrepreneurs do not stay within organizations, they leave and start their own. Some, such as the brilliant innovator who founded Apple Computers, Steven Jobs, do it more than once. Their knack, their accomplishment, and their success comes from starting organizations, not from managing mature ones. In fact, they often find the management of mature organizations to be boring. This perception of entrepreneurs as anti-managers is so closely held that it has come to be accepted as an obvious truth.

For the library profession this dichotomy is perceived to be equally stark. Libraries are, after all, very mature organizations. They have a hardening of decision arteries brought about not only by the risk avoidance tendencies of many librarians, but by the preference for minimal or no changes by the library's clientele, be these academic faculty members, special library users whose preconceptions come from what they have seen as university students, or the public library patrons heavily skewed toward children and the elderly. All are groups that have an affinity toward the library just as it is. Individuals who do not like the library just as it is do not tend to try to change it. They just ignore it and as we already know from a variety of research investigations the existence of an inadequate library does not pose an insurmountable barrier. Users adapt to poor service, find other approaches to information, or pretend they never needed the information in the first place.

All this tends to create a scenario which, in libraries as in other organization structures, but perhaps particularly in libraries, stresses an environment of cooperation and coordination, of "getting along," of working "as a team," and of not being aggressive or confrontational, or even assertive and outspoken. As a library educator I see recruiters who search for those who work well within groups, and who avoid the students whose academic brilliance and articulateness makes them unique. As an administrator I can certainly understand and even appreciate that preference. At the same time, we must recognize, as our colleagues in the more generic management field have recognized, that this will almost inevitably deprive us of entrepreneurs and the strengths that such individuals bring to an organizational dynamism. Entrepreneurs are not usually good team players. They can be opinionated, rude, loud, stubborn, even obnoxious. The redeeming quality only comes into play when they are right. Some organizational management consider it too great a price to have such people around disturbing the equilibrium.

Not all. The aforementioned Thomas Watson, Jr., having created for IBM a balanced structure combining delegation, authority, and responsibility, and certainly based in large measure on committee input and coordination, nevertheless argued passionately for the protection of what he called the organization's "wild ducks"—those individuals who march to the beat of a different drummer, create difficulties and tensions wherever they go, but can also, just once in a while, be counted on to make the major breakthroughs that "organization men" could never make. We now know enough about hiring and selection policies to recognize that nobody would, in the 1980s, hire Thomas Edison as a junior research scientist. And yet, presumably, somebody should.

For libraries, oriented toward tradition and risk avoidance to a greater extent than most organizations and without the incentive of profits to justify chance taking, the temptation to hire a long line of inoffensive looking "grey" people is just about insurmountable. Nowhere is this pattern clearer than in the hiring of administrators for major academic libraries. Candidates for these posts come from three pools: (1) administrators of smaller academic libraries; (2) assistant administrators of large and even larger libraries; and (3) faculty scholars who would like to take a crack at running the library. All three of these candidate pools are almost automatically conditioned in support of the status quo, or at best of carefully suggested miniscule change. As this article will argue later, such attitudes will not serve us in the face of the crises we now face. Nevertheless, the climate is not ready for entrepreneurs in this setting. Entrepreneurs would without doubt make major changes, and there is no awareness that major changes are needed. Such changes could of course dramatically improve the library. They could also harm it and that is a chance nobody is prepared to take.

In addressing the issue of entrepreneurship in the library and information industry, Helena Strauch's chapter in "Careers in Information" assumes at the outset that entrepreneurial careers will be outside the structure of the traditional setting and outside the present library.[1] She stresses that such entrepreneurs leave their present employers and blaze new trails for themselves.

She emphasizes quite correctly the dangers, misconceptions, and myths that accompany entrepreneurship. The most significant of these is the point that while entrepreneurs are indeed free to follow their own hunches and implement their initiatives, their success will nevertheless be dependent on their ability to get others to see and accept the validity of what they see so clearly. The examples of library and information science pioneers she cites are Mortimer Taube, Saul Herner, Eugene Garfield, and Earl Coleman, among others. All fit the classic definition of the entrepreneur—brilliant, individualistic, visionary, courageous, impatient of the weaknesses of others—not builders of teams, delegators of authority, or developers of subordinates.

If that perception of irreconcilable differences between entrepreneurs and team managers were allowed to continue into the last 15 years of this century, then the impact on libraries of individuals with entrepreneurial spirit would indeed continue to be minimal. Bureaucratic organizations have efficient mechanisms for driving out the person who is different from the norm, because even those who are brighter, quicker and more efficient than the norm tend to make others uncomfortable. This is of course true throughout organizations, because human behavior is fairly generic. It is nowhere more true than in libraries for reasons already stated in part and to be elaborated later in this article. Students do not normally choose this profession in search of wealth or notoriety and the admonition of the 1970s that we should seek a consensus through consultation and participation has found an eager audience among librarians. That consensus decisions are invariably "safe," that they are usually unimaginative in conception and slow in development have been recognized as well for some time. Some administrators in the for-profit sector such as Thomas Watson, Jr., though, sought ways to balance individual initiative and innovation with the characteristics of a large slow-moving bureaucratic structure. They had the motive and incentive for greater profits and a greater market share, however. Libraries have no such performance measurement criteria and neither their staffs nor their users have come to expect any. We could therefore perceive ourselves as in a trap, discouraging entrepreneurs from entering our midst and driving away those who wander in by accident.

A recent development named by its originator, Gifford Pinchot III, as *in*trapreneurship seeks to differentiate his argument that entrepreneurs do not have to leave and that they can work within the organization.[2] Pinchot's ideas are worth examining, because, as will be argued later, probably no profession has a greater need for this newly termed intrapreneur than librarianship. Pinchot stresses the importance of entrepreneurial approaches within organizations, with examples drawn directly from the for-profit sector—and argues persuasively that organizations that depend on "style" of organizational behavior as opposed to a concentration on results pay a heavy penalty.

While the term "intrapreneur" may be new, the ideas are really not. Other managers and teachers of management have stated that a continued reliance on innovation is essential for success in any organizational setting. William Zucker, professor at the Wharton School of Business at the University of Pennsylvania, has argued that entrepreneurship is a part of the warp and woof of any organization. Robert T. Grohman, president of the clothing firm Levi Strauss, has stated that "Scarcity of innovation is the surest path to slackened competition, to emphasis on maintenance of effort, and finally, to inertia."[3] These writers, and others, argue that an atmosphere open to innovation requires a tolerance for failure, and an openness to risk.

It is perhaps Peter Drucker, the articulate and outspoken guru of management concepts, who puts the idea into its most useful perspective and who permits us to apply it to librarianship. It was Drucker who, a number of years ago, pointed out that managers only get credit for two activities, innovation and marketing, because operational maintenance of the status quo is assumed and earns no recognition. It was he who noted that managers needed to be innovative to avoid the risk of being boring, because boredom was a deadly sin in any management environment. Librarians, of course, can take the example from there. If we are taken for granted, if we are trivialized, and if our decisions not to generate an atmosphere of crisis then causes others to rush to solve them, it may be because we have not taken these injunctions to heart.

In a 1985 book *Innovation and Entrepreneurship* Drucker examines these issues in greater detail, and he makes some statements which librarians might find startling.[4] He argues, for example, that the last 15 years have seen the emergence of a truly entrepreneurial economy in the United States. This timing is interesting, because it would relegate the concept of "team management" to the 1960s, and replace it in the 1970s and 1980s with a more rugged individualistic model. For libraries, as always well behind their industrial role models, such a suggestion becomes particularly ironic. Our literature is still filled with urgings that we develop concepts of greater participation, consensus seeking, and committee decision structures, when Drucker now suggests that such an approach has been passé for some time.

The suggestion of the 1960s sociological argument was that people will work harder if they are happier and that what we really need are managers who are sensitive to the concerns and needs of people. That this "fad" has now run its course can also be seen from a general examination of the longevity of management theories and from an examination of recent newspaper accounts. It is most directly evident from the actions of corporations in the mid-1980s, which are ruthlessly stripping their organizations of middle management layers of coordinators, staff assistants, and facilitators, and relying on keeping individuals who "do things" and who "make things happen." The change, of course, is never total. Management fads have a way of swinging like pendulums, overcorrecting perceived imbalances and then precipitating a counteraction against an activity that had gone too far. Certainly no one would argue that sensitivity to individuals, an ability to listen, and a willingness to compromise are bad. What appears clear, however, is that these values as virtues in themselves have fallen by the wayside. Organizations do want individuals with these values if possible, more importantly they want people who will make a direct and personal contribution to the program of the organization, if necessary by cutting through the red tape and caution flags set up by the bureaucracy's "people people," the ones who do little but convene meetings and report the consensus achieved there. I attempted to address this fascination in our own field with style as opposed to substance of decision making in a column entitled "Participative Management is the Answer, But What Was the Question?"[5] The column drew little direct response, but at least some comment that I had rather cleverly exposed some of the weaknesses in an excessive use of participative processes. This exposure only pointed out that we had to work harder to make the process work, because participation was desirable as a social good and we needed to make it effective. Why, for heaven's sake? Because it makes for more efficient and effective libraries? Because it makes for more fulfilled and happy librarians? Neither point can be "proven," but in the 1960s such things did not have to be proven if they were "obvious." What we do know about job fulfillment would suggest that protecting staff members against abuse, unfairly low salaries, and objectives for which there are no resources of implementation are far more effective techniques than the recognized absurdity of sitting around in lengthy meetings pondering the undoable. I cannot help noting that as this is being written the radio reports the death of Admiral Hyman Rickover, one of the great, most effective, and to some, most obnoxious entrepreneurs. Rickover developed the atomic submarine, and in that process his unflagging enemy was the bureaucracy of the U.S. Navy, most particularly those admirals whose route to success was through the socialization process of getting along with others. The country club is still an effective route to success in the United States, as school ties are in Great Britain, party membership in the Soviet Union, and important relatives in the Middle East.

I hope that the reader will forgive the digression, which somehow seemed a necessary tribute at the time of writing. For libraries, the developments in management practice, and our own approaches to seeking collegiality and cooperation just as others turn to individuality and contribution may suggest that we are still, or perhaps once again, out of phase. As an educator and administrator I know that some libraries shun candidates who are "different," even though they know that in this case different may mean brighter and more articulate. I also know that some educators assign group projects and assign group grades, although they know that they cannot really tell who contributed what portion to the overall outcome, except that this contribution was almost never equally distributed. Hyman Rickover, by contrast, prided himself on refusing to accept recommendations with several equal signatures. He wanted to know who was taking responsibility and who would ultimately be credited or blamed. Rickover was unusual because he insisted on this practice in the 1960s when such behavior was considered bizarre. It is bizarre no longer, except perhaps in libraries and similar institutions.

In discussing entrepreneurship within the organization, Peter Drucker stresses that opportunities for innovation come from unexpected successes (the development of data base access services for libraries comes immediately to mind), or unexpected failures (here the obvious example would seem to be our failure to secure adequate financial support for our historic and traditional approaches). Drucker further argues that innovation should be based on an analysis of opportunities, that it should be kept as simple as possible, that it should start small, and that innovation should be for the present and not the future.

Although Drucker does not specifically discuss libraries, his book points to the particular difficulty of public service institutions in attempting to deal with innovation. The problems he identifies are certainly descriptive of libraries; yet it is his unswerving conclusion that ways must be found around these difficulties:

1. We are judged by budgets rather than by results. True enough, but the solution is self-evident. It lies in the concept of program budgeting, of starting with proposed activities and moving from these to budgets, rather than the other way around. Program budgeting, of course, has been in vogue in responsible administrative circles for 20 years. If it has not been applied to library budgets it is because we have not developed either the justification or the insistence that it should.

2. We depend on a multitude of constituents, any of whom has at least a partial veto over what we do. Again, this is certainly an accurate description of libraries. It opens questions of "turf," of who controls the decision process of how libraries function, the professionals or the amateurs. Turf battles are not uncommon in any discipline, but doctors and lawyers won theirs long ago. Teachers are presently involved in the struggle to determine who decides curriculum and classroom size. Librarians, by contrast, have generally been loath to broach the issue. Some, particularly in academia, even argue that users know better than we what the library should do, a statement made specious by the recognition that most users do not even know what the library *could* do, only what it does.

3. Public service institutions see their mission as one of "doing good," as a moral absolute rather than in economic terms. If we do not succeed, we assume either that we must try harder or obtain more resources. It does not readily occur to public service institutions to exam-

ine what they do and why they do it. Drucker must have been looking over our shoulders when he wrote that.

Drucker's most telling points for us come when he describes what is needed to develop an organizational climate hospitable to entrepreneurship and innovation. It is my preference to list these all at once and then comment on them in greater detail. Drucker's points are:

1. A clear definition of organizational mission
2. A realistic statement of objectives
3. The recognition that a failure to achieve objectives requires the redefinition of these objectives in terms that can be achieved
4. The need to look at innovation as an opportunity rather than as a threat

The application of Drucker's points to the scenario of the library is quite evident. Libraries do tend to have mission statements, but these tend to be open-ended and unsuited to quantification. Such mission statements as "provide library services to all the citizens of the community" or "support the research and teaching mission of the university" are not inappropriate as slogans, but they suggest a clear need for translation into objectives. Objectives, management theorists remind us, are statements of what is specifically going to be accomplished in a finite period of time. They are allied to an identification of needed resources, and to the development of plans and strategies for accomplishing these objectives.

It is here, and in Drucker's third point which argues that a failure to achieve objectives (particularly because of an inadequacy of resources) requires a redefinition of objectives, that libraries, and by inference, other public service institutions, fail so badly. It may be because we do not control our agenda and instead depend on constituents to tell us what to do, constituents who may not be the same individuals as those who control our resources. It may be, as Drucker has also suggested, because we believe in the "goodness" of our service, and therefore take a personal responsibility for providing it, regardless of resources. Certainly, when our managers suggest to us that "they have confidence in our ability to cope" or that "we do the best we can," those statements contain a tacit admission that the job really cannot be done. We are often reluctant, though, to make that necessary statement to complete the scenario. As library managers, we give our subordinates assignments that cannot be satisfactorily completed because there is not enough time or not enough resources. When we knowingly perpetrate this fraud by urging *them* to "do the best they can," we do so much damage to organizational morale that management styles of autocracy, consultation, or participation become irrelevant by comparison. When individuals are given jobs in which they cannot succeed that injustice transcends the style in which we do it.

And yet, as a wholly emerging literature on the management of declining resources suggests, we do badly in relating our resources to our objectives, likely because we are measured on the basis of budgets rather than results. If this is the case, and I am sure it is, it becomes puzzling that we are unwilling or at least unable to renegotiate those expected results based on the resources provided. The clue may be found in the last and by his definition most important characteristics in the Drucker description of public service institutions. Because we are here to do "good" and because we see our mission as a moral imperative rather than in more mundane down to earth terms, it may be precisely because we do not *want* to limit our objectives that we fail to tie them to the resources provided. However, in this noble and perhaps understandable aim, we make two fatal mistakes. The first is that by a failure to tie accomplishments to resources we insure both decreased resources and ultimately decreased accomplishments. In other words, we doom ourselves to failure because we are unwilling to take the risks necessary to be managers. We also fail to recognize, as Thomas Galvin has reminded us, that "management is a contact sport."[6]

Our second mistake is even more serious, because it makes victims of our subordinates. In our unwillingness to fight for the resources they need to accomplish their jobs or to restructure the job to meet the resources, we sentence subordinates to play a game they cannot win. It seems ironic to me that in this profession we spend so much time trying to implement in the 1980s a 1960s philosophy of personal decision involvement. At the same time we ignore a reality that has been around a lot longer and is not going to change—that we owe our subordinates a job they can accomplish with the training and resources provided—and that we owe them a chance to win, if they are willing to try. It takes no genius to figure out what happens to the morale of individuals who learn that they cannot win no matter how hard they try.

A number of recent articles dealing with the management of declining resources in the public sector, but more directly that by Bo Hedberg written a decade ago, tell us quite directly how to deal with this phenomenon.[7] Hedberg outlines the stages through which a management confronted by declining resources must pass to ultimately deal with the problem. The first is the premise that the decline is temporary and that nothing needs to be done because the problem will disappear on its own. This is of course occasionally true, but not nearly as frequently as we would like to believe, or as often our managers urge us to believe. The most obvious test for such a hypothesis is to ask what situation is likely to improve and why this will occur. Frequently, the hope for better days ahead is nothing more than wishful thinking. As often as not the cut presages further cuts in the future. The prudent manager, of course, deals with realities and not with fond hopes. In contrast to the teaching of children's fairy tales, wishing will not make it so.

Hedberg's second stage recognizes that the cut is not temporary, but that somehow "it can be absorbed." Many libraries allow themselves to be cajoled or pressured into accepting this scenario, but Hedberg notes quite clearly that the argument is bankrupt, for two reasons. The first is that it creates yet more pressures on efficiency, on doing what we do as rapidly and cheaply as possible, rather than allowing a concentration of effectiveness, an investigation of why we are doing what we are doing and a determination of possible alternatives. The second is that as we suggest to our subordinates that they must "do more" because the budget has been cut, we create two unacceptable premises. The first is that they must somehow bear the brunt and accept the blame for our failure to succeed as managers, because clearly one of our jobs as managers is the obtaining of resources. The second is that we entrap them into an admission that they can absorb more work, and thereby into a self-indictment of not having worked as hard as they could have. Subordinates are smarter than that. The suggestion that more work can be absorbed must be categorically rejected whether or not it has validity. If higher production quotas are unilaterally imposed, they are met with dire warnings that quality will suffer. Of course, having been issued, these warnings must be made to come true and therefore they do come true.

Ultimately, Hedberg argues, organizations can only deal with declining resources by reexamining and changing the premises of what is to be done, how it is to be done, or both. That clearly involves us in renegotiating the "contract" with our constituent groups. Sometimes it is these individuals who also directly or indirectly provide our funds and that negotiation should be relatively simple. In other situations, the constituents and source of funds represent different communities. It is then necessary for the librarian to clearly establish the relationship in the understanding of both groups—so that constituents know whom to blame and that budget cutters understand whatever risks they incur in cutting budgets. It must be obvious to all readers that if there are no perceived risks in the cutting of budgets or alternatively no credit to be gained in restoring or augmenting a library budget, then library budgets will indeed be automatically cut. This is true because there is inevitably credit to be gained for frugality and economy. If that action has no price it becomes an absurdly simple decision to make. Librarians who do not understand that political reality participate in their own destruction and fail to protect their organizations or their staffs. It is these individuals who are our truly incompetent managers.

Budget cuts and other failures of programs and initiatives, Drucker reminds us, provide excellent opportunities for innovation. It is important in this case to stop harboring grudges, to cease looking for scapegoats, and not to engage in lengthy and paralyzing analysis. Rather, Drucker suggests that the potential innovator and entrepreneur simply look around. Options will suggest themselves as long as we concentrate properly on objectives and not on processes themselves. It can be argued that declining environments not only provide opportunities for innovation, they make the process essential. For, as my college tennis coach well advised me, "always change a losing game. The worst that can happen is that you will still lose. You therefore risk nothing."[8]

As librarians have the opportunity to examine the admonitions of Drucker and others dealing with nurturing innovation and entrepreneurship within the organization structure, there are a number of concerns that must be kept in mind.

The first is that libraries, perhaps even beyond other public service institutions, tend to attract and then promote individuals with other than entrepreneurial and innovative characteristics. Entrepreneurs, we must remind ourselves, are not necessarily the most pleasant and affable of individuals. We can see this from the list of information entrepreneurs identified in Helena Strauch's chapter, all of them personally known to this writer. The point is that what they have done shows courage and it works. The biographical synopses of Admiral Hyman Rickover which now flood the media stress that same contradiction. Entrepreneurs and innovators are not likely to win popularity contests, if for no other reason than their advocacy for change, and most of the organization resists change. The job of the manager in this environment is to separate what is perceived to be beneficial change from change which can have negative implications or which is change simply for the sake of change. However, as libraries, rushing to implement the 1960s sociological model of governance, seek individuals less noted for iconoclastic brilliance than an ability to fit into a collegial mold, the likelihood of the survival of innovators and entrepreneurs becomes lessened. Protecting entrepreneurs in an organization requires effort as Thomas Watson, Jr., in his admonition to nurture and protect "wild ducks," constantly sought to remind IBM lower level administrators. I recall telling one of my subordinate supervisors in one of my information industry assignments: "You cause me more trouble than any three of my other subordinates put together. But you are worth it." It was the nicest compliment I could think of. Of course, this puts us in mind of one of the premises that management theory has recognized all along. Good subordinates make trouble. They are impatient for change, for improvement, and for personal reward. Only a self-confident supervisor can handle this. When organizational dynamics demand that the individual first "persuade" his or her co-workers, the cause is likely to be lost. Groups are unlikely to foster innovation. Group decisions tend to foster compromise and safe approaches. When we deliberately opt for such a tensionless environment, we give up a great deal. It was indicative to me that at least one of the criticisms about my article that questioned the blind adherence to participation as a management style conceded that indeed participation did not always work, but that we should strive to make it work. That approach has nothing to do with organization objectives and it has nothing to do with the role of the library. Nor, as we have learned, does it have much to do with making people "happy." Giving people job assignments at which they can succeed is more likely to do this, but such an action of course requires protecting them and the library from the imposition of objectives that cannot be accomplished.

Innovation and entrepreneurship involve risk. There is clearly the risk of failure, and would-be innovators must know that we are not just looking over their shoulder waiting for them to fail. Failure, in institutional initiatives and for individuals, is a normal thing to be expected, as long as there is some reasonable balance with success. It was interesting to note that Coca-Cola conferred a substantial salary increase on the executive who made the decision to implement the new formula Coca-Cola. That decision, marketing statistics clearly indicate, was a mistake and corporate management obliquely acknowledged that fact. The reward was not for success, it was for the courage to try.

Public service institutions such as libraries, we are reminded by Drucker, are not expected to take risks, because they are judged by their budgets and not by their accomplishments. If budgets were adequate that *might* be an acceptable approach, although not for the innovators and entrepreneurs who had accidentally drifted into our profession. However, we know that budgets are not adequate, and they are becoming less adequate all the time. We therefore must, for our own professional survival, concentrate on results rather than budgets, and apply a healthy dose of innovation and entrepreneurship to the process.

Drucker also notes that unexpected successes, unexpected problems, incongruities between what is and what ought to be, and the development of new knowledge and new technology all provide a fertile ground for the consideration of innovation. All these can be seen to apply to libraries and only a few examples will suffice to make the point. The reader can easily find his or her own.

1. The application of technology to the cataloging process, most specifically through the development of the MARC system, allows us to reexamine the premises and redesign the parameters of how we analyze.

That is particularly true for subject analysis. Subject analysis for books is sparse in the library cataloging process for a number of reasons, but two immediately come to mind. The economics of manual card filing limited the number of cards to be produced and filed. Having opted for a detailed analysis on each basic card of the descriptive features for the book and having decided to file at least under author, title, and other applicable descriptive tags, only at most two or three subject cards appeared affordable. Moreover, the difficulty with card catalogs of performing coordinated multi-term searches suggested the use of more generic subject terms, even though we recognized (or at least presumably recognized) that such broad headings with many cards would make subject searches difficult. If anyone doubts this he or she need only spend a little time at the divided catalog of a major academic library. Most subject searches are begun in the author-title catalog. Whatever the rationale for this historic approach, it is valid no longer. Computer access to bibliographic information permits not only the economic storage of more records, but also the coordinated searching of several access points. It provided for us the innovative and entrepreneurial opportunity to take advantage of the new technology by developing new analytical approaches, rather than just transferring manual cataloging rules to machines. It is perhaps ironic to note that one entrepreneurial commercial information service is now bringing out a tool with which to search for book information through greater subject detail. It is a need we have failed to address and at least somebody perceived the gap.

2. The development of computerized access for bibliographic searching has made that exercise far more productive, far more worthwhile, far more interesting, and at the same time far more complex. It makes historic reference department budgets based on the manual perusal of card files and published indexes totally irrelevant. This development also suggests a relatively simple justification for a manyfold increase in the public service budget of libraries, based not on history but on need and opportunities. It is, in any budgetary setting that concentrates on results, relatively easy to do. In the case of bibliographic searching, it is easy to demonstrate that the funds will be spent in any case and undoubtedly spent less efficiently if outside the library budget. A budgetary increase is also easy to do because the management literature reminds us that large increases with significant results are far easier to justify than small increases which produce no noted change. The sad indictment is not that we have failed, it is that by and large we have not tried. Instead, we have produced a tortuous literature that argues that teaching individuals to do their own information searching work is the "better" approach. This argument runs counter to evidence that we do it more economically and more effectively and that most users would rather delegate the process if they could. What we have done here is to

continue to define the library's tasks as we have always defined them and to expel all tasks that do not fit priority definitions. We have of course applied new techniques to the tasks we have always performed, but that is neither innovative nor entrepreneurial. It is safe, it is sure—it is also boring and in the long term probably suicidal.

3. As a corollary to increased bibliographic access we have also developed a heightened demand for document delivery, as users and reference librarians are no longer restricted to finding out about things in our own card catalogs. Statistics indicate a growing reliance on interlibrary loan. We ought to be thrilled at that opportunity to broaden our services, although these increases are usually reported in our literature as troublesome problems. The reason, of course, is that we have never developed an updated strategy for dealing with the issue of shipping material from one library to another. We prefer to avoid the problem by pretending that this is nothing more than a mutually shared exchange. That, of course, becomes the ultimate trivialization of the process. Fortunately, technology has developed techniques to help us with this problem and these techniques are widely in use. Paper copy can be reproduced by bouncing it off a satellite, or by transmitting it via telephone lines to a printer at the receiving end. I recall a demonstration of this process at the Library of Congress over 30 years ago. The quality was not very good, but the inventor clearly saw value for libraries as soon as quality improved. Little did he know that quality had nothing to do with our use of this technique. Our concern was and remains cost. However, we do not need to be as esoteric. Many commercial services, and even the formerly traditionbound U.S. Postal Service, now have mechanisms for one day delivery. Why do we not utilize this service? Why do we continue to insist on using package delivery and lower class delivery at that? That process, added to delays at both library ends, can result in a wait of four weeks or longer. Is it because we really believe that what we do is so trivial that it is not worth a greater effort? I hope nobody will suggest that it is not because we do not have the money, because that excuse, if accepted, would effectively prevent any change from ever taking place. We obviously don't have the money, but the answer is to get some.

Innovation and entrepreneurship in this profession are rare enough that when some example does come to mind, it really stands out. Several years ago one of our brightest Indiana graduates accepted a position with an industrial firm to provide on-line search services in that organization's small library, services never offered previously. The corporation made it clear that this was only a one year appointment, funded by appropriations that would not and could not be sustained and that under no circumstances would the job extend beyond one year. Many students were and are reluctant to take such a position, but this young entrepreneur and innovator had no reservations. She told me that she had a full year to make herself totally indispensable and that long before that year was up management would be convinced that the funds had to be found somewhere to maintain her service. Of course, she was completely correct. The decision to turn this into a full-time position was made before the end of six months, to make sure she did not start looking for another job. Peter Drucker has also told us this. He reminds us that if we can create utility, price is almost always irrelevant. Put another way, we know, or we ought to know, that corporations, universities, and even small municipalities find ways to afford what they really want to afford, and that could include library activities.

Entrepreneurs and innovators know that too, probably instinctively. I am not sure that one can really develop entrepreneurial and innovative perceptions in individuals unless the germ is already there. What we must do is find such individuals, attract them to our profession, and then nurture and protect them from all of the organizational forces that demand that they resemble everybody else.

Entrepreneurs are not often themselves the managers of large enterprises, including major libraries, although small and special libraries can function with entrepreneurs in charge. There is in management too much of the administrative, of the routine, of the maintenance of stability to allow senior executives in charge that much flexibility. It is an old management axiom that the higher one progresses within a management structure, the less freedom one has. What senior library managers can and should do is create a climate that welcomes and encourages innovators and entrepreneurs, that protects them from second-guessers when they fail, that guards them in their "difference" from colleagues and coworkers, and that makes it clear that risk is welcome even when it leads to failure, and is still preferable to never trying or suggesting anything. Finally, upper level library managers must create an environment in which people care about the organization, in which they understand the importance of their own contribution, and in which they are given assignments with a relationship to the resources provided—assignments in which they have a chance to succeed. That is of course true in all organizational dynamics, but it is particularly true in settings such as libraries, in which such a climate does not automatically develop. This, as already noted, is because those outside the library with whom we deal expect little and least of all innovation and change. By and large, our users want us to continue what they already find comfortable, only they want more of it. Our bosses want the same thing, only they want it all at lower cost.

It is an intolerable no-win strategy, and it can only be changed by individuals with the foresight to seek a better way, and the courage to fight for it.

Intrapreneurs are revolutionaries. They cause trouble but they are worth it. Hewlett Packard, one of the organizations mentioned by Pinchot as supportive of entrepreneurship and innovation, goes so far as to issue a Medal of Defiance, awarded in recognition of extraordinary contempt and defiance beyond the normal call of duty.

It is not at all certain that even Hewlett Packard, which encourages this process among its engineers, either welcomes or expects it from its librarians. As we already know from Drucker, librarians are not judged by their accomplishments, only by their budgets. Because it is for us a no-win situation, we have to change it in our dealings with those who fund us.

However, we have to do more. We have to attract innovative and entrepreneurial individuals into our profession, we have to hire them knowing that they will make trouble and protect them when they do. Obviously, only if their contribution turns out to be constructive. However, our 1980s application of outmoded 1960s management values which concentrate not on accomplishment but on getting along within an overall group model, a team approach whose theme is consensus, compromise, conformity and comfort, will quite effectively weed out whatever entrepreneurs we might attract before they can even begin to make a difference. We must have the discipline to change this model ourselves. We have no choice. Our present system of management structure and decision distribution is safe and comfortable, but it doesn't work. It would not work in a corporate profit center setting, either, but at least there we would find an executive like Thomas Watson, Jr. to worry about it. The discipline must come from within, because as already noted nobody else cares what we do, only how much we spend. Many in our user communities, of course, would just as soon we changed nothing that is already comfortable. That is unacceptable, because it trivializes our own professional role.

Most of all, we must search for individuals who seek to destabilize the status quo and who are willing to take risks in search of improvement and change. Not high risks. Calculated moderate risks, but risks all the same. Why? Because what we are doing now does not work and I do not think I need to prove that contention. In the final analysis, my old tennis coach is still a good management philosopher. Always change a losing game.

References

1. Strauch, Helena M. *Entrepreneurship in the information industry.* In *Careers in information,* edited by Jane F. Spivack. White Plains, NY: Knowledge Industry Publications, 1982, pp. 73–101.

2. Pinchot, Gifford III. *Intrapreneuring: Why you don't have to leave the corporation to become an entrepreneur.* New York: Harper & Row, 1985.

3. Nelton, Sharon. *Finding room for the intrapreneur.* Nation's Business, 72, Feb., 1984, pp. 50–52.

4. Drucker, Peter F. *Innovation and entrepreneurship.* New York: Harper & Row, 1985.

5. White, Herbert S. *Participative management is the answer, but what was the question?* Library Journal 110 (no. 13), Aug. 1985, pp. 62–63.

6. Galvin, Thomas J. *Maxims for managerial survival in tough times.* Conference handout available from the author.

7. Hedberg, Bo and others. *Camping on seesaws. Prescriptions for a self-designing organization.* Administrative Sciences Quarterly 21(1), pp. 41–65, 1976.

8. White, Herbert S. *Bjorn Borg and the library materials budget.* Information and Library Manager 1, June 1981, pp. 3–4.

OH, WHERE HAVE ALL THE LEADERS GONE?

Some in our field have decried the end of the "great man" era. I am not really sure this is true, and certainly for our field in the present time the sexist terminology is misnamed.

Leaders are rarely recognized until after their time. In part this is because we can't really evaluate contribution until the dust has settled. It is a fascinating game to watch historians revise our historical view of presidents, and to determine which have gone up over time in a more objective historical perspective (Truman), and which have gone down (Kennedy). British Prime Minister Margaret Thatcher is without doubt a leader, but opinions about that leadership vary widely, and cannot really be resolved while she is still in office.

... BUT YOU CAN'T MAKE THEM DRINK

In part this is because leaders are not necessarily popular. They want to take us somewhere, and some of us don't necessarily want to go there. Others, with something of an anarchist streak, don't want to go anywhere at all. Where we find leaders who indeed are popular we worry that style rather than substance governs the persuasiveness of their success. The contradiction is perhaps best expressed in the realization that we believe in leaders and in leadership, but that on a personal basis few of us want to be led.

Nor do any of us really want to be characterized as followers, although leadership implies followership. The emotional success of the descriptive phrase participative management, and the huge popularity of committee decision processes, is precisely because it appeals to the most

From *Library Journal* 112 (1 October 1987):68–69.

democratic of all instincts in us. We believe in equality, without probably ever thinking that equality is unfair because talent and dedication are unequal. The important goal is equal opportunity. We find the populist emphasis in approaches that blur individual distinctions by a reference to the "team" approach, frequently borrowing from sports terminology, and we fail to recognize that teams work only when each member knows what he or she is supposed to do and what he or she is not supposed to do.

PRESERVING THE WILD DUCK

There is considerable danger, to my thinking, that the uniformity and blandness of consensus decisions will lead straight to mediocrity. The risks of depending on the group process, and the safety that comes from a consensus in the sense that even if we are all wrong we are all safe, has been dealt with facetiously in such musical comedies as *How To Succeed in Business Without Really Trying* and, seriously, in the musings and writings of business leaders such as Thomas Watson Jr., who constantly exhorted his IBM subordinate executives to tolerate and protect the "wild ducks," those individuals who can be difficult and even obnoxious but who may have tremendous contributions and insights within them.

The term wild duck was carefully chosen, because Watson recognized that as ducks become tamed to human feeding and control they lose their survival skills as ducks, and the process is fundamentally irreversible. When librarians decide it is most prudent to promotional opportunities to keep quiet and go along with the system, much is lost to the library.

Probably the most obvious example of the "get along by not rocking the boat" syndrome is found in the very closed system of research library administration. Major research library directors emerge from a candidate pool of directors of smaller research libraries, or of assistant directors of still larger libraries. It is of course possible for unique and distinctive leaders to rise to the top in this process because we have examples of it, but they are really swimming upstream. The system is geared to protect the collegial and the conformists.

Harried supervisors frequently find that employees who are "different" are a lot of trouble. One of the reasons is obviously the fact that much, and perhaps most, of the time an obnoxious co-worker is simply obnoxious, without redeeming virtues. And yet the management literature tells us that we are supposed to encourage and support individualism, that we should seek aggressive or at least assertive subordinates who want their own way. That sounds ugly, and the reader will note how much better it reads as "the will to win." Style counts for at least as much as substance in this process.

IT'S A MATTER OF STYLE

It has been suggested that people come in one of four work-style packages: inert, reactive, responsible, and creative, and I doubt that these terms require further description. We obviously don't want inert people, but we have them and we have difficulty in getting rid of them unless they start breaking rules. At the other extreme, creative people are generally considered too much trouble. They are damned with the statement that they are not team players, without the clarification that in management's interpretation team players are the ones who block while we carry the ball. Responsible people are, of course, the ideal, but for the most part we settle, gladly, for reactive people—the individuals who will do exactly what they are told and don't make trouble.

AUTHORITY IS A FOUR-LETTER WORD

Leadership, much as we admire it in the abstract, is something we suspect in the specific. This is because leaders seek authority, and authority is a dirty word in organizational communications. Responsibility is the clean word, but responsibility without authority becomes frustration. The most obvious source of authority is the legal power that comes with a higher-level job. Because it is the most obvious, it is also the one that should be used as little as possible. Managers who resort to legal power primarily or exclusively are certainly not leaders, because they have no credibility.

Competent and referent power are far more acceptable and far more workable sources for authority. Under the former, subordinates accept the premise of your expertise and greater knowledge. Under the latter, even more successful type, they have accepted you as a role model, and want to please you because they want to emulate you.

It is the referent authority users who are also natural leaders, but there is no obvious connection between the authority of management and the mystique of leadership. There is clear evidence all around us that, despite our insistence on democratic and participatory processes, the emergence of leaders is a natural and perhaps unavoidable process. Not all leaders are managers, and not all leaders are necessarily either "nice" or "wholesome." Some leaders are destructive of organizations and of individual lives and careers, but the process of recognizing and following leaders continues.

THE EVOLUTION OF A LEADER

The characteristics of what makes a leader are pretty clearly understood by behavioral scientists. They include social sensitivity and ability to judge others and anticipate their reactions; active participation, a characteristic involving energy and enthusiasm; intelligence and good communications skills, particularly as persuasive oral communicators. The most potentially sinister leadership characteristic is charisma, and we know what harm charismatic leaders can do. However, although we recognize that leadership is a process that can take place for good or for bad, we also realize that leaders evolve out of any setting, even the most democratically structured.

As Laurence Peter has reminded us, promotions are not based on either leadership skills or management orientation, they are most commonly presented as a reward for outstanding work as a nonsupervisor. We take this largely irrelevant action because promotion to management is the only mechanism available to us to provide salary increases. Most organizations have not realized, and certainly libraries have not, that reward for outstanding performance can take place through a process of dual career ladders, and that there is no rule that says that a subordinate cannot earn more than his or her boss.

Disasters can occur particularly when the supervisor is a nonleader, and the priorities between that individual and the real group leader are in conflict. This is why it makes perfectly good sense to notice natural leaders within the library and groom them for management promotion, to try to merge the two processes and minimize potential conflict. In one of my corporate posts I encountered on almost my first day the presentation of a long-standing group grievance. I found the grievance valid, and the group spokesperson, who presented the case reasonably and articulately on behalf of his fellow workers, immediately became my prime candidate to be the group's new supervisor. It turned out to be both a wise and a popular choice, but wise was more important than popular.

While I believe that leadership qualities are probably more instinctive than learned, as a profession and as individuals we can do much to encourage leaders to develop. This is because potential leaders don't necessarily need nurturing but they do need mentoring, and they need protection from those who see any new idea not their own as a threat.

LEADERSHIP VS. SUPERVISION

Does librarianship need leaders? Are things really so perfect that anyone can be uncertain of the answer? What sort of leaders? In his book, *The*

Classic Touch: Lessons in Leadership from Homer to Hemingway, John Clemens tries to argue that we have been dealing with a continuum all along. He notes that Plato, in examining Athens's demise, had few kind things to say about democratic, people-oriented management. Excellence, innovation, and creativity, he argued, could not flourish by committee.

In an attempt to update their now somewhat jaded 1960s jargon, some of the "warm fuzzies" in the behavioral sciences who preached as Dr. Pangloss did, the "best of all possible worlds," now try to tell us that anybody can be a leader. However these writers confuse leadership with supervision. I agree that almost anyone can be trained to become at least an acceptable manager, and it is essential that we work at this because lots of people are named to managerial posts for the wrong reasons, in our field as in others. They can be taught at least to be passable managers, and they must be taught.

But leadership skills are not the same as management skills, and primarily they are instinctive although they can be refined. The confusion becomes most apparent when it is suggested that leaders seek consensus and learn to compromise. The search for consensus is the very opposite of what they do, and if they agree to compromise it is part of a pragmatic process of yielding a little bit now in order to win a lot later.

Of course leaders are manipulative. Some are nice about it and some less so. Leaders seek to win first of all for themselves, but good leaders win for all of us. However, as noted, leadership is not necessarily an issue of popularity. Our own field's undoubtedly greatest leader, Melvil Dewey, has been described as both arrogant and bigoted. We remember that, but we forgive it for leaders like Dewey whose accomplishments we recognize and appreciate.

TOO MANY CHIEFS?

It is just as well that not everyone wants to be a leader and that some prefer to be followers, because an organization populated only with would-be leaders would be chaotic, although that never happens in libraries. Clemens notes that in the corporate world as things get tougher there is a greater call for leadership management style, for individuals not afraid to take risks, to make difficult and sometimes unpopular decisions, and to take personal responsibility without hiding behind faceless committees.

Potential leaders are not really hard to spot. Even as they enter library school as students they are easy to notice, because there aren't that many. I worry about whether or not our institutions will provide a hospitable climate for them, as contrasted to those who may do better in the promotion game because even as students they take an informal poll before they ever express an opinion. We can "ordain" managers and perhaps even make those with little management potential passable, but we can't ordain leaders or make leaders out of nonleaders. We can, however, develop and assist those with leadership potential, or alternatively frustrate and even kill their will to lead.

HOW TO COPE WITH AN INCOMPETENT SUPERVISOR

That librarians might report to incompetent supervisors should hardly surprise us. The work of Laurence Peter shows us that managers are not necessarily created because of a perception of management skills. That problem is accentuated in libraries: few librarian managers initially chose this profession because of a desire to manage, and many of the non-librarians to whom we report have no real interest in libraries. The following article examines this problem and suggests tactics for dealing with it.

There is very little in the otherwise voluminous management literature that discusses the care and feeding of incompetent bosses. There is a great deal written about motivating, challenging, and otherwise stimulating indifferent or unproductive subordinates, and one can assume that the reason for this imbalance is either the presumption that managers are competent by definition or the fact that these articles are written by managers or by those who aspire to become managers. Nevertheless, much of what is written about "managing" the relationship with subordinates also applies to dealing with one's own supervisor.

The purpose of management communication in either case is to get something accomplished. What that is depends on organizational objectives, plans, and strategies. Libraries, while long on eloquent goals, are short on realistic objectives and strategies for implementing them. The interpretation of what the library is to do therefore becomes inevitably a highly personal one, with which others up or down the management chain may or may not agree.

We also know from much management writing that since individuals personalize their decisions they have no trouble in unifying personal and organizational objectives, usually by adjusting the latter to fit the former. This is done innocently and usually without even awareness, and it helps explain why being urged to "cooperate" so frequently falls on deaf ears. We do believe in co-operation, but to most of us it means doing things our way, not because we are selfish (we never see ourselves as selfish) but because we are right.

Interaction with an incompetent therefore only affects us negatively. Incompetent subordinates are usually seen as concerns because they don't produce either qualitatively or quantitatively what they are supposed to, and this becomes a waste of resources.

Incompetent bosses are something else, because in general bosses don't really "do" anything of a directly productive nature in relation to operational plans. Their competence or incompetence is related directly to whether they help us or thwart us, and frustration comes especially when we can't even fathom why they have acted as they have. A consistent and predictable approach is always preferable in any management communication, and we will probably happily settle for incompetent bosses who nevertheless do as we ask them. That issue of what we want them to do for us will be explored later in this article, but let it suffice now to point out that incompetence among subordinates and incompetence among superiors are entirely different issues.

SELECTION PROCESS

We must note whether the supervisor is also a librarian or a non-librarian who may have been selected as the librarian's boss without having demonstrated either aptitude for or interest in the job. The latter situation is common in special libraries, but it is even possible in public libraries. Individuals may seek a board post because they love children or literature or because their main concern is to see that taxpayers are protected against expensive library programs. Sometimes appointing them is a handy thing to do. When the supervisor is a non-librarian we must factor in at least two additional causes for incompetence—lack of interest and confusion. Supervisors who are themselves librarians at least don't have those excuses.

However, it should not really surprise us to find that there are incompetent librarians who are supervisors. Peter (1969) eloquently and humorously points out that supervisors are not usually created because of any perceived aptitude for this process, but rather because they excel in some pre-supervisory or non-supervisory activity. This may not only be irrelevant, it may even be counter-productive, because when the best cataloguers become heads of cataloguing they may bring unrealistic expectations to the interactive process with subordinates or become impatient with those who don't learn as rapidly as they did.

It is of course mediocre employees who require the most supervision. For outstanding subordinates, a great deal of supervision is unnecessary and perhaps counter-productive, and for imcompetents and willfully destructive employees, our energies are better spent figuring out ways to remove or at least isolate them so that they can't poison the atmosphere. Outstanding performers who have been promoted to management without further guidelines and training may think that everyone not as good as they is incompetent, which includes most of the employee pool.

In addition to that general observation about the supervisory pool—that we don't pick good supervisors because we don't seek good supervisors—a further injunction must be introduced that applies specifically to librarians. Librarians do not usually choose this profession because they are either seeking power or because they are anxious to manage. In fact, the overriding need to manage comes as a huge and unwelcome surprise to many library school students. Finally, until recently (and even now in part) women were categorically excluded from management opportunities in our field as in others. In librarianship, however, the impact was much greater, because we deprived ourselves almost automatically of eighty per cent of our potential management pool. We chose specifically from the small segment of male librarians and then often for the wrong reason.

And yet, the situation is not as catastrophic as one might expect. This is because successful management involves much common sense and implementation of the golden rule. If we do unto others remembering how we might feel if someone did the same thing unto us, it is not a bad way to start. Except for a fortunately small, mentally ill segment of managers who crush and destroy for the sheer pleasure this gives them, most supervisors, in our field as in others, think that they are decent individuals trying to do their best under difficult circumstances and that they are as fair as they know how to be. We as subordinates may not agree with this evaluation, but if we pitch our arguments on that plane of their own self-assessment, there is a reasonable chance of success.

RESPONSIBILITIES

The formal and assigned role of supervisors has two ingredients: to exercise control and to make decisions. Supervisors definitely govern the control process, most often seen in budgetary, hiring, and space constraints. However, it is the smaller of the two requirements, because computer programs can be developed to exercise control, sometimes more consistently and effectively than can be done by people. What computer programs cannot do is to make necessary unprogrammed decisions; this is fundamentally what supervisors must do. They must decide. One hopes that they will decide well, but in any case they must decide.

Even that statement requires some modification. We don't really, in most cases, want our bosses to decide. We want them to approve, and we need that approval simply because they have authority and we don't. There are situations in which we require our supervisor's intellectual input for a problem we have been unable to solve, but that is not a frequent occurrence. Most of the time we know what we want to do, and what we seek are support and approval—in authorizing funds, in clearing political roadblocks, in dealing with a difficult interpersonal problem affecting a manager or a client in a high place of authority.

We want our supervisors to use their power on our behalf far more often than we seek their advice on how to answer a reference question or assign an elusive classification number. In fact, we recognize quite instinctively that supervisors who are full of ideas and suggestions about what we should be doing drive us crazy, even if, and perhaps especially if, they are correct. If there is one thing we have learned from Japanese models it is that subordinates and groups of subordinates should be left alone as much as possible and should be permitted to develop their own methodologies and internal value systems as long as these do not conflict with the organization's objectives. That is delegation as contrasted with assignment, and of course it assumes that the organization does have objectives, plans, and strategies and not just idealistic goals.

Even when managers need to make negative decisions, that process is necessary, because a negative decision is better than no decision at all. Managers (or supervisors as they are usually called lower in the management chain) are therefore expected by the organization to exercise control, but they are also expected to make decisions. Much of the management literature addresses the concern that managers have about being able to make correct decisions in an environment in which their own subordinates try to keep important facts from them. Managers, we are told by the general literature, want to make decisions. This is probably an accurate generalization, but it applies far less in libraries. Why is this?

QUESTIONS AND ANSWERS

Are our managers stupid? Some undoubtedly are, but certainly not nearly as many as we might want to think. Drucker (1985) suggests that we never assume our managers are stupid. Chances are it isn't true, but even if it were, giving them credit for intelligence only serves to flatter and compliment them.

Don't they care? This can be the case particularly when dealing with non-librarian supervisors if these individuals have no understanding of what difference their decision will make and, even more fundamentally, what differentiates a good library from a poor one. If they lack the ability to make that distinction, they will inevitably seek refuge in the control half of their managerial model, because in the absence of any other accomplishments they will at least get credit for having saved the organization money. One certainty in any management communication environment is that if we can't get our bosses to talk about the ideas and programs we want to implement we will end up talking only about money. That is for the library, as for any overhead organization without products to sell or income to generate, a disastrous level of discussion.

As noted earlier, most of our uncaring supervisors tend to be non-librarians, because they don't understand what difference their decisions make, because we have failed to articulate our needs in terms that they understand and care about, or because the stated goals are so grandiose and impractical that they sense they are not achievable and they might as well save money. However, some uncaring managers are librarians, and this raises questions as to what they really care about.

Are they afraid? Some managers are afraid of their subordinates, but a far greater number are afraid of the decision process itself, primarily because they fear they might make a wrong decision. They fail to understand not only that their primary responsibility is making decisions, but also that the absence of a decision represents a decision, albeit often an unattractive one, just as the absence of communication ("I don't have time to talk to you") is a specific form of communication that sends very clear messages.

For managers who are afraid to make decisions, it is unfortunate that recent developments in management faddism (and management is very much given to fads) provide them with excuses for not making decisions. Participative management and consensus decision structures are appropriate when properly utlized in settings in which they make sense. When they are simply used by managers as a decision avoidance device, it is bad for the organization, and those kept busy in this committee process know perfectly well they are being used.

Don't they know how to supervise? This is of course a classic problem, not only because supervisors are often improperly selected, but also because they are almost never trained. Surprisingly, this is not necessarily a major problem for the subordinate, although for the employing organization inefficient supervisors are a considerable waste and expense. It is not as significant a problem for the subordinate because, in actual fact, we ask very little of our bosses.

What we do ask can be encapsulated in only five brief phrases: Let us make sure that I understand what you expect of me; Leave me alone to do my own job in my own way; Help me if I ask for help, and then do so without moralizing and lecturing; Tell me how I did; Reward (or at least treat) me in accordance with what you have just told me. These are basically simple requests, and even an unsophisticated and raw supervisor can become at least passable at carrying them out.

If we bear in mind that once individuals know their jobs they only want to be treated fairly and rewarded properly, left alone and helped only if they seek help, the manager's job is not really that complex. For the employing organization concerned about goal integration and maximum allocation of resources, requirements can be greater, but if managerial selection is improperly made and no training is provided to supervisors, relatively little can be expected.

THE OCTOPUS AND OTHERS

There are of course other reasons for incompetent, malicious, and manipulative supervision. Perhaps the most common is what Belker (1978) has referred to as the octopus manager, an individual who smothers subordinates by insisting on making all of the decisions. Even when the octopus is competent, the results are destructive because individual development and initiative are smothered. However, most octopus managers are not all that competent. A variant of the octopus is the boss who does not necessarily want to make all the decisions, but wants to take all the credit.

Management problems come in all shapes and sizes. Some supervisors are paralysed by the decision process because their fear of errors outweighs their desire for recognition and advancement; these managers are difficult to deal with because they have no interest in being persuaded, only in being left alone. Other supervisors are faddists or "technology happy," and they represent the opposite problem because they seek change for its own sake.

Whatever the problem, it must be faced by subordinates at least to the extent of allowing them to function. When the subordinate is also a manager, this means being permitted to carry out assigned duties with adequate support or authority. It is a recently recognized classic in management that responsibility, as a "clean" word, is generously assigned. Authority, as a "dirty" word in management parlance, is often withheld. And yet even common sense tells us that there must be a balance.

STRATEGIES FOR COPING

How do subordinates deal with these problems? They must start by developing a plan to manage their own managers. Threats do not work here, and neither does the use of naked power, because subordinates do not have any. However, managers can frequently be manipulated into making the proper decision (at least from the subordinate's point of view) by the presentation of at least two alternatives, perhaps only one of which may really be acceptable. The supervisor can choose one of the two alternatives or develop a third alternative, if indeed there is one.

The supervisor cannot simply reject all options and send the subordinate away empty-handed, and this is stressed because some supervisors will try it. "I don't care for any of these alternatives! Bring me some others." To refute that management strategy, we must fall back on the premise that managers want to appear fair and reasonable, at least to themselves and members of their families. What they have just said is neither fair nor reasonable, and they must be forced to face this.

Other strategies are possible depending on the problem. If the manager is afraid to take risks, then a scenario must be created in which the absence of decisions creates even greater risk for the manager.

The management truism that suggests that responsibility can be delegated but is always also retained may have to be called to the boss's attention, and it can be found in the literature. If my operation (or my library) functions badly, it is presumably my fault, but it is equally your fault. That is basic management at its simplest, but your manager may not know it. Find him or her things to read on decision making, good management, communications, etc.

If the manager perceives (quite correctly at times) that credit will be given for cost reductions, then the scenario must be created in which the manager also understands that even greater credit can be given for developing a unique environment and that risk can be encountered when, despite cheapness, there is no real economy. Doing this requires something all subordinates must do, but something librarians in general often do badly. We must differentiate—for our managers and for those who have power over our managers—between a good library service and a poor one, and we must make sure that just as they seek credit they also are willing to accept blame if their decision caused poor service.

Drucker, in writing about service professionals (a group which includes librarians), stresses that they are known and expected to accept the "moral imperative" of seeing to it that proper services are provided, whether or not they are funded and supported. In other words, we now try to interpose ourselves between incompetent supervisors and at least potentially irate clients in order to protect them, rather than provide road maps to their homes and offices.

Service professionals (including librarians) are also considered fair game for the management ploy that suggests that objectives are somehow independent of resources and that budget cuts can be absorbed without anything happening. Hedberg (1976) was among the first to point out the bankruptcy of such an approach, because it is of course sheer nonsense and everybody knows it. It causes you to betray your own subordinates by accepting on their behalf tasks at which they cannot possibly succeed, and this makes you an incompetent manager. In adddition, one implementation of the suggestion that we do more (or the same) with less only leads to an endless succession of such implementations.

When resources are reduced, programs change, and in general they become smaller. If anyone complains or asks why this happens, the answer must come from the management that made the decision in the first place. It seems fair because it is fair, and ultimately managers, even the most recalcitrant ones, must acknowledge that fairness. Most of all, we must get managers to deal with reality. Paradoxically, the management literature tells us that this is what they want to do, but the management truisms in the literature sometimes don't reach down to libraries.

Do these strategies work all the time? Can we ensure that somehow we can take an incompetent boss and inevitably create a successful situation in which we either retrain the incompetent or at least get that person to function for our support and to our requirements? No, we can't. If there is one thing we know about management, it is that nothing works all the time.

If you have realistically assessed the problem as insoluble, there are two remaining options:

1. Quit if you can, and find something more satisfying to do. Life is too short to endure endless torture.

2. If you can't quit because the pay is too good, the job is convenient, or retirement benefits are too attractive and can't be transferred, then stop feeling guilty. If your job cannot be properly performed despite all of your efforts because of an incompetent manager about whom you can do nothing, then the fact that the users are not properly served is not your fault. Channel your energies into something else: gardening, contract bridge, learning a new language, improving you bowling average. Anything will do, but retain your sanity.

Some incompetent supervisors can be persuaded or trained to achieve a modicum of competency, and some, if properly motivated, can even become supportive. Others can be successfully evaded. However, some will, for reasons that vary, block and thwart all of your initiatives and good intentions. Only in television programs is there a successful settlement of all problems, which allows you to happily heed the sponsor's last commercial message. Learn to differentiate between problems you can solve and problems you cannot solve, and develop your strategies accordingly.

References

1. Belker, Loren B. *The First-time Manager: A Practical Guide to the Management of People.* AMACOM, New York, 1978.

2. Drucker, Peter F. *Innovation and Entrepreneurship.* Harper & Row, New York, 1985.

3. Hedberg, Bo, et al. "Camping on Seesaws, Prescriptions for a Self-Designing Organization." *Administrative Sciences Quarterly,* vol. 21, no. 1, 1976. p. 41–65.

4. Peter, Laurence J. *The Peter Principle.* William Morrow & Co., New York, 1969.

MANAGING LIBRARIES AND THE SOCIETAL MORAL GOOD

My column "Library Managers—Female and Male" (White Papers, *LJ*, February 1, 1987, p. 58–59) triggered more reaction, most of it personally addressed to me, than anything else I have written. In general that would please me, but the vitriol in some of the comments surprised me. They included both a questioning of my commitment to equal opportunity for women and flat statements that management could never be a sex-neutral process. Indeed, it was suggested that because women were "nurturing" they were better managers, and that my comments represented nothing more than a restatement of the tedious old male viewpoint.

LIBRARIANS AT WAR?

That what I thought was a rather innocuous statement of the obvious would be taken as a salvo fired in a war between sexes disappointed me, and that for some my own sex made me an automatic enemy chagrined me even more. If I am in such a war, my own role in trying to educate assertive "opposition soldiers" would appear particularly incongruous.

However, my earlier column really said very little that was new. I noted that managers were managers regardless of sex, and that is was because of their qualifications that I assumed they ought to be appointed. The job of managers is to help articulate and accomplish organizational objectives as translated into plans and programs.

When it comes to personnel management the requirements can be simply stated as two in number, and they are not remotely contradictory. One is to see to it that the organization that has appointed you to management gets its money's worth from the resources (largely people) entrusted

From *Library Journal* 113 (15 April 1988):60–61.

to your stewardship. The other is to see to it that these same people receive what they deserve from the employer. I have no patience with those who take advantage of the financial naïveté and vulnerability of librarians by paying them only what they must, and not what they should, and many of the perpetrators of this inequity are other librarians.

As individuals are complex and different, so issues do not lend themselves to simplistic approaches. I attempted to address that concern in "Participative Management Is the Answer, but What Was the Question?" (White Papers, *LJ*, August 1985, p. 62–63). My point was that participation had taken on a moral quality of its own, a "willed" goodness, rather than the plausible and easily supportable premise that one should let individuals shape the methods and tools of their own work as much as possible, and that there was no benefit in managing what does not need to be managed. It is that line that managers have to know how to draw. Again, some of the reaction to this column supported my premise. Writers would grudgingly acknowledge that I and others had done a "slick" job of raising questions about participative management that were difficult to answer, but they argued that we ought to do it anyway "because it was the right thing to do."

THE ULTIMATE IRRELEVANCY

My main concern with "nurturing" as a recently promulgated management value system is that it can lead us into that most dangerous of management traps, being satisfied with answers of *why* rather than insisting on answers of *what*. Ultimately, if work is being done satisfactorily it is not really urgent that we find out why, although it might be useful. However, if work is not being done satisfactorily, knowing why not and then stopping at that as though it were an answer is the ultimate irrelevancy.

I am also concerned at the damage that we can do, at the very moment when we have finally and belatedly opened management opportunities for women, by some sort of self-serving insistence that women as managers are "different" and must be judged differently. It won't work any more than the suggestion of "separate but equal" worked in civil rights cases. Management values are not pluralistic, they measure results. Appropriate support mechanisms are essential if we are to allow individuals to achieve their potential, but the ultimate responsibility is still their own, and sometimes good intentions lose sight of the forest because of all of the trees.

The kooky experimentation by one magazine with encouraging women (never men) to bring their small children to the office and let them play amidst the workers never achieved broad acceptance, precisely because it doesn't work in the organizational setting, any more than (as an A. J. Anderson case study noted) having children underfoot in the library staff lounge works. Surely the promulgators of the magazine policy must have known this, but they were willing to ignore management values for something they considered more important. It doesn't work, because for managers the ground rules of management must predominate.

Employers are not generally stupid, and they know perfectly well that when an employee is absent not only for his or her own illness but also for every illness or school emergency of one of the children or for home repairs, those factors are relevant to hiring and to promotion decisions because they are expensive. When that individual is inevitably female the negative implications for women competing in the workplace are obvious. It does not then help us face this issue to publish papers that tell us confidently that women are not ill more often than men, when we know that illness is only one and sometimes a minor reason for lost work time. Such papers are at best irrelevant, and at worst mischievous because they are distracting and misleading.

CHANGING FAMILY RESPONSIBILITY

Government agencies clearly have the responsibility for dealing with this problem, and child care centers that shelter not only preschoolers but ill children and children displaced from school because of teacher conferences and strikes are part of the solution. A clearer understanding of changing family responsibilities in two-career families is also important. Unless both careers are equally important in the reaction to disruptions and potential relocation, then a secondary job in the family also becomes a secondary job in the marketplace.

We really know all this, but we are disturbed by "research" that suggests something else. Some of it is immediately suspect when it is undertaken by individuals with a prestated will to prove the validity of what they claim. This is unfortunate for all of us, because it forces us to slog through a lot of rhetoric to get to reality. It has taken us ten years to get over the myth of "super-mom," the working professional, caring parent, supportive spouse, social butterfly, and community leader who could have it all.

Quality time, we were assured, was more important than the amount of time, because this is what we wanted to be told. It would have helped to face these issues more quickly and directly, because solutions require an honest assessment. Certainly the individuals confronted by the multiplicity of these concerns know better. They know that multiple responsibilities bring painful choices and a shuffling of priorities. Perhaps the greatest danger to the importance of the issue faced by women comes from people like Shere Hite, who sensationalizes and trivializes whatever she touches, and of whom Ellen Goodman has written: "She goes in with a prejudice and comes out with a statistic."

We must also be aware that when librarians espouse special treatment not for the benefit of the organization but for the individual, they undermine the seriousness of our demand for equal pay for equal work. One of the arguments used by those who defend unequal pay structures is that men work for careers and women work for convenience. It is an ugly generalization that is totally unfair to the many dedicated career-oriented women in our field, but sometimes it is our own insensitivity to how others see us that causes us problems.

The point that the use of flex-time scheduling, part-time employment, and job sharing may indeed benefit the employer by increasing the hiring pool, particularly in specialized and hard-to-find skill areas, should not be hard to make where it is true. However, where it is not true, rigging the library's priorities to fit the preferences or needs of its employees only trivializes our profession. Ultimately, we pay dearly for such a value system. We have recently seen studies that confidently predict the proven organizational value of flex-time, and conclude, in our own research literature, with the whimper that perhaps we can't prove it but we know it to be true.

THE MANAGERIAL COMMITMENT

Our need is to create good managers, and make good managers better. I will stress again that this should be a sex-neutral process, and there is every reason for women to be every bit as good at this as men. I hope that the reader will settle for this statement, because the argument recently made, charitably as an angry overreaction, that women will be better managers is generalized bigotry at exactly the same level as the bigotry to which it responds. There can be no doubt that management requires a special kind of commitment that short-changes other commitments, and we are finally reading articles in women's magazines such as *Savvy* that honestly acknowledge that reality.

Management is hard and it requires sacrifice, at least for those who take the process seriously. Of course it evolves and changes as values shift and as leaders change our perceptions, but when these change they change for everybody. It can perhaps be demonstrated that men may have a greater tendency toward assertiveness, women toward consensus seeking. If this is true, and it is at best a generalization because there are consensus men and assertive women we all know, then we benefit because it broadens the options and the spectrum. But that is all. The crime of the past and the present is that we haven't allowed women to be managers no matter how willing and how qualified. The potential nonsense of the future is the suggestion that we can have two kinds of managers, male and female, with different value systems and different ground rules.

Practical and sensible writers like Eliza Collins who "tell it like it is" give me hope, but if we allow this process to be messed up the great losers will be the so-called women's professions like librarianship. We have historically been denied access to our largest pool of potential managerial talent, and therefore, not surprisingly, had many poor managers, almost inevitably male because they were chosen for wrong reasons. We can't afford this and we certainly don't need to play games with it. We need better managers, and in our field most of them will be women. We don't need "different" managers just because most of us are women.

The process of trying to reconcile individual and organizational needs and values is an ongoing one, and it is important that we not con ourselves into believing something to be true simply because we wish it were. From my educator's vantage point I can see almost daily how our students try to balance their career objectives with their family responsibilities. It is a difficult and often intensely painful process, but suggestions that such decisions don't really have to be made will only confuse the issue and delay solution. Up to now, they have been decisions exclusively for women. That isn't fair and it must change. But let us not deceive ourselves with fairy tale endings. Some of us go back far enough to remember a lovely and wistful song, "Wishing Will Make It So." No, it won't.

LIBRARY OPERATIONS AND THE LIBRARY USER

A colleague whose business is developing thesauri once told me that terms with multiple meanings in different disciplines (such as the word mass) were never recognized as having this ambiguity by the specialists in any one field. To them, the meaning was clear and unique. It has occurred to me often since that this is exactly the way library users feel about "their" library. They know what they want the library to do for them, they are positive that what they "know" is correct, and they see no basis for any other library activity. It is not necessarily bad for users to accept the premise that the library is uniquely for them. In teaching management I stress the importance of building one-to-one bridges with both supervisors and subordinates, so that in effect every manager has a whole range of interactive styles geared to the perception and value system of the other participant in this communication process. The development of an interactive style with library users that addresses them directly as individuals is a worthwhile objective. However, we cannot allow such narrowly focused priority to control the library and what it does, because we have a whole range of clients to serve.

This is perhaps clearest in academia, in which the term "research library" can be used to ignore completely all of the other things that happen in a university community, all of which require information support. Instead, we throw all of our energies into supporting the research of the faculty, although according to Ladd and Lipseth it is only a small percentage of any faculty that do any real research. What happens to the other unserved library users is not difficult to determine. The teaching mission and the needs of students gets short shrift, but students have no power base and must shift for themselves. If student needs had any ranking in library decision hierarchies, we would never cancel the heavily used duplicates in order to protect the one subscription of the unused esoteric title. We have known for some time that collection development and library use support can have antithetical values, and we also know from the studies of Trueswell (that half of what the library owns can not be supplied when it is wanted) where that value system lies. That represents ownership at the expense of access, and it is what the researchers who tend to keep things in their own offices anyway prefer.

We can ignore students even if our service profession value system suggests that in addition to offering them bibliographic instruction we should be offering them reference service, but there are other service constituencies not as easily ignored. These include faculty working not on basic research but on applied studies and even on implementation development, and we know that in the search for federal and corporate funds universities have accommodated to a whole new coterie of researchers who do not have the teaching and publication requirements inherent in the tenure process, but who are brought in specifically to do project work, something that begins to resemble the corporate sector. The greatest unserved constituency for the university library is university administration, which is faced with planning and business decisions every bit as complex as those faced in industry.

Academic libraries are not the only ones that ignore a part of their constituency, because all of their energies have been absorbed with one rather shrill and insistent group of users. Public librarians fall into this trap when they concentrate on service to children, the elderly, and the illiterate. These are of course worthwhile activities, but they cannot allow us to ignore the rest of our constituencies, simply because these do not come to us of their own volition. Corporate librarians sometimes report that they work in the Research Library. I tell them that if there is no other library, theirs is the corporate library. Individuals unserved by their library in what may even be a conspiracy of silence between "busy" librarians and users who agree that their needs are too esoteric have at least two other options. One is to bypass the library and obtain their information in some other way. There is clear evidence that pseudolibraries spring up both in academia and in industry as the real library fails to fill the vacuum, and the cost is financial as well as political. Certainly the individuals and organizations offering information for a fee service are doing nothing that a responsible library could not do. The other option is to do without information, and to pretend that it wasn't really needed. What that costs may not be measurable, but it is certainly frightening.

Several conclusions follow from these observations:

1. The library's appropriate role will vary, depending on the user, and may range from amusement to education to research support to specific fact recall to information packaging for decision making. Every library must be prepared to play several of these roles, and some libraries must be prepared to play all of them.

2. The user's information need cannot be defined simply by the user. That determination results from an assessment of many options, many of which are probably unknown to the user. It starts with the

statement of what the user thinks he needs or thinks he wants and proceeds from there.

3. In this process of interaction the librarian is the expert, dealing in a professional and client relationship exactly as doctors and lawyers do. Professions, it has been noted, share the characteristic of controlling their credentialing process (nobody can be a member without their permission) and of defining the terms of the user interaction.

4. The library is a service institution. It does not necessarily follow from this that it is a self-service institution, although it might be. End user searching provides little advantage and certainly no moral justification if the end user does the work badly or expensively, or if he simply abdicates the process to a secretary or to a graduate assistant.

5. It is usually far preferable to have dissatisfied rather than satisfied users. In part this is because users will settle for almost any level of professional service and complain only about the clerical routine that irritates them. In larger part it is because mainly through user dissatisfaction that echoes our own assessment, recommendations, and predictions can pressure be brought to bear on our own management. User dissatisfaction or the threat of it then becomes a weapon we can use in our funding battles, and they are battles because money is never a pleasant topic and because there is never enough of it. For these discussions, two things are worth remembering. The first is that even in the absence of money there is always money, if enough of a case can be made. The second is that it is almost always far easier to get a lot of money than a little bit of money if the dramatic difference can be demonstrated. One additional clerk is just about impossible to get, precisely because the impact is seen as so trivial.

GROWING USER INFORMATION DEPENDENCE AND ITS IMPACT ON THE LIBRARY FIELD

INTRODUCTION

The now widely accepted description of the new post-industrial society as defined by Daniel Bell clearly points to an emphasis on the provision of services rather than on the production of goods. In part this is true because improved technologies for agricultural and industrial production allow a smaller and smaller proportion of the population of the Western world to supply even the increasing demands for the food, the clothing, the shelter, and the material goods which at one time took all of our strength and all of our energies. The growing emphasis is on the provision of services—in part because having others do things for us is an indication of our growing affluence—in part because the number of potential services increases as our imagination and desires constantly stay one step ahead of what we have—and in part because increased efficiency and increased performance have also brought with them increased complexity.

Through the nineteenth century and into the early twentieth, man was relatively self-sufficient and in control of his own course of action. Now we sit by the side of the road for several hours waiting for a tow truck, because the car has broken down and because arrangements under the hood have become so complex that one can't even get at anything any more. One hundred and fifty years ago our forebears might have been able to build their own house. Now we wait two weeks for

---

Paper presented at the 52d Aslib Annual Conference, Edinburgh, 19–22 September 1978. Reprinted from *Aslib Proceedings* 31, no. 2 (February 1979):74–87.

someone to come and give us an estimate on fixing a squeak in the heating system.

How does all this apply to information? We certainly know that the provision of information, in its various guises and forms, is among the most rapidly growing if not the most rapidly growing of the service professions. Although we might find the definition of information somewhat too broad for the concerns of this audience, it has been suggested that we already spend or are about to spend more on information (if you include the media) than on capital goods.

THE GROWTH OF INFORMATION

However, even applied to the more narrowly prescribed bounds of information as we are more accustomed to using it, the growth has been startling. Georges Anderla[1] has projected the world's literature growth in science and technology at eight per cent per year. While others have quarrelled with this projection of rapid increase, Dale Baker[2] of the Chemical Abstracts Service reported in 1976 that the chemical literature, at least as covered by his service, was still taking less than ten years to double, a projection which closely matches Anderla's. Baker reports that, in 1975, Chemical Abstracts included the abstracts of 324,000 papers and books, and with the addition of patents, over 454,000 total documents, more than twice the figure for 1965, and a rate which will have put just this one information service at a level of over 1,000,000 document announcements per year by 1986. However, the growth does not simply stop there. Because, with the increased availability of machineable data bases, our access to this growing file of literature has also increased. To what extent? Nobody really knows. But certainly we are beyond the constraints of information access as defined by the holdings of the card catalogue of your local library for books, and shelf copies of abstract-index journals for the periodical literature. The growth of data bases has been estimated by Martha Williams,[3] in her 1977 article in the *Journal of the American Society for Information Science,* to be from fewer than twenty in 1965 to over 300 publicly available data bases in 1977, with better than fifty of these now available on-line. These are, of course, far and away the largest of the data bases.

Lee Burchinal,[4] the former head of the US National Science Foundation's Division of Information Science and Technology, projects even larger numbers than Professor Williams. He goes on, in a paper presented at a US–India binational seminar, to describe the startling growth in on-line searches. In the US alone, and from a beginning in about 1968, on-line searches grew to 1,000,000 per year in 1975, and are expected to surpass 4,000,000 by 1980. Where is the potential limit? It is impossible to predict with any accuracy, and experience tells us that, in dealing with new concepts, while we are usually overly optimistic in predicting what will happen in the next year, we are invariably well below target in estimating what will happen ten years from now. Even assuming that all of the 1975 searches were performed by or for scientists or engineers, an assumption both simplistic and inaccurate, it would still only amount to a half a search per year per scientist or engineer, and even the 1980 projection of 4,000,000 searches only permits the average technical professional one search every six months.

It seems inevitable that, in an atmosphere of so much growth and development, change will be rapid and continuous. It seems almost as inevitable that complexity will increase, despite the protestations that this ought not to happen. Part of the reason, it seems to me, is built into the growing inter-relationship of subject disciplines, at the very time when these disciplines become ever narrower and more specialized. Another part of the reason comes from the political and economic factors which govern the generation and dissemination of data bases.

DATA BASE DEVELOPMENT

I think it can be argued that rapid development of machine-readable files has been greatest precisely where artificial interference and constraint has been the least. Data base development, in the western world, tends to come from three sources—government, professional societies, and private industry. While the publicly avowed motivations and value systems of professional societies versus private corporations may differ, in reality the factors which drive decisions are basically the same. In both cases there is usually a genuine belief that the data base being created will meet a need—if it did not how could you sell it? The need for financial validation is equally important. Neither societies nor companies have hidden gold reserves from which to finance a money-losing abstract-index service, and members of a society are as loath to subsidize a charitable undertaking as are stockholders in a corporation. Studies which the Indiana University Graduate Library School Research Center has undertaken for the National Science Foundation on the economics of the publisher-library interaction convince us that the economically motivated decision model differs only in the nomenclature applied. What is labelled a profit in industry is called a surplus in professional societies, and both are essential if there is going to be further innovation, development, and growth, as there must be in any meaningful and dynamic system.

It is interesting and coincidental that, as I was preparing this article, a regional network of academic libraries in the United States was criticizing *Psychological Abstracts,* a professional society product, for a price increase for on-line data base access. I am not sufficiently familiar with the financial constraints, nor do I want to be, to be able to comment on the validity of this price change, but the simple and perhaps simplistic suggestion that the publisher should forgo a price increase because the information for the data base is already in machine-generated indexes and therefore relatively free of cost ignores both the economics of publishing and the factors which motivate pricing decisions. The determination of the extent to which a database competes with, or perhaps in some instances enhances, the sales potential of published indexes, is part of the overall marketing strategy which any publishing organization must develop, professional societies no less than commercial organizations.

It becomes an absolute essential that for a data base to be developed effectively, to meet the aims of its originators, it must be developed selfishly. By that I mean that if the charter which your program has set for itself requires the inclusion of certain information, that inclusion is no less valid simply because some other data base also decides, for its own reasons, to cover the same information. In fact, while the material being included may be the same, it is likely that the difference in orientation of subject scope will almost automatically account for differences. Even data bases which presumably cover relatively neatly defined subject areas are not immune to interpretation. Take chemistry. Does anyone really know where chemistry ends and biology begins? Or physics? What is the difference between physical chemistry and chemical physics? If academic departments within universities cannot agree on lines of demarcation, it is hardly reasonable to expect that producers of abstract/index publications and data bases who, if they err, must err on the side of inclusiveness, would do so. The problem is further compounded by the emergence of interdisciplinary problem-orientated data bases, concerned with such broad topics as energy, pollution, and nutrition. It can be assumed that virtually everything covered in these data bases will be contained in subject data bases as well, although the emphasis of approach might very well be totally different.

Government-produced data bases generally show this same lack of consistency, depending on the mission statement of the agency involved. Thus, within the United States, the Department of Defense concerns itself with controlling and announcing all documents produced by and for the Department of Defense, regardless of subject, while the National Aeronautics and Space Administration is concerned with all documentation related to space, regardless of originator, and definitely including Department of Defense reports concerned with space, as NASA defines it. I am sure that Great Britain can point to similar examples.

REDUNDANCY OF INFORMATION

Producers of abstract/index tools and data bases have been quite defensive about the extent of their overlap coverage. A study undertaken by the National Federation of Abstracting and Indexing Services[5] and published in February 1977 points out that, among fourteen major scientific and technical abstracting and indexing services, only 21 per cent of the 26,000 journals scanned were scanned by two or more services. Furthermore, only 23.4 per cent of the articles in those journals which were covered by more than one service were in fact included more than once, a two-level approach which could lead you to conclude that less than 5 per cent of the articles were in fact double covered.

Perhaps so, but it would also be of significance to know whether or not these articles were any more important (in terms of frequency of retrieval) than the body of literature as a whole. I suspect they might have been. In addition, the fourteen abstract/index services in the survey (thirteen US and one British, INSPEC) represent primarily subject disciplines, with perhaps three or four which could be considered interdisciplinary or mission-oriented to any appreciable extent.

In any case, the presumption that duplication is unnecessary duplication is easily open to challenge. As the NFAIS report points out "Even when two or more services do index the same article, this does not really imply *unnecessary* duplication, because the intellectual analysis of the article content by each service is intended to serve the particular needs of its users. For example, a research chemist's approach to a secondary service for identifying the literature he needs may be entirely different from the approach by an engineer, whose subject terminology may be completely different from the chemist's."

Any assumption that an item of the literature belongs in one abstract/index tool or data base only is probably an extension of the premise in librarianship that every item in the collection deserves one particular place. We therefore spend a considerable amount of time worrying about where exactly to park a specific item, letting users then worry about figuring out where we have hidden it. The totally reasonable suggestion that perhaps we ought, if we have more than one copy, to place one in each of several locations within the system, is of course anathema to the values of the library profession.

Depite the somewhat defensive nature of the NFAIS study, and the almost obvious relief with which the investigators report the relatively small amount of overlap, it raises in at least this commentator's mind the perverse thought that perhaps there isn't overlap enough— that perhaps some degree of redundancy is still one of the most effective techniques for insuring retrieval. Those of us who have worked with retrieval problems from subject files probably realize, although we may be loath to admit it, that only the multiple approaches provided by computerized access have enabled us to do meaningful subject searches. The one or two or three necessarily broad subject headings attached to a manual catalogue card make searching of subject headings highly unprofitable, and many if not most subject searches are in fact carried out through the author or the title file. If any of you doubt me, find a divided catalogue in a research library and observe the number of patrons. Chances are, the people you find at the subject catalogue are in fact library employees putting more cards in.

DIRECT USER ACCESS

One of the main reasons we continue to be concerned about the avoidance of duplication, and about the growing number of data bases, is because we are still wedded to the forlorn and injudicious hope that somehow we must allow the researcher to maintain direct contact with the publications in this field. Forlorn because there is little evidence that he is either interested or competent in doing so. Injudicious because the best hope for this profession and its practitioners, be they called librarians, information officers, or documentalists, is that of assuming the crucial role of information intermediary between the researcher and his literature.

Strategies for the development of information systems have consistently been based on the premise that the researcher or scholar is anxious to have more and newer esoteric tools to permit him to access additional information sources. I am sure that there are some individuals who fit that description, but most researchers and certainly decision makers with whom I have come in contact are not looking for more to read, they are looking for ways to cut down the amount of reading they are doing now. This is behind much of the concern about overlap and presumed redundancy of information which prompts studies such as the NFAIS abstracting and indexing overlap study referred to earlier. My dealings, in particular, with scientists and engineers in industrial settings as part of my consulting assignments, yield a highly cautious reaction to the suggested implementation of SDI profiles. Their thoughts immediately turn to stacks of unread journals, and then fear that these stacks will ultimately topple over and bury them. They don't want the material, they want to know if it is germane to the solution of their present problem. I find these users generally dissatisfied with the tried and true library technique of routing journals. They arrive at inconvenient times, they contain much information of no interest, and yet there is a sense of guilt, at least among some, about holding up the journal from further distribution. And so many of them cross their names off the list and pass it on, pretending they have read it.

The designers of our abstracting-indexing services, data bases, and major information systems insist on and perpetuate the myth that their output is going to be used directly by technical professionals. I teach a course in the literature of science and technology at the Indiana University Graduate Library School, and my students learn quickly enough that with some significant exceptions such as *Chemical Abstracts*, the AI and data-base services pay not the slightest attention to the real needs of the real users of these information tools. Most of them, particularly those produced by professional societies, but also certainly including government services, are self-perpetuating clubs which pay little attention to the needs and preferences of the real users, in part because it is an embarrassment to acknowledge them.

An embarrassment? Certainly politically so. I served for five years as Executive Director of the contract-operated NASA Scientific and Technical Facility. During that time the agency persisted, in its program-design strategies and financial justifications, in describing the users of its information services as scientists and engineers, when we knew that virtually all of the document requests, and most of the machine searches, were performed for and by librarians and other information workers. The reason for this stratagem was perfectly obvious. Funds are far easier to justify and obtain for the support of front-line bench researchers than for the support of libraries.

When the National Library of Medicine first designed its on-line MEDLARS system, it was with rosy justifications about men and women in white lab coats sitting at terminals, and perhaps rushing back to the laboratory or even the operating room, if you care to be melodramatic, to use the results of their information searches for instantly successful application. It never happened. The people at those terminals are librarians. A number of projects, including MIT's Project INTREX, were aimed at the implementation of the premise that information systems should be geared to the common denominator of the interests and capabilities of the untrained scientist and researcher. A number of other research projects at various universities are aiming at this same premise, at making information access systems fit the level of competence of the ultimate user. It would be a harmless exercise, except for the fact that by reducing file structures and access software to a common denominator, we back away from the optimum capability which sophisticated file design and search strategies for uniquely structured data bases frequently offer us.

The premise is, as I suggest, based on a myth—the myth that the ultimate users of information enjoy the process of search and discovery in the literature, and that they would prefer to do this themselves, given the option. It is more likely that they do it, when they do it, because they don't trust anyone to do it for them, or because somebody has told them they *should* do it themselves. Furthermore, they do it badly—I'll come to that later.

Perhaps except for those involved in basic research (and even there only perhaps) individuals need information not for its own sake, but for the purpose of doing something else—of making a decision, of writing a report, of choosing an experimental alternative. They usually want and need the information quickly, simply, and with as little work on their part as possible. Mooer's Law, that if it is easier to make assumptions and guesses than to dig for information you know is there somewhere, people will pretend there is no information and make assumptions and guesses, has been demonstrated over and over again to every information professional. Furthermore, most professionals fail to see the information-gathering and evaluation process as one of particularly high gratification and reward. As George Shapiro[6] of the University of Minnesota has pointed out, they identify with the library in terms of their own childhood, when they felt somewhat overawed and overwhelmed by the power structure which confronted them and the rules with which they had to comply. Now they have achieved power, prestige, and a salary at least twice that of the people who work in the library. They are certainly not going to reveal to these people that there are tools they don't know how to use. So they stay away entirely and pretend they don't need information, or they send their secretaries.

I started this talk by pointing to the growth of service functions, and of the acceptance of delegating work to specialists, while at the same time feeling superior because, after all, these people work for us. One of the symbols of power is the ability to delegate work to others, particularly work we don't want to do ourselves.

About eight years ago a major corporation developed what was one of the earliest on-line interactive management-information systems. They placed a keyboard and cathode ray display into the office of every senior executive, with the promise that by using these terminals they could get instant reporting and updating on such important considerations as production status, unfilled orders, inventory, and cash flow. The system worked perfectly, but the executives wouldn't use it. They wouldn't use it because they perceived, and still perceive, sitting at a keyboard as a clerical function, and having to ask and interpret their own questions as lowering of status. And so these executives were provided with information intermediaries, and the terminals were given to these staff assistants sitting in outer offices. These intermediaries would perform the searches and provide the information, either after being asked, or on an automatic updated basis. The executives went back to their comfortable methods of information access befitting their status—

receiving digested reports and analyses, summoning people to their office for oral briefings, and using the telephone.

USERS' EVALUATION OF THEIR NEEDS

However, in addition to dealing with the myth that information systems should be designed for direct access by the ultimate user, despite the fact that he neither uses them nor cares to use them, and despite the risk that fitting the system to his level of understanding and training may dilute and downgrade information access, we deal with an additional myth. That is the myth that professionals know the literature of their field, and can make evaluative judgments about that literature—at least to do it better than librarians and information officers.

I was surprised when I came to an academic community after twenty-five years in government and industry, at the extent to which academic libraries have conceded the selection process to their faculties. During times of affluence, when the real test of a high quality library was its ability to identify and locate obscure materials, library bibliographic specialists and acquisition officers had a prized and valued role. However, now that the number of easily identifiable acquisitions far outnumber the available funds, many librarians have reported, paradoxical as it may seem, that decision and evaluation procedures within the library have all but disappeared. Instead, we are engaged in a tortuous and highly political process of buying or renewing what we must, frequently involving the allocation by formula of materials budgets to various departments and schools, a process which guarantees that whatever imbalance and inequities now exist within the collection will be perpetuated and exacerbated. In fact, many of these highly prized libraries have disintegrated into little more than free book stores for the acquisition of materials for storage in faculty offices. I am not suggesting that the same practice does not also exist in many industrial or governmental libraries. It undoubtedly does, but perhaps not to the same extent.

I would be the last person to suggest that libraries and information centres be operated without paying attention to the needs of their users, but there is, I think, considerable danger in running them simply in response to the priorities and desires which users express, and the needs as users perceive them. To suggest that we may have more valid perceptions about their information than our users is, for the information sector, a radical new thought, but it is totally consistent with the acceptance of service specializations developing in other fields.

What can we say about information operations run to the specifications of their user communities? Well, for one, that expectations of information service are abysmally low. It might be expected that, by contrast, expectations for materials collection might be high, and this is generally true, but only for the very narrow and specialized area of the user's own competence, and not for the collection as a whole. Our users don't really care about the quality of the library, only about the quality of their part of it.

Almost without exception, in my experience, the determination that an information service was poor and needed substantial improvement came either from its own staff, or from a higher level of management, and never from complaints from its users. Expectations for analytical and evaluative services are almost non-existent, and this appears to be true even when this service could be provided by individuals whom the user might accept as fellow-professionals and practitioners in his own field. Certainly the concept of information analysis centres, so fervently put forward by Alvin Weinberg[7] twenty years ago, has never really taken hold. In fact, the last several years have seen the demise of a number of information analysis centres, ostensibly because of budgetary pressures, but in reality because of a lack of interest. There is always money for things which people really want done.

My own experience in dealing with, in particular, scientists and engineers, points to their strong insistence on the development of a materials collection, but a materials collection based on tradition and experience rather than on newly evolving needs. The self-perpetuating and self-validating "invisible college" system is simply not geared to an awareness of newly evolving publication sources and publication formats, particularly when these require access to information in related or even unrelated disciplines in which the user has neither experience or training. This is not intended as a criticism. I believe that the fact that professionals in various disciplines can no longer keep up (if in fact they ever did) with needed information in their fields is neither surprising nor disturbing. They have other, perhaps more important things to do. What I think is disturbing is that we, as information professionals, expect them to keep up themselves, or allow them to pretend that they do.

User evaluations of their information needs tend not only to be narrow in scope, but also conservative. Known things will invariably outrank unknown things. One of the most disturbing findings of our NSF-sponsored study,[8] to me, although many others hardly noticed, was the pattern of decision priorities which emerged when large academic libraries no longer had enough money to maintain their historic practices of journal acquisition—namely to renew everything already bought and subscribe to everything newly published.

Forced to make reductions in their periodicals subscriptions, these libraries failed to renew some existing subscriptions, to be sure. However, to a far greater extent, their budget-trimming took the form of not subscribing to newly published titles. In fact, when compared to their pre-economy 1969 pattern of activity, the strategic choice of failing to purchase a new subscription which would otherwise have been bought was exercised seven times as frequently as the option of cancelling an existing single subscription, and this, of course, in the face of the evidence from the University of Pittsburgh[9] study that huge chunks of the periodical literature, perhaps half or more, is never looked at over a five-year period in a major academic library.

Librarians, of course, must bear their share for this non-evaluative value system under which existing titles, no matter how useless, take precedence over new ones. Some of these are bound to have at least some potential, particularly in view of the recognition that many emerging disciplines are covered only by new publications and not at all by old stand-bys. Certainly, the library workload system would be geared to renewing the existing subscription and forgoing the new title. This requires no additional work in the Serials Department, rather than cancelling an existing subscription and placing a new one, which involves double work. However, the complicity in this process of our subject specialist users, and in many cases their outright insistence on this value system, calls sharply into question the assumption that professionals in various subject areas are indeed the best qualified monitors of their own literature. On an after-the-fact basis, of literature they have once seen, without a doubt. But how can they judge the usefulness of information about the existence of which they know nothing, when in fact they believe they already see everything of importance to them? It is an absurd assertion, but nobody has ever challenged it. And so we have individuals working on similar projects, some the beneficiaries of large sophisticated information services, others dependent on the routing of twenty journals by the departmental secretary. And yet each insists that his information system is adequate. He must; how can he admit the contrary?

CONCLUSION

Addressing myself finally and circuitously to the topic assigned to me in the program—the user's view: hopes and expectations, the effects on the user and his operation—we must first address the question of who this user is.

If, by user, we are talking about the ultimate recipient of information service, be he or she bench chemist, economist, or business executive, then I doubt that hopes and expectations have very much to do with the case. These individuals have for a long time suffered from a severe case of information oversupply, and they have rationalized what they find time to do as being adequate to their needs. After all, they are not paid to digest information, they are paid to do productive work. They have no choice, and if necessary they will lie to themselves and to others, or perhaps even train themselves to believe, when they assert that they have all of the information they need—or that they would have all of the information they needed if only we would provide them with these five journals which contain everything they need to know.

The development of new abstracting and indexing services, progressively narrower, more specialized and therefore less self-sufficient, and of new machine-readable data bases with unique and complex search strategies and differing vocabularies or free text search, does nothing for these individuals except increase their anxiety. They don't need more information services. They already have more than they can possibly cope with. They want, if anything, less information, but they need answers to their problems.

If, on the other hand, the user is an information professional, trained and expert in the knowledge of data bases and search strategies, then not only do I see a meaningful utilization of the world's growing literature and the tools with which to access it, but also a promising future for those who now labour in this vineyard, unappreciated and underpaid. Not all of them, by a long shot. But enough of them, and enough of the new recruits attracted by the challenge and opportunity, to fill the ranks. However, to do this they must understand nomenclature, technology, and the problems confronting the organization they serve. More importantly, they must understand that the need is not for reports and journal articles, but for answers. I am, of course, talking about the concept of the information intermediary, and I am talking about a conscious and planned approach to remove the user from primary contact with the literature, not to bring him closer to it. He's never been that enamoured of it in the first place.

However, old value systems and old prejudices die hard, and the implementation and acceptance of this professional intermediary concept will not be sudden or automatic. It requires, first of all, a belief by ourselves in our own role and our own importance. It requires an assertion and insistence that in fact the ultimate user professional really knows damn little about the literature of his field, that he knows less and less all the time, and that the problems of solving his information needs are beyond his scope. Or, if it seems preferable, that he has more important things to do than worry about books, journals and reports. Acceptance of the need to rely on specialists is, after all, not that strange. We do it to an increasing extent in all other areas of our daily activities.

It requires, additionally, a shift from the preoccupation with materials to a concentration on answers. It is, if you like, Weinberg's information analysis centre in new clothing, but with new participants. Scientists selected for information work were frequently handed these tasks because they were considered unsuited for what was believed to be "more important" work. I foresee the information function as demanding and exacting, and its practitioners as meeting those requirements. The question to be addressed is: what is the need? Don't ask the ultimate user what he would like you to look at or where he thinks the answer might be found. Fine if he volunteers suggestions, but don't simply assume that he knows, or embarrass him if he doesn't know, or force him to pretend he knows.

Finally, it requires an understanding by abstracting-service and database producers for whom their services are being produced, and some input by the real users regarding those services. In an increasingly interdisciplinary world it is foolish to insist that information services in a subject field are produced specifically and directly for the practitioners in that subject field. If these information-service producers recognize their audience, then perhaps, and only then, can we achieve some consistency of approach, arrangement, vocabulary, and format. But only where this can be accomplished without dilution. Common denominators tend to be small numbers.

What I am suggesting has, of course, major implications for the philosophy of the present self-service library. There are fields in which self-service will continue, either because the field is truly narrow, clearly defined, and highly specialized, or because research investigations are carried out, as they sometimes are in the humanities, over a lifetime and not in preparation for tomorrow's meeting. These, however, also tend to be the fields in which information tools are sparse or primitive.

In applied science and technology, business and industry, and government, however, the need is not for more sources of information for the ultimate consumer to scan—the need is for answers. If any of you doubt this, look at the recent development of commerical organizations whose sole purpose is to analyze and digest information contained in our libraries and information centres, and to apply it to problem-solving—or at least, to synthesize, boil down, and comment on in terse, directly applicable statements. It is this need which the growing group of on-demand information services has recognized and addressed, because we have either failed to recognize the concern or refused to involve ourselves in it.

The capabilities of computer technology, and the funding support of concerned governments and industries, have allowed us to make remarkably rapid progress in the development of tools in many fields for coming to grips with the problems of expanding literature, expanding inter-dependency, expanding specialization, and increasing time constraints. At present our tools, which will most certainly continue to develop as pressure increases and technology improves, already outstrip our abilities to use them because of an insistence that somehow they must be geared to the ultimate user's interests, abilities, and available time.

Optimum simplification consistent with or in conjunction with the maintenance of other values is always a worthwhile goal, but simplification as an end in itself in a desperate rearguard attempt to make the system fit the wrong user is not the right answer.

References

1. Anderla, J. G. The growth of scientific and technical information—a challenge. *Information,* **2–3**(3), 1974, p. 1–52.

2. Baker, D. B. Recent trends in growth of chemical literature. *Chemical and Engineering News,* **54** (20), May 10, 1976, p. 23–7.

3. Williams, M. E. Data bases—a history of developments and trends from 1966 throught 1975. *Journal of the American Society for Information Science* **28,** March 1977, p. 71–8.

4. Burchinal, L. G. The ST communication enterprise in the United States: status and forecasts. *Library Science with a Slant to Documents (India)* **14,** June 1977, p. 53–61.

5. Bearman, T. C. *and* Kunberger, W. A. *A study of coverage overlap among fourteen major science and technology abstracting and indexing services.* Philadelphia, National Federation of Abstracting and Indexing Services, 1977.

6. Shapiro, G. Talk presented at the annual conference of the Special Libraries Association. Minneapolis, Minnesota, 1966.

7. U.S. President's Science Advisory Committee. *Science, government, and information* (Weinberg Report). 1963.

8. Fry, B. M. and White, H.S. *Publishers and libraries, a study of scholarly and research journals.* Lexington, Mass., D. C. Heath & Co., 1976.

9. Galvin, T. J. and Kent, A. Use of a university library collection: a progress report on a Pittsburgh study. *Library Journal* **102,** November 15, 1977, p. 2317–20.

FACTORS IN THE DECISION BY INDIVIDUALS AND LIBRARIES TO PLACE OR CANCEL SUBSCRIPTIONS TO SCHOLARLY AND RESEARCH JOURNALS

Under a grant sponsored by the National Science Foundation, the Indiana University Research Center for Library and Information Science sought specific information, through a series of survey questionnaires, on the factors which prompted both individuals and libraries to place new subscriptions or cancel existing subscriptions to established scholarly and research journals. The survey sought particularly to evaluate the impact of library action on individual subscriptions and to determine how library decisions were affected by the recent emergence of consortia and networks and the development of cooperative acquisitions policies. The study suggests that the availability of a journal in a library has little impact on the decision by individuals to place subscriptions. However, while the vast majority of cancellations of individual subscriptions are caused by a loss of interest in the journal, a minority of individuals, perhaps 10–15 percent, canceled subscriptions unwillingly for purely financial reasons and now depend on the library for continued regular access, without which they might not have canceled. We found that the financially induced decision by libraries to cancel subscriptions is beginning to be affected by an increasing awareness of consortium and network policies and knowledge of the availability of titles in other libraries.

The past several years have seen an increasing amount of interest in the economic interaction between publishers and libraries. This fascination is not difficult to explain. The curtailment of library budgets, or at least their inability to keep pace with increases in the scholarly literature and in prices, has forced even major academic libraries to back away from

From *Library Quarterly* 50, no. 3 (July 1980):287–309.

the process of simply buying and then renewing subscriptions to every journal that is identified as appropriate or is actually requested. Moreover, in addition to not placing subscriptions, libraries are canceling them—a practice almost unknown, except in special libraries, before the early 1970s.

This heretofore unknown phenomenon is causing mistrust and suspicion among librarians and publishers, up to now and still close allies in dealing with funding agencies and potential censors. Publishers who see their subscriber base declining have blamed library cooperative activities, including expanded interlibrary loan, consortia, networks, and the proposed national periodicals center for some of their woes. Some library spokesmen have replied that this sort of conjecture is sheer nonsense, that librarians are spending as much on periodicals as they can, and that the drop in subscriptions is caused simply by a lack of funds. Although this assertion may be generally correct, it is also simplistic, because individual publishers care not only about why libraries cancel journals but primarily why they cancel *their* journals. It is important to recognize that, while some segments of the publishing community in the commercial sector are flourishing, other small nonprofit publishing enterprises are in desperate difficulty.[1] Completing this already strained relationship is the individual subscriber market for scholarly and research journals, which is declining even more rapidly than the library market, and it is an attempt to bolster this customer community which underlies part of the strategy of differential pricing.[2] Some publishers may fear that, as library service improves, particularly through expanded bibliographic access via terminals and enhanced lending, individuals will feel encouraged or at least free to cancel their own subscriptions if assured of library availability.

There has been no substantiation for any such assumptions. Librarians have ascribed cancellations to the economic situation or to high prices and have argued that in any case they had no responsibility for what individuals did or did not do.[3] Their job was to provide competent service, and if the perception of that service allowed an individual user to cancel his own subscription, that was his own concern. It might even serve as a validation of the worth of the library. After all, libraries historically have existed to provide access to scholarly resources that individuals could not acquire personally except on a very selective basis.

Some libraries, however, have voiced aggressive counterattacks, even suggesting that expanded library service, including interlibrary loan, increases rather than decreases the probability that individuals will place subscriptions, because it permits individuals to learn about titles they previously had not encountered.[4]

Our own attempts, in earlier studies, to try to determine the impact of cooperative practices on library policies in placing and canceling journal subscriptions led to scattered and confusing responses. Many libraries responded that increased availability through interlibrary lending made no difference in their decisions to subscribe or cancel subscriptions; others were almost equally divided between those who believed that expanded access through interlibrary cooperation had led them to decrease their own subscriptions and those who felt that these activities caused them to purchase more titles.[5]

We became quickly aware that these responses dealt not with occurrences but with perceptions, and that librarians were answering in terms of what they thought happened or perhaps even of what they would like to think happened. We therefore proposed to undertake a study which would determine reasons for specific decisions to cancel or to subscribe made by specific individuals and libraries with respect to specific journals. We believed that certainly individuals, and in all probability libraries, would be able to tell us what had prompted them to enter a new subscription or to cancel one already in effect if we asked them within several months of the decision. A study to accomplish this was proposed to and approved by the National Science Foundation Division of Information Science and Technology and undertaken during 1978 and 1979.

CONDUCT OF THE STUDY

As indicated, the intent of the present study was to deal with specific actions by specific individuals and specific libraries—to determine what they did, what prompted them to do it, and what had happened since they did it. We broke the impact of library policies into four categories: (1) impact on new subscriptions by individuals; (2) impact on cancellations by individuals; (3) impact on new subscriptions by libraries; and (4) impact on cancellations by libraries. The study, we knew, would require the cooperation of publishers in supplying us with names and addresses of both cancelers and new subscribers, information which is usually considered sensitive and proprietary. It would require the willingness of individuals and librarians to respond to our questionnaires, although responses might indicate inconsistencies and might, for libraries, lead to a possible second-guessing of decision processes. We were able to secure the full cooperation of all participants. A number volunteered that they would be happy to participate because they considered the work timely and important.

This paper will not deal in depth with the development of the sample or of the study methodology. Those who may be interested in following this in greater detail are referred to the project final report.[6] It will suffice to indicate that we asked publishers to furnish us with the names and addresses of individuals and libraries in the United States who had newly placed or newly canceled subscriptions to scholarly and research journals (these were defined in our first NSF study) published in the United States.[1] We restricted the sample to journals (the word "journal," which is publisher terminology, is used interchangeably with the word "periodical," which is preferred by librarians) which had been in existence for at least five years. We wanted to minimize the impact of individuals or librarians discovering a new title or canceling a subscription because the publication was so unsettled that it had to be evaluated before a decision could be made. We attempted to structure the sample to provide responses by four types of publishers (commercial, professional society, university press, and other miscellaneous not-for-profit groups), four types of subject disciplines (pure science, applied science and technology, social science, and humanities), and two types of circulation (those with more than 10,000 copies and those with fewer). All of these definitions had been used in our earlier NSF studies.[1,5]

These breakdown combinations would permit thirty-two different types of combinations, to enable us to determine whether differences in treatment by type of journal existed. Our second NSF study,[5] had identified 2,672 U.S. scholarly journals. Of these, 857 were eliminated as being in existence for less than five years or not providing information from which the age of the journal could be discovered. The distribution of the remaining 1,815 journals into each of the thirty-two categories is shown in table 1.

It is readily apparent that some combinations have far greater populations than others. For example, there are many large-circulation applied science journals distributed by commercial publishers, and there is also a substantial number of social science journals with small circulations distributed by professional societies. By contrast, there are very few university press journals in the pure sciences, and even fewer if we further specify larger circulations. After consultation with the project

TABLE 1
DISTRIBUTION OF THE JOURNAL FILE INTO 32 CATEGORIES FOR JOURNALS IN EXISTENCE AT LEAST FIVE YEARS (1,815)

Publisher	Applied Science (617)		Humanities (270)		Pure Science (185)		Social Science (743)	
	Small	Large	Small	Large	Small	Large	Small	Large
Commercial	60	239	23	36	25	17	67	106
Society	64	203	24	29	32	66	123	188
Other, nonprofit	19	19	38	4	21	10	134	78
University Press	7	6	82	34	11	3	26	21

Note.—N's shown in parentheses.

statistical adviser, it was decided to request data initially from a greater group than would finally constitute the sample. This was done because it was assumed that many journals would not respond to the request and that others would be unable to furnish the information requested. Initial letters requesting lists of new subscribers and cancelers were sent to ten journals selected by random numbers in each category. Where there were fewer than ten journals in the category, all were contacted. In all, 419 letters were mailed. As weakness in response levels for certain categories became apparent, an additional seventy-seven journals, also randomly selected, were contacted. We found that many publishers, while cooperative, were simply unable to identify new subscribers and recent cancellations. Cards or records for new subscribers were interfiled with those for other subscribers; canceled subscription records were discarded. This is mentioned not only to stress that much of the scholarly publishing community is poorly organized and unable to organize its own records, let alone take remedial action, but also to reinforce the point, frequently ignored amidst librarian-publisher debates, that half the scholarly and research journals (unlike trade journals) in the United States are issued by small organizations, such as university departments, which issue only one journal. A study undertaken for the Commission on New Technological Uses of Copyrighted Works (CONTU)[7] found that 84.6 percent of the U.S. scholarly publishers publish only one journal and that they account for 46.5 percent of journal publication. Publishers distributing five or fewer journals account for 61.3 percent of scholarly journals distributed in the United States. The understanding of marketing techniques and pricing strategies by such groups is hazy, at best.

The journal response rate to our letters of request is shown in table 2.

STUDY RESPONSE LEVELS

We decided to use a larger sampling for individuals than libraries because we thought—correctly, as it turned out—that individuals would

TABLE 2
JOURNAL RESPONSE TO LETTERS OF REQUEST ($N = 496$)

	N	%
Returned by Post Office as undeliverable	7	1.4
Did not respond	235	47.4
Declined to participate	6	1.2
Could not supply data	148	29.8
Promised data but did not furnish them	30	6.1
Supplied data	70	14.1

TABLE 3

DISTRIBUTION OF LIBRARY CANCELLATION QUESTIONNAIRES (1,334)

Publisher	Applied Science (476)		Humanities (301)		Pure Science (360)		Social Science (197)	
	Small (187)	Large (289)	Small (199)	Large (102)	Small (185)	Large (175)	Small (74)	Large (123)
Commercial (146)	22	10	32	17	10	6	6	43
Society (602)	4	213	32	0	135	169	8	41
Other, nonprofit (256)	57	0	49	45	6	0	60	39
University press (330)	104	66	86	40	34	0	0	0

Note.—N's shown in parentheses.

not be as motivated to respond as librarians, who had an interest and stake in the outcome. We also made the individual cancellation sample somewhat larger than the new subscriber sample, on the premise that some cancelers would not be reached because of change of address or death.

The distribution of questionnaires in the survey is shown in tables 3–6. It can be readily seen that for some response categories no sample could be developed, and that for others the sample is sparse. Although we were able to achieve the questionnaire distribution levels projected in our proposal and recommended by reviewers, the need to find candidates for certain sparsely populated cells curtailed and even negated our attempts to achieve a random distribution. We were concerned that this would affect overall response validity and that the far greater populations in certain samples would bias any attempt at survey conclusions. We were, therefore, very careful to undertake detailed analyses of responses under

TABLE 4

DISTRIBUTION OF LIBRARY NEW SUBSCRIBERS QUESTIONNAIRES (703)

Publisher	Applied Science (213)		Humanities (208)		Pure Science (113)		Social Science (169)	
	Small (100)	Large (113)	Small (168)	Large (40)	Small (70)	Large (43)	Small (169)	Large (0)
Commercial (87)	15	25	10	0	19	10	8	0
Society (232)	8	40	41	0	32	33	78	0
Other, nonprofit (172)	65	0	16	0	8	0	83	0
University press (212)	12	48	101	40	11	0	0	0

Note.—N's shown in parentheses.

TABLE 5
DISTRIBUTION OF INDIVIDUAL CANCELLATION QUESTIONNAIRES (1,643)

Publisher	Applied Science (512)		Humanities (517)		Pure Science (238)		Social Science (376)	
	Small (103)	Large (409)	Small (322)	Large (195)	Small (115)	Large (123)	Small (197)	Large (179)
Commercial (441)	30	67	143	82	32	4	23	60
Society (481)	4	142	56	0	61	119	45	54
Other, nonprofit (410)	0	93	71	50	2	0	129	65
University press (311)	69	107	52	63	20	0	0	0

Note.—N's shown in parentheses.

each of the variables and under the possible combinations. These analyses, reported in detail in the project final report,[6] indicate no significant differences in response patterns. Libraries or individuals subscribing to or canceling journals in one subject discipline, of a given circulation and distributed by one type of publisher, did not report the reasons for their actions any differently from those who were dealing with journals in other disciplines, with different circulations and distributed by a different type of publisher. This became, in fact, one of the most significant findings of the study and had not been wholly expected. Decisions, we found, were based on more fundamental concepts.

Our overall response rates were very gratifying, with 832, or 64.0 percent, for individual new subscribers, 736, or 48.5 percent, for individual cancellations, 514, or 73.4 percent, for library new subscribers, and 853, or 64.4 percent, for library cancellations. This is shown in table 7.

A totally unexpected and yet highly significant factor served to

TABLE 6
DISTRIBUTION OF INDIVIDUAL NEW SUBSCRIBER QUESTIONNAIRES (1,317)

Publisher	Applied Science (469)		Humanities (321)		Pure Science (166)		Social Science (361)	
	Small (296)	Large (173)	Small (260)	Large (61)	Small (97)	Large (69)	Small (300)	Large (61)
Commercial (226)	35	70	64	1	26	9	21	0
Society (401)	14	57	95	0	57	60	117	1
Other, nonprofit (507)	244	0	32	0	9	0	162	60
University press (183)	3	46	69	60	5	0	0	0

Note.—N's shown in parentheses.

reduce the response level. Almost as a formality, we began each questionnaire by asking whether the information supplied by the publisher, on which the questionnaire was based, was correct. A total of 15.3 percent of those individuals whom the publishers described as new subscribers, 34.1 percent of those described as cancelers, 42.4 percent of those libraries described as new subscribers, and 50.9 percent (more than half!) of those libraries described as canceling titles responded that they were incorrectly described, that the change alleged had not taken place. These responses and the number of returns which had to be eliminated are also shown in table 7.

Reasons for the discrepancies were not difficult to determine. Some respondents volunteered suggestions, and upon further questioning publishers not only confirmed these but also added some more. Because of a lack of system organization, which frequently extends to both manual and machine circulation files, address changes and late renewals from individual subscribers are frequently handled as cancellations and new subscriptions, and there is no attempt to differentiate between a cancellation (which requires the reporting of a decision) and a nonrenewal (which may only be because of delayed action). Address changes for libraries are less frequent (although "attention" lines do change), but changes in subscription agents occur frequently. Since the publisher ships to the library but gets paid by the subscription agent, many publishers treat a change in agency as though it were a cancellation and a new subscription.

Although we have been assured by our statistical consultant that the remaining valid responses left us with ample data for the completion of our survey, this startling result leads to a point which needs to be made before consideration of specific responses begins. As a general group, publishers cannot hope to develop meaningful information on the basis of which to draw conclusions and develop strategies until they make greater efforts to improve the quality of their subscriber database. Although certain individual publishers may have accurate data, industry-wide claims about what is or is not happening to scholarly journal subscriptions will continue to be highly suspect until far more publishers make changes to insure accurate records.

INDIVIDUAL NEW SUBSCRIBERS

Motivations for Subscription

As shown in table 8, the primary factor in the decision to subscribe is the individual perception that the journal is important to the subscriber's work. Thus, about half of the responses (even allowing for overlap)

TABLE 7
OVERALL RESPONSE RATES

	Questionnaires Distributed	Undeliverable	Total Usable Distribution	Response as of 5/14/79	Response (%)	Incorrect Publisher Information (%)	Returned Questionnaires Eliminated	Usable Response for Analysis
Individual new subscribers	1,317	18	1,299	832	64.0	15.3	127	705
Individual cancellations	1,643	125	1,518	736	48.5	34.1	251	485
Individual total	2,960	143	2,817	1,568	55.8	24.1	378	1,190
Library new subscribers	703	3	700	514	73.4	42.4	218	296
Library cancellations	1,334	10	1,324	853	64.4	50.9	434	419
Library total	2,037	13	2,024	1,367	67.5	47.7	652	715
Overall total	4,997	156	4,831	2,935	60.6	35.1	1,030	1,905

TABLE 8

INDIVIDUAL MOTIVATIONS FOR SUBSCRIPTION

Since this journal has been in existence for some time prior to your subscription, we are interested in the factors which prompted you recently to subscribe (please check all statements which apply)

Rank	Responses*	%
1. I am relatively new to this professional activity	255	36.2
2. I now feel I can afford to subscribe	234	33.2
3. I formerly used a library copy, but this is now impractical	142	20.1
4. I have recently changed to this area of specialization	116	16.5
5. I have joined a society which supplies the subscription as part of my membership	105	14.9
6. I have outside funds (such as grants) which permit this purchase	57	8.1
7. This journal is important enough so that I have canceled other journals instead	38	5.4
7. I formerly used a colleague's copy, but this is now impractical	38	5.4
9. The quality of the journal has improved	19	2.7
9. The journal is needed to fulfill the demands of my research	19	2.7
11. The subscription is furnished to me free as part of an exchange	8	1.1
11. The subscription was given to me as a gift	8	1.1
11. I formerly used a library copy, but the library canceled its subscription	8	1.1

Note.—Duplicate numbers indicate ties.
*Multiple responses permitted (*N* respondents = 705).

indicate that a new subscription to an older journal (in existence for at least five years) has been placed because it is the subscriber who is new either to the profession or to this particular field of specialization. Financial considerations are second in decisions to subscribe and include a perceived ability now to being able to afford the journal or to having grant funds available. While 20 percent of these new subscribers indicated that they had formerly used a library copy but that this was now inconvenient, the other answers of this group force us to redefine "convenience," not in terms of distance from the library, unattractive reading rooms, or limited hours of opening, but rather in terms of wanting the journal at hand rapidly and continually because of its importance to them. Only 1 percent or respondents gave as a reason for placing a subscription the fact that their library had canceled its subscription, and this reason was in each case combined with others. The conclusion that most individual subscriptions arise from the interests of those new to a field and that the library has little to do with their decision to subscribe is also supported by the fact that 80 percent of new subscribers placed their subscriptions within three years of becoming aware of the existence of the journal, although all of the journals had been in existence at least

TABLE 9

INDIVIDUAL AWARENESS OF JOURNAL

How did you first become aware of the importance to you of this journal?

Rank	Responses*	%
1. In school	254	36.0
2. Through professional contacts	241	34.2
3. References in the literature	225	31.9
4. Browsing in the library	116	16.5
5. Promotional activity by publisher	24	3.4
6. Borrowing through the library	5	.7
7. Abstracting and indexing services	2	.3

*Multiple responses permitted (N respondents = 705).

five years and some much longer. Furthermore, the decision to subscribe is a decision made for that journal alone. Subscribers do not rank their journals, at least not consciously, to choose between placing one subscription or another. As the results of the individual cancellation study will also confirm, the perceived importance of the journal to professional activities is central to the determination of whether or not to buy it or to renew it.

Awareness of the Existence of the Journal

As shown in table 9, the great majority of respondents became aware of the existence of the journal during the course of their education, for example, as a result of assigned readings, or independent research, or as part of their work assignments. Even the third-ranking answer, learning of the existence of the journal through references in the literature, can be considered a part of this same educational process.

It can be seen from table 9 that interlibrary loan requests for references obtained in various ways do not tend to lead to individuals' subscribing to new titles, a finding which contradicts the assertions made by the Alaska Health Sciences Information Center.[4] This is probably not surprising. We already know that the titles borrowed on interlibrary loan are not primarily the esoteric journals nobody has but rather the popular journals a library has but cannot produce on demand.[8] It is also true that the journals which the individuals ultimately find important enough to purchase are already owned by the libraries at the institutions at which they received their academic preparation or at which they currently work. They are the titles known to an individual's professors and coworkers and are the ones to which he is referred by references in his other readings.

Conclusion

It can be fairly concluded from this part of the study that a library's policies and activities have little impact on the decision of an individual to place a new journal subscription, although the library may play a part in permitting the subscriber to become familiar with the journal in the first place.

INDIVIDUAL CANCELLATIONS

Reasons for Cancellation

As shown in table 10, reasons for cancellation tend to center on a perceived change in the value of the journal to the reader's professional work. This is not necessarily something the publisher can do anything about. A change in the subscriber's own focus of interest, which outstrips all other responses by more than two to one, tends to lead to a cancellation. Similarly, cancellation of a membership in a society in many cases could be another indication of shift in interest.

Financial pressures, while evident from this survey, are not the primary reasons for cancellation. Allowing for overlap in responses, only about 20 percent of the respondents mentioned money at all in various

TABLE 10

INDIVIDUAL REASONS FOR CANCELLATION

The subscription was canceled in consideration of the following factors (please check all statements which apply)

Rank	Responses*	%
1. I have changed my focus of interest	200	41.2
2. The journal did not contain the kind of information I thought it would	91	18.8
3. Substitution of a more appropriate journal	81	16.7
4. I am no longer a member of the society through which I received this journal	71	14.6
5. I have less money available and/or inflationary pressures	65	13.4
6. The library purchased a subscription which I can use	53	10.9
7. Outside (such as grant) funds originally used no longer available	33	6.8
8. Sharp increase in price	21	4.3
9. Poor publisher service	18	3.7
10. The journal has changed its scope	14	2.9
11. I forgot to renew or I did not receive a renewal notice	12	2.5
12. Death of subscriber or elimination of subscribing institution	10	2.1
13. Deterioration of quality of the journal	6	1.2

*Multiple responses permitted (*N* respondents = 485).

explanations, and many of these also checked nonfinancial reasons for cancellation.

Similarly, while 10.9 percent checked the availability of a library copy as one of the reasons for canceling subscriptions, many of these individuals also gave other reasons which centered on the journal's content and their changed interest in it. Only 6 percent checked availability of a library copy alone as their reason.

Continued Readership

We sought to ascertain the sincerity of the answers listed in table 10 by asking individuals whether they were still reading the journals they had canceled. More than half, or 53 percent, of the respondents indicated that they have not read the journal at all since the cancellation of their subscriptions to it; 39 percent indicated that they read it only occasionally; and only 8 percent still read the journal regularly. Clearly, for the great majority the availability or unavailability of library copies had nothing to do with their decision. They canceled the subscriptions because they no longer wanted to read the journal, at least not regularly, and they have not read it regularly since they canceled. It is primarily the 8 percent who still read the journal regularly who canceled their subscriptions not because they wanted to but because they had to, usually for financial reasons. These individuals now rely far more heavily on library subscriptions. We found that 70 percent of those who continue to read the journal regularly or who continue to read it occasionally now rely on a library copy in preference to other approaches, such as reading the copy of a colleague or depending on an alerting service.

Another series of questions elicited similar responses. More than 78 percent of respondents indicated that they were aware that they could find the journal to read elsewhere, most frequently the library, after they had canceled their subscriptions to it, and 11 percent of this group considered this availability as the primary factor in their decision. An additional 16 percent considered this assurance important even if not crucial, but for 73 percent continued access was not important because they foresaw little if any need to read the journal again. Two questions dealt with reinstating canceled subscriptions: "Do you think you are likely to reinstate this subscription in the next several years?" and "Under what circumstances would you consider resubscribing?" Only 15 percent of the sample considered reinstatement likely, 62 percent considered it unlikely, and the rest were not sure. In responding to the second question, those that considered reinstatement unlikely either indicated that there were no conceivable circumstances under which they would subscribe again or identified circumstances that would influence them to change their minds—such as a change in the scope of their own work to fit the journal or a change in the journal's scope to fit their work—that were so improbable that they can be discounted. Improvement in financial conditions was mentioned by 22.1 percent of individuals canceling subscriptions as a condition for renewing them, a response that may be considered surprisingly low in view of the tendency of some publishers to attribute financial reasons for most cancellations. An additional 5.4 percent of the cancelers indicated they might resubscribe if the quality or timeliness of the journal improved or the publisher's service got better—a discouragingly small target at which publishers can aim their qualitative improvements. The same number, 5.4 percent of the cancelers, blamed a lack of reading time for their cancellation and indicated they might resubscribe if they had more time, which seems unlikely to happen. Finally, 5.1 percent indicated that they might resubscribe if they lost access to the library's copy.

Conclusion

As with new subscriptions, the majority of cancellations by individuals have nothing to do with the library, and they are concerned only secondarily with money. Subscriptions are canceled, as they are placed, because of the perceived importance or lack or importance to the professional activities of the subscriber. Many of these changes result simply because people change fields and therefore change journals. There is a small group of subscribers, perhaps 10 percent, who cancel their subscriptions unwillingly because of financial pressures, and who then depend on the availability of a library copy.

LIBRARY NEW SUBSCRIPTIONS

Before we begin consideration of library responses, one point should be reemphasized. As noted earlier, in 42.4 percent of the cases, libraries disputed the publishers' claims that they had entered new subscriptions for a journal; and 50.9 percent of the libraries which publishers believed had canceled subscriptions disputed this. Together these figures account for 47.7 percent of subscription data supplied by publishers. There is little doubt that in virtually all of these disputed cases library records are correct, and the aberrations are caused by the way in which publishers handle late renewal, attention line changes, or changes in subscription agents. This is unfortunate, because it makes it virtually impossible for any publishers with such circulation records to draw meaningful conclusions about their library market. The survey results described below have the advantage of having culled these spurious records from the file, although this was done at a cost of having to lose almost half of the library response sample.

Fortunately, the size of the initial sample (it was providentially increased at the suggestion of proposal reviewers, although none suspected the nature of the situation ultimately revealed) and the excellent response rate provide us with enough data for useful analysis, despite the possibility of bias introduced by the variation in the sampling procedure.

Type of Subscription

As shown in table 11, a sizable majority of all subscriptions placed in libraries represent titles not previously held, even though the titles themselves are at least five years old. If newly published titles had been included in the survey, it is probable that the percentage of first-time subscriptions would have been greater. About a quarter of the subscriptions placed are reinstatements; this supports the finding from later questions that, while libraries may be reluctant to cancel subscriptions, once having gone through the process of deciding to retain or to cancel a subscription, they are not likely to reopen the question. Only about one in sixteen subscriptions represents an additional subscription for a title already in the collection. Since the initial wave of cancellations reported in the 1969–76 data from our earlier studies largely involved elimination of duplicates,[1,2,5] it is interesting to note from these statistics that there is no rush to reinstate these, despite the implications for service cited by Trueswell[9] and others who have studied collection usage.[10] It seems clear that collection building, or at least the maintenance of the integrity of the collection, still outranks service availability in libraries holding research journals.

TABLE 11
IDENTIFICATION OF TYPE OF LIBRARY SUBSCRIPTION PLACED

Rank	Responses*	%
1. A new subscription to a title not previously held	182	61.5
2. A reinstatement of a subscription previously held	78	26.4
3. An additional subscription for a title already in the institution	19	6.4
4. A formerly free (exchange or gift) subscription	12	4.1
5. Other miscellaneous responses	5	1.7

*N responses = 296.

The Library Subscriptions

As shown in table 12, the process of deciding to place a new subscription, even to an older journal, still consists primarily of a specific action in response to a specific request. That is, the library entered a subscription because somebody suggested, requested, or demanded that it do so. Four of the top five reasons for placing a subscription involve users, either as individuals or as groups. While it is possible that the suggestion to subscribe to one journal was accompanied by a suggestion to cancel another, there is no reason to suppose that this was so. The practice of "relative ranking" of journals in a particular subject discipline to determine subscription priorities usually involves existing subscriptions. Suggestions for new acquisitions, which can come at any time during the year, frequently fall outside this ranking process, although some libraries, by allocating dollars to subject disciplines and in effect abdicating selection to their users, force these users to face a ranking process at the time of renewal.

There is no evidence that libraries make any significant use of formal measurements or criteria in deciding to place a subscription. The

TABLE 12

LIBRARY MOTIVATIONS FOR SUBSCRIPTION

Since this journal has been in existence for some time prior to your subscription, we are interested in the factors which prompted you to subscribe at this time.

Rank	Responses*	%
1. Evaluation by a user group or department has recommended this title	93	31.4
2. Evaluation by library staff has recommended this title	76	25.7
3. This title was specifically requested by a continuing user	70	23.6
4. We are developing new areas of specialization	63	21.3
5. This title was specifically requested by a new user	55	18.6
6. Easing of budgetary restrictions	31	10.5
7. Special funds available for this purpose	21	7.1
8. General collection development	20	6.8
9. We find we are borrowing this title frequently	19	6.4
10. The library just learned of this title from citations and other literature references	16	5.4
11. The library just learned of this title from abstracting/indexing tools	9	3.0
12. The subscription is for a new facility or branch	5	1.7
13. The journal has improved in quality	2	.7
13. This title has been assigned to us as a network or consortium responsibility	2	.7
15. An extra copy was needed for routing to users	1	.3
16. The library just learned of this title through interlibrary loan	0	.0

Note.—Duplicate numbers indicate ties.
*Multiple responses permitted (N respondents = 296).

process appears to be primarily subjective; nor is there any comparative evaluation implied in reasons 6 and 7 given in table 12, which deal with the availability of funds, although such evaluation would not have been precluded. It may be, for example, that these journals were selected from a want list when funds became available. It appears that the availability of funds, comparative ranking of a title, and the holdings of other libraries are far less important in the decision to subscribe to a specific title than they are in the decision to cancel. It is not until the ninth-ranked factor (listed as a reason for subscribing to a title by only 6.4 percent of respondents) that we begin to arrive at evaluative factors which consider use, demand, outside availability, or the assignment of specializations by networks or consortia. Obviously, it is far more difficult to develop quantitative criteria for a title not held than for one already held. There is little evidence of much planning in the selection of new titles, which appears to be a subjective and perhaps political process. Frequent borrowing of a title is listed as at least a partial factor in deciding to resubscribe in only about one case in sixteen.

Permanence of New Subscriptions

Over 58 percent of the libraries in the sample indicate that a decision to subscribe to a new title will be reviewed at the time of renewal; the new subscription, therefore, is at a far greater degree of risk than historically ensconced subscriptions. These libraries report that their review involves a case-by-case evaluation in which users, staff, and usage statistics, as shown in table 13, are consulted. Of particular significance are the 12.5 percent (although some respondents may have checked both answers 5 and 6) who report that, in deciding to renew (as contrasted to deciding to subscribe), they will consider the holdings and acquisition decisions of other libraries as well as the policies of networks and consortia to which they belong. Since these factors have not heretofore been mentioned in our earlier survey[1, 2, 5] responses, it is reasonable to believe that use of these criteria for retention will grow. Since it is decisions not to retain subscriptions which result in cancellations, it is relevant to observe that responses to the cancellation questionnaire indicate that interlibrary evaluations, both formal and informal, play a larger role in deciding to cancel than in the decision to subscribe initially.

LIBRARY CANCELLATIONS

Of subscriptions canceled by libraries in the survey, 81.7 percent were the only subscription in the collection, 14.6 percent were duplicate sub-

TABLE 13
LIBRARY DECISION TO RENEW SUBSCRIPTION

If you plan to review this decision at the time of the next renewal, whom will this involve?

Rank	Responses*	%
1. User evaluations	98	64.5
2. Staff evaluations	84	55.3
3. Usage statistics	67	44.1
4. Rank ordering with other titles	17	11.2
5. Acquisitions decisions of other libraries	11	7.2
6. Network or consortium policies	8	5.3
7. Did not indicate specific procedures although review is planned	2	1.3

*Multiple responses permitted (N respondents = 152).

scriptions within the same library, and 3.7 percent were subscriptions in a branch library with a copy still available somewhere within the system. This high proportion of cancellations of unique titles is a distinct change from the survey data we reported for 1969–73,[1,2] which indicated that the cancellation of duplicates was the first priority. The apparent shift in priorities to the cancellation of unique subscriptions may be partly attributable to a greater concern for collection use than for collection continuity, but it seems more likely that at least some of the unique subscriptions are being canceled because the duplicates—at least the most obvious duplicates—are already gone.

Factors in Library Subscription Cancellation

As shown in table 14, budgetary curtailments underlie the majority of library cancellations. This is similar to the finding from our earlier studies[1,2,5] that, until confronted by budgetary constraints, libraries tended to renew subscriptions automatically, regardless of need or use. For large academic libraries we found the 1969 cancellation rate to be 0.2 percent, although it was considerably larger for other types of libraries, approaching 5 percent for special libraries. At the same time, while budgetary curtailments underlie most cancellations, it does not therefore follow that expensive journals get canceled. There appears to be a reverse of the selection process for new subscriptions, which, as noted earlier, takes place as an independent judgment outside the scope of other evaluations. The cancellation process seems to start from the amount of dollar savings to be achieved; the journals to be canceled are then selected. While it is true that cancellation of one expensive journal would eliminate the necessity of canceling several cheaper ones, libraries seem not to choose this option. One of our earlier studies indicated that the mean

TABLE 14

FACTORS IN LIBRARY CANCELLATIONS

The subscription was canceled in consideration of the following factors (please check all statements which apply).

Rank	Responses*	%
1. Budget curtailments	238	56.8
2. Staff evaluation	192	45.8
3. Shifting priorities	148	35.3
4. User recommendations	117	27.9
5. High price	36	8.6
6. Closed facility	14	3.3
6. Other factors (miscellaneous responses)	14	3.3
8. Increase in price	13	3.1
9. Not included in major indexes	7	1.7
10. A gift subscription not picked up	3	.7
11. Physical format of publication	2	.5
11. Poor publisher service	2	.5
13. Microform availability	1	.2
14. Available in computer databases	0	.0

Note.—Duplicate numbers indiate ties.
*Multiple responses permitted (N respondents = 419).

price of canceled journals was no greater than the mean price of retained ones,[5] and the relatively low rating given to the present study to price factors as a reason for canceling specific titles suggests that this process has not changed.

It is interesting to note that, while users played the predominant role in the selection of new titles, it is librarians who play the larger part in determining what subscriptions are to be discontinued.

Interlibrary Activities in the Cancellation Decision

When asked whether the decision to cancel was based to any degree on membership in a consortium or network whose policies formally encourage cancellation of titles available elsewhere, 329 of 358, 91.9 percent, of the libraries replied in the negative. What is surprising is that twenty-nine, or 8.1 percent, actually did indicate that membership played a part in deciding to cancel. As late as 1976 we could find no indication whatsoever that cancellation decisions were anything but specific action taken by a library in an evaluation of its own needs and priorities.[5] This present survey gives some indication of a role of cooperative planning in cancellation decision—something which publishers have feared. It is likely that this process, once begun, will accelerate, though the responses indicate that the process is still informal. Over 72 percent of the twenty-nine libraries for which group membership played a role in their decision to cancel a subscription indicated that the decision was theirs alone and based on the knowledge, or at least belief, that another library or a central resource center had the title. Only 27.6 percent of these respondents, or eight libraries out of the total sample, based their own cancellation at least in part on the specific information that either the subject specialization or the specific title had been made the responsibility of another library.

There are, of course, two ways of looking at this information. Libraries may look at it as providing some confirmation of the economic value of consortium and network membership and may argue, as they have done in the past, that, since the total funds expended for periodical subscriptions are set by outside forces, all that results is perhaps a shifting of funds from one journal to protect retention of another. That is, cooperation agreements may influence which journals are retained or canceled, not how many.[3, 11] Publishing groups, particularly individual publishers, who in the long run care less about why libraries cancel journal subscriptions in general than why they cancel their particular publications, may not be as easily assuaged.[12]

Important as the beginning of a trend like this is, it is also important that it not be stressed too much. Primarily, the decision to cancel is still an internal decision made without consideration of outside factors. When specifically asked whether probable availability on interlibrary loan was a factor in the cancellation decision, 65 percent of the libraries responded that it was not; and of the remaining 35 percent for which it was at least a partial factor, only slightly more than half *knew* they would be able to borrow the title if they needed it. The rest just assumed it or planned to purchase individual copies from either the publisher or a central service if they could not conveniently borrow them. About 10 percent indicated that a national library or a major resource center for the particular discipline to which the journal belonged would be certain to have it available. Of course, the 65 percent who did not consider loan availabililty in their cancellation decision may simply have an abiding faith that somebody, somewhere, will be certain to subscribe to the title and will lend it to them.

Use of Title since Cancellation

An analysis of the next set of responses indicates why libraries are frequently not particularly concerned about whether the title is available. They frequently cancel subscriptions which have had little if any use in the library and for which they expect little use in the future, and their judgment appears to be correct in this. We know that some of the cancellations which become part of the survey had occurred only a few months ago and that others were almost two years old. An average of one year may be assumed to have elapsed since cancellation at the time of the present survey. Asked whether they had had any call or request for the now canceled title in the last year, only thirteen of the responding 362 libraries, or 3.6 percent, indicated that they had, while 269, or 74.3 percent, replied without hesitation that they had not. The eighty libraries (22.1 percent of the sample) which are uncertain are a surprisingly large group, and there are several possible explanations for this. It may be, particularly in large libraries, that the serials staff which generally completed this questionnaire was not aware of interlibrary loan activities. It may be that some librarians, despite the anonymous nature of the questionnaire, were being vague to avoid possible self-incrimination in copyright infringement. And, of course, it may be that some simply do not know, although the new copyright law requires that libraries maintain records of what they borrow.

In any case, the specific positive indication of further use of the canceled title is small indeed.

Review of Cancellation Decision

Earlier in this paper it was reported that a large proportion of libraries planned to review their new subscription decisions at the time of renewal. The same is not true for cancellation decisions. Having made a decision to cancel largely based on financial exigencies, librarians tend not to review this decision subsequently. They probably see no point in reopening the question as long as financial constraints are still in evidence.

Only 15.5 percent of canceling libraries, or fifty-six of a responding total of 362, planned any sort of formal review of their decision, and even of these only nine, or 16.1 percent, estimated the possibility of resubscription as good.

General Library Conclusions

The survey indicates that placing new subscriptions and canceling existing ones seem to involve different processes, mechanisms, and value systems. Placing a new subscription is largely a subjective process, perhaps a political one. The subscription is placed because a user or a user group wants it placed. Little account of usage statistics, citation patterns, interlibrary borrowing, or availability of the title in other libraries is taken in the decision. That is, the library tends to see its role as purchasing the faculty's materials as requested or instructed. Cancellation, by contrast, results not from desire but from financial need, and it is a process in which the user tends to participate to a lesser extent. The library staff tends to select for cancellation those titles that are thought to be little used and sometimes those titles which can be readily borrowed if the library has guessed wrong.

The two processes of new subscription and cancellation appear to have little to do with one another. Libraries cancel because they do not have enough money to maintain existing subscriptions, but they do not cancel in order to place new subscriptions. Once placed, however, these new subscriptions become part of the overall pressure when they come up for renewal. There appears to be no attempt to rank a new title with existing subscriptions before deciding to purchase it. Such a ranking seems to be a part of the cancellation decision, but the ranking is based on a complex variety of factors, including perceived need and political considerations; actual price is a secondary factor. It seems also that librarians are beginning to look at networks, consortia, and other formal cooperative programs for protection against the risk of making a wrong cancellation decision. This process, long expected by librarians and feared by publishers, appears just now to be getting under way.

References

1. Fry, Bernard M., and White, Herbert S. *Publishers and Libraries: A Study of Scholarly and Research Journals.* Lexington, Mass.: D. C. Heath & Co., 1976.

2. White, Herbert S. "Publishers, Libraries, and Costs of Journal Subscriptions in Times of Funding Retrenchment." *Library Quarterly* 46 (October 1976): 359–77.

3. De Gennaro, Richard. "Escalating Journal Prices: Time to Fight Back." *American Libraries* 8 (February 1977): 69–74.

4. Alaska Health Sciences Information Service. "Effect of Photocopying on Journal Subscriptions." *Medical Library Association News* 82 (September 1976): 7–9.

5. Fry, Bernard M., and White, Herbert S. "Impact of Economic Pressures on American Libraries and Their Decisions concerning Scholarly and Research Journal Acquisition and Retention." Final Report. National Technical Information Service PB 283874. Bloomington: Indiana University Graduate Library School, June 1978.

6. White, Herbert S., and Fry, Bernard M. "The Impact of Periodical Availability in Libraries on Individual and Library Subscription Placement and Cancellation." Final Report. National Technical Information Service PB 80111883. Bloomington: Indiana University Graduate Library School, December 1979.

7. Fry, Bernard M.; White, Herbert S.; and Johnson, Elizabeth L. "Survey of Publisher Practices and Present Attitudes on Authorized Journal Article Copying and Licensing." Final Report. National Technical Information Service PB 271003. Bloomington: Indiana University Graduate Library School, June 1977.

8. Stewart, Blair. "Periodicals and the Liberal Arts College Library." *College and Research Libraries* 36 (September 1975): 371–78.

9. Trueswell, Richard W. "Growing Libraries: Who Needs Them? A Statistical Basis for the No-Growth Collection." In *Farewell to Alexandria,* edited by Daniel Gore. Westport, Conn.: Greenwood Press, 1976.

10. Kent, Allen; Cohen, Jacob; Montgomery, K. Leon; Williams, James G.; Bulick, Stephen; Flynn, Roger R.; Sabor, William N.; and Mansfield, Una. *Use of Library Materials: The University of Pittsburgh Study.* Books in Library and Information Science Series, vol. 26. New York: Marcel Dekker, Inc., 1979.

11. Line, Maurice B., and Wood, D. N. "The Effect of a Large-Scale Photocopying Service on Journal Sales." *Journal of Documentation* 31 (December 1975): 234–45.

12. Van Tongeren, E. "Documentation Notes: The Effect of a Large-Scale Photocopying Service on Journal Sales." *Journal of Documentation* 32 (September 1976): 198–206.

Ownership Is Not Always Availability: Borrowing May Not Satisfy Access Needs

I am pleased to contribute a paper to this volume dealing with access to scholarly information, with an emphasis on the word access. I make this point at the very outset because most of our preoccupation as a profession, and particularly in academic libraries, has been with the evaluation and measurement of libraries through their ownership and holdings. Access not very many years ago meant the ability to find an item in the library's card catalog. If that location was successful, then the library's role in providing access had been successfully fulfilled. Whether or not the item could be retrieved for the individual requestor within 30 minutes, one hour, one day, two days, or one week, was a secondary and perhaps irrelevant question which had nothing to do with the values of the library. If the material was already charged out, that was hardly our fault. Lest the reader think that my statement is a gross exaggeration I would note that to this day, few if any libraries have any statistics concerning their ability to respond to the need for items in their own collections. If the material is in the catalog, what percentage of it is available immediately? What percentage within two hours, one day, one week? It has been stated that half of the material in the catalog is not on the shelf on the day it is requested, but to my knowledge we don't have hard core information, or really any way of getting it. It would require us to implement a policy under which we somehow got indivi-

From *Access to Scholarly Information: Issues and Strategies,* ed. Sul H. Lee (Ann Arbor, Mich.: Pieran Press, 1985), 1–11.

duals who looked for a book and didn't find it to report that to us. Right now, many of them simply take another book (whether or not it is as good we will never know nor will they), or leave the library, and say nothing to us.

Concern with collection rather than access is of course the faculty view. Faculty are not as concerned with access questions. Much of what they need they have already pre-empted away to their own offices, so that in this case ownership equals access. Ownership concerns also get in the way of fostering interlibrary cooperative activities, and will continue to as long as we are counting volumes. My response at a cocktail party to the question "Why don't academic libraries cooperate more in their acquisitions programs?", was "libraries are likely to cooperate more when the president of the university stops having cocktail parties to celebrate the x millionth acquisition." I almost ended up with a drink dropped on my foot.

Access as differentiated from ownership is of course a major concern for secondary users, but many of these are students, and library policies are rarely made for the benefit and with the input of student concerns. Trueswell postulated his 80–20 rule as long ago as an article in the *Wilson Library Bulletin* in 1969.[1] Most simply, his rule is an expression of the Bradford distribution curve; 80% of document needs can be satisfied from 20% of the collection. Of course, the Pittsburgh study by Galvin and Kent[2] said the same thing, and I found it fascinating that at least some of the criticism came from individuals who didn't really attack the methodology or conclusions, but stated the premise that such a study should never have been done, because it played into the hands of the enemies of libraries. I consider that nonsense.

That ownership and access can present contradictory value systems during times of budgetary stress (such as for the last 10 years, now, and for the foreseeable future) becomes clear in the results of an Indiana University National Science Foundation funded study[3] on which I reported in an Oklahoma University sponsored conference several years ago. We found that as budget cuts required decisions on what *not* to buy, the most immediate candidates were duplicate copies and duplicate subscriptions. Not necessarily because they weren't being used—they presumably were—but because from the standpoint of holdings these duplicates were "frills" which didn't count. Over a period of only about five years, the duplication rate of periodical subscriptions in academic libraries fell from 5% (a figure I would already consider suspiciously and unnaturally low given the number of branch collections) to less than 2%. It is only after we have cancelled these "frill" duplicates that we are prepared to tackle the question of what we might have that nobody is using, or is unlikely to use. Those predictions are not hard to make. As Kent and Galvin noted, material not used in the first year or the first five years is not likely to be used in the next hundred years, either. Yes, the possibility exists, but the probability does not, and collection decisions should at least be based on an estimate of reasonable probability, unless you are prepared to acquire everything. Not even the Library of Congress does that.

It is clear that the academic library materials budget is aimed at ownership and not at access. Perhaps the most blatant example is the practice of charging users for the cost of interlibrary loan, but not charging them the cost of a book they have appropriated as soon as it was cataloged and have kept in their office for the last ten years. Charging for interlibrary loan represents, for me, a logical absurdity in any case. It amounts to a double penalization for the user. The first comes from the fact that you didn't buy what I am now asking you for. I am sensible enough to recognize that you can't buy everything, but I could probably make a case that this acquisition would have been more reasonable than some of the things you did buy. However, I won't even do that, because I realize that second guessing is unfair. I am therefore willing to forgive you for not already owning what I have just requested. However, your insistence in now penalizing me twice—first from the standpoint of time because I have to wait and secondly by attempting to charge me—stretches all credulity, and I refuse to play along.

I realize, of course, why academic libraries have so much difficulty in paying for so-called peripheral activities such as on-line searching and interlibrary loan. They are peripheral only because they weren't anticipated, at least not in the budget. Most library budgets I have seen spend about ⅔ of their money on staff salaries, and of course that is never enough, certainly in our view. Most of the remaining third goes for material purchase, and of course that is never enough, for either the librarians or the faculty. The materials budget will certainly never be adequate no matter what it is. Nothing or virtually nothing is held back for contingencies or unexpected expenses. This then is why we can't pay for on-line searches. Not because they are more expensive than manual searches. Perhaps they are and perhaps they aren't. The point is that the budget may not have anticipated any such costs, or at least certainly not enough.

An emphasis on collection subverts an emphasis on access because of the continuing competition for funds. As noted in our NSF study, it simply is no contest. It also means that in looking for access alternatives we are looking for the cheapest and not necessarily the best way, or ways to stick the user with the cost of anything we didn't buy. The emphasis on holdings count as a measurement of value goes back to days when there was plenty of money and the strategy worked. Both faculty and library administrators were first and foremost collection builders—only incidentally if at all managers or with a service orientation. The statement "we will be remembered not for the service we gave but for the collection we left behind us," which some of you may recognize and identify, correctly characterizes the period. At the present time, when many academic libraries are indeed being run by qualified and competent administrators capable of making alternative value judgments, we find that the faculty is still playing the old game by the old rules.

We should recognize very quickly that when faculty (and you will already see that I identify faculty as the major obstacle to progress and change) talk about the quality of the library, they are really talking about quality stated as the size of their part of the collection. To faculty the library is a balkanized organization, and they watch to make sure they get what they perceive as their fair share of the acquisitions pie. There is really no way for us to deal with this problem except ultimately directly and in a straight-forward manner. The size of their collection piece becomes part of their own security blanket, and part of the mechanism by which they seek and achieve recognition and approbation from their own colleagues in the same field in other universities. The problem reaches its critical and most tragic point when we have a faculty member who stubbornly insists that the library develop a collection expertise in an area totally outside the university mission, because it is an area in which he or she *wishes* the university were active. Faculty, who can be useful in ranking two books or two journals in their own field to see which is better, but not in deciding that both should be bought (they must work within finite guidelines) don't in all honesty know anything about what makes a good library. This is why concerns of access haven't really permeated faculty bodies. There is really no reason faculty should know very much about this—I don't know what makes a good cyclotron or a well-structured fugue, either. But who is going to tell them?

The proper and, obviously at this stage, idealistic answer to the question asked so often from outside but also inside the field—how many books and journals do you have?—is "I really don't know and I don't care. Does it matter? What is it that you need to know?" The exercise works for me at least in principle, although I recognize there might be more difficulty in applying it in practice. I have asked faculty colleagues "If I promised to deliver to your office within 72 hours any book or journal article you have requested, would you care where I get it from?" Their answer is always that they wouldn't care. Actually, 72 hours probably provides me a margin of safety, because I am quite convinced that even present technology would comfortably permit it in 48 hours or even 24.

If we are to extricate access as a significant priority, we need access budgets, and we need them as a broader substitute for the far more specific materials purchase budgets. By far the greatest portion of the expenditure will still go for purchase, but some for interlibrary loan costs, some to bibliographic access, some to copyright royalty payments, some to photocopying, some to payments for commercial services, some for the development of even faster, more accurate and higher quality delivery mechanisms. It is after all part and parcel of the same problem.

Satellite accessibility for the transmittal of text has been available for some time, and individuals in Hawaii long ago stopped relying on airplanes to bring them films of football games. I served in 1975 as a member of the consultant team for what was to be the new Pahlavi National Library in Iran. The library never happened, for reasons I am sure you understand. However, the report still exists at least in fragmented volumes, it could be reconstructed, and it has some value even nine years later. We planned interlibrary loan from the British Museum and the Library of Congress to Teheran via satellite, with local delivery via helicopter because the roads were not good enough. That was 9 years ago, and it was not then nor is it now a far-flung technological breakthrough. All of the technology was available then, and it is old technology now. We don't need to be nearly as esoteric or expensive, but we do need to do a great deal more than we are doing, if we are serious about doing for the access problem what we have done for the collection problem.

In our attempts to develop systems for access beyond ownership, we immediately turn to "funny money" solutions such as interlibrary loan. They are funny money approaches in part because we don't really want to know what it costs to lend—certainly not in the true economic sense of burdened expense categories. The best we will do is identify out of pocket expenses, and we do even that reluctantly. Interlibrary loan is still justified as a cooperative activity, and buttressed by the insistence that it provides a mutual benefit for all of us. There is even the suggestion that it involves a moral or higher duty to the profession. Of course, we know that services provided as a favor are furnished at the convenience or pleasure of the provider, and will usually take a low priority when compared to other and more important functions. I find this sad, because it has burdened us with an antiquated and archaic mechanism, which stands out particularly in contrast to the rapid strides we have made in developing bibliographic access systems. Alternatives are available, but they cost more. What is saddest of all is the fact that users have accepted this value system and these delays as reasonable. Users are not critical of library services, and almost any survey of user reactions to the local library will produce a favorable response—except perhaps with regard to materials purchase. We pay dearly for this lack of critical expectations, although it does make things easier for us. Please allow me to give you three specific examples from my own observation and background.

I do a fair amount of industrial library and information center consulting, much of it oriented to an evaluation of present library services. Even though hardly anyone ever complains, sometimes the librarians and sometimes upper management know there are problems which should be addressed. As part of this process I try to schedule interviews with a random sample of professionals in the organization, some heavy library users, some non-users or very peripheral users. All are high in their praise of the library, and all blame themselves for any lack of further use of the facilities. Ultimately, the one service virtually all of them use is interlibrary loan. I ask them how the service works and they say it works fine. I ask them how long it takes to get a response and they tell me it varies, usually from a few days to several weeks and sometimes more than a month. I then ask them if they think that is reasonable. I invariably have to repeat the question because they don't understand it. They believe it is reasonable as a delay because we have told them it is reasonable, and of course that is nonsense. For some users a lengthy delay causes no problems, for others it makes the entire process irrelevant. We have no real way to adapt to the specific situation and to change our procedures to suit. We might if the client is willing to pay more, and we will happily let him use his own resources to satisfy his request.

I know a faculty member at another university who once shared a particular problem with me. He is a full professor, a graduate of an Ivy League institution, and not easily intimidated—except by library policy. Confronted by the need to verify a reference from a work he planned to use for a class assignment, he proceeded confidently to the library catalog and located the call number of the item in question. There was no copy on the shelf, and his inquiry at the circulation desk produced the information that there were two copies, one lost and one charged out. It might return any time but was not due for two weeks. Defeated, because he needed the material by Friday, he returned to his office and deleted the reference from his reading list.

Why? Why did he accept an inventory report instead of a plan to furnish him with the needed material? If the library's copy is out, or lost, or at the bindery, and the need for a copy by Friday is realistic, is it really true as assumed that the interlibrary process could not meet the request in time? Of course not, if we are prepared to deal with individual need rather than with organizational procedure. A rapid contact of the OCLC file will indicate quickly if the material is included in the collections of one of the neighboring state universities, located less than 200 miles away. A telephone call will determine whether the material is on the shelf, with the request that it be charged out on interlibrary loan and left at the main circulation desk. The paper work, if indeed there must be multi-carbon paperwork, can follow. A further call to the university travel office will identify at least a half dozen faculty members on the neighboring campus, planning to return (probably by car) within the next 24 or 48 hours. Would they be willing to pick up the material, as a favor to a faculty colleague if not the library? Of course they would. Why don't we ask them? Because it never occurs to us. It also never occurs to us that offering a status report, or an explanation of why the item is not available, is neither a solution nor an answer.

A doctoral student at Indiana University is currently completing a dissertation under my direction. In it, he compares and contrasts the interlibrary loan practices of chemistry librarians in industry and chemistry librarians in universities. There are substantial differences, and they are largely attitudinal. Some of them involve a greater expenditure of funds, but not all. Industrial librarians of course never charge their users for the cost of interlibrary loan. They recognize, or at least someone does, that such a practice would be pointless because ultimately the cost would still be borne from parent organizational funds. Of course, the same thing is also true in universities, because I doubt that very many faculty members pay the interlibrary loan cost from their own personal pockets. At least, not in the universities with which I am familiar.

There are other differences. Industrial chemistry librarians are free to use their ingenuity and interpersonal contacts to obtain needed material as quickly as possible. Many requests are made over the telephone. Academic libraries, which usually have a greater access to terminal equipment, rarely use it for this purpose. Most academic chemistry branch heads are not even allowed to make their own requests, but must rather submit the request to a central interlibrary loan office. That function, which has no direct contact with the original requestor, places the request through its own procedures, and either mails the material to or contacts the requestor. The branch librarian doesn't even know when or whether the request was filled.

Industrial chemistry libraries report that they make heavier use of commercial services during peak load periods or when the interlibrary loan clerks are backlogged. In academic libraries the user just waits longer, because the process doesn't change. Of course commercial services cost more. Why don't we budget so that we can use them as necessary?

For librarians to face issues of access we have to separate them from issues of ownership, because ownership is only one form of access. Even ownership does not guarantee access—not if somebody else has the material first. As a teaching faculty member who both adapts library procedures to my own needs and my own strategies to procedures I can't change, I note with some assurance that the reason that individuals such as myself don't return things to the library is in part because of a value system which makes books in our offices (even if we didn't buy them) appear impressive. It is also because if we have any expectation of needing material again it is safer to hang on to it. I don't return it because I don't trust it to be there if and when I want it again, and of course that becomes a self-fulfilling prophecy. I trust the library's purchasing system a lot more than I trust its access system.

Once we begin to look at all aspects of access as alternative solutions to one and the same problem, we can perhaps begin to dismantle the present antiquated and obsolete system of interlibrary loan which has choked off response quality for so long, and substitute for it a system which validates itself on economic grounds. That is, economic ground for the librarian, because that individual now has the choice between purchase and a more temporary or request-driven form of acquisition. Richard de Gennaro,[4] in his talk at Indiana University's own copyright seminar in 1977, was not making that point directly, but it emerged at least peripherally. The copyright borrowing limitations for a particular periodical title posed no problems for him, and as far as he could see should pose none for other academic libraries. Anything borrowed so frequently as to approach the CONTU guidelines should be bought, because it is certainly being used more frequently than much of the material which is being bought. De Gennaro is correct, in his appeal to reason. I would feel better if I could buttress that point with an appeal to the pocketbook. What should be the crossover point economically where repeated borrowing is more expensive for the borrowing library? We need such an economic motivator because the motivator of anticipating the user's requests by having more copies of fewer things obviously does not persuade us. And, of course, if librarians pay for purchase but individuals pay for borrowing, we have destroyed the ability to compare.

Interlibrary loan will work well when it is economically driven to motivate the supplier, as of course it now does with commercial services. That should also apply to academic lenders, who should be encouraged to charge not only out of pocket cost, but all direct cost, burdened with overhead as in any proper accounting system. In fact, if we can provide a little extra beyond that, we might even get lenders to compete in service quality and speed for the privilege of lending. Will it cost more? Of course it will cost the borrowing library or whoever is subsidizing it more, although the money will presumably stay within the larger system, and those libraries which both lend and borrow will break even. Lend is an outmoded term when applied to the periodical articles which comprise most of scholarly transactions, anyway. Articles are not lent, photocopies are sent for retention.

To the extent to which the acquiring library can successfully seek subsidies for this process, I wish it good luck. Those subsidies can perhaps be furnished by the parent institution, perhaps by the state, perhaps the federal government, perhaps some benevolent foundation. The options are as open as they are for the support of other library activities.

However, to charge the user for this transaction when he is not charged for the books the library has bought for him to keep in his office, and when the need to acquire from the outside really results from your decisions and not his, is illogical and unfair.

What is the cost of supplying material at a proper reimbursement rate? Commercial services provide something of a clue of bottom line cost, because it certainly costs the supplying academic library, bureaucratically structured as it is, more than that. Perhaps $10 on the average, perhaps as much as $15. We really can't control that figure, or at least shouldn't try, to any greater extent than to which we influence the cost of books and periodicals we purchase. The relationship between the economics of purchase or of other forms of access can then be easily established, and we can even establish a cut-over point between purchase and each-time-we-need it acquisition for every title. Obviously, there is a cost involved in all of this and we don't have enough money. But then, we never have had enough money, don't have it now, and won't have it in the future. But we have failed to accept the fact that other costs of access (bibliographic as well as document) are as legitimate a kind of library cost as the purchase of material which will sit on the shelf and, at least according to Trueswell, Kent, and Galvin, be used by nobody. Our attempts to diffuse or minimize the cost of interlibrary access leads us into all sort of nonsensical ground rules designed to even up the burden of lending, precisely because it is still a burden. Requesting libraries are supposed to go through a geographically based system of priorities in deciding from whom to request material. The doctoral dissertation to which I referred earlier found that industrial special libraries, perhaps because they are more pragmatically driven, ignore that injunction. I could have told the student that, too. When I was an aerospace industrial special librarian in Texas in the late 1950s we acquired almost all interlibrary loans from Georgia Tech. Why? Because they had almost everything we wanted, because they were accurate, and because they were fast. If someone had demanded I first try the Texas Engineers Library I would have responded that I used to try the Texas Engineers Library first, and that was why I now requested from Georgia Tech.

Georgia Tech never complained, and never asked why they had been singled out for an attention level which sometimes exceeded 25 requests/week. They never charged me, either, and perhaps that was wrong. If they had charged me, I would have had to make my case to my own management for budgeting this cost, and perhaps this would have allowed me to make a stronger case for a larger purchase budget. As management then saw it, and perhaps in many libraries still does, the difference between purchase and other forms of access was between a cost and no cost, and that made decisions easy. Too easy.

Although I have been addressing this issue in more general library terms, and drawing some of my examples from the special library sector, I believe that it applies just as well to research libraries and the use of scholarly materials. We have known for some time, or at least should have known, that the acquisitions emphasis difference in scholarly libraries comes largely from what librarians and faculty members historically perceive, and not from what they do. They want large inclusive collections because of the security and prestige which this brings to them and their academic department, not necessarily for the way the material will be used. We have known for some time that scientific research as funded by federal agencies (and these are the source of funds for most scientific research projects) tends to be applied research. There is very little basic research carried out in universities, and where it is, it still does not start out with an exhaustive literature review, except for doctoral students who carry no real clout. It starts with a premise, with a hypothesis, with a paradigm, and then seeks evidence to support the conclusion already reached. Evidence which refutes or clouds it is definitely not welcome. As social science research became more and more heavily dependent on government priorities and wishes in the 1950s, 1960s and 1970s, the same description applied here as well. However, there is now at least some evidence that even humanities research may not in all cases be as massively collection-oriented as we have assumed. A member of our NSF study advisory committee, a distinguished professor of theology, stated with confidence that virtually any doctoral program in theology could be supported from a collection of 2000 books, and that in fact he had already identified those books and seen to it that they were moved from the main library to the Theology Department of his university.

Questions of whether or not we provide adequate access services are in any case a matter of concern primarily to us librarians, because for our users alternatives to the library increasingly exist. These include alternatives in bibliographic access, available on a terminal to anyone with an electric outlet and a few dollars. They also include alternatives in document delivery services, available increasingly as an output option of the bibliographic process, and available via telephone line, telefax, or one day delivery service. How often do most libraries use Federal Express or Purolator to acquire information? How often is UPS used to ship material?

Access, both bibliographic and document, can increasingly be done by just about anyone. It only costs money. And, yet, at the same time, I consider it suicidal for libraries to attempt to pass off this process directly to their users, or to users urged to work directly with other information intermediaries. This is something some academic libraries have begun to do increasingly with regard to on-line searching for the silly and correctable reason that it costs money and staff time. In neither case does the refusal to take on this responsibility result in cost reduction for the institution, it only shifts the cost and the responsibility, and as I have already noted in other writings it is a very unwise ceding of library responsbility, or library turf. We certainly don't understand turf as street gangs understand it. It is unwise for us to ignore this concern because control over the bibliographic and document access process is only the preamble to the much larger and much more important struggle we must fight and we must win if we expect to retain our significance in a technologically shifting information era. That struggle will concern the role of librarians as information intermediaries and information interpreters, and it is that struggle we must undertake as soon as we put access concerns behind us.

References

1. Trueswell, Richard W. *Some Behavioral Patterns of Library Users: The 80/20 Rule.* Wilson Library Bulletin 44:458–461, Jan. 1969.

2. Kent, Allen, and others. *User of Library Materials; the University of Pittsburgh Study.* New York, M. Dekker, 1979.

3. White, Herbert S. *Publishers, Libraries, and Costs of Journal Subscriptions in Times of Funding Retrenchment.* Library Quarterly 46: 359–77, Oct. 1977.

4. De Gennaro, Richard. *The Major Research Library and the New Copyright Act.* p. 147–162 of The Copyright Dilemma, edited by Herbert S. White. Chicago, American Library Association, 1978.

THE USE AND MISUSE OF LIBRARY USER STUDIES

User studies are frequently carried out in all kinds of libraries and information centers to determine how individuals like the libraries which serve them.

Some of these projects have consisted of questionnaires or sampled interviews, and some have even used the simple mechanism of asking users to pick up and complete a questionnaire left at the circulation desk. The latter approach is, theoretically at least, as amenable to ballot stuffing by librarians as fans voting for the annual baseball all-star team, long a farcical exercise in convenience and popularity but not in performance evaluation. In library questionnaires the stakes aren't nearly as high, and the results are far more predictable.

I am not sure why user studies in libraries are so popular. Perhaps in part it is because they are so easy to do, and so easy to tabulate. Perhaps it is because we carry, since library school, the injunction that ours is a service profession, and this is one way to validate that service. To some extent such studies may mask librarian insecurity at not knowing how well we are doing the job unless somebody tells us. In some instances the survey is prompted by a management dictum which seeks confirmation from others because of mistrust of the opinions and recommendations of the library staff.

Whatever the reasons, library user studies pose no particular threat, because they always come out complimentary and positive, regardless of the level of library service provided. In the final analysis, that may be the major reason we do user surveys. They always make us feel competent and valuable, and this may compensate for the lack of appreciation and support from our own management.

If that is the purpose, I have no quarrel with it. Librarians receive

From *Library Journal* 110 (December 1985):70–71.

few enough gratifications, and being told by our adoring public how wonderfully we are holding up in spite of all of our problems may be the only reward available. If the purpose of user studies is to gather information for planning and decision making, however, then given the framework in which most are currently carried out, they are next to worthless.

"THEY CAN BE DANGEROUS . . ."

More important, user surveys can be dangerous. If the librarian has been trying to make the point that service is inadequate and even deteriorating, that argument is not likely to be supported by user surveys. Deterioration of a collection, yes—deterioration of services and in particular of professional services—or the continued absence of needed services, probably not.

There is, in our literature, an unfortunate tendency to confuse user needs, user wants, and user demands (or requests) as though these were the same things. Most of our studies do an excellent job determining what users say, but what they say is conditioned by what they think they ought to say, or it would be "reasonable" to say.

Fundamentally, this means that users ask for the library service they get and get the library service for which they ask. Where this may not apply is in user expectations of collections or of hours of opening. Here users can be unreasonable, but only because, in their own backgrounds and our training of them, they have come to believe that the quality of a library is measured in the number of books it owns and in the number of items it circulates. We even publish statistics for our users to transmit this nonsense. Unfortunately, it is the only ranking device they know.

Holdings and circulation do not require librarians at all, they require clerks to purchase and clerks to charge out. Now *we* know that professional librarians do more than that, but *users* don't, and the common perception of the librarian as someone who stamps dates into the backs of books comes from the fact that many think that this is what we do.

The expectation of library service is for the routine transaction of "buy what I tell you and then send it to me." It is only in the failure of that fundamental transaction that we risk client censure. Such censure is then easy to avoid, particularly when we recognize that the user doesn't even care whether or not we catalog the book before he gets it, and would just as soon we didn't if it is going to delay matters.

In my consulting assignments, primarily in industrial library settings, I have been involved in the evaluation of library services which have ranged from the excellent to those which both librarians and high-level management agreed was poor. In all of these circumstances a randomly drawn sample of users and nonusers was unanimous in its praise for the library and its staff. Except for some very minor and localized annoyances concerning the failure to agree to purchase a specific book or specific journal subscription, praise was unstinting.

This unanimity of praise even extended to nonusers, the names of whom were sometimes extracted from reluctant librarians with great difficulty. They need not have feared. Nonusers were as enthusiastic in their praise of libraries as heavy users, and they blamed the library's failure to have what they needed on the esoteric nature of their own work, and never on a library failure to plan or anticipate.

This user passivity is surprising and, as will be noted later, also disastrous. I am forced to wonder whether or not individuals whose trash is not picked up on schedule just naturally assume that one of the trucks broke down or one of the garbagemen is ill, rather than call City Hall to complain.

In my gentle prodding of these enthusiastic and loyal supporters (or apologists) I eventually get to the question of what the library does when the material they are seeking is not available. I am assured that the library is always willing to make the effort to borrow the material for them (the implication of a favor being done comes through quite clearly), and I learn further that this process varies in time from several days to several weeks and occasionally a month or more.

My question of whether or not they consider such a delay reasonable invariably draws a blank stare. The question of reasonableness has never occurred to them. As Allen Veaner has recalled for us in his excellent article on the future of academic libraries, libraries have not improved document delivery time, but have done an excellent job of convincing users to wait.[1] We even convince them to pay for what they are waiting so patiently to receive. It does not occur to them to suggest snidely that perhaps the reason they are waiting is because we failed to anticipate their request.

Asking users to tell us what they want (an expression of demand) is nothing more than an exercise in regurgitation. They tell us quite faithfully what we have prepared them to tell us. Collection is the bottom-line requirement, any extension of service beyond delivery from that collection is "a favor." It is little wonder that our users have fastened onto ownership (first in the library and then, at least in academia, in their own offices) as the ultimate criterion. They remember what we have told them.

We have no difficulty in determining what users say. What do they want? This is a far more difficult exercise in extraction, because it requires that we remove them from the "reality" of current budgets, time constraints, and delivery mechanisms, and allow them to think both idealistically and selfishly. Both librarians and library users have very severely clipped wings, and the free flight of fancy is not encouraged and seldom seen.

A former research director at General Electric is reputed to have argued that he always gave the most difficult problems to junior professionals, because senior professionals not only knew it couldn't be done, but could prove it. By contrast, junior researchers at least occasionally would succeed because they weren't smart enough to know they couldn't. In the field of aerodynamics the bumblebee comes most easily to mind. Given its body weight and wing-lift capability, the bumblebee cannot fly. Fortunately (at least for bumblebees) they cannot read aerodynamic reports.

NEEDED: IRASCIBLE GROUCHES

Perhaps what our profession needs is a few more idealistic dreamers, and what our user communities need is at least a handful of unreasonable and irascible grouches who demand that presumed professionals figure out a way to provide professional services.

My own consulting approach to getting users to tell me what they want is to ask them to idealize an information service specifically oriented to their work, and the way they would like to work, regardless of whether or not such a concept is reasonable and implementable. The "real world," I assure them, will tell them soon enough. It is extremely difficult to get users to fantasize in this manner, just as I have found it nearly impossible, in the two cases in which this was appropriate, to get librarians to develop blueprints for proper service without at least initially worrying about cost.

If we succeed at this, we can perhaps determine what users want or prefer. We still don't know what they need, because they don't know either. User expectations are shaped by environmental pressures, and needs are never discussed because such discussions are not practical. And yet, countless studies which are nothing more than user responses to their Pavlovian stimuli are passed off as user-needs studies, and are then implemented with pomp and solemnity as though they had merit.

The determination of user needs is important, because only with that knowledge can we identify the gap between the present and the potential, between the actual and the ideal. The determination of user needs requires an analytical approach in which both users and librarians can participate, but which of course neither can be permitted to dominate.

User needs go back to the purpose of what is being done—by the user, by his or her group, by the larger organization. This is a complex issue which involves a blend of cost constraints, time pressures, political considerations, and other factors too numerous to mention. All of these affect "need," because a conclusion which does not pay heed to one of these very real limitations is no conclusion at all.

Where time constraints predominate, the "need" may be for the best available information deliverable by 4 P.M., because after that it not only doesn't matter what else you found, I don't want to know about it because I am already committed to a course of action.

Herbert Brinberg has pointed out quite clearly that different users have different needs.[2] Some need information for evaluation, some need specific answers as an input to a larger issue, some need an arrangement of acceptable alternatives which have already eliminated the unacceptable ones.

I would add to Brinberg's argument that these individual and distinct users with unique priorities don't necessarily know what their real needs are, because their evaluation processes have been stunted by the realities of what we and others have told them. Which of these groups are libraries supposed to serve? Obviously, if our frame of professional reference has any meaning, all of them, and in terms of their own needs. And, of course, this array of needs is found in the clientele or potential clientele of just about any library—public, special, or academic.

SELF-FULFILLING PROPHECY

The reason this exercise in discipline in determining requirements is important is because in its absence we encounter a self-fulfilling prophecy. If our clients adapt to the kind of library service we are prepared or authorized to provide and find it adequate or even superior, then reductions in budgets and service levels will continue to go unchallenged as long as the basic requirement of purchase and delivery of material from the home collection is maintained at some rationalized level.

Here the innate conservatism of our profession returns to plague us. Crisis management is not a recommended tactic, but crises do lead to actions. A carefully developed scenario of user preferences and expectations based on a critical examination of need will create imbalances, and only when imbalances become dangerous for decision makers are many decisions made.

The figurative howling mob of faculty threatening to throw rocks at the librarian may be difficult to contemplate, but in any case the mob leaders should then be told that their more appropriate target is the president, who is the real culprit because of his failure to provide funds. We might even provide road maps to his home. Some librarians might get fired (or stoned) but so might some presidents, and others might decide it isn't worth the risk.

The present concept, in which we equate user need with user responses to our little surveys, does not serve us, because there is no library so rotten that many users won't think it is just fine. Expectations are geared to resources and to our explanation of reasonableness based on those resources. In time, balance is always regained, and library service is rated as acceptable. We know well enough why this happens.

Calvin Mooers[3] told us a long time ago that in an information environment in which getting service is too much trouble people will pretend they didn't really need it. That was true 20 years ago, and it is probably truer still today. The individuals who write books, complete reports on research grants, and prepare presentations for a management presentation on Monday morning cannot ever admit that their work is based on ignorance. Whatever they know is all they needed to know, and stonewalling is a highly sophisticated skill.

At worst, there are also alternatives to the library for anyone who has access to funds, and usually expenditure controls for library materials apply only in the library itself. In some cases, the smaller the library budget the more money is spent. Individuals in my corporate library consulting assignments who had come from another organization with a stronger tradition of library service tried for a while to get the library to provide service at the higher level, but they soon stopped fighting. They either pretended they no longer needed what they thought they did, or they found another way to get it. After a while they even began to believe that the library was really pretty good considering all of its difficulties and problems, and rated it as excellent, or at least as satisfactory.

If we allow service levels as provided by our funding agents to determine expectations, we will have started on the death spiral which is sometimes used to describe what happens in public transportation. There is a lesson in this for us. Nobody really wants to pay for more library service, least of all the politician nonusers found in every sector. They will pay what they must, and of course that cost is so trivial that it is easily afforded if they have accepted the need, in even the most crisis-plagued setting.

No, our profession has not yet developed user-needs studies. But we sure could use some.

References

1. Veaner, Allen B., "1985 to 1995: The Next Decade in Academic Librarianship, Part I," *College and Research Libraries,* May 1985, p. 209–229.

2. Brinberg, Herbert R., "The Contribution of Information to Economic Growth and Development," in *Organization and Economics of Information and Documentation.* Proceedings of the 40th FID Congress, Copenhagen, Denmark,

August 18–21, 1980. Federation Internationale de Documentation, The Hague, 1982, p. 23–26.

3. Mooers, Calvin N., "Mooers' Law: or, Why Some Retrieval Systems Are Used and Others Are Not," *American Documentation*, July 1960, p. 204.

THE OTHER BARRIERS TO INFORMATION ACCESS

Our professional concern about barriers to our clients' access to information is widely and frequently asserted. Those barriers can be intentional or not. This profession takes its responsibilities in the gathering of materials for public use and in the battle against unreasonable barriers quite seriously. We are quite right to take the leadership role in confronting intentional barriers.

On the other hand, how seriously do we take the parallel responsibilities for making the accessible information available for use in the library—for helping individuals find what they need, even when they don't know what it is or that the information exists? What clients need is not necessarily what they ask for.

It is easy to provide vivid anecdotal information about the growth of information sources, and the term "information explosion" has been with us for decades. In my course dealing with the literature of science and technology, I sometimes point out that more than half of the chemists who have ever lived went to work this morning.

Special librarians have known for a long time that even highly educated specialist users are not as knowledgeable about the literature of their speciality as they like to pretend they are. That should be no surprise, as specializations become more narrow and information needs become increasingly interdisciplinary.

As users become aware of their own uncertainty they can become increasingly defensive, even belligerent. It requires both delicacy and tact to create an environment in which advanced scientists and scholars feel comfortable asking for help from librarians. It also requires making this responsibility our priority.

In academic libraries that issue is never really broached, and professors are allowed to continue pretending that they really have mechanisms for learning about new publications of importance to them. In public libraries this is rarely a barrier to information requests. Reference librarians in public libraries could do much more business if they could handle it. Here the limitations are caused by us and not the user.

MORE IS NOT BETTER

Part of the users' unwillingness to admit an information need stems from the very real fear that "better" information systems will bring them *more* information, when their real hope is for *less* but more germane information. In my consulting assignments in corporations there is often immediate user concern when an improved information system is suggested. Users remember the stacks of unread material already on their desks. They recall that librarians tend to measure quality in quantitative terms. They are reassured when they learn that an improved information system means a finely tuned information system from which they will receive preferably less, but more *useful* information.

When I was director of the NASA Scientific and Technical Information Facility, it was common for individuals to exclude foreign-language materials on their SDI profiles. They had enough to do to read all of the English-language materials they were expected to study. To suggest that material they could not or would not read contained information important to them only added to their insecurity and frustration. Calvin Mooers has written that individuals will often prefer to pretend there is no information available rather than to go through a painful, time-consuming process of searching for it.

Libraries are large; some of them are enormous. To the extent that we insist (quite properly) that users have access to *all* pertinent information, we face the responsibility for assuring that users can indeed *find* what they need. We must acquit this duty by charting a path for them through all of the stuff they don't need. That process of information intermediation is the active aspect of our craft. It may be the only aspect that is professionally appreciated.

There is some evidence that librarians who think that our functions end with acquiring materials and ringing a bell to "come and get it" are still in the majority. They include a library school dean who once argued that it was our responsibility to make materials available, but not to determine whether they were found or used. Also among such people are those who believe bibliographic instruction should not provide users with an alternative, but should lighten the workload of librarians and simply help clients hear the "come-and-get-it" bell more clearly.

Library instruction courses would be far better if we instructed users in what they had the right to expect of librarians, in addition to the lessons on bibliographic tools and techniques.

The Carlyle quote, "The true university is a collection of books," heard whenever university presidents speak at library conferences, glorifies the size of the library while it trivializes the role of librarians. Most of our criteria deal with quantity, not quality. Academic libraries are still primarily ranked by size of holdings (rather than the number of times the reference phone rings before it is answered).

It is difficult to defend these priorities using the old argument that they are what the faculty prefer. We have not made any attempt to offer them other options, or to put forward our own priorities.

For public libraries, the concentration on circulation as the measure of the "good" also suggests a perverse scenario. When information response is inexact, it tends to spill out into greater volumes of less useful information. For an information source, increased circulation may be an inverse indicator, showing either the lack of specificity of the response or the physical unattractiveness of the library as a place to read and work.

Trueswell argued some time ago that the likelihood of finding in the library what was wanted did not exceed 50 percent, *when the library owned the material.* We don't seem to worry about that. I find little if any internal data that measure satisfaction from the collection at the time of request, although satisfaction here is simplest, only requiring that we furnish a document the user has identified for us. We seem to feel that once we purchase and catalog an item our responsibility has ended. To the user, only the delivery of the document matters, not whether we own it.

Common sense suggests that if we can't supply it, we had better borrow it even if we already own it. The reasons we don't do that are inherent in interlibrary loan barriers. Interlibrary loan is an imposition on the supplying library. In any case, it is so slow that the unfortunate client might as well wait the two or three weeks until the copy we own is returned.

HOW MUCH REFERENCE SERVICE?

To the suggestion that libraries don't do enough reference work, reference librarians always respond that they are already swamped. That is often true, but who set some preordained level for reference service, rather than to let it grow as needed?

When academic libraries avoid doing online searches for faculty and students with the happy thought that individuals would rather do it themselves and do it better (both statements we know to be generally untrue), they confirm and validate the status quo. The same validation results when public libraries limit reference service to five minutes per user.

It would be better to provide the reference service at the level appropriate to the request. Corporate special librarians know how long that takes—anywhere from 30 seconds to three weeks. If that means that long lines form at the reference desk, we will have made a point to the administrators who decide whether we will get the resources to do what we should.

Beyond these familiar confrontational tactics, however, there are two other dimensions of the problem of information access that are under our control and of our own making: processing backlogs and weeding.

WEEDING OUT BACKLOGS

My training in backlog management came at the NASA Facility and the Institute for Scientific Information, where backlogs no greater than two weeks were the maximum allowed. I can understand academic library backlogs of one or two months, but certainly no more. I'm surprised that the role of backlogs as barriers to access is so rarely discussed in our literature.

When material has not been bought, it is not available to users, but at least no funds have been invested. When a processing backlog reaches or exceeds two years, that much of the library's acquisitions budget has been temporarily squandered. That money could earn investment interest if material was not bought until it could be processed.

There are backlogs that remain the same size or even slowly decline, and others that continue to grow. The solution is relatively simple for the first type. Ongoing staffing and expenditure are apparently adequate, but a one-time staffing and expenditure effort to eliminate the backlog must be undertaken. Budget officers who balk at such a suggestion should understand the waste incurred in repeated shuffling through the backlog to find and retrieve some volume a user needs.

If the backlog continues to grow, then there is an inherent imbalance that must be corrected. It can be corrected by purchasing less, increasing the investment in the processing operation, or changing processing procedures. Managers who watch backlogs grow and do nothing are not really managers.

Weeding is a more emotional issue, particularly for librarians brought up on the philosophy that big is good and bigger is better. We know from studies performed at Indiana University that hardly any library weeds unless it is forced to do so by space shortages. Yet we know from fundamental principles of operations research that it is easier to find information in a smaller collection than in a larger one. Recognition of this fact is at least partly responsible for continuing pressures to establish branch libraries, or to allow individuals to keep material in their own offices where they think they can find it.

Operations research suggests that material that is not needed should be weeded even if there is plenty of room, because it interferes with the process of finding the material that is needed. A few special librarians know that, but hardly anyone else. Weeding should be an ongoing process, and it has nothing to do with space availability.

All of these arguments finally bring us back to the beginning. Our profession has a responsibility for assuring that information is made available to and through our libraries. In particular, it should not be withheld because somebody finds it awkward to allow it to be seen. That vigilance and that battle may never end because information suppressors and dissemblers will probably always be among us.

Surely, however, the reasons we want to obtain this material go beyond just having it. They include the responsibilities to ascertain that those who need it can use it even if they don't know what it is and to assure that we can lead them to what they need by guiding them through minefields of trivia, redundancy, and misinformation.

That describes reference service at its most germane. That is information intermediation. For me, at least, that is the kernel of this profession's responsibility. Long after computerized national and international document analysis and dissemination systems have changed everything else, the need to deal with information problems will remain. Increased volumes, increased access, and increased sensitivity to delays will make that process far more complex, not simpler, as some hardware manufacturers suggest. Computer access has broadened our opportunities, but it has further complicated the process, and user friendly systems either fail to keep up, or trade sophistication for ease of access. Our role is there for us, if we want it and take it. At least it is there for somebody.

The *Wall Street Journal* uses an intriguing slogan in its national TV advertising: "Information isn't power. Knowing where to find it is." What a magnificent motto that would be for our profession! What a fine yardstick against which to measure our own performance!

INTERLIBRARY LOAN: AN OLD IDEA IN A NEW SETTING

Computerized access to bibliographic information and rapid delivery techniques based on mechanisms as routine as jet planes or as advanced as telephone and satellite transmittal have brought us to the reality that access to information is not dependent on information ownership. For users it is access, not ownership, that really matters.

If the librarian provides the needed information, it should not be necessary to inform the requester whether it came off the shelves or from across the continent. Why should the user care? Even commercial services based on old technology promise to deliver packages anywhere in the Western world in 24 hours. Those packages could certainly include books and periodical articles. Yes, it costs money, but it may be worth it. Rapid and assured delivery has a price, and it certainly has a cost.

TRAINED TO BE PASSIVE

In our desire to ignore that ugly financial implication, we continue to undermine what is, at least potentially, the most significant change to affect the management of libraries in the last 50 years. We continue to make it appear trivial and unimportant, a sidelight activity to whatever else we do. Allen Veaner captured that attitude when he pointed out that we had been less successful in improving the rapidity of interlibrary loan than in convincing people that they ought to wait (*College and Research Libraries,* May 1985, p. 209–229).

In my own interviews in the corporate sector, library users inevitably find completely unexpected my question of whether or not they consider loan delays to be reasonable. "However long it takes" is the definition of reasonable. We have trained our users to be passive.

ILL: A MARXIST IDEA

Why do we deal with this important issue of information delivery so cavalierly, so unprofessionally? Primarily, our attitude comes from acceptance of interlibrary loan not as a pragmatic commodity, but as a moral precept. "From each according to his ability to each according to his need," is a quote from Karl Marx. Librarians might be surprised to recognize to what extent this philosophy serves to define the interlibrary loan process for us. I find nothing terrible in this realization, because socialist doctrine always sounds much better than it works, but this premise now conflicts directly with our evolving responsibilities as resource managers accountable to those who fund us and those we serve directly.

HIDING THE FACTS

We run into particular difficulty when our predetermined conclusions cause us to want to hide the facts. We don't really know what interlibrary loan costs, primarily because we don't want to know. Attempts to define a cost basis over a decade ago by Westat were emotionally attacked as yielding too high a cost by articles which also failed to establish any sort of basic accounting ground rules for the allocation of overhead and management costs, the most significant part of any cost equation. The costs of the environment in which all of this takes place are far more significant than the cost of photocopying, mailing, and even student labor.

CONVINCING THE UNCONVINCABLE

All of our attempts to rig an acceptable cost for interlibrary transactions have failed to be convincing to those who most need to be convinced, the individuals responsible for authorizing the supply of materials. How do I know this? Because the librarian suppliers exhibit no enthusiasm for their role in the process.

Commercial providers understand their motivation, and compete for the privilege of supplying needed materials. Major academic libraries, with access to infinitely larger collections, could do it not only better but also faster because they have much more under one roof, but they don't encourage the process because they see no incentive for themselves.

COOPERATION: A ONE-WAY STREET

As resource managers, they now recognize that supplying another library becomes the lowest priority after supplying their own client needs. The net lenders know who they are, and they also know that they provide far more than they receive. "Cooperation" is a one-way street, and they know it. The value system will change only when they perceive that participating in the process will provide enough income so as not to inhibit and perhaps even to improve services to their own clientele. That is the selfish profit motive, and even classically socialist countries such as China, Yugoslavia, and the Soviet Union are discovering that it provides a more tangible incentive for performance than ideology. Lest anyone has failed to notice, the 1960s are over.

Accepting the premise that resource sharing, with concentration on access rather than ownership, is the priority of the future, what are some of the things we ought to do?

HONEST COSTS

1. Treat the determination of costs honestly, in terms that meet the accounting criteria of the supplier whose perception is ultimately all that matters. Cost is not the same as price. Strong arguments can be made for government subsidy of the process of acquiring, but it can't always be subsidized by the supplier. That supplier's good will and willingness to participate are essential.

We have tried to bludgeon lenders with a club of moral suasion, but it hasn't worked. It will work even less in the future as library managers understand their priorities in accountability and responsibility. Technology has helped speed the request process, but delivery still works at the pleasure and pace of the supplier, whose incentive to perform poorly may be to discourage the interaction.

2. Recognize that we are in the business of supplying materials and answers, not of building monuments. The old truism about railroads' failure to understand that they were in the transportation business applies here. Like them we must shape our procedures to the needs of our clients, rather than adapting their expectations to our procedures. To expect material within 48 hours (wherever it comes from) is perfectly reasonable. It can certainly be done in academic as well as corporate libraries. Some corporate librarians can be fired for failing to perform in

terms of that value system, but most of us have no such dramatic trepidations. Instead, as Veaner noted, we spend a great deal of effort explaining why we can't do something—as though anyone cared! I have listened to careful explanations of why library material wasn't on the shelf that completely miss the point. All the client wants is a copy.

3. Budget in the realization of the importance of this process. Interlibrary loan is an alternative to purchase. We are currently trapped into budgets that allow us no alternative to purchase. We place an inordinate value on ownership as opposed to access. We have also allowed others who may have their own reasons to prefer ownership (perhaps they use very little but get pleasure from collecting) to control our priorities.

Charging our clients for interlibrary borrowing costs is the greatest injustice of all. We have already penalized them by not having the foresight to buy the item, and now we want to penalize them again, to charge them for the honor of waiting. It would be more rational to adopt the Chinese concept of paying doctors only when people are well and not when they are sick to provide some incentive for cure. If we have the material available for you immediately you pay us! If we force you to wait we pay you a forfeit, which grows the longer you have to wait! It is impractical, but it provides the correct emphasis.

"TEMPORARY ACQUISITION," NOT ILL

4. Get rid of the term "interlibrary loan." For periodicals it is inaccurate, we don't lend, we make photocopies. Even for books the term confuses the process. The real decision is between permanent and temporary acquisition. Permanent acquisition costs more initially, but that cost is not repeated for each future use.

Temporary acquisition costs less one time, but if it is repeated the costs reach an equal level, a point we should be able to estimate if we keep honest statistics. Each library should also calculate a cost for delay. That would make availability, not ownership, the primary issue. It would be perfectly acceptable to obtain another copy temporarily even if it is something you already own, because that will be faster than waiting for your own copy to return from wherever it now is.

The concept of temporary acquisition is acceptable as long as the supplier is not being asked to do you a favor. Richard De Gennaro was completely correct when he observed at a conference on the new copyright law a decade ago that the fair use provisions should eliminate all problems for academic libraries. Anything "borrowed" often enough to endanger fair use criteria should be bought immediately. There are many titles already in the collection not used nearly as frequently. In some cases that means buying two or three subscriptions to the same title. That's perfectly plausible in any true economic setting. We don't do it because we believe in cooperation as a self-evident good. That resembles seeking the appearance of economy, no matter what the cost.

The process will work when it is perceived as a straightforward economic process for the supplier. The acquirer can be subsidized from any number of sources. That kind of subsidy already exists for purchase. It can be broadened to encompass acquisition for access—for ownership or temporary use.

RAISING SERVICE QUALITY

In his book, *The Failure of Resource Sharing in Public Libraries and Alternative Strategies for Service* (ALA, 1986), Thomas Ballard says that the effort and money spent by public libraries supporting interlibrary loan and cooperation are not worth it. He may be right. I would simply argue that *if* interlibrary interchange of materials *is* worth doing, then it must be done in a manner insuring timeliness and quality service. There is nothing worse than a good idea implemented badly. Doing interlibrary loan badly provides another barrier to doing it well at a later time.

Corporate special librarians sometimes feel a tremendous sense of guilt at being labeled "moochers" in what we now call interlibrary loan. Special libraries are people poor, and the best thing they can contribute to the process is money, something still far easier to obtain in corporations than staff. Academic libraries, on the other hand, are usually money poor but at least potentially rich in inexpensive student help. It seems an obvious symbiotic relationship.

AN ANNOYING INTERRUPTION

The way in which we acquire material we don't own and don't plan to acquire permanently is another example of the way we downplay our own profession by pretending that such a process is a surprising and annoying interruption, rather than part of the day's regular activities. When we select for purchase we make a conscious effort to anticipate what our clients might ask for, and most librarians do it well. However, permanent acquisition through purchase cannot be a perfect process. We can't always anticipate what one user might want, nor can we anticipate that two or more users might want the same thing at the same time. Limitations of budget and space constrain even the largest research library, and the interest in certain material could peak and decline rapidly.

None of these occurrences should shock us. We have all experienced them many times. Why, then, do we treat them as somehow different? Why do we insist on providing our clients with inventory reports when what they usually want is a copy of something. Given our new tools of bibliographic access and document delivery, satisfying that request isn't hard at all, and certainly not nearly as hard as it used to be. All it really requires of us is realism and pragmatism.

THE SEVERAL FACES OF LIBRARIANSHIP

Librarianship has several value systems and emphases, as teaching in a major university and a library education program with specialized faculty expertise makes clear. At times, these value systems emit contradictory signals. Students are sometimes initially confused at what they perceive as contradictions in what they are supposed to learn. It is only after a while that they realize that there are no rights or wrongs in this process, that librarians and libraries serve a variety of clients with different desires and needs, and that not even the desires and needs always match.

There is probably no more cogent argument for the value of formal education. It is a value that cannot be obtained through job experience.

One great problem for our profession is that we deal with outsiders who think they understand libraries and what we need to do, and try to impose their unilateral value system on us. That is, of course, the issue of turf, which I have addressed ("Library Turf," *LJ,* April 15, 1985, p. 54–55).

LIBRARIANS FIRST

It is easy to allow our profession to be fragmented. We can lose our professional uniqueness in many ways. We lose it if school librarians think of themselves first as teachers and only secondarily as librarians. We lose it if academic librarians insist on trying to look like faculty and ignore their major differences in teaching and research. We lose it when special librarians forget that their job is to provide information expertise

From *Library Journal* 112 (1 November 1987):42–43.

and not primarily cost-slashing economies. We lose it when public librarians fail to realize that their clientele is the entire community and that they must never take political sides, for example, between tenants and landlords but assist both because anything else automatically narrows their constituency.

I see at least four separate and distinct roles for the library and the librarians, and readers may identify others: support of amusement and recreation, support of education, support of scholarship and research, and support of decision making.

However, even these four can cause us enough problems, for at least two reasons. The first is that they can impose value systems that have the potential for being contradictory, for virtually all libraries need to function in more than one role. The second is that our users, who are sometimes also our bosses, tend to see only the one role that affects them most directly.

TO DELIGHT . . .

The role of the library in recreational and amusement activities is probably easiest to see, and therefore requires the least description. It is relatively simple to gain instant recognition and visibility when we do this, and providing video exercise tapes and huggable toys most directly reaches down to the common denominator of giving people "what they want." At the same time it is also the most dangerous for us as our mission statement because it is precisely these activities that we do not perform with any unique ability or cost effectiveness. As cost cutters prioritize, and as the winds of privatization (not having the government do what the private sector can do) blow about us, it is these activities that can appear to be frivolous and frilly, and perhaps correctly so.

. . . AND TO INSTRUCT

The role of the library as a part of the educational environment is the one I know least about from my own professional experience, and yet I have come to recognize it as the one that dominates our professional image. Indeed, the placement of library programs within the Department of Education is based on the assumption that libraries are a part of what teachers and schools do, and this makes it as difficult for us to establish an agenda based on priorities of the library profession within the federal education hierarchy as within a local school corporation.

The battle to determine what school librarians need to study was unfortunately lost a long time ago. When school librarians are prepared in "media only" library education programs they may be well *trained* for what their bosses want them to know. They are not, however, nearly as likely to have been exposed to the rich heritage and the complexities of the library profession more likely to be available in diversified library schools.

Public libraries also willingly accept their teaching role, particularly in their work with children and with adult illiterates. Nobody can quarrel with this mission, but it becomes dangerous for us when the inevitable shortage of funds keeps public libraries from fulfilling other community roles in the information process.

Academic libraries also accept their teaching mission, particularly as it applies to undergraduate students. The academic literature is filled with articles that complain that in college we end up teaching students what they didn't learn in high school but should have, so that the college library becomes an extended high school library. This may result from a faculty disregard for what the library can offer students, in both schools and colleges. With a few exceptions, concern about the adequacy of undergraduate bibliographic instruction is a librarian and not a professor concern.

A SELF-SERVICE COLLECTION?

The university faculty perception of the library as a collection of materials, if necessary a self-service collection, has already been explored in an earlier column ("Trouble at the OK Corral University Library," *LJ,* September 1, p. 154–155). It was noted that faculty have little interest in library automation and almost never initiate a demand for new services, although they can be weaned to new services when these are properly marketed. However, by and large the library's perceived role is in support of scholarship and research, and both of these are seen largely as self-service processes. The library's task is viewed as restricted to the development of ever larger collections.

I can understand why faculty would rather not have librarians diverted from full-time attention to their own expensive collection habits, but what is in it for us? Why would we not rather expand our service base to include administrators and trustees, as perhaps public librarians would also want to serve mayors and chambers of commerce? A number of recent studies suggest that few faculty do basic research involving the stretching of intellectual frontiers. Most academic research, like corporate research, is now applied in nature. Applications research shifts the need from masses of raw data to specific proofs. Librarians can do this faster, better, and cheaper than full-time faculty members, especially in the expanding realm of interdisciplinary research.

For special librarians, and particularly those in the corporate sector, the issues are simpler. It is those with which I have had my greatest experience prior to my present academic teaching and research assignment. Special librarians have a key role in providing information for decision making, and in furnishing needed pieces for research jigsaw puzzles. That role is more easily claimed because nobody tends to find it threatening. Even here, we find the academic and school value system occasionally creeping in. We find hard-boiled profit center administrators insisting that users should do their own information searches because "it is good for them." It should not surprise us when we realize that these individuals are all the products of earlier library role imprinting.

What is the appropriate role of the academic, special, public, and school library with regard to these differing and contradictory missions? We must offer tribute to all four, in some proportion it becomes our professional responsibility to determine. If we have not yet done so, it is because we have allowed our special interest user groups to determine our larger priorities and agendas. That is not the characteristic of a profession. It is not even the characteristic of a responsible service enterprise that gives clients what they need rather than just filling orders.

THE HISTORIAN OF CONGRESS

The argument that "democracy" demands that we allow user groups to set our agendas continues to be heard. In testimony before the Senate Subcommittee considering the proposed White House Conference on Libraries and Information Science, then Librarian of Congress Daniel Boorstin argued that the conference should address the nation's most urgent cultural needs, not the problems of the profession (News, *LJ*, May 15, p. 16). There may be a need for a conference to assess cultural needs, but this isn't it, and I think Boorstin should find his own conference to champion.

Serving cultural needs is only a part of what libraries do. Boorstin is tragically wrong when he states that a conference on libraries and information science should *not* address the problems of the profession. It is only through the profession that we can deal with the complex and contradictory issues we now face. We must be charitable enough to recall that Boorstin is a distinguished historian and not a librarian, and that he brings the preconceptions and biases of his own discipline to the evaluation of ours.

It is not my aim to denigrate Boorstin's scholarship, intentions, or eloquent defense during his term of those things in librarianship he considered important to defend. However, during that term he quite consciously and successfully isolated himself from anything in our profession that might have changed his value systems. He made no attempt to learn to get to know us or to attend our meetings, seminars, or workshops.

We recall that at one point early in his career Boorstin argued that he was *the* librarian, not *a* librarian. Even as a bad joke this is sophistry at its worst. The President of the United States had appointed him *a* librarian, and if Boorstin cared to stretch that term to call himself *the* librarian, that little bit of arrogance is probably forgivable. After all, it is a BIG library. It was then within his power to also determine whether or not to become a competent one, and it became clear that he couldn't be bothered.

As the term of our next Historian of Congress begins, it is my hope that this individual will recognize that he has much to learn about the new profession of which he has agreed to become a part. Fortunately, there are some excellent library education programs in the Washington area.

THE ROLE OF INFORMATION IN THE MODERN AGE

It has now been 14 years since Daniel Bell predicted the start of a post-industrial society.[1] Although his prediction has not yet been implemented in all parts of the world, the evidence is clear that in the developed countries there has been a decreasing emphasis on the production of goods—through manufacture and farming—and an increase in what has been called the service economies. Those patterns clearly become the model to which less developed countries aspire, and there can be little doubt that what Bell has predicted has come to pass or will come to pass. Only the time-table is in question. For more highly developed countries, predictors and analyzers have now gone one step further, and assert bravely that not only is there a concentration on the service rather than production sector as economies continue to develop and mature, but that beyond this half or better than half of the workers in these countries are now concerned with the broad area of information. Information is indeed broadly defined by these individuals to include all forms of communications, and some of these would not necessarily fall within the framework of this conference and its emphasis. However, even in a narrower framework there can be little doubt of the growth not only of information sources—because a growth in information sources would only be of narrow importance if those sources were not used—but also a tremendous increase in the reliance on information and in the recognition that ultimately it will be those nations, those corporations, and those individuals with the best capability to analyze and apply information who will succeed.

I am pleased that the sponsors of this conference have assigned me the topic of information without attempting to define or limit what

Paper presented at ICIK 87, the International Conference on Information and Knowledge, Yokohama, Japan, 11–13 November 1987.

information is, or what forms of communication it excludes. We who work in this field tend to think of the term far too narrowly, and librarians think of it most narrowly of all, in restricting its consideration to formal published sources, most specifically books and journals. Even in published literature any special librarian can attest to the central importance of technical reports, newsletters, memoranda, data bases, and even correspondence. Of course information is not limited to what can be compressed into presentation on a disk or on a printed page of paper. The forms of electronic journalism, and even the most informal communication mechanism—face to face meetings and telephone conversations—are part of the information process. Indeed, studies undertaken in the United States by such diverse sources as the Rand Corporation and Auerbach Associates in the 1960s concluded that individuals inevitably preferred informal to formal information mechanisms. Their preferred access to information was to consult their own files, then to visit a colleague down the hall, then to call a friend who might know the answer. Derek Price, in his reference to the invisible college, has documented a phenomenon of which we are all aware.[2] When individuals turn to the formal information sources, as contained in data bases or in hard copy library materials, it is in one sense because their preferred information gathering techniques have already failed. In considering the questions at this conference I doubt that we can deal with these informal and casual information gathering habits and preferences to any significant degree. And yet, at the same time, it is essential that we remember them, because if we understand one thing it is that information sources, no matter how excellent, will be useless unless they are utilized. Computer professionals attempt to address this problem when they argue for "user-friendly" systems, but their definition, while useful, is immediately far too narrow. It presupposes a willingness of the individual to engage in some sort of formal search as a process. This requires of the person an admission of ignorance, an admission that is never easy, and in some societal structures is most difficult of all. This is a problem that I have seen addressed only rarely—the crucial point that information systems depend for their success on a user admission of ignorance. The developers of user friendly systems also assume a willingness of the individual to do all of this information searching himself or herself, and there is clear evidence that this is not necessarily true. To a great extent information searching, either through a manual search of libraries or a computer search of a terminal, is perceived as a clerical process, to be avoided as beneath one's dignity and one's own sense of self-importance, and to be delegated or abdicated to a subordinate.

As those of us who consider ourselves information professionals now deal with this complex problem, we must recognize that our success will depend on our ability to adapt what we do to what the ultimate user is able to do, and more importantly is willing to do. Some individuals, without doubt, have developed superb invisible college networks of information exchange with colleagues—over lunch, over the telephone, at professional meetings, and enjoy the process. They will not give it up just because we tell them to, although they might be willing to supplement these sources with whatever else we can provide for them. Other individuals enjoy the process of formal information searching, and want to do as much of it themselves as they can. These individuals are not nearly as numerous as some information systems designers assume, but they do exist, as part of a phenomenon to be discussed later in this paper. Another group of individuals detest the need to search personally, either because they believe they have more important things to do or because they are made to feel inadequate and stupid by the process, and for us ultimately it is not really necessary to know which is the case. Finally, there are individuals whose use of information sources is severely limited because they simply do not know what to ask, or do not know what an information system might provide.

Our job as information professionals is to assist all of these individuals, and ultimately the phrase "user-friendly" has a far broader meaning than the design of computer use instructions. It is the process of dealing with each user in terms of that user's needs, but also in recognition of his or her preferences. We know by now, as Calvin Mooers told us many years ago, that the best information system is useless if the people for whom it is designed decline or refuse to utilize it.[3] In the last analysis, the most effective user friendly system may be a friendly, knowledgeable, non-judgmental and sociable human being, an information intermediary.

Having defined the problem broadly, let me now seek to narrow it a little so that we can deal with it. Certainly information companies such as AT&T and IBM provide some guidance, and it is important to note first of all that these organizations have long ago stopped calling themselves telephone and computer companies and have adopted the more generic term of information. These organizations, and the many others they represent in what is surely the most rapidly growing industrial development of all, have also recognized the need to support the informal and casual information gathering process. The ability to construct individual files on personal computers, and the increased convenience in telephone technology, are both clearly indications of this. However, we as information professionals have enough to occupy us even if we, for the most, ignore these narrower and specialized personal approaches to information, and concentrate on the more formal information files, manual or computerized, accessible through us.

There can be no doubt that we are dealing with a segment that is growing beyond anyone's wildest expectations, indeed even beyond our ability to measure it. The more formal scholarly publication mechanisms give us the most tangible indications, but only make us aware of the fact that we are measuring the tip of an iceberg. Back in 1974 Georges Anderla projected the growth of scientific literature at 8%/year.[4] If Anderla was correct, then in the 13 ensuing years that literature of science and technology has almost tripled. If anything, librarians challenged to afford this formal segment of scientific literature would argue that Anderla understated the case. At a recent meeting, one publisher stated that in the last five years his company had started 180 new journals while canceling only 5, and that of course represents only one organization, although a large one, out of a scholarly publisher population that numbers in the thousands. And that is only in scholarly communication, and certainly the growth in other fields, such as business, has been far more rapid. Only ten years ago Martha Williams reported that there were then 300 publicly available data bases, compared to less than 20 in 1965.[5] How many are there today? Can we even begin to guess as the thousands, or more likely tens of thousands? Dare we project an end to this growth, or even a slowing of this process? Not likely. Similarly, Lee Burchinal, then with the U.S. National Science Foundation, estimated in 1975 one million on line searches, and predicted a world-wide growth to four million by 1980.[6] We know that he was understating that growth then much as he thought he was shocking his audience. My point is not to criticize Anderla, Willams, and Burchinal, but only to note the impossibility of their task. What is the number for 1987? What will it be for 1997? Futurists tell us that we consistently underestimate what will happen ten years from now, because we tend to frame our projections in terms of known technology and known behavioral patterns, and these will change in some direction as yet to be determined. We face exactly that problem in trying to project information growth and information availability. Surely there can be no doubt that technology will continue to proliferate, and bring us new possibilities. Once we have those possibilities, there will be pressure on us to utilize them, and we can only hope that we utilize them effectively.

Those who have been in this field for some time recognize that our work as information professionals has been largely shaped by developments that came about without us in mind. The use of microform technology in the 1930s was not developed for libraries and information centers, and as late as 1965 the use of microfiche was still severely limited because the various user groups could not agree on a standard of reduction or even on a format for a resulting microform, while an entire industry stood poised to serve this market as soon as it could be sure what that market was. The development of digital computers was not initially for information operations but for accounting, purchasing, and inventory control, but these large, fast and in one sense stupid machines were ideal for the information process—a process that at least in libraries deals with large files and many relatively simple questions. The use of distributed processing, time sharing and on line access to a centralized file from decentralized terminals came from an attempt to make computers more effective, because the central processing unit was far more rapid than input/output devices. Miniaturization has allowed us to move from large main frames to minicomputers, microcomputers, and personal computers as stand-alone devices and as part of a large system, and cost and size reduction continue under the inevitability of constant competitive pressure. It has been suggested that if the improvements in computer technology had been replicated in the automobile industry, we would now be driving cars that weighed less than an ounce and cost less than one cent, and not even our Japanese colleagues, superb as they are in automotive engineering, have been able to accomplish this. The changes in computer technology pose both an opportunity and a threat for us, as I will attempt to elaborate later in this paper, but that threat becomes sinister only when we are unable or unwilling to articulate what we want, and rather just take what we are given. Changes in computer technology even alter their own profession. Twenty years ago, when I was managing large national information files, there was a considerable emphasis on careful and elegant programming to conserve computer memory always in short supply in our configurations. That is a problem no longer. When we run short of memory, we simply add some more, because it is very cheap. Programming is now fast, simple, and sloppy—and correctly so.

  I could go on to list some of the other capabilities available to us—satellite and telephone transmittal of hard copy, computer graphics and computer art in multiple colors, the availability of CD ROM technology and file downloading to allow us to develop small and personalized data bases out of large and impersonal ones—but at some point these examples become redundant and this paper has limitations of time and space. You certainly accept the premise I have presented—that our progress as information professionals is not really limited by the tools or toys that the industry has given us, but by a lack of an overall strategy of what we want to do with them.

  Our use of information tools in service to a whole range of client communities—business decision makers, government planners, manufacturing engineers, agricultural specialists, military strategists, sportsmen and recreation specialists, artists and musicians—present us with a new range of problems, problems of which those with new hardware designs on the drawing boards are totally oblivious. A very incomplete list would include the following:

1. Information at this point is individually prepared and packaged. It is inconsistent in format and in coverage (giving us both gaps and duplication), and it creates problems of interchangeability between hardware configurations and software packages.
2. Information has a cost, and we recognize that the information itself, and the software with which to manipulate it, are far more expensive than the hardware on which we store it. Many if not most of us have at some point been convinced to invest in the hardware, and yet the hardware becomes rapidly obsolete, even as we still endeavor to pay for it. The rapid dynamism of this process also has severe international implications. Rich countries get information richer, the poor get poorer even as they struggle to spend more in relative terms, and the gaps widen. And, yet, this process cannot be stopped even if some were to argue that it should be stopped.
3. Information access is still limited by barriers of language interchange. Forty years of effort have not yet produced completely successful programs for machine translation, and although we are getting better idiomatic problems still keep us from being good. Nowhere is this isolation clearer than in the United States. Americans, perhaps because of geographic distance and perhaps because of the confidence that everything will be written in English sooner or later, are disastrously unilingual. In an example of the phenomenon already described by Calvin Mooers, individuals who find that accessing important information is simply too much trouble will pretend that it does not exist.
4. There are political barriers to the communication of information. Some of these are international, some are intranational. There is really no need to examine this issue at this meeting, but it is important to acknowledge that this problem exists.
5. Closely tied to this is the issue of disinformation, the conscious use of the mechanisms so conveniently provided to furnish lots of information—only it is wrong—willfully and deliberately.
6. The related problem of having access to a great deal of information—information access in abundance—is information overload. The information process can be as easily distorted by strangling it through overfeeding as by starving it. Users are quite correctly concerned when information professionals suggest more available information sources, because they haven't yet been able to examine what we gave them last month. As important as the issue of what we provide for

our users is the issue of what we consciously do not provide for them. While this issue is directly applicable in a computer environment, it has always been known even in the traditional library environment. Operations research analysts told us a long time ago that it is easier to find something in a small file than in a large file. When library patrons in academia remove material from the library to store indefinitely in their offices they are simply applying instinctively what operations research specialists know. They are creating a small file, in their own offices. Data base access has potential for this same problem, and downloading is at least one of the solutions.

7. Finally, the complexity of the world in which we live forces decision makers to deal increasingly with interdisciplinary data bases, including work in areas in which they were not academically prepared. Pollution, nutrition, population control, space exploration—these are just some of the interdisciplinary issues we face. Such issues are difficult to address in narrowly oriented data bases—and the results are difficult to understand and use even when once searched.

This wide range of information issues and user preferences suggests that we as information professionals cannot impose a unilateral solution, because no such solution can possibly exist. It is rather our task to help the user identify his or her information need, and then to help identify strategies for dealing with that need. Even that very simple statement hides a tremendous amount of complexity. What is it that the user *needs?* Is it simply what the user wants, or thinks he needs? Or is it, even more simplistically, the further filtering of the request into what the user thinks it is "reasonable" to request? These approaches will not get us to identifying and fulfilling needs, only to revalidating old and sterile superstitions.

The important new role that all of this suggests is that of the information intermediary, a person probably educated in one or more subject disciplines, a person familiar with computers and what they can do, but a person whose specific contribution is in information. These are not research scholars who have a vast knowledge of a tiny fragment of the world, nor are they bibliophiles who love dusty old books. Nor are they computer specialists who understand what machines can do, but not necessarily what they should do, nor graduates of business administration programs who can measure the financial impact but don't understand the process. The responsibility of tomorrow's information professionals is the gathering, processing, analysis, dissemination and application of information, and information as we already know is not uniquely tied to any one format. Information intermediaries must have interactive people skills, not only because individuals have different preferences about what they want to do themselves and what they want the intermediary to do, but also because we must assure some of these now rather hesitant requestors that there is no disgrace in asking, and that the problem of finding an answer can be ours rather than theirs, if that is what they prefer. Herbert Brinberg, speaking at a meeting of the International Federation for Documentation, made a clear case for differentiating information users and their styles and preferences.[7] Researchers, Brinberg argued, sought raw information for analysis. Engineers sought answers to specific questions, while managers sought neither of these but rather an indication of available options. Brinberg's example suggests enough complications, because there is yet more, because these are not the only kinds of information users (there is, for example, also education and recreation), and because the same user may have different values in different settings. Libraries are known for developing techniques for self service, through bibliographic instruction, pathfinders, and end user training. These are not improper techniques WHERE THEY ARE APPROPRIATE. They are totally inappropriate when we impose our value system to override what the user needs. The problem is not moral, it is pragmatic. It was suggested many years ago that our appropriate role is to take the burden off the user's back, and to assume the tension of the information process. That advice was wise even when presented in the absence of the multitude of information options now available to us. It is even wiser today.

Technology becomes our servant rather than our master when we remember to tell it what we want, rather than have it tell us what it can provide. Peter Drucker probably put it most succinctly and directly. Automation, he argued, is not about machines. It is about how people work.[8] And this is also true of information technology.

References

1. Bell, Daniel. *The Coming of Post-Industrial Society; A Venture in Social Forecasting.* (New York: Basic Books, 1973).

2. Price, Derek de Solla, *Little Science, Big Science.* (New York: Columbia University Press, 1963).

3. Mooers, Calvin, "Mooers' Law or, Why Some Retrieval Systems Are Used and Others Are Not," in *American Documentation* 11 (July 1960):204.

4. Anderla, J. Georges. "The Growth of Scientific and Technical Information—A Challenge," in *Information,* parts 2–3, no. 3 (1974):1–52.

5. Williams, Martha E., "Data Bases—A History of Developments and Trends from 1965 through 1975," in *Journal of the American Society for Information Science* 28 (March 1977):71–78.

6. Burchinal, Lee G., "The S T Communication Enterprise in the United States: Status and Forecasts," in *Library Science with a Slant to Documentation* 14 (June 1977):53–61.

7. Brinberg, Herbert R., "The Contribution of Information to Economic Growth and Development." Theme Paper at the 40th Congress of the International Federation for Documentation, Copenhagen, Denmark, 18 August 1980.

8. Drucker, Peter F., *Technology, Management, and Society* (New York: Harper and Row, 1973).

ECONOMIC ISSUES

In a society that deals increasingly in phrases such as accountability budgeting and return on investment even for service activities, economic justification for libraries becomes a necessity. Some librarians have found this difficult, and some have bitterly resented the need to demonstrate what they have considered to be self-evidently good, but being judged as self-evidently good has not served us very well in the past, and will serve us even less as the competition among such services for scarce resources continues to grow. Moreover, the emphasis in a noneconomic justification environment is always on the library as a collection of materials and never on librarians and what they do. We have in the past given those who fund us little reason to suspect that they cannot have libraries without librarians, or that libraries without proper staffing are not cost effective.

We should welcome the opportunity to discuss economic issues, both because libraries when properly staffed are cheap in providing the throughput of services they offer, and because they are efficient as compared to the alternatives. They are clearly affordable, in a corporation in which their cost cannot begin to affect the organization's financial statement, and in a community that finds the funds to fund fads such as video games, at least several such fads to the decade. They are certainly affordable in a society that holds the importance of information to be virtually irrelevant of cost, but has not made the connection between information and libraries.

Despite this very upbeat framework, we can also recognize the problems. Some of these result from the fact that from a financial standpoint our services have never been properly evaluated, and are taken for granted. Drucker has noted that service professionals accept the moral imperative of accomplishing whatever they perceive as necessary with or without funds by taking the guilt on their own shoulders. Because of this, we have grandiose goals but no specific objectives within a given time frame, and no plans and strategies tied to alternative resource allocations. Instead, we allow ourselves to be entrapped in a scenario in which we try to do more and more with less and less. Management communication, the literature tells us, distributes credit for support and blame for nonsupport. In large part we do neither.

We are a very visible overhead expense, and overhead expenses are vulnerable because their contributions are not obvious. We bring no credit hours and registration dollars to the university coffers; no sales dollars to the corporation, at least not directly. Our funding in the public sector is from the most fragile, vulnerable, and visible of all tax bases, the property tax. Nevertheless, we own a tremendous reservoir of good will. Libraries are considered worthwhile and basically efficient, and it is not libraries that those seeking to eliminate bureaucratic boondoggling through tax initiatives have in mind. We suffer when such initiatives take hold even more than the average public community service, but only because of our ineptness in failing to make the economic case in advance.

It is difficult to "prove" what we contribute, because we cannot construct laboratory experiments to determine the impact of information or its lack on either a growing child or a stressed corporate official, both because they have access to other information resources the library fails to provide and because it has already been noted that a lack of information does not have to be admitted. Cost benefit determinations that hunt for specific dollar savings are certainly useful when they can be done, but they are fragile tools at best. The claimed cost reductions are usually not recoverable, because research directors may be willing to agree that the library saved time and effort but are not willing to reduce their own staffs because of this.

All of this suggests several strategies. The cost of library services is important, particularly in a growing atmosphere of accountability. But it becomes irrelevant if only the library's portion of incurred information costs is being monitored. If these costs are of concern, and they should be, then what faculty or corporate officials spend with university or company dollars is equally important. The controlling and brutalizing of library budgets may simply drive such costs underground. What we have then is not economy but irrelevant pseudoeconomy. In the recognition that no self-respecting officials can agree to the desirability of such a scenario, I usually begin consulting assignments designed to evaluate the "efficiency" of the library by asking the officials who have hired me two questions: (1) Are you interested in economy or the appearance of economy? (2) Do you care only about what the library spends, or do you care about the total drain on your budget? There can be only one answer to each of these questions. What libraries must address is not just their own budget but the total expenditure on librarylike activities and materials. If part of it is to be controlled and monitored, then it must all be controlled and monitored.

Allocation mechanisms used to measure impact on various user groups within the concept of centralized responsibility are not unreasonable, but they must be meaningful and not simply games to implement a predecision to reduce the library budget. When user groups are allowed to decide what to spend in a carefully documented exercise of charging back every photocopy or interlibrary loan there are at least two risks. The first is that library service falls victim to the expectations we already know to be sublimated. The second is that as long as these same groups have other alternatives that bypass the library's charge-back mechanisms, the game becomes silly. However, it is costly both as an accounting exercise and also because record keeping of such minute detail only serves to trivialize the library and makes us the innocent victims of the stereotypical view they already hold. They may think that we keep all those records because we want to. There is yet another reason in a political environment. Your budget represents your power base, don't give it away! Don't look cheaper, look more important!

Library costs can be charged to user groups if organizational philosophy so dictates. But these costs cannot be negotiated with users, because it is one of the fundamental premises of much of my writing that users cannot be depended on or trusted to understand what they need or what you can do for them until after you have shown them. Personnel, accounting, and purchasing departments and the president in selecting staff assistants have never allowed others to determine the needed level of activity, except in one-to-one negotiation with direct management. Unless the case that our budgets are not negotiated with the world at large but only with our own bosses (who must then take responsibility for what does or does not happen) can be made, I see little of a professional role for us.

Our costs can be allocated, but that allocation should be on a basis that never penalizes or challenges use, because use is too fragile to start with. If we can transfer the preconception in favor of information use to an understanding that we are talking about the library when we say that information is power, then we can develop mechanisms that allocate on the basis of some independent determination such as size of professional staff, and that then penalizes nonuse rather than use. When that happens, not only is library service allowed to develop to its proper level, but the justifications for further growth (or for that matter decline) are based on what the librarians are able and willing to do in support of their clients.

The amount of money that we spend is truly trivial in any larger budget setting, and our problem is not that we spend so much but that we spend so little that we are hardly noticed. When C. Northcote Parkinson observed that the amount of time spent on an issue was inversely proportional to its importance, he was only reporting accurately what we all know. Our greatest potential contribution to economic accountability is not in doing less but in doing more, and not in spending less but spending more. The essential corrolary to this is that we also insist that others not be allowed to spend *our* money to do what they really do not know how to do, and in the process waste *everybody's* money.

Publishers, Libraries, and Costs of Journal Subscriptions in Times of Funding Retrenchment

A study funded by the National Science Foundation and carried out at the Indiana University Graduate Library School examined the economic interaction between libraries and publishers of scholarly and research journals for the period 1969–73. Drawing from the findings of the study, the validity of the fears of librarians of growth in the number of journals published and publishers' profits and the fears of publishers of unlimited photocopying in libraries are examined. The complex price structure of journal subscriptions, their increasing cost, and the problems these pose both to publishers and librarians are discussed. How libraries allocate their budgets is also examined, and problems requiring further investigation are identified.

In the spring of 1974 the Indiana University Graduate Library School began work, under a grant from the National Science Foundation, on a study on the interaction between the publishers of scholarly and research journals in the United States and the libraries which form their primary customer base. These libraries are largely academic, particularly major research libraries, but smaller academic libraries, special libraries, and larger public libraries are also included. It is not the purpose of this article to repeat, or even to summarize, the findings of this massive study.[1] Instead, this article will examine what the survey revealed about the total network of economic relations which tie these publishers and libraries inexorably to one another. It will examine the validity of the assumptions which each group has made about the other. It will look at some strategies either employed or contemplated by librarians and pub-

From *Library Quarterly* 46, no. 4 (October 1976):359–77.
Best Paper for 1976–77. American Library Association Resources and Technical Services Division.

lishers to minimize anticipated or actual economic difficulties and comment both on the rationale for, and success of, these strategies.

First, some delineations and disclaimers are in order. The survey was carried out under the direction of Dean Bernard Fry of the Indiana University Graduate Library School. I participated actively in the evaluation of data and in the writing of the final project report. We began by trying to establish a common meeting ground on which librarians and publishers could at least agree on the form and kinds of questions and the populations to be asked to respond in the study we proposed. We recognized that this survey required participation in both the formulation and evaluation phases from a broad range of interests, including commercial, society, university, and miscellaneous nonprofit publishers and academic, public, and special libraries. The study also required contributions from economists and statisticians, as well as from representatives of those sectors of the governmental community concerned with the formulation of policy.

Definitions of periodicals for inclusion and exclusion are described in some detail in the final project report. Periodicals produced by countries other than the United States were not included, not because they were not important, but because they are a major group with different characteristics which require a separate study. A group of 2,459 periodicals was identified as U.S. scholarly and research journals, a group smaller than earlier estimates[2] because of the more stringent criteria used to determine membership. Approximately half of these periodicals were then selected for inclusion in the survey.

We anticipated that, because of the length and complexity of the questionnaire, publishers were less likely to respond than libraries. We further anticipated that commercial publishers would be particularly reluctant to participate because of concern about disclosure of proprietary financial data, despite the use of an intermediary to process all responses. The techniques developed were designed to minimize these problems and to ensure that no individual publisher was asked to complete an inordinate number of three-hour questionnaires. The procedures were as follows: (1) Of all publishers publishing only one journal, half of those in each category of publisher except commercial publishers were randomly selected. All commercial publishers of only one journal were included. (2) For all publishers publishing more than one journal, half of each publisher's journals were randomly selected. However, no publisher was asked to respond to more than ten questionnaires even if, as in one or two cases, he published more than twenty journals.

Despite all these precautions, the rate of response from publishers was disappointing, ranging from almost 50 percent for university presses to 14 percent for commercial publishers. Not all lack of response was caused by reluctance to participate. In many instances organizations were simply unable to supply requested information.

The response rates from larger academic and special libraries, those most directly affected by the economic structure of scholarly and research periodicals publishing, ranged between 50 percent and 70 percent of the sample population. This rate was achieved despite the necessity of a rather formidable, lengthy, and complex questionnaire, which took several hours to complete. It seems clear that the high level of participation is indicative of a high level of interest and concern.

The data and conclusions are clearly limited by the fact that the survey encompasses only the years 1969–73. While much information was obtained for this time period and many trends could be seen, the survey stops short at the very time when pressure on library budgets, decreases in government subsidies, and the rate of domestic inflation were just beginning to reach their peak. The absence of information concerning the pivotal years of 1974 and 1975, in particular, only serves to accent the significance of conclusions which can already be drawn from the earlier data, since there can be little doubt that many of the problems already evident in 1973 have since been exacerbated.

THE RATE OF GROWTH OF SCHOLARLY AND RESEARCH JOURNAL LITERATURE

There has been considerable speculation among librarians, publishers, and government officials concerning the rate of growth of the published research literature. These speculations, based on fragmentary data, have ranged from projections of zero growth[2] to rates as high as 8 percent per year[3], a rate which would cause a doubling approximately every nine years. Concern about this assumed rate of growth among librarians and others has been so great that suggestions have ben made[4] that libraries refuse to purchase newly published journals in order to force publishers to limit their output. It appears clear, however, that most new journals arise from the needs of scholars and researchers to communicate the results of their research and the needs of others to learn about that research rather than from some preconceived notion by publishers that new journals in particular fields must be issued.

The results of this study would indicate that, at least during the years 1969–73, the growth in publication of new American scholarly and research journals was not as rapid as many librarians had supposed. Of the 2,459 journals identified in 1973, 403, or 16.4 percent, did not exist in 1969; this suggests a gross annual growth rate of approximately 3.9 percent. *Ulrich's International Periodicals Directory* indicates that 200 scholarly and research American journals ceased publication between 1969 and 1973. The net annual rate of growth, therefore, approximates 2 percent, a figure considered neither alarming nor abnormal when compared to growth in research, particularly academic research, during the same time period. It is possible and even likely that foreign scholarly and research journals grew at a more rapid net rate. Since American libraries appear far more willing to cancel foreign titles which receive little use or are available through networks or consortia, even this problem may not have the dimensions attributed to it.

The publication rate of new journals in the commercial sector was double that of the overall average and approximated 8 percent a year, compared with an annual rate of less than 2 percent for journals published by societies and university presses. The 200 journals which ceased publication during 1969 and 1973 were not categorized by publisher, but I suspect that a correspondingly large percentage of commercial publications were represented. Commercial publishers, guided by a profit motive, can be expected to take risks. At the same time, they are probably also more willing, for the same motivation, to cease publication of a journal which is not economically viable. Other publisher groups, particularly university presses and small not-for-profit publishers, are known from the survey data to go to great lengths to keep economically unviable publications alive, frequently through transfers of funds and direct subsidies. Such publications, which might be expected to disappear in a laissez-faire economic environment, struggle to stay alive for reasons involving perceived professional responsibility rather than economic gain.

THE RATE OF PRICE INCREASES FOR AMERICAN SCHOLARLY AND RESEARCH JOURNALS

Studies of price increases, as compiled by various universities, subscription agencies,[5] and even publisher groups, already abound, and this survey adds only more specific data, although perhaps significant in its specific orientation to American scholarly and research journals.

During the period 1969–73 the American publishers represented in the survey increased publication prices at an annual rate of between 7.5 percent and 9.8 percent per year, with the small not-for-profit publishers at the low end and commercial publishers at the high end of the spectrum. University presses fell roughly in between, with annual increases of 8.7 percent, while professional societies at 9.4 percent come close to the commercial publishers' rate.

These statisitics are consistently less than the average annual periodical price increases reported by the libraries in the survey. Academic libraries reported an annual price increase for all periodical titles of 11.2 percent, while special libraries reported an annual rate of 12.4 percent. There are several possible explanations for the difference. First of all, it must be recognized that the responding libraries were commenting on all periodical subscriptions, including such nonscholarly publications (as defined in the survey) as newsletters, general and popular publications, translations, and publications generally not covered by abstracting and indexing services. These may have increased their price at a greater rate, although we do not know.

Second, it must be noted that the price changes in foreign periodicals, not included in the data provided by publishers, could not be separated out in the responses from libraries. There is a considerable amount of evidence to suggest that, during the period 1969–73, the price of foreign periodicals increased more rapidly than that of domestic publications. This may be true, in part, because of greater inflation rates in many other countries than in the United States, and also because the general weakening of the dollar increased prices in terms of rates of international currency exchange. Finally, it must be pointed out that the prices reported by libraries usually include the charges of subscription agencies, while publishers' price rates do not. Service charges applied by subscription agencies have increased sharply over the last several years, from what was a discount from list price not many years ago to present service charges ranging from 4 percent to 10 percent and more. Furthermore, some subscription agents impose other, less obvious, costs, such as handling charges for address changes and currency conversion hedges of as much as 10 percent for foreign periodical titles. All of these factors would be represented in the periodical prices reported by libraries, but not in the price reported by publishers. It must be recognized that the relatively sharp price inflation seen in subscription-agency activity has been caused in large part by decreases in discounts offered to these agents by publishers, and this reduced discount becomes, in effect, a hidden price increase passed along to the ultimate library purchaser. It is unfortunate that the role of the subscription agent in the economics of the journal publication system has not been adequately explored, particularly since this role appears to be having an increasing economic impact and since substantial differences in practice between various subscription agents exist.

Despite the general unhappiness in the library sector with the rate at which periodical subscription prices have been increasing (certainly as contrasted to changes in their own budgets), there is no evidence to suggest that this has resulted in the accumulation of large profits in the commercial sector or operating surpluses in the noncommercial group. With operating income defined as revenue minus costs of sales and operating expenses but excluding such items as interest paid or received, capital expenditures, and taxes, both university presses and the small not-for-profit publishers show deficits which, for the period 1969–73, are not only consistent but increasing. By 1973 both groups had annual operating deficits in excess of 6 percent of income. This problem can be hidden for a while by the fact that periodicals customers, unlike book purchasers, pay for subscriptions before the issues subscribed for are produced and before costs are incurred. But this is a situation which ultimately can be resolved only by the death of the publication, increased subsidization by the sponsoring body, substantial increases in circulation, or even greater price increases. Increased prices can, of course, have a negative impact in turn on circulation, and the resulting spiral of increasing prices followed by decreasing customers followed by increasing prices, ad infinitum, will be recognized by those with some familiarity with what has happened to urban public transportation systems.

Publications of professional societies, which report an operating surplus of about 3 percent in most of the reporting years, appear to have kept pace with their cash requirements. Like other not-for-profit organizations, societies obviously yield no return to investors or stockholders. A 3 percent surplus can be considered only marginally sufficient to meet capital expenditures such as new equipment or facilities or to provide operating capital to permit the start of new projects and their sustenance until they can reach financial stability.

Commercial publishers of scholarly and research journals, however, report an operating profit, which increased from 11.3 percent in 1969 to 14.1 percent in 1973. That commercial publishers make a profit cannot be surprising, since the financial pressures under which for-profit organizations operate tend to be self-purging in nature. Inefficient or unlucky entrepreneurs who are not successful tend to drop out, although new candidates are frequently found to take their place.

Although the sentiment of some librarians may be against the principle of publication of scholarly and research journals for profit, the achievement of a 14.1 percent operating profit by a commercial organization cannot be considered exorbitant or, for that matter, even impressive. The low esteem in which publishing stocks have traditionally been held on the stock market is ample evidence of this. It must be recognized, too, that, in addition to extraordinary expenses such as interest, the remaining profit is then subjected to a 50 percent federal income tax, in addition to various state and local taxes. It is highly unlikely, therefore, that from an operating profit of 14.1 percent, more than 4 percent or perhaps 5 percent would remain for reinvestment or distribution to owners or stockholders. When this is compared to the 8 percent which money can earn in safe tax-free bonds, the operating profit seems even less attractive. It can, in fact, be argued that the return of $104 in one year for $100 expended in a previous year represents no return at all because of inflation, which dilutes the dollar's purchasing power in the interim.

It is clear that, for the scholarly and research publishing community as a whole and for the commercial sector in particular, whatever the reasons for increases in journal prices, large profits are not among them.

PRICING STRATEGIES WHICH DISCRIMINATE AGAINST LIBRARIES

Many librarians have maintained that they are the victims of discriminatory pricing stratagems, under which they are asked to subsidize lower subscription rates charged to individual subscribers. This is considered to be particularly true in the case of subscription rates for individual members in professional societies. The charge, as evidenced by the data from this study, is not without foundation. Some publishers, however, would argue that libraries should pay higher rates, since their copies are used by more individuals and the cost, therefore, can be amortized over a number of users. Although this is often posed as a moral issue, the statistics of this study indicate that the publisher's decision to charge libraries more than individuals is based on economic rather than moral considerations. Apparently these are so compelling that the discrepancy between individual and institutional subscription rates is increasing.

An increase in the number of customers is the major alternative to an increase in prices and is, for most publishers, the course they prefer in attempting to raise additional revenue. By and large, however, the publishers of scholarly and research journals have been unsuccessful in significantly broadening the total subscriber base, even allowing for growth in foreign subscriptions. Neither commercial nor society publishers were able to increase domestic subscribers at a rate of more than 1 percent per year during the period under investigation. The 2.2 percent annual growth in subscriptions to journals from university presses was caused by increased foreign subscription. By 1973, foreign subscriptions represented 44.1 percent of all the subscriptions of commercial publishers, and, while the percentages were considerably lower for other publisher groups, they also showed substantial growth in foreign subscribers. This increase was essential because American commercial, society, and university publishers all had overall decreases in domestic subscriptions in the period 1969–73. Without exception, this decrease was caused primarily by drastic reductions in individual subscriptions, ranging from 2.7 percent for the commercial sector to 12.9 percent for university presses, with society journals at 4.0 percent. Increases in institutional subscriptions, usually libraries, were unspectacular but steady. From this information it appears, as it must have appeared to publishers, that even with the difficulty which libraries have had in meeting increases in periodical prices, the difficulty for individual subscribers, supported either by grants or their own checkbooks, was even greater.

Reaction to this problem of differential subscription rates by the publishing community is scattered and appears confused, probably representing uncertainty concerning appropriate strategies. Some publishers charge single rates to all subscribers and perceive this either as the most equitable or the most practical pricing structure. Other publishers have a variety of intricate pricing structures including library rates, individual subscriber rates, student rates, and sometimes even student subscriber rates. Those publishers who had already differentiated between library and individual subscription rates tended during the period 1969–73 to increase this differentiation. In general, commercial publishers appear to be moving away from a structure of differential rates toward a single rate. While 67 percent of the commercial publishers surveyed had different rates in 1969, only 56 percent retained them in 1973. By contrast, both society and university publishers, who already were more likely to charge differential rates by which libraries pay more than other kinds of subscribers, increased this practice during this period; 76 percent of society publishers and 65 percent of university publishers had different price rates by 1973.

Publishers who charge differential prices have been increasing the gap between institutional and individual subscription rates. Librarians, therefore, can argue that they are in fact subsidizing unrealistically low individual subscriber prices. Publishers undoubtedly tend to counter by saying that price differentiation is necessary to protect what little remains of a personal subscription base. Without this, library prices would have to be set still higher. They also tend to argue that there is at least some suspicion that cancellation in individual subscriptions is accelerated by the availability to the library user of expanded interlibrary loan through networks, consortia, and photocopying.

The increased differentiation between library and individual rates for publishers who differentiate is marked for all publisher groups. In 1969 the median library price for commercial publications with different price structures was 165 percent of the individual subscriber price. By 1973 it had grown to 172 percent. The change was from 135 percent to 137 percent for society publications and from 133 percent for publications issued by university presses to 150 percent. The smaller not-for-profit publications exhibited an even greater increase, from 106 percent to 145 percent.

The charge that libraries are increasingly being asked to bear a larger share of the subscription price than in the past appears to be true. Librarians argue that they are being singled out because they are largely a captive market with little ability to make competitive decisions. Publishers respond that librarians are singled out to shoulder increased prices because, despite their poverty, they are still the most affluent group of subscribers available.

PRICES CHARGED BY COMMERCIAL PUBLISHERS AND THOSE CHARGED BY OTHER PUBLISHER GROUPS

Librarians have tended to believe that commercial publishers of scholarly and research journals charge the highest prices. The survey indicates that, without question, this is true. The reasons for this, however, are not obvious. In 1973 median prices charged libraries by commercial publishers were 168 percent of the prices charged by society publishers, 181 percent of those charged by university presses, and 253 percent of those charged by other not-for-profit publishers.

There are several possible explanations for these higher prices in addition to that of profit motivation. Commercial publishers are less eligible for subsidy than the other groups of publishers in the survey, and are generally ineligible for government-paid page charges, although it must be added that neither subsidies nor page charges provide much revenue for any group. The higher prices charged by commercial publishers are also a function of the higher prices generally charged for journals in the pure and applied sciences, as compared to the humanities and social sciences. The median pure science journal, regardless of publisher, is sold at twice the price of a social science journal and at almost three times the price of a humanities journal. Applied science journals are also more than twice as expensive as humanities journals. Commercial publishers are most active in the pure and applied sciences. Whether pure science journals cost more because commercial publishers put them out, or whether commercial publishers are forced to charge more because pure science journals cost more to issue (because of composition costs for diagrams and formulas, for example) is difficult to ascertain.

More significant, in my view, is the fact that commercial publishers publish larger journals. When price per page is used as the basis of comparison, commercial prices, while still higher than those of other groups, appear more realistic. The page price of commercial journals is 117 percent of the page price of society journals, 182 percent of those issued by university presses, and 122 percent of those of other not-for-profit publishers. University presses continue to charge the lowest prices per page. Perhaps not coincidentally, university presses are also shown from earlier data to be in serious financial difficulty.

WHAT LIBRARIES ARE DOING ABOUT THE PROBLEM

Although the problem of acquiring materials for libraries has many ramifications, at least that part of the problem concerned with the obtaining of scholarly and research journals published in the United States can be quantified in a relatively simple way. In order to maintain an equivalent position over time, libraries would have to be able to afford the price increases of existing journals and also absorb the estimated 2 percent net growth in the literature that has been reported above; for example, on the basis of our survey data, academic libraries would have to spend an additional 13.4 percent of their serials budget, and special libraries would have to increase expenditure by 14.6 percent. This approach ignores the impact of the cost of foreign publications, the prices of which I suspect are rising more rapidly than domestic journal prices. It also ignores the responsibility of both academic and special librarians to expand journal holdings as specialized subject areas become increasingly interrelated and as fields once considered peripheral become more important and even crucial to their users. Nevertheless, it can be argued that during the period from 1969 to 1973 an annual increase in expenditure of 13.4 percent per annum for academic libraries and 14.6 percent for special libraries would allow them to maintain their position with respect to the number of scholarly and research journals to which they subscribe.

Survey returns indicate that the total budgets of large academic libraries increased at an annual rate of 8 percent during the years 1969–73. Small academic libraries fared considerably worse, with an annual growth rate of only 5 percent. Special libraries, by and large, had budget increases at an annual rate of 10 percent for small special libraries and 13 percent for large ones. None of these library groups (public libraries simply do not spend enough of their budgets on scholarly and research journals to be heavily affected) had budget increases proportional to the increased cost of subscriptions to scholarly and research journals during the period from 1969 to 1973. It should be noted that the years 1969–73 are still considered by many library administrators as "good" years, at least relatively good compared to what has followed.

The 1969–73 budgetary picture for academic libraries is even more bleak than is apparent from the data presented. In large academic libraries, while the overall budget rose by an annual 8 percent, salary budgets rose by 9.5 percent. Staff costs in smaller academic libraries rose 6.5 percent. In 1969 the figure for labor costs was about 54 percent of the budget of small academic libraries and 57 percent of that of large academic libraries; in 1973 it was a remarkably consistent 59 percent of the budget of both large and small academic libraries. While costs generally classified as "other" (equipment, supplies, miscellaneous expenditures) do not require a large overall portion of the library budget, even these costs showed a percentage growth.

There was, therefore, a decrease in the percentage of the library budget available for the acquisition of materials. This decrease ranged from almost 3 percent in large academic libraries to almost 4.5 percent in small academic libraries. As shown above, this was at a time when even the maintenance of the same percentage of the budget would have been insufficient to maintain the same level of periodical subscriptions.

Material budgets in libraries, as defined by our survey, consist of three categories: books, serials, and "other" (this contains such items as audiovisual materials and microforms, for example). As a percentage of budget allocation this last category is so small (about 0.1 percent of the overall academic library budget and less than 0.5 percent of the materials budget) as to be insignificant in strategic decisions. The most significant and dramatic shift revealed by the 1969–73 survey data was the transfer of funds from the book to the serials budget.* Since it is known from the experience of subscription agencies that there is a parallel trend of shifting nonperiodical serials into the book budget to permit an easier annual review of purchase decisions, it can be assumed that the transfer from the book budget is primarily, if not exclusively, for the purchase of periodicals in an attempt to maintain and even expand library holdings, despite the budgetary difficulties.

Despite the decrease in the percentage of their budgets expended on all materials, a large proportion of academic libraries in the survey increased substantially the percentage of the total budget spent on serial publications: 12 percent in 1969 to 15.5 percent in 1973. This is a 29 percent increase in a four-year period. I suggest that, for the years 1969 through 1973, large academic libraries not only maintained the existing level of their serial holdings despite price increases, but that they also managed to absorb the estimated 2 percent net growth in the literature.

This was accomplished at a price, and that price was a drastic reduction in the level of acquisition for books. The percentage of the total budget for book purchase in large academic libraries dropped in the four-year span from 24.3 percent to 18.1 percent, a decrease in level of expenditure of 25.5 percent. When this decrease is interpreted in light of what is already known of book price increases,[6] the effective decrease in level of spending becomes even greater. Stated in different terms, it can be shown that in 1969 large academic libraries were spending more than two dollars on books for each dollar spent on serials. By 1973, this had

---

*It is unfortunate that the term serial, which includes both periodical and nonperiodical material, had to be introduced for purposes of budgetary comparisons. Responding libraries were asked to differentiate between periodical and other serial expenditures, but to a large extent they were unable to do so.

dropped to $1.16 for books for each dollar spent on serials, and it is probable that 1975 data would show that the order of the two categories has been reversed. Small academic libraries, which, according to the survey data, have historically spent far more on books than on serials, show the same trend, although the proportions are different. In 1969, small academic libraries were spending $4.60 on books for each dollar spent on serials. By 1973 this was down to $2.70.

Both publishers and librarians who have been privy to the analysis of these data agree that this trend is highly disturbing. It can be shown that, even at the 1969–73 rate (and there is evidence for assuming an acceleration in the rate), by the late 1980s large academic libraries will have ceased to purchase books entirely; all of their materials budgets will be expended on serials. Such projections, of course, are only useful as an exercise and for their shock value. First of all, little can be said at this stage about either library budgets or materials prices in the late 1980s. Second, the percentage of materials dollars spent on books must, at some point, reach an irreducible minimum, although no one can predict with any level of confidence what that will be. When this occurs the full impact of budget constraints will hit the library periodicals budget if, indeed, this has not already happened in the time elapsed since the 1973 cutoff date of this survey. The expedient of shifting dollars from the book to the serials budget to avoid difficult decisions about discontinuing periodical subscriptions was and is temporary. Sooner or later academic libraries must make these decisions about what subscriptions to place, what subscriptions to keep, and what subscriptions to cancel.

FACTORS AFFECTING DECISIONS ABOUT LIBRARY PERIODICALS

Academic librarians tend to attempt to maintain continuity of periodical runs by retaining subscriptions already in effect, even at the cost of severely curtailing the addition of new titles. From everything known about the half-life of information use and the application of Bradford distribution,[7,8] this attitude would tend to confirm the findings of Wasserman and Bundy[9] that the value system of academic librarians tends to rate completeness and continuity of collection above actual information use. Academic libraries were still successful in the period 1969–73 in adding periodical subscriptions at a more rapid rate than the rate at which subscriptions were canceled, although the ratio of new subscription to cancellations declined sharply. In 1969 large academic libraries were adding forty-seven titles for each title canceled; by 1973 this ratio had fallen to 7.3:1. By the same token, in 1969 academic libraries were canceling existing subscriptions at a trivial 0.2 percent of their collections, giving credence to the belief that, until budgets became tight, subscriptions once placed were generally automatically renewed without evaluation. By 1973 the cancellation rate had more than tripled, but even a 0.7 percent rate of cancellation indicates little in the way of continuous evaluation or analysis.

The impact on the ordering of new titles (at least of titles not previously held) during the period 1969-73 was far more severe. In 1969 the percentage of new titles ordered in large academic libraries as related to the collection as a whole was 9.4 percent. By 1973 this had dropped to 5.1 percent, without any comparable indication that there were fewer new or worthwhile periodicals among which to choose. Stated another way, confronted by the choice of canceling an existing subscription or not placing a new one, large academic libraries opted to forgo a new order forty-three times for every five times they decided to cancel an existing subscription, a ratio of better than 8:1.

During the period 1969-73, large special libraries, on the other hand, actually increased subscriptions to new titles as a percentage of the collection, and by 1973 were doing so at a greater rate than large academic libraries. Moreover, special libraries, which in 1969 canceled titles at a rate more than three times that of large academic libraries as a percentage of the collection, continued to do so at a rate almost twice that reported by academic libraries in 1973, the year in which they canceled the most subscriptions. It would seem, from the above, that special libraries are far more willing or able critically to evaluate and weed their periodical collections and make room for new subscriptions by cancellation of duplicate subscriptions or titles no longer judged important enough to be retained. This is particularly significant, because there is every indication that the ability to decide what to do without while at the same time maintaining as much as possible of the value of a collection will develop rapidly into a new and highly sought after skill.[10]

It might be assumed that when librarians make cancellation decisions, they do so in large part on the basis of their knowledge of the availability of titles through consortia and networks. In fact, network boosters[11] have claimed this to be so, while publishers have feared and decried it. The survey information suggests that, at least through 1973, such rationalizations by academic librarians are infrequent. While this may change and may already have changed, in 1973 the priorities for developing and maintaining the integrity of the overall collection were simply too strong. In large academic libraries elimination of duplicate subscriptions, despite the fact that there was not much duplication of titles to begin with, was the strongest factor in cancellation decisions. In 1969 the incidence of duplicates (or triplicates or more) in the entire collection of large academic libraries was 4.9 percent; by 1973 this had decreased to 3.0 percent, a drop of 39 percent. This offers further credence to the belief that, as a priority, integrity of collection exeeds optimization of use, particularly since other studies tell us[7,12] that the greatest incidence of interlibrary loans is of titles which the borrower already owns but cannot locate in response to a request. In small academic libraries, which are not likely to have branch collections, the tendency to have no more than one subscription of any one title is even more pronounced. The incidence of duplication is consistently less than 1 percent, and in many cases as low as 0.2 percent. For those libraries an irreducible minimum appears to have been reached, and whatever duplication exists continues and may even increase slightly. Large academic libraries appear to accept, whether willingly or grudgingly, the concept that one copy on the campus is sufficient for access, whether or not this is, in fact, realistic on a large and scattered campus, for example.

In cancellation decisions there is also a noticeable tendency to cancel foreign titles, particularly those in languages other than English, in preference to domestic titles. Whether this is because these titles are thought to be less significant, are used less because of language difficulties, or cost more than domestic periodicals was not ascertained.

Increases in prices for specific periodical titles appear to play a small and relatively unimportant role in decisions to cancel or retain them. In large academic libraries the mean price of canceled titles exceed that of retained titles by only 13.6 percent, a significant but certainly not dramatic difference. When academic libraries do cancel subscriptions, they tend, perhaps paradoxically, to cancel in subject disciplines in which the subscription price is generally lower to begin with. The subscription price of canceled social science journals exceeds that of those retained in the same discipline by a price differential of 24.8 percent; the difference for humanities journals is 22.0 percent. By contrast, for pure science journals, by far the most expensive as a discipline group, the price of canceled titles exceeds that of those retained by only 1.2 percent. Publishers who insist that quality journals tend to survive in libraries whether or not they have increased their price may be correct. In fact, it can be surmised that periodicals which have not increased in price at all may be canceled to provide funds to meet the increased price of important publications.

VALIDITY OF A PUBLICATION LAISSEZ-FAIRE SYSTEM

The discussion so far may seem to suggest that a totally laissez-faire system under which quality publications survive and marginal or substandard periodicals die a natural death is desirable. This has been suggested by some librarians and even by some publishers who obviously believe that their journals are of sufficiently high quality to survive. While such an approach has the attractions of being clean-cut and simple, it is rather simplistic. The fact that university presses and small not-for-profit publishers as a group are less and less viable economically, in that they have increasing annual deficits, has already been reported. Their financial position may sometimes be the result of the poor quality of a publication, but more frequently it results from the fact that the publication, while perhaps unique and important, is addressed to a small and specialized reader population. In addition, small publishers such as these usually have neither the marketing expertise nor advertising dollars to attempt to reach a worldwide market. A major factor in the marked differentiation which exists between commercial and noncommercial publishers in tapping foreign markets may well be the commercial publisher's ability to mount extensive market-penetration programs. Such programs normally require both overseas advertising and the employment of local sales representatives abroad, and are expensive. While university publishers in particular are increasing their share of the foreign market, that share is still quite small.

Of perhaps even greater concern is the uncertain support entire subject disciplines would be able to provide for journals published under a laissez-faire system. Journals published in the applied science and technology disciplines are the only ones demonstrating continuing operating surpluses or profits. Pure and social science journals hover at the break-even point, while publications in the humanities consistently and increasingly report operating deficits across the disciplines which comprise them. Clearly, a system without subsidies or other buttressing devices would have devastating consequences for research and scholarship in the humanities and could even lead to the demise of all journal publication in certain humanistic specializations. It seems unthinkable that something like this should be allowed to happen.

CONSORTIA, NETWORKS, INTERLIBRARY LOAN, AND PHOTOCOPYING

Publishers, whose economic position has been shown above not to be particularly strong, have been understandably concerned about the rise of photocopying, particularly as this is facilitated by organized networks of libraries. They are also concerned that such networks or consortia have an impact on library purchasing decisions, particularly since some consortia claim as a benefit for their members the possibility of reduced purchasing.

In previous sections of this paper I have commented on the lack of evidence from this survey that the existence of networks and consortia has much impact on a library's decision concerning the level of its funding for periodical subscriptions. There is a similar lack of evidence concerning interlibrary loan and photocopying.

There is no doubt that within the survey period we were experiencing dramatic increases in interlibrary borrowing and lending of periodicals at all levels. Large academic libraries, traditionally large-scale lenders, were also becoming borrowers on a greater scale. It is not clear that the titles being borrowed were those the library did not in fact own. Other studies[12] have suggested that borrowing is frequently prompted by an inability to locate a copy which the library does own. If this is true, the reported elimination of duplicates for frequently used titles could spur interlibrary loan to an even greater extent than the elimination of single copies.

In the survey, libraries were unable or unwilling to differentiate between interlibrary loan of an original article in loose or bound form or the supply of a photocopy. The distinction does not seem significant to me. Libraries lend the original document because this has a real or perceived convenience for the lender. There may be a truck service which avoids mailing costs; there may be no copying equipment, or it may be broken down. The survey did not provide for any indication, in these instances, if the borrowing library made a photocopy before returning the borrowed material. I have observed that this practice is followed in virtually all cases in which the material is found to be useful, and even in some cases when it is not. Many libraries are unwilling to entrust a valuable bound volume which belongs to another organization to an internal user and will, as a matter of policy, make a photocopy to give the requester.

Despite the undoubted increase in interlibrary loan periodical lending, and given the probability that many libraries consult holdings lists of neighboring libraries or of other members of consortia and networks before making decisions as to which periodicals to retain and which to cancel, there is still no evidence that all of these practices affect, in any significant way, the totality of the library-journal publisher relationship. This assertion is based on the evidence, as presented earlier, that libraries are already doing everything possible, and perhaps more than may be reasonable, to make dollars available from their meager budgets for the purchase of periodicals. It is a highly doubtful proposition that the elimination of networks or the imposition of photocopying charges paid from library funds would do anything other than simply increase the competition for fixed quantities of dollars and accelerate decisions about which titles to cancel and which titles not to add. There is no doubt that the present availability, through consortia and interlibrary loan, of photocopies of periodical articles can damage specific publishers, and in some cases perhaps cost them a great deal in lost revenues. However, this problem is one of revenue allocation and distribution among publishers rather than one of increasing total sales dollars for publishing as a whole.

No argument is raised here that, for this reason, photocopy charges should not be imposed. The question is at this moment before Congress. However, without a broadening of the funding base to include the ultimate user's own budget in both academic and public libraries, or without some outside support through a subsidy mechanism, little will be gained on an overall basis by the publishers' success in imposing controls and charges. In most special libraries, of course, the alternative of charging the ultimate user becomes meaningless, since such libraries, particularly libraries operated in the for-profit sector, are usually supported out of corporate overhead allocations. Unless the imposition of charges is paralleled by increased budgets for special libraries and either increased budgets or outside user charges in academic and public libraries, publishers will have gained little if any advantage. Most publishers with whom I have talked agree with this analysis.

ATTEMPTS TO ALLEVIATE ECONOMIC PRESSURE

Publisher Community

The survey attempted to elicit information from both publishers and librarians concerning actions either being taken or being contemplated to alleviate the economic problems of which both groups are clearly aware. Responses from both groups, unfortunately, were more rhetorical than substantive.

Publishers perceive little alternative to reliance on subscription income for the support of their publications. Neither advertising revenue nor page charges is a major source of funds. Advertising revenues, together with subsidies, have never been significant and are in fact declining as a percentage source of funds. Publishers resort to page charges with reluctance and hesitation, in part because they are keenly aware of the danger of losing significant articles to rival publications. The reliance on subscription income, which represents more than 80 percent of the revenue of commercial and university publishers and represents a smaller percentage for society publishers only because part of membership dues are transferred to the support of societal journals, is increasing for all publisher groups. Increased subscription income can come from only two sources: more customers and higher prices. Publishers obviously prefer the former, but largely they end up with the latter.

In addition, publishers see little prospect that new technologies or publishing practices will ease their financial pressures. On the contrary, they are disturbed by increases in the cost of paper and other raw materials and by imposed or threatened increases in postal rates. Publishers respond without enthusiasm to microform publication, publication of abstracts in lieu of full articles, or publication on demand. They see as their biggest source of potential support the development of spin-off publications from existing machine-processable data bases. Since such additional spin-off publications will only result in greater competition for the library's purchasing dollar, there is no potential benefit for libraries in this development.

Library Community

Little emerges from responses of librarians in the survey to cause optimism about the identification of significant solutions for their financial problems. As shown, labor costs, already the predominant category of expenses in all types of libraries, are taking a still increasing share of library budgets, leaving smaller percentages of budgets already inadequate to cope with materials costs. Nor is there any indication that the increase in personnel costs is brought about by an upgrading of existing user services or by the implementation of new ones. This is particularly true for academic libraries, which have been shown to be under the greatest financial pressure during this survey period and to be preoccupied primarily with maintenance of the status quo.

Many of the responding libraries pointed to technical services as potentially the most important area for cooperative activities and cost reduction. Pooled or shared acquisitions and cataloging operations and the use of centralized services such as the Ohio College Library Center (OCLC) were all mentioned frequently. However, while respondents extolled the potential benefits of such activities, they rarely indicated any specific commitment to cost reductions by reducing staff levels. Rather, they claimed such benefits as the avoidance of the need for increased staff and the reduction of backlogs. Since it is unlikely that, in such financially difficult times, staff size would have been allowed to increase in any case, the savings in terms of personnel costs tend to become hypothetical. However, it appears clear that a reversal of the trend of allocating larger percentages of library budgets for the labor cost of ongoing services will only be possible if libraries find ways to operate with smaller staffs—not smaller than they would like to have, but smaller than they presently have. Cooperation or shared technical services at least offer this potential.

It may be that the 1973 cutoff date of the survey was not late enough to identify specific savings which have become possible through the implementation of cooperative or shared technical services. It may even be possible, despite evidence to the contrary, that since 1973 networks and consortia have caused a reduction in expenditures for library materials. It can only be stated here that not only had these reductions not occurred by 1973, but respondents gave little indication of expecting them to occur in the near future.

The ambivalent attitude toward automation is indicative. A significant number of librarians pointed to automation as an area in which cost reduction had been achieved and as one in which more was possible. However, while some respondents talked of cost reduction by means of the implementation of automation techniques, others projected savings through the elimination of machine processing.

There is some evidence, but not much, that some attitudes about the need for binding are changing. However, they are expressed most frequently in terms of the marginal economy of acquiring microforms as second copies in lieu of binding for retention and not in terms of the use of microforms as an initial substitute for a full-size current subscription.

CONCLUSIONS

While the shortcomings of study limited to American scholarly and research journals and ending in 1973 prior to a period of serious economic dislocations have already been pointed out, the study does permit major conclusions. It is no longer viable to consider the increasingly unstable interrelationships of American research publishers and American research libraries as a closed system. The difficulties of their relationships are not the result of unreasonable behavior or practice by either the publishing or library communities, although both can perhaps be criticized for a lack of imagination in confronting their problems. Unless new attitudes toward the need to publish in formal refereed formats are adopted, little can be expected except an exacerbation of the present problems. In fact, there is evidence of a series of spiraling economic disasters which accelerate by feeding on themselves. Thus, as the relative purchasing power of libraries decreases and subscriptions are discontinued, journal prices are raised to offset falling revenues and the process starts anew. The "new attitudes" referred to above, which would allow for research disclosure through abstracts and summaries, flash publication, or publication on demand, would require that such techniques be accepted for research "credit" in the academic and research community. These matters have been discussed for many years, but there is no indication that any change is likely to be forthcoming. Unless they are accepted by researchers, neither publishers nor librarians can proceed very far with them.

The alternatives presently envisaged to the economic dilemma do not appear to be of much help. A laissez-faire approach to publication survival would lead to a thinning of the ranks, but not necessarily one in which only marginal journals would disappear and communication remain largely unaffected. The present approach in academic libraries, concentrating as it does on the elimination of duplicates, preserves collection integrity only temporarily, while immediately undermining access and use of material in heavy demand.

The shift of dollars from books to periodicals reported in the survey has almost certainly had a drastic impact on the publishing of books intended for purchase by academic and other research libraries, although this was not investigated in this study. In any case, such a shift can only provide a temporary solution in freeing dollars for the purchase of periodicals.

It is unlikely that a drastic change will occur in academia concerning the importance of scholarly and research publications. It is equally unlikely that libraries will receive increased funding or that there will be a dramatic breakthrough in publishing technology. My conclusion, therefore, is that the entire system will need to be subsidized, most probably at the federal level. My colleagues and I were not particularly disturbed by this conclusion, since the research process which leads to publication is already heavily subsidized. To provide financial incentives for the completion of research, but to stop short of enabling the researcher adequately to report and disseminate his findings, appears to be inconsistent and even foolish. What remains for intensive study and evaluation by appropriate bodies is the amount of subsidy required and to whom it should be granted. Alternatives are to help the author to meet page charges, to provide the publisher with a direct subsidy, to assist the library in the purchase of publications whose price reflects interplay of normal economic factors, or to enable the user to pay for library services.

References

1. Fry, Bernard M., and White, Herbert S. "Economics and Interaction of the Publisher-Library Relationship in the Production and Use of Scholarly and Research Journals: Final Report." National Technical Information Service Report no. PB 249108. Bloomington: Indiana University Graduate Library School, 1975.

2. Gottschalk, Charles M., and Desmond, Winifred F. "Worldwide Census of Scientific and Technical Serials." *American Documentation* 14 (July 1963): 188–94.

3. Anderla, J. Georges. "The Growth of Scientific and Technical Information—a Challenge." *Information, Part 2* 3, no. 3 (1974): 1–52.

4. Ballhausen, C. J., et al. "Too Many Chemistry Journals." *College and Research Libraries* 35 (July 1974): 268–69.

5. Clasquin, Frank F. "Periodical Prices: A Three-Year Comparative Study." *Library Journal* 99 (October 1974): 2447–53.

6. Brown, Norman B. "Price Indexes for 1974." *Library Journal* 99 (July 1974): 1775–79.

7. Gore, Daniel. "The View from the Tower of Babel." *Library Journal* 100 (September 1975): 1601–4.

8. Garfield, Eugene. "Citation Analyses as a Tool in Journal Evaluation." *Science* 178 (November 1972): 431–39.

9. Bundy, Mary Lee, and Wasserman, Paul. "The College and University Library Administrator Technical Data Summary, Preliminary Analysis." National Technical Information Service Report no. PB 192123. College Park: Manpower Research Project, School of Library and Information Services, University of Maryland, 1970.

10. *De-Acquisitions Newsletter.* Bimonthly, 1975-.

11. Williams, Gordon Roland. "Inter-Library Loan: The Experience of the Center for Research Libraries." *Unesco Bulletin for Libraries* 28 (March 1974): 73–78.

12. Stewart, Blair. "Periodicals and the Liberal Arts College Library." *College and Research Libraries* 36 (September 1975): 371–78.

COST-EFFECTIVENESS AND COST-BENEFIT DETERMINATIONS IN SPECIAL LIBRARIES

> *Mechanisms to establish and evaluate cost-effectiveness in the administration of libraries are as feasible and necessary as for any other operational unit. The determination of cost-benefit to the sponsoring organization is far more difficult, and probably cannot be made on a consistent and continuing basis. However, user perception that such cost-benefit exists, even if unsupportable in an accounting sense, can suffice to justify the validity of the library operation. It is this perception and appearance that library managers must seek to cultivate.*

One of the things which differentiates libraries in the for-profit sector from academic, public, and school libraries is that in these latter institutions the library is assumed to have value *per se*. In part this is because there is perhaps a greater tolerance for knowledge and learning as a self-evident good, rather than simply as a contributor to bottom line figures. However, academic librarians now report that much of this tolerance for the library is eroding under financial pressures. Nevertheless, it should be safe to assume that a university president would not, and could not, shut down the university library and sell its books, even if the administration was absolutely convinced that the library contributed nothing to academic excellence on the campus. The faculty would not allow it, the school would lose its accreditation, the graduates would not get jobs, and the Board of Trustees would fire the president at its next meeting.

By contrast, the author cannot envision any such restraining pressure on corporate officials, or company presidents comparing notes on the quality and size of their libraries.

From *Special Libraries* 70 (April 1979):163–69.
H.W. Wilson Award for SLA Best Paper for 1979.

CORPORATE DECISION-MAKING

Although many companies are beginning to soften their public image, the fundamental purpose of the for-profit organization is still precisely that—to make a profit. What size profit? Stockholders never set limits on their appetites for return on investments, and when short-term profits are plowed back into the business for plant expansion and enhanced research programs, all that is being done is to trade in a present return for the expectation of an even larger future profit. Corporate executives are hired to make good decisions, and if the decisions work out well for the company, no one really cares whether or not they were scientifically based. If the decisions turn out badly, nobody cares how they were arrived at either.

Most business decisions of the 19th and early 20th centuries, as well as management philosophies in existence today, were and are based on instinct and innovation. Success rates were never high, but those who did succeed were glorified and lionized, and the impression grew that such bold and incisive courage was the key to business success.

We still have some such instinctive innovators, but they are a dying breed, replaced by groups of professional managers whose objective is frequently the avoidance of a bad decision rather than the formulation of a good one. These managers, who did not necessarily start the business or grow with it, need tools with which to make good, or at least safe, decisions.

Cost-benefit and cost-effectiveness analysis programs are designed to assure the effective allocation of scarce resources. In a production environment this works reasonably well. Parameters can be established for determining the relative merits of starting a second shift or of building a new assembly plant. Models can be drawn to determine whether or not price increases will depress sales sufficiently to offset the gain in unit profitability.

THE LIBRARY AS OVERHEAD

Cost-benefit analyses become more difficult when applied to overhead operations such as the library. In accounting terms, overhead is cost applied to gross profit; overhead turns profit into a smaller operating or net profit, or even a net loss. Since overhead always has a negative impact, it is always assumed to be too large. Furthermore, the advantages of overhead expenditures, while perhaps easy to claim, are difficult to justify. Why renovate the company cafeteria? Because it improves employee morale? Does it really, even if there were complaints in the last survey? Would employees prefer this to a raise? Will renovation decrease turnover or improve productivity? If productivity later increases, how do we know that this renovation was solely or even primarily responsible? It makes for happier employees? So what? There is no tangible proof that happier employees are harder workers. We have all seen organizations with so much staff camaraderie that most of the day was spent in planning parties, picnics, bowling tournaments, and bridal showers, and almost no work got done.

The author is forced to conclude, from his own experience in operations and management, that a true cost-benefit analysis of an overhead organization such as the library, in terms of what it contributes directly to organizational goals, may be neither practicable nor even possible. There are libraries, of course, whose operating budgets are allocated to user groups, either by formula or by actual use. In theory, to the extent to which the group has the right to reject library service, such an acceptance can be argued to represent cost-benefit acceptance, but in point of fact there is organizational pressure for each group to pay its so-called fair share. Part of this pressure still comes from the belief, even in business environments, that libraries are good things, and not to be reviled. Part of it comes from the recognition that, if one group refuses to pay, the others will probably have to pay more. Most importantly, they are willing to go along because their share of the allocated library expense is in fact rather trivial, and really does not make all that much difference.

Generally, corporate measurement criteria have not extended to the evaluation of one overhead service against another—of a better library versus hot cafeteria lunches versus new electric typewriters versus expanding the parking lot versus doubling the number of daily mail deliveries.

Usually, the library is treated as part of the overhead pool, and a fairly insignificant one at that. Overhead funding is decreased when sales and earnings fall, or when they do not approach expectations. It can be convincingly argued that bad times are in themselves the worst times in which to cut back on research and, by extension, library activities, but those arguments are usually fruitless. Stockholders are interested in this year's dividends and this year's stock market quotations. Five years from now somebody else may own the stock, and the present owner will not care.

If decisions affecting specific overhead services such as the library are not made within the organization based on any specific or scientific cost-benefit formulation, how are they made? By and large, these decisions are based on perceptions by individuals on how the continuance, strength, growth, or decline of the library will affect their own performance. It should not be assumed that individual profit center managers will be sufficiently altruistic to vote for things that will hurt them or their performance, but which may help the organization. Managers are encouraged to be selfish in their thinking; they are rewarded for their own successes and punished for their own failures. Credit and blame are not generally shared.

THE LIBRARY'S "USEFULNESS"

Individual managers have little idea of how the operation of the library affects the success or failure of their own performance. They cannot admit that they would have committed a serious blunder, if not for certain help from the library. Nor can they accept that the existence of a strong library allows them to decrease their own technical staffs or to increase their sales targets. While they may happily agree that the library saves them time, they will never agree that this allows them to operate with fewer people, and there is therefore no tangible cost reduction.

The lesson for librarians in this is clear. The library is perceived as being useful (these words are chosen carefully because it cannot actually be proven to be useful) to the extent that its services and activities are felt by operating profit center managers to be of positive influence on their group. Only "positive" counts. An evaluation of "having no impact" is just as deadly as a negative one would be. Having postulated that cost-benefit studies of the role of the library in the achievement of overall organization goals are probably not practicable, it could then be argued that cost-benefit analysis of operations within the library can be measured quite effectively if objectives for the library are established in terms of their impact on the performance of operating groups.

INTERNAL COST-BENEFIT ANALYSES

What this requires, first of all, is that librarians think of themselves as entrepreneurs running a business. The success or failure of that business comes from the acceptance and appreciation of its products and services—its operating capital comes from the willingness of the customers to provide it with a stake.

Most corporations pay little attention to how libraries allocate their funds. The budget may require line item descriptions, but the only real interest is in the cost total. In addition, most organizations impose headcount ceilings, in that additional money cannot usually be spent on full-time permanent employees without additional permission. However, it usually can be allocated to purchased services or contract labor, and sometimes even for in-house employees, as long as these are either part-time, temporary, or both.

In order for the library administration to perform its own internal cost-benefit analysis, it must obviously know both costs and benefits. Costs are easy to calculate; they come monthly from the accounting department. If we assign functional or task codes to time sheets we can get cost breakdowns by functions performed and even user groups for which services are performed.

One of the traditional management communication problems that libraries have had is that library objectives are usually inwardly directed. We will purchase and process books and periodicals to projected numbers, we will compile a certain number of bibliographies, we will achieve a 10% increase in circulation and an 8% increase in interlibrary loan. These statistics, while they may impress fellow library professionals, are meaningless to management, which is not in the book processing and material lending business. It is to the real business, or the many businesses, of the company that library objectives must relate. What does the library plan to do in support of program A and program B? At least as importantly, how do we assure that the directors of programs A and B are aware of what we are doing for them—are they direct recipients, are they told by their own people, or do we make sure we tell them ourselves?

Unless the library manager has a specific direction for the library and feels convinced that success in this endeavor is good both for the library and for the organization, then the library will inevitably drift. The librarian was hired to run a good library and to serve the needs of the organization, even if management cannot articulate them.

That is our objective; saving money is not our job. Economy may become a requirement, but corporate profitability is a factor that someone else is hired to monitor at a considerably higher salary. In fact, we can cost reduce our way into being fired for not doing our job, which is to run a library that is both an effective library and one which is perceived to be an effective library. Both are important, and both are inexorably tied together. The first because that is our professional responsibility, the second because it is a prerequisite for being able to do the first. It is sometimes difficult to convince library managers in for-profit environments, who are usually conservative to start with and who have been ground down by corporate propaganda, not to worry about requesting a tripling of their budgets for a program addition or a program expansion if that program makes sense. The library cannot spend enough, no matter how extravagant we get, to affect earnings by even one cent per share, and new programs are far easier to sell than a 20% increase in existing programs.

JUSTIFIABLE COSTS

It is possible, then, to make cost-benefit determinations in the for-profit special library, but only if there is first a determination of what will be beneficial. That determination is not practicable in terms of overall corporate goals and objectives. These are too broad to permit the library to measure its performance against the achievement of corporate performance. In fact, it might be misleading in that corporate performance may be excellent despite a poor library, or that corporate performance may be poor because of a marketing strategy decision in which the library had no part.

Nor can the library's contribution be measured simply in terms of its own internal statistics. Technical processing unit costs, circulation unit costs, or circulation per volume owned are useful tools in any library, and they may be sufficient in an academic setting in which the need for a library, and even the largest possible library, is accepted as a premise and not subject to question by the faculty. However, in a for-profit library, located in an organization for which library service is an incidental and suspect miscellaneous expense, the only meaning of benefit can come in terms of impact on those profit centers and revenue earning programs which are subject to close scrutiny, and even more importantly, in terms of the perception of that impact by profit center managers.

With this as a yardstick, consideration of alternatives within the library is possible. Bibliographic access, which is now expanding so rapidly through various time-shared access systems, inevitably carries a cost; the cost of providing bibliographic availability must be related to the cost of providing document delivery. This can be done through library purchase of single copies and subscriptions, through the purchase of multiple copies and subscriptions to assure rapid access, through effective recall procedures for material already in the system, and through providing rapid and reliable document delivery from outside the collection. Should the librarian, from the labor budget, designate one individual on a half-time basis to make a daily trip to the nearby university library, make the necessary interlibrary loan copies personally, and bring them back the same day? It obviously depends on many factors, including the volume of material requested, its relation as a percentage to the material supplied internally (missing the tenth article is not quite so important when you have been able to immediately supply the other nine), and the user perceived importance of rapid service in general and for specific items. Of course, we must also consider what we give up in other services by detaching this half-time clerk, or by cutting $4,000 from our other budget categories to contract for twenty hours per week of a student to do this work. That option is usually ours. Management neither knows nor cares, nor should it bother.

Academic libraries are not as fortunate. Since the concept of information service has not really been developed and no expectation for it has been aroused, except in small departmental collections which function more like special libraries, the academic library is basically expected to maintain the size of its acquisition program. It does not have the option of transferring materials money to services or to the development of effective computer systems.

If we look at our stewardship of the library as running a private business, we will quickly see that making wrong decisions is a luxury we cannot afford. Store owners will rapidly go bankrupt if they sink capital into stock which does not move from the shelves. The comparison to libraries is apt. If we spend our money to have staff perform useless tasks, if we subscribe to bibliographic data bases in which no one is interested, we are not only wasting organizational money, we are stealing money from ourselves which we could use for more meaningful purposes. This is not to suggest that we return it as surplus. Our job, as previously stated, is not to save money. There is a whole financial control organization; let them worry about that. Nor is it our job to help out the personnel department by accepting protected misfits into the library. Our need for a high quality staff is as great as that of any other unit. Perhaps our need is greater, because our staff is unusually small.

COORDINATION WITH COMPANY PROJECTS

The library cannot make tangible contributions to the specific programs which are carried out within the organization without first knowing what these are. This may seem obvious, but it is surprising to what extent these programs are only dimly perceived. Start by making a list of programs and activities within the organization, and then determine to what extent these can benefit from library support, and to what extent they are already supported. There are two kinds of projects that should be starred or underlined. The first consists of the ones run by individuals in a position to affect library funding and library support. Frequently these individuals, in general administration and finance, are not natural or instinctive library users, but that does not mean they do not have information problems. Lack of complaints in this instance does not necessarily imply good library service. It may mean poor service, or no service.

The second group concerns newly started projects, because new projects are most in need of information, and timeliness is crucial. Frequently a new project team is put together and given specific and demanding assignments, with little if any understanding of what has transpired in the past, what documentation already exists, or what services might be available. The manager of this new project has no time to spend on literature searches. More priority must be given to logistical problems, concerns about justifying, interviewing and hiring staff, fighting for and arranging space and equipment, getting a budget established, and developing the necessary contacts with the accountants and purchasing agents without whom life in the organization is impossible. These managers of new projects need help most of all. Yet they do not know what they need; neither do they have time to think about it.

How do we find out what projects exist, particularly what new projects are just coming into being? We must work hard at developing informal communications channels, because most decisions are made long before they are formally reported. Depending on the librarians' position in management chains, they may be participants in meetings in which decisions are made. If not, then somebody in the management chain is such a participant, and we must make it clear that it is part of their job to help us do ours by keeping us informed.

Part of the information process simply consists of talking to people, informally or through formal appointments, to find out what they are doing and to suggest support the library might be able to provide. People like to talk about their work, like to explain what they are doing. They usually do not consider this an imposition, even if it requires translation into very basic English. At the same time, their perceptions of and expectations for services from the library are frequently restricted to the clerical provision of documents on request, and they require education just as we do.

CONCLUSION

The implementation of cost-benefit determinations within the library is a long overdue process. Librarians have continued, far too long, to perform their jobs in a traditional way, partially because they report to a management which is neither knowledgeable enough nor interested enough to suggest any changes. At the same time, the premise of the library as an inherent good is coming under growing challenge in the public and academic sector. In the private sector this is nothing new, as the "bloodbaths" of the early 1970s attest. Libraries, unable to demonstrate their specific contribution to this year's profit growth, have tended to avoid financial analyses entirely. It is a third alternative, a middle ground, which this paper has sought to address.

WHY DON'T WE GET PAID MORE?

Last year I participated in a state library conference which had the above title as its theme. It will not surprise readers to learn that the meeting drew an overflow audience. Our growing sense of impatience with inadequate remuneration is a useful and encouraging trend. The image of librarians as individuals who willingly opt for genteel poverty has earned us respect from a few, contempt from quite a few more, and genteel poverty for most of us.

To some extent this awakening belligerence can be traced to the feminist movement, and if this drive is successful in opening professional positions in library administration to the best qualified candidate regardless of sex, women and men will both benefit.

THE ULTIMATE VALIDATION

Salary, we know from personnel management studies, is very important for all of us. This is not only because of the creature comforts that increased pay brings (and librarians are not required to be ascetics who forswear Caribbean vacations), but because salary is recognized as the ultimate validation of the esteem in which we are held. As some sage noted many years ago: "Talk is cheap." Nowhere is it cheaper than when mouthed by library boards, campus administrators, and corporate executives.

One of the more recent approaches to increasing librarian salaries has been through the legal channel of pay equity, or comparable worth, developed as an issue by the women's movement. This approach has had some significant local successes, and has achieved increasing impor-

From *Library Journal* 111 (1 March 1986):70–71.

tance within the priorities of the American Library Association, particularly in the eyes of some of its present officers. To the extent to which court action, or the threat of court action, succeeds in improving the salaries of the so-called "women's professions," all of its practitioners, regardless of sex, will benefit.

At the same time, I have doubts about the ultimate success of this strategy, and I am particularly concerned lest this become our only or even our primary strategy. Legal threat and legal action have succeeded primarily in communities largely predisposed to the acceptance of the premise. In those communities in which there has not been ready acquiescence, the process is now bogged down in what will undoubtedly be a lengthy legal process that may surface before several sessions of the Supreme Court.

A SUBJECTIVE PROCESS

We know how the present federal administration feels about this issue, and decisions of the court are increasingly difficult to predict. What bedevils the issue of comparable worth most of all is the recognition of all who have worked on the development of job descriptions and evaluations that this is a highly subjective process. In fact, it would not be farfetched to state that job descriptions like much research result from the process of retrofitting—of first reaching conclusions and then "proving" them to be correct.

To present just one simple if rather garish example in what is not intended as an essay on job descriptions: the comparable evaluation of librarians and garbage collectors depends a great deal on the value placed on the unique activities of each group. For garbage collectors, unlike librarians, that includes outside work in potentially inclement weather. What is that job description factor worth?

There are no real guidelines, and if there were, they would undoubtedly differ between southern California and northern Minnesota. Evaluation factors also include a higher risk of exposure to disease and hazardous materials. How does this compare to some of our stresses and pressures? Have we even made the point that our work includes stress and pressure? Not to the general public, which thinks that librarians lead gracious and relaxed lives in which they do a lot of reading.

THEY CAN AFFORD MORE

If the drive for legal solutions to our pay dilemma has a particular positive emphasis, it is that it disposes once and for all of the myth that we are paid so little because our employers cannot afford to pay more. That is as absurd for a small town as for a major corporation, and even if it were not absurd it would still be irrelevant. Ultimately, nobody is required to hire librarians, or for that matter to have libraries. However, if they do, then those with fund-raising authority have the responsibility for finding the money. Comparable worth lawsuits say that, and it should be clearly true even without the need for legal enforcement.

My greatest concern about the legal strategy toward salary equity is that it not distract us from the recognition of what the problem really is. There is no doubt that there are salary preconceptions about "women's professions," but those preconceptions, like the stereotypes about librarians, are based on generalized (generally accurate if specifically unfair) observations.

Most wage and salary administrators I have known are neither saints nor sinners, and they pay what they must and little more. If they pay librarians less and truckdrivers more, it is because they can get away with it. If they could get away with paying truckdrivers less, they would.

It is important that we recognize that we are not surrounded by a gigantic conspiracy. Librarians tend to be a little paranoid in any case, but nobody is out to get us. We have no real enemies, because only those with power have enemies. We will change the perception when we take ourselves and our roles more seriously, and when we concentrate on economic issues just as other professions do.

THE PRICE OF "DEDICATED"

I see some progress in this direction. My students of the 1980s reject as irrelevant the suggestions that pay be based either on employee need or on the employer's ability to pay, and of course in the American free enterprise system that is totally correct. I shudder to think what the sobriquet "dedicated" has cost us in economic terms.

In the economic environment, being called dedicated is being cursed. It is of course harder to change this perception in a "women's profession" and to eradicate the suggestion that we work for convenience and not for reward. However, teachers, also a characteristically female profession, have made progress in changing this view. There is probably no more confrontational work force in the nation today than school teachers, and the most articulate representatives seen on TV are women. Teachers were once paid about the same starting salaries as librarians, but there is now a gap and that gap is growing.

Ultimately the question asked by all administrators and pay analysts is, "What do I get for my money?" Is there a benefit in hiring better-qualified librarians and paying them more? This difference is not well understood by those who fund libraries, and we do virtually nothing to emphasize or explain it. I have addressed some of that remarkable reluctance to stress our unique expertise in earlier columns on turf (*LJ,* April 15, 1985, p. 54), the White House Conference (*LJ,* October 15, 1985, p. 51) and self-respect (*LJ,* February 1, p. 58), and I will undoubtedly do so again. It is clear to me that our unwillingness to articulate that difference between good and inadequate libraries, and between the work of librarians and nonlibrarian poseurs, lies at the root of much of our salary problem. In the words of the immortal Pogo Possum: "We have met the enemy, and he is us."

In the long run, the marketplace and not legal initiatives will continue to be the determinant for salary distinctions. In academia, assistant professors in computer science and law earn more than full professors in comparative linguistics, and that difference has nothing to do with sex bias. That distinction may be unfair, but it is real and it will be with us for the foreseeable future. What is at work here is the law of supply and demand, and it is a powerful force.

A SHORTAGE OF LIBRARIANS

Paradoxically, librarianship is turning from a surplus to a shortage profession, and it is an interesting question of what we will do about an economic force that can now at least potentially work to our benefit. There would be no salary difference in academia between comparative linguists and computer scientists if unemployed linguists were hired to teach computer science, but of course that doesn't happen. Computer science vacancies remain vacant until they are *properly* filled. Who may do what in a library?

We have always had certain shortages in our field. A lack of qualified physical scientists to work in special libraries comes immediately to mind and their salaries are higher. However, there was never in any case the overwhelming surplus of librarians that was claimed in the library literature of the early and mid-1970s, much of it in articles and letters that bordered on the hysterical. The thrust was invariably one that suggested that because the writer couldn't get a job, there must obviously be a glut of librarians. It wasn't true.

Even in the mid-1970s, library school graduates were able to find positions far more readily than graduates of humanities programs, and the placement rate in 1985 of close to 90 percent would be considered by economists to be too high for natural selection, if economists cared about library placement rates. Then, as now, but particularly now, an inability by the graduate of a respected education program to find a job is brought about primarily because of geographical inflexibility. The need to be willing to go where the jobs are has always been a prerequisite to selectivity, in our field as in others.

The present shortage falls unevenly on certain specializations, as it inevitably does. We have seen recent articles bemoaning the shortage of catalogers, and of course missing the point of why that shortage exists. Educators are even accused of conspiring to keep students out of cataloging posts, but students have minds of their own. Moreover, at least half of the students in most library schools have present or recent job experience in libraries. They may not know what catalogers specifically do, but they know what they see.

CHILDREN'S LIBRARIAN

The most intriguing shortage to me is that of children's librarians. It is intriguing because if there is one stereotype to which the public holds, it is that librarians work with kids. Of course, we created this shortage ourselves, by hammering away at publicizing the presumed glut until guidance counselors and college students interested in working with children believed there were no jobs. The guidance counselors still think so. It takes a while to repair misconceptions.

It is true that a number of library schools have reduced or even eliminated their educational programs to prepare children's librarians, and at least in public institutions I consider such actions unconscionable. However, it is also important to recognize why this has been done. The number of students interested in taking these courses has declined, and academic administrators must also be responsive to that other marketplace, student preferences.

In any case, the imbalance will repair itself, if we let it. Attractive job opportunities draw candidates to educational programs, and fortunately there has never been nor can I see real shortage of young people interested in working with children. We drove them away, but we can also bring them back. In part with money, because that is the way the system of supply and demand works. Under supply and demand, shortages and surpluses cure themselves.

Part of me looks at shortages such as this with eager anticipation because I know what it could mean for the salaries in the profession. Another part of me looks at them with dread, because I am afraid we may foul up this opportunity as we have fouled up others.

We now find public library systems unable to lure qualified candidates for children's library posts at the advertised salary of $10,000, $12,000, or $14,000. The exact salaries offered don't really matter, because cost of living rates vary widely. The point is that children's librarians, like computer scientists and law professors, are not applying in sufficient quantities at the salaries being offered. It is a classic example of the supply/demand model, except that for once it favors librarians. Maybe.

WHOM WILL THEY HIRE?

What will these public library system administrators do? Will they leave the positions unfilled, if necessary for months and years, incurring the wrath of both patrons and library boards in their stubborn insistence that the qualifications are realistic and must be met, and that the salary structure must be brought into line with the new reality? Or will they adjust their expectations and, failing to find qualified candidates with accredited MLS degrees, the proper specialization courses, and an interest in children, who are willing to work at the posted salary, hire whatever they can get at that salary? What will be the governing determinant, qualifications or dollars? In the answer to that question also lies much of the answer to the question of pay equity.

DIFFERENTIAL PRICING

Here is another in what may unfortunately be an endless series of essays examining the remarkable passivity of our profession. International scholarly journal pricing is something I will claim to know something about. I have been an officer of a corporation which published journals on an international basis. I have been president of a subscriptions agency, and much of our business consisted of purchasing scholarly journals from Western European countries for American academic libraries. As director of the Indiana University Research Center for Library and Information Science I engaged in several major studies for the National Science Foundation on the financial interaction of libraries and scholarly publishers.

I even have some understanding of the rationale by some publishers for a two-tiered pricing schedule under which individuals pay at one rate and libraries pay at a higher rate. It is argued that individual subscriptions serve one client and library subscriptions serve many, and that therefore differential pricing is "fair." If you say it fast enough it may even sound plausible. However, I know, and certainly the publishers know, that fairness has nothing to do with it.

Libraries are charged higher prices because experience has shown that they will pay higher prices, and that the cancellation rate in response to price increases is much greater for individuals than for libraries. Economics govern these decisions and all others. Publishers believe that libraries have little if any price resistance, and their statistics and our Indiana studies bear them out.

I will even go along, to a point, with the suggestions that those paying for a foreign journal in U.S. dollars should pay a surcharge over the currency exchange rate to reimburse the publisher for the inconvenience of currency conversion. That process does have a cost, and a surcharge of perhaps $5 is not unreasonable. So does international air

From *Library Journal* 111 (1 September 1986):170–71.

shipment, although for a quarterly publication it isn't that great, and bulk shipment to a redistribution point can reduce this further, if the publisher thinks it is important to save the customer's money.

However, when foreign publishers tie their dollar prices to conversion schedules which bear no relationship whatsoever to the rates published daily in the newspapers, only five possible conclusions occur to the casual observer: 1) They think we are so rich that we don't care. 2) They think we are so stupid that we don't notice. 3) They think we are so spineless we won't object. 4) They think we are only the clerks who order what users tell us to order and therefore have no power base. 5) They think we will pay anything to continue to be invited to their ALA cocktail parties. There may be other opinions.

Libraries astute enough in the management of their money have had ways around what I can most charitably only call a scam. They can place their subscriptions through agents who have the capability of paying in foreign currencies, and watch to make sure they get the benefit of that leverage. Alternatively, major libraries can, without too much trouble, establish accounts in banks in major foreign countries, and pay directly with local bank drafts or checks.

What has truly outraged me has been the reported action of some international publishers to foreclose even these options, by insisting that U.S. libraries continue to pay in dollars, and that they continue to pay at the price scale reserved for "rich Americans only." I don't know about the legality of such actions, but I do know about their morality. They assume, somehow, that differential pricing can be justified on a presumed ability to pay. That works for United Nations dues, and even for the U.S. Tax Code, but it isn't supposed to work in the business world. If I wanted to be contentious I could argue that American libraries should be charged less than local clients for British and German journals, because our large number gives us negotiating leverage, but that wouldn't be fair either.

I don't think I lack understanding of the problems that scholarly publishers have, and I know that while some of them make huge profits others barely survive. They operate in a very narrow and highly segmented market, and our National Science Foundation studies clearly indicated that library subscriptions represent a very large and increasing percentage of their customer base. American libraries are the largest part of that library clientele. Even more importantly, readers of these journals through U.S. libraries represent a crucial rationale for publishing the journal in the first place, and for convincing authors to entrust their manuscripts to this editor and to this journal. They need us badly, even desperately. Get the idea?

In that context I was pleased to note the beginning of some "discussions" between American librarians and European scholarly publishers. However, tactics employed by American libraries in these meetings would cause any veteran labor negotiator to shudder. One is quoted in the press as stating: "We can only ask them to reconsider, because we need their journals for our readers."

One publisher has responded by suggesting that American libraries have to pay more because of the publisher's cost in maintaining a U.S. office, and that is really a funny answer. I had always assumed that these publishers had opened American offices because it would help them make more money, by increasing the U.S. market, by the process of bypassing subscription agents entirely and keeping all of the income, or by a greater ability to reach potential authors to improve the quality of the journal. If that is not the case, they should close their American offices. We did not ask them to open these offices, and the great majority of libraries which purchase through subscription agents don't need them.

Do American libraries need foreign scholarly journals? Of course we do, but nowhere nearly as much as they need us. In part that is because of the subscription dollars generated, but far more importantly because they need their readership in American academic institutions. Without that readership they would lose something far more crucial than even their subscribers. They would lose their authors. Why do you think all the German, Swedish, Italian, and Japanese scholars write in English? They want their work read here, and they know that Americans are by and large unfortunately unilingual. Yes, having access to American scholarly and scientific readers is crucial to these authors, and therefore to the journals that solicit their manuscripts.

To counter this unbelievable ripoff I would suggest a very simple strategy, and it requires only agreement among the largest of the academic libraries, the members of the ARL. It doesn't even need unanimity, half will do.

If 50 or 60 of the top U.S. academic libraries banded together to announce cancellation of all campus copies of the offending journal until a pricing structure which did not discriminate against American libraries or any other single group of libraries were put into effect, I doubt that the threat would ever even come to fruition. However, just in case it does, you must tell your faculty colleagues what you have done and why. Note that I suggest telling them, not asking them.

There are even additional options of access while you wait for a response, although you must never let targeted publishers know what these are, because they must really think that nobody on your campus now has access to their journal. You could distribute the current tables of contents to faculty members, and obtain interlibrary loan photocopies of requested articles.

If you want to take a page out of the tactics of the nonviolent civil disobedience movement, buy one copy and photocopy the entire issue for distribution to all other libraries. That will of course make you subject to a suit for copyright violation, but that suit would have to be filed in a U.S. court, would take years to come to trial, and would include very specific testimony regarding the pricing tactics which prompted the response. American judges and American jurors would find all this fascinating.

The other journals (the nonrapacious ones) would love to cover the proceedings, and we might even qualify for *60 Minutes*. Would these foreign journals sue American academic libraries in a U.S. courts and explain their tactics to a U.S. jury? They may be greedy, but they aren't that stupid.

None of this would need to happen if the publishers thought you meant it, and if you gave them six months to shape up or face the consequences. The great majority of responsible publishers on both sides of the Atlantic would applaud our actions, because we are talking about a very small number of bad apples who give their own community a bad image. These few publishers, whose marketing ethics consist only of a search for the easy buck, are opting for their strategies simply because they think you lack the organization and the backbone to fight back.

Prove them wrong once, and you'll never have to do it again.

THE FUNDING OF CORPORATE LIBRARIES: OLD MYTHS AND NEW PROBLEMS

> *Economy drives in corporations never end—particularly for overhead organizations, such as libraries—since management does not know what it should spend on support services and feels that it does not hurt to try to cut. Unfortunately, some librarians, ground down by incessant propaganda, accept the suggestion that we "do more with less"—a suggestion recognized as patent and dangerous nonsense, even if it must be publicly endured. Our job is to run effective libraries, not cheap ones, which may require that we spend more, even as it requires that we insist on spending wisely, by establishing priorities and eliminating the trivial and pointless tasks now assigned to us.*

Corporate libraries, like their counterparts in the academic and public sectors, have always led a precarious existence. They are the beneficiaries of a great deal of good will, being judged, in one sense, as "self-evidently good." At the same time, there is no clear indication of what defines good, and of what it takes to provide library service at that level. Unlike academia, which measures libraries by the size of their collection, and municipalities, which tend to compare circulation statistics, corporate libraries have no such criteria that organizational statisticians either collect or care about. It is interesting that many corporate libraries, perhaps out of habit or out of a dearth of anything else to report, still carefully report holdings, acquisitions, and circulation statistics on a monthly basis, as though that mattered to the parent organization and its programs.

Corporate libraries are part of the organizational overhead structure, that is, what they do does not contribute directly to the preparation of a marketable product or the generation of income. As such, they are

From *Special Libraries* 78, no. 3 (Summer 1987):155–61.
H.W. Wilson Award for SLA Best Paper for 1987.

immediately suspect as potential "waste." We do not hold that distinction uniquely; we share it with purchasing, accounting, personnel, public relations, and even research. However, these organizations have probably been more successful in establishing the premise that without them the rest of the organization could not function.

Corporate libraries are also part of a general category of service institutions, which exist directly for the purpose of assisting others in doing whatever it is that they are supposed to be doing. In writing about the service professions in his most recent book on entrepreneurship and innovation, Peter Drucker does not mention libraries, but his characterization of service professions (he specifies nursing and social work) certainly fits us as well.[1] Drucker argues that service professions exhibit three characteristics: 1) Their performance is measured by how much they spend rather than by what they do; 2) their agendas are controlled by others or even by groups of others, whose priorities may even be conflicting and contradictory; 3) service professionals accept the "moral imperative" of somehow doing whatever it is they are supposed to do whether resources are provided or not, and they consider it their own fault if this does not happen.

When these general characteristics of overhead and service organizations are applied to corporate libraries, several indicators appear. For example, organizations do not know how much to spend for support services, and specifically for libraries. Since they do not know, the safest thing to do is to cut. Economy waves, therefore, run through the organization continuously. At times they peak, but at least the appearance of a drive for economy is never over. At an attempt at humor, I once responded to the announcement of a new economy drive with feigned amazement, stating that I had not realized that the earlier economy drive had ever ended. I cannot recommend this tactic to my colleagues. Economy drives are taken very seriously by accountants and bureaucrats, and librarians are supposed to take them seriously as well. Scientists, by contrast, tend to shrug them off as minor annoyances, and, therefore, they do not let economy drives get in the way of what they planned to do, or what they planned to have the library do.

Furthermore, since the appearance of economy is at least as important in a bureaucratic environment as economy itself, there is an immediate attempt to reduce the visibility of library costs. This is most often done by either getting users to buy things out of their own budgets, or through charge-back mechanisms under which users agree to accept the costs of books, subscriptions, online searches, or interlibrary loan. These exercises of moving peas from one shell to another accomplish nothing in the way of savings, because the assumption that users will constrain their appetites if they are to be charged has no substantiation. The amount is too trivial for them. However, the process looks good, and that is frequently what matters. As one cynic once observed: "We will have economy no matter what it costs us." However, this scenario, aside from being absurd, also causes some real problems for the corporate library professional.

First of all, it is based on the assumption that the user is the best judge of what needs to be purchased, and of what will satisfy his or her information gap. That concept is not necessarily true; users can only judge on the basis of what they already know. As one user commented with a rare insight of honesty: "My problem is not just that I don't know, it is that I don't even know that I don't know." That, of course, defines precisely the appropriate role of the professional librarian. Furthermore, reliance only on a response to user requests tends to clericalize the entire process. What users ask us for (as trained in school and academic libraries) is material—specific books, articles, and reprints. Obtaining these for users may require some ingenuity, but it is still a clerical process, and is recognized to be exactly that.

The appearance of a low-cost service, through the various techniques of squelching the proper level of information access, can end up costing more. Hiding and distributing costs can lead to duplication, as well as to a lack of control. If the process really works as it is intended, then an absence of needed information can end up costing the parent institution even more. The fact that we know what we have saved but don't know what we have lost is poor comfort.

The low-cost approach deprives librarians of a professional role and of a professional visibility. As Drucker has noted, we are judged by how much we spend and not by what we accomplish. In fact, the pressures for cost cutting can become so ingrained that I know of situations in which substantial increases in materials and service budgets have been approved, sometimes with such a strong mandate that no dollar ceilings are even imposed. Some librarians, when confronted by this sudden largesse, simply have forgotten how to spend money. It is as though they were starving prisoners suddenly presented with a banquet, and the sight of so much food makes them ill. The lack of professional identification for what librarians do has, in some special libraries, led to the insistence that all new librarians have subject degrees, sometimes advanced subject degrees. Where a case for a real need to understand the materials in such depth can be made, the need is justified, but when the requirement is cosmetic and simply serves to placate personnel officers or to make users feel more comfortable, the emphasis is misplaced and becomes wasteful. In addition, all libraries are, as we well know, clerical traps. Clerical work takes precedence over professional work, and is also what users specify most immediately as their primary priority when they are unaware of the ability to delegate professional interactions. At a minimum, the library becomes nothing more than a purchasing department. In the final analysis, the library can become so small and so useless that closing the library, rather than cutting its budget again, becomes an act of euthanasia, as Matarazzo has noted.[2]

Ground down by organizational propaganda, librarians, as the good soldiers they are, begin to believe that their primary job is to save money. This produces several ugly side effects. When librarians do receive funds, such as for the hiring of a clerk, this is presented by management as a favor, rather than simply as a carrying out of management's responsibility for judgement and action. The need for a clerk has presumably been justified, not as largesse for the librarian but for the organization at large. One does not normally like to look gift horses in the mouth, but this point must be made; otherwise, management is likely to establish its own quid pro quo, one "favor" for another. Usually, librarians are expected to repay by being cooperative, often by accepting problem employees nobody else wants (the phenomenon of the library as the personnel dumping ground is too real to assume coincidence), by accepting undesirable space not needed by "more important" groups, or by taking on an undesirable project that nobody else wants to do, probably with good reason.

Under incessant pressure and propaganda, librarians sometimes forget what their job is: to run an effective library—not necessarily an expensive one, but not necessarily a cheap one either. The cost of running the library is truly irrelevant to the profitability of the parent organization, since you, as a librarian, would not be able to squander enough money (although nobody suggests that you should) to affect earnings by one cent per share. Besides, others are paid a great deal more with the specific responsibility for seeing to it that neither you nor anyone else spends the organization into oblivion. Furthermore, the library budget is in most corporations only the tip of the iceberg of what the organization spends for information. Depressing that tip under water does not save money; in fact, it may cost more money, since it also leads to a loss of control.

Saving money is *not* your job. In fact, if you are successful enough in implementing a program in which that becomes your prime priority, the ultimate savings you will be able to engineer will be your own salary. Avoiding waste of money in information operations (yours or others in the corporation) *is* your job. Running a productive and efficient professional information service *is* your job, and sometimes suggests spending more money in order to establish the likelihood of greater profits, or the avoidance of other expenditures. Sometimes it suggests aggressive action to save the corporation money by insisting that others don't spend it wastefully. It is recognized that economy drives are more cosmetic than real, but a cost reduction exercise that affects the library but has not addressed the list of *Wall Street Journal* subscriptions does not mean a great deal. There is something of an assumption that only money spent by overhead organizations is potentially wasteful, and that money spent by direct profit centers carries its own presumed justification. However, any controller would agree that a dollar spent in a direct operation impacts profits just as directly as a dollar spent in an overhead operation, particularly if that dollar is wasted. Controllers know this, but even controllers must work through a certain level of accommodation. Unfortunately, nobody accommodates to libraries. If economy is to be meaningful and effective, it must function across the board. I can accept the knowledge that my budget is being cut a lot more easily if I learn that everybody else's is also being cut. Who besides the service departments is affected by the economy drive?

Another vestige of what is largely a stylistic approach to economy comes in the fascination with decentralized decision making. It is assumed that decentralization of authority means better control over decisions. To a large extent that is even true, because if people can be made to care they can be made to be more careful. However, such decentralization does not work for library costs, because the implications of any transaction (one book, one photocopy) are simply too trivial for any user or user group to monitor or care about. What we are left with is simply the cost of record keeping, and that is pure waste. Controllers cannot condone waste if the point is made directly and forcefully enough.

Moreover, decentralization can also lead to inequities of information access. Such varying levels of information service, as between the information informed and the information ignorant, cannot really be tolerated by organizational management once management understands what is happening. These individuals often move to other parts of the organization where their ignorance penalizes innocent bosses. There needs to be at least some level of minimum information service to which every professional is entitled, regardless of what his penny-pinching boss thinks. That is a corporate responsibility in order to establish a level of consistency of approach. It is understood clearly enough with regard to legal services, which are almost never decentralized precisely because the organization cannot afford the risk of inconsistent actions and decisions. The organization cannot afford it for library services, either. Management just does not realize it.

How do we deal with across the board cuts? First of all, why do organizations use such meat axe approaches anyway? Sometimes, of course, cuts occur out of dire necessity. If a company has just filed for protection under the Bankruptcy Laws, the librarian presumably knows this. Other times, however, across the board cuts result simply from a desire to improve profits further, or from the suspicion that over time organizational fat has accumulated. The suspicion is, in fact, often correct. Corporations have found that a 10 percent layoff every five years will not only reduce costs but also improve productivity IF the cuts are made through qualitative selection of the lowest performers and not through longevity rules. Union contracts inevitably specify this, but even organizations not bound by such restrictions usually follow a unionized approach because it is easier to explain and to justify. Most recently, organizations—driven by a sense of responsibility to their employees that is commendable, but not necessarily consistent with the achievement of the objective—have achieved staff reductions simply by not replacing retiring or resigning employees, or by finding homes for surplus personnel whether they fit the new job or not. The result for libraries from such action can be particularly disastrous. While personnel departments usually understand that there are minimum requirements that must be met for a reactor safety engineer, it is assumed that anybody can answer reference questions, and most certainly anybody who has been with the company for 30 years.

Across the board cuts are usually accompanied by the admonition that these cuts are to be absorbed without reductions in service—the old suggestion that we do more with less. For fat and overstaffed units (which, unfortunately, rarely turn out to be libraries), doing more with less is possible. Since management cannot really determine whether it is possible, they consider the effort worth making. Such slogans cannot be openly challenged; however, they can be, and usually are, ignored as the simplistic nonsense they represent. Only a few individuals, which inevitably includes librarians, ground down and brainwashed by propaganda that tells us that our primary job is to save money and that every clerk assigned to us is a favor, tend to believe the premise that we can indeed do more with less.

How, instead, should we deal with budget cuts and retrenchments? A number of articles in the last 10 years have suggested approaches, but the work of Hedberg[3] represents perhaps the clearest and most direct exposition. Hedberg makes it clear that budget cuts cannot simply be absorbed, and he suggests several reasons:

Absorption, without impact, is a self-indictment, for yourself and for your staff. If cuts are made and nothing happens, then indeed you were overstaffed; however, even if it were true, you could not admit to the premise. Most importantly, you cannot make such a commitment on behalf of your subordinates—that they can do more because you said so. Their disillusionment and rage will be reflected in one of the two ways they have of fighting back—increased backlogs or increased errors, perhaps both.

Attempting to do more with the same staff, or as much with fewer people, or, more absurdly, more with less, puts an even greater emphasis not on reducing costs, but on hiding and distributing them to others in the organization. It is the great shell game we already play, and on which we spend a considerable amount of our energy. Furthermore, such an emphasis stresses *how much* is done, not *what* is done or what *ought* to be done. The concentration is on efficiency, not on effectiveness. As I have noted in an earlier article,[4] even when you do the wrong things you should do them as quickly and as cheaply as possible. However, surely there are better ways. Unfortunately, under the pressure of doing more with less, we are usually so busy doing things that we do not have time to think about what we are doing. The answer, as we should know, is not working harder, it is working smarter. For librarians, this means an examination of the entire premise of what we do. This is particularly important, because to a great extent what we do is not necessarily any sort of cogent plan we put together, but rather an accumulation of tasks devised by others, and sometimes these are junk tasks. We need to remind ourselves of Drucker's second injunction. The work of libraries is controlled by a number of other groups, and these groups have differing and sometimes contradictory objectives for us.

Hedberg tells us that the answer to the dilemma lies in program budgeting. It is perhaps ironic that program budgets were developed initially not at the behest of subordinates, but at the insistence of superiors who were disturbed that they were constantly being asked for more money in a line-item budget scenario, but never understood what happened because of the money. For libraries, for which line-item budgets mean only cuts in the face of cost increases and increased demand, program budgets offer the only possible salvation. Program budgets must be prepared even when the organization operates on a line-item budget arrangement, as most of them do. The program budget, once approved, can be turned into a line-item budget to serve the needs of the accounting department. Libraries that have no budgets, except through the whims of their managers, or that have budgets but the librarians have not been told what they are, clearly have even more fundamental problems that must be addressed before any of this makes sense.

A program budget is a contract, and it is a mutually negotiated contract. It can start with a management specification of what services are to be provided, with a librarian implementation plan that then leads to a negotiation of dollars. Alternatively, it can start with dollars; in which case, we then negotiate the services to be provided. Management cannot specify both—common sense tells them that—but that does not mean they will not try, particularly if they have taken Drucker's third characteristic to heart, that librarians, like other service professionals, will "somehow" find a way.

When a contract reached through a determination of funds and programs is changed, then it must be renegotiated. Bear in mind that management has the right to change the financial terms of the equation by cutting the budget at any time, but only if it is then willing to discuss the implication for activities. Alternatively, management can insist that the library take on additional functions, or the proposal for this can come from within the library itself. Again, this changes the premise, and we must then discuss cost implications. As already noted, management is not necessarily anxious to renegotiate, and some bosses are pretty good poker players, particularly if their bluffs have worked with you in the past, or with your predecessor. However, the suggestion that something can be done with nothing is not a serious one, and they know it. Tell them that, and ask them when they want to talk meaningfully.

A budget cut does not simply mean an equivalent cut in all activities, because a budget reduction of 10 percent, translated into a 10 percent (or even 8 percent) reduction in everything we do, suggests a simplistic style of nonmanagement. However, a cut in budget requires that things *change*, although we may even do more of some things and less of others, or eliminate some activities entirely. Similarly, the addition of a new task of high priority without additional funding means the identification either of another task to be eliminated or the discussion of alternatives that will ease and simplify how we do what we now do.

The process of contract negotiation provides the librarian with risk, but also with opportunity. The emphasis on working smarter, which usually accompanies an announced budget cut, allows you to recommend getting rid of activities and procedures you consider annoying, or dumping useless routines and record keeping. There will never be a better time! It also provides the opportunity for cleaning house, for getting rid of a chore that does not really fit your mission, but was only handed to you because somebody else was arranging his or her own budget cut. In general, in staff-poor organizations, such as corporate libraries, you should concentrate on doing what you can do uniquely, or what you can do better. If anybody else can do it just as well, and the task adds neither prestige nor importance, it forms a poor premise for building your empire.

The primary advantage in this process is that it allows you to take the initiative in proposing changes that your boss can either approve or replace with his or her own changes. Chances are that your boss has few, if any, alternatives, and that his or her real approach was to test your willingness to try to "absorb" this budget cut. A sense of humor for both parties is helpful here because it allows you to smile and say "Nice try. Now when can we talk seriously about this?"

You need to be aware of one final injunction. During periods of budgetary curtailment, just as you are looking for opportunities to unload dead weight projects, so are others. The process may yield for you "offers" to take on additional activities, sometimes made to you directly, sometimes through your boss. (If your boss has already accepted the assignment for you without even consulting you first, you obviously have BIG problems that transcend this issue.) Your response obviously depends on whether or not taking on this assignment is good for you and/or good for the company, and usually it is not difficult to rationalize a consistent answer so that the two questions, in fact, become one. If you see this as an opportunity, you may even want to propose reshuffling priorities to do this instead of something else. You probably have some activities you would be happy to dump. If, conversely, you are not really anxious to have this new assignment (it can be assumed that much of what others are willing to give you is dull, routine, troublesome, and clerical) then, at a minimum, you should insist that acceptance of this task depends on a full and total funding transfer and that the job stays only as long as the money stays.

Bear in mind that you are not being paid to save money (although there is no reason to squander money), and that you are not being paid to be charming and cooperative (there is nothing to be gained in being either more or less cooperative than anyone else). Management is not a popularity contest. It is, however, as Thomas Galvin noted, a contact sport. Your job is to provide a professional ingredient that nobody else can provide and to provide a level of information service that nobody else really understands as well as you do, although some bosses have to be trained to that realization. You will succeed or fail specifically on the basis of how well you meet these obligations. In one sense, the drive toward corporate cost effectiveness provides (or, at least, should provide) strong opportunities for corporate libraries to establish their importance, and even to grow while other parts of the organization are declining—this is because strong corporate libraries are cost effective and far more of a bargain than any alternatives. By contrast, weak, ineffective, and so-called "cheap" libraries are probably not worth what little money is spent on them, and the risk for you is that sooner or later management will find that out. There is no safety in being small, and there is no safety in being cheap. There is only safety in being unique and in being valuable.

References

1. Drucker, Peter F. *Innovation and Entrepreneurship.* New York: Harper and Row, 1985.

2. Matarazzo, James M. *Closing the Corporate Library: Case Studies on the Decision Making Process.* New York: Special Libraries Association, 1981.

3. Hedberg, Bo et al. "Camping on Seesaws: Prescriptions for a Self-Designing Organization." *Administrative Science Quarterly* 21 (no. 1): 41–65 (March 1976).

4. White, Herbert S. "Cost-Effective and Cost-Benefit Determinations in Special Libraries." *Special Libraries* 70: 163–169 (April 1979).

SCHOLARLY PUBLISHERS AND LIBRARIES: A STRAINED MARRIAGE

A librarian with close ties to publishing trenchantly argues for increasing the dialogue between scholarly publisher and librarian

Scholarly publishers and librarians have long enjoyed a warm and cooperative relationship. Publishers seek to distribute their publications through libraries to reach their scholarly readers, and librarians have historically gained both pleasure and credit for building ever larger collections by buying what publishers had to offer. That this relationship has now come under strain because of growing financial pressures on both communities, and that an atmosphere of distrust and suspicion has developed, is clear to all readers of this article. That a balance must be restored should be equally clear, along with the recognition that it will require communication, consultation, and an end to arbitrary and capricious decisions. A report prepared for the National Science Foundation (NSF) over a decade ago by the Indiana University Graduate Library School Research Center included a cartoon that showed a librarian and a publisher sitting in a single leaky rowboat. It is important that we remember, then as now, that when a boat sinks both ends of it go under water.

I suspect that I bring qualifications that are at least unusual to the examination of the issue. I come from library practice through a background of journal publishing (albeit secondary journals), and I have been president of a subscription agency. I have undertaken a number of

Paper presented at the Society for Scholarly Publishing Sixth Annual Top Management Round Table, Toronto, Ontario, Canada, 17 September 1987. Reprinted from *Scholarly Publishing* 19, no. 3 (April 1988):125–29.

economic analyses and research studies of the interaction of libraries and scholarly publishers for the National Science Foundation. Finally, as an academic administrator, I write and speak on the issue of library priorities in a political environment. My work has been extensively reported in the literature, through monographs, research articles in such publications as *Library Quarterly,* and expository articles in *Library Journal.* I will, therefore, not repeat what has already been published in great detail, but rather summarize these findings as a starting point for comments and discussion. It should be noted that many of the specific findings concerning funding difficulties in libraries, and in particular academic libraries, are now more than ten years old. However, the financial strains that had begun to be evident at that stage have now intensified, and the problems already evident then are now far greater.

Libraries do not control the decision about what journals to purchase. This is clearly understood by the marketing executives of scholarly publishing organizations, who tend to bypass the library with advertising literature in order to reach the ultimate users within the organization. It is also understood by those publishers who package their journals into ever more specific and narrow areas designed to attract what only may be an academic constituency of one user per institution, and who place considerable effort on impressing that one user through such tactics as the appointment of a prestigious advisory board, which in fact may or may not advise but certainly looks good on the masthead. We know that libraries do much of the buying of these journals, and for some titles virtually all the buying. However, libraries are not treated as if they were customers, and are not consulted in the development of marketing plans as customers normally might be. Librarians are considered to fulfill only the roles of purchasing agents.

Confronted by this power structure of publishers who bypass them completely to reach ultimate users perfectly willing to agree to the purchase of anything that they do not have to pay for, librarians have exhibited virtually no defense and no resistance. They have complained but done nothing about dual pricing structures affecting individual and library copies, or pricing structures in dollars for European journals that have no relationship to the reality of foreign exchange. They have even accepted the instruction that they must pay in dollars at an inflated price, even when (either directly or through a subscription agency) they could have done their own currency conversion. In short, libraries have done what they were told to do by an informal consortium of publishers and readers, with the latter caring little if at all about the financial pressures on the library. As unwilling to confront faculty members as publishers, libraries have adopted several somewhat dubious strategies. They have continued to plead with their own administrations for additional materials budget funds, even at the cost of abandoning all other initiatives in such areas as automation and bibliographic service. They have also plundered the monograph budget by transferring funds to the serials budget. In general, faculty members have supported and even encouraged such actions because cuts in the monograph budget are visible only in terms of individually requested book purchases. Serials cuts, by contrast, are highly visible and confrontational actions that librarians have not been willing to take.

Libraries have, of course, made some cuts in their own journal holdings. These have largely involved duplicate subscriptions, even where these have been the backbone of service availability. Libraries have also shown a greater reluctance to subscribe to new (and therefore untested) journals, a strategy publishers have effectively countered by tailoring these publications to the one key user who will, in each case, demand them. Libraries have little if any data on the use of journals, and what information they have is largely based on observation and instinct. In fact, when they attempt to gather hard data on the use of journals, faculty members become alarmed.

We know from NSF studies that library subscription decisions, cancellation decisions, and interlibrary-loan activities have little impact on personal subscription decisions, despite assertions by publishers that library copies depress individual ordering, and librarian counter-arguments that interlibrary loan spurs individual subscribing by identifying new titles for interested faculty members. In reality, neither happens. Libraries by and large order the journals they must order, and not those they found on interlibrary loan. Individuals subscribe to journals they know and like (the role of colleagues and teachers is far greater than the role of the library), and they cancel subscriptions because they no longer want to read the journal, perhaps because their own work area has changed. When individuals cancel a journal, they don't read it in the library, either. On rare occasions the loss of grant or contract funds, or changes in interpretation of spending policy, will lead to an individual cancellation, but the library plays no part in this process.

The number of scholarly journal titles to which libraries are expected to subscribe continues to grow. Natural selection and the pressures of the marketplace simply do not apply here. In part this process results from the phenomenon of front-end cash flow, which will protect even a marginal journal for a considerable period of time. By contrast, monographs can die quickly, and their death can discourage further monograph publishing. Old journals do not die, nor do they fade away. They simply continue along, except when, like amoebas, they split to form two journals.

Everything up to now has been a description of the existing process, and I could not blame publishers for wishing it could continue exactly as at present, because for them the process works. However, even mild and non-confrontational librarians are beginning to understand that this scenario cannot continue. They cannot request and obtain serials budget increases of 15 per cent and 20 per cent in an overall budget in which other things increase at the rate of inflation, or perhaps by 5 percent. The money is not there—and even if it were, there are too many other deferred priorities that librarians must address. Until and unless the funding basis for higher education and research changes, librarians will have to tie their serials budgets to 5 per cent increments, and publishers will have to understand that the goose has no more golden eggs to lay.

It will not be simple. Publication costs, I am told (and I have no reason to disbelieve), continue to rise at a rate greater than that of inflation. Currency exchange rates, which favoured the US dollar in the 1970s (something we enjoyed but never mentioned) are now sharply swinging in the opposite direction. This assists US publishers trying to sell in Europe; it creates problems for European publishers trying to sell in the United States. However, the simplistic strategy of passing along all increases from greater production costs and weaker dollars to the customer simply assumes that the customer has no option except to pay, and that will no longer be true because it can no longer be true. However, before publishers can adapt to this reality they must first adapt to an even more fundamental one—that of the librarian as the customer and not just as the purchasing agent who does what he or she is told to do.

Once this process begins, negotiations are now possible. I realize the publishers are examining alternative options for cost reduction, including electronic publishing, cheaper and more rapid approaches to the refereeing process, and less expensive (even if less attractive) alternatives for typesetting, justification, and the inclusion of illustrations. Librarians may be as reluctant to see a reduction in visible quality as anyone else because they also like attractive journals. However, if publishers and librarians discuss these questions, some acceptable middle ground can be found. At this moment publishers discuss these issues with nobody. Perhaps the scholars who serve as editors discuss them with their fellow scholars, but ultimately we must remember that these scholars do not really buy anything.

The issue of size and birth control must also be addressed. I have already noted that natural selection and the survival of the fittest do not work very well in journal publishing, because hardly any species die. And so we must find ways to kill the weakest, although that will not be easy because simply leaving cancellation decisions to the political process within the institution will not protect the best—only the biggest and loudest—and entire sub-disciplines might disappear from the publishing scene. We must also examine the relationship between price and size, and I realize that some publishers can make the case that, on a cost-per-page basis, the journals had not really increased 30 per cent in price, although the invoice would suggest so. I understand well enough why journals continue to grow. The literature grows, and each journal tries to cover its own turf completely to prevent the start of a new and competing journal. However, is meaningful scholarly communication really growing that rapidly, or are the journals simply a mechanism for feeding egos and tenure dossiers for multiple restatements of the same idea? What is the role of the refereeing process, with tough criteria from the publisher, in rejecting articles that contain a new title but no new ideas? Ultimately, if your customer does not want the product to grow larger if it means an increase in price, can the supplier continue to completely ignore that preference? Do Japanese automobile manufacturers ignore market surveys in designing next year's hatchback? Do they simply pass along to the customer the variations in currency exchange, or do they tighten their belts and absorb the bad news through more efficient production techniques and perhaps even lower profit margins?

I have raised far more questions than answers, and indeed I am not sure of what the answers are. However, I am quite sure of what the problem is. The problem is that unbridled growth in the number of publications, in their size, and in their price, with all of this then dumped on one pliant customer community, cannot work in the future. Not necessarily because librarians will become more assertive, although even that is possible, but because they simply will not be able to play the game. The process of unbridled and continued growth in scholarly publishing cannot work, because there is no growth in the resources of what continues to be the one and only customer community. Unless some planning and restraint enters this process, there is bound to be a bloodbath. I also know that some of my colleagues in publishing do not fear such a scenario, because they are confident that their journals will survive and prosper no matter what happens to other "weaker" journals. However, self-delusion has always been one of the risks of marketing, and some of the publishers are wrong.

What Price Salami? The Federal Process of Contracting Out Libraries

The use of contractors to perform parts of library operations is certainly not new. Such contracting can make sense based on a lower cost or a greater convenience, and libraries have for a long time had the option of paying their book vendors a higher premium to receive books with catalog cards, with spine labels, or with circulation pockets. The use of contractors to undertake special tasks of high effort but relatively short duration is also not unusual, because it avoids the need to add staff for a finite period.

A whole industry of supplying temporary staff has arisen in support of the premise that special needs are sometimes more effectively met through this process of contracting. It probably costs more than doing it yourself, but the extra cost may be worthwhile, or it may be the only option available. Libraries, like other management structures, have the option of using contract services at the two extremes of the spectrum—work that is so routine and mundane that we have better things to do with our own small staff, and work that is so specialized that we need to purchase unique skills for limited assignments.

ROUTINE BY ROTE

Corporate libraries, which sometimes operate under hiring freezes and head count ceilings that allow money to be spent but not people to be hired, have long used the avenue of contract services. The primary, and I would think most justifiable, emphasis has been on routine functions, such as photocopying. The absence of sufficient clerical staff (and clerical staff is usually much harder to justify than professional staff) makes this particularly attractive, because we already know that libraries are clerical traps in which the routine must be done ahead of the professional.

Some libraries have also contracted out professional and intellectual activities such as database searching and bibliographic compilation. This is something I would be far more reluctant to recommend from a political standpoint, unless the application is narrow and specific. An environment in which management thinks that the librarians do the routine and vendors do the unusual does not bode well for the librarians. At a minimum, if there are specialized intellectual contract services in our field, they should be hired, monitored, and paid by the librarian.

IDEOLOGY VS. COST EFFECTIVENESS

In one sense, this issue is nothing more than a variant of the old "make or buy" models with which business students are thoroughly familiar. The issue is not ideological, the issue is overall cost effectiveness. In an article written many years ago but still relevant ("Contract Services in the Special Library," *Special Libraries,* April 1973, p. 175–180), Herbert Landau discussed contracting options for librarians and examined scenarios in which this might be appropriate. He indicated that there might be advantages of cost, availability of specialized talent, convenience, quality, and the objective of making unemotional external decisions. He also stressed quite correctly that librarians using contractors must control the process, through performance objectives and measurement criteria clearly spelled out and administered.

I had a personal involvement with what was an example of contracting out an entire information operation. When Melvin Day developed the NASA Scientific and Technical Information Program in the early 1960s, he opted for an operation run by a contractor rather than a staff of government employees. His reasons were a perception of greater flexibility in hiring and firing based on competence, and greater opportunities for innovation because, for the contractor, risks also carried rewards.

The process worked well, at least in these early years for NASA, because the space agency maintained control over goals, objectives, the formulation of specific plans and strategies, and even the delineation of specific tasks. There were frequent meetings at which the agency supervisory staff and the contractor operating personnel discussed not only specific activities, but directions for future planning and service potential.

Reward and punishment mechanisms were devised that measured not just cost but time response, quality of service, innovation, and continuing development. Cost was a factor, but the reason for contracting was not economy but the hope of a better functioning operation. It was called a Scientific and Technical Information Facility, but I, as its executive director, certainly knew it was a library. The premise so innovatively created by Day worked. It is now generally recognized that in the mid-1960s the information programs at the National Library of Medicine and at NASA were at the forefront of the development of information services.

SOMETHING ISN'T KOSHER

This contract succeeded because overall control remained in the contracting agency, and the agency retained and even recruited a staff of professionals qualified to specify for the contractor what he was to do, and to make sure he did it. The lesson in this for federal agencies now considering the contracting option should be clear. It is indeed possible that the use of contractors can, under carefully controlled circumstances, improve performance.

It can even reduce cost, but cost reductions outside the context of qualitative evaluations are meaningless. Any intelligent grade school student is smart enough to respond that if I pose a scenario in which I suggest that store A sells salami for $2 and store B sells it for $3 and then ask which is the better buy, I have not provided enough information to answer the question. How much salami for that price? What grade salami? Imported salami? Kosher salami?

It seems clear to me that if government agencies decide, for political or economic reasons (generally it is the former because the appearance of economy in government is more important than actual economy), to contract out all or part of library operations, they can probably dispense with clerks and junior professionals on the government payroll, but is it a good idea? The cost may or may not be smaller and that may be important, but mechanisms must also be devised to assure the quality of work.

What these agencies must retain is the cadre of professional librarian managers to establish goals and objectives, specify contract provisions, select the contractor, monitor performance, and reward or punish accordingly. And of course, this is precisely what has *not* happened.

INTO THE HANDS OF ACCOUNTANTS

The process has been placed in the hands of accountants who may understand cost but not professional performance evaluation, and may not even realize that there is professional performance to be evaluated. Nor need they understand, but it is important that they recognize their own ignorance.

I have recently looked, primarily from morbid curiosity, at some of the requests for proposals, or RFPs, issued for the operation of federal libraries. Some are major information centers, some are small and scattered locations such as prison libraries. All look, to this writer, like pure garbage, because they measure libraries as a series of quantified activities, and not by results achieved in information use. It is not the first time this has occurred.

A number of years ago one of the military services put out an RFP for a large quantity of dictionaries. It specified only cost and number of terms included, and it was revised only after it was pointed out that what was being demanded was simply a cheap dictionary, not necessarily a useful dictionary. In fact, the specifications as written virtually guaranteed that the winning bid would be for a poor dictionary.

ACHIEVEMENT-BASED RESULTS

Cheap libraries, like cheap dictionaries, are not necessarily worth the money, and ultimately governmental concerns ought to be not with cost, but with cost effectiveness. This in turn requires a concentration not on the mechanical processes performed in a library (circulation, books cataloged, periodical issues checked in), but on the results to be achieved as these serve the needs of our users. And yet it is mechanical tasks that are specified in the contract, without a competent qualitative evaluation.

How do we define and describe the information services needed by our users in a contract document? As I noted in an earlier article ("The Use and Misuse of Library User Studies," LJ, December 1985, p. 70–71), we are at fault by allowing the process of user communication to degenerate into determining what they ask for, rather than what they want and, most importantly, what they need. By allowing this to happen we have lost control over our libraries, and that is a catastrophe for our users.

To deal with needs requires a development of library objectives based on the objectives and activities of the organization we are chartered to serve. This is of course program budgeting, and everybody in Washington is in favor of program budgeting. They just don't know it also applies to libraries.

In the absence of a clear determination of what a good library needs to do, as determined by competent librarians at every stage of the process, we cannot really have adequate contracting. Contractors may or may not have qualified librarians on the staff, but the contractors do not make policy, they work to specifications spelled out in the contract. It is this focus on what is to be done, rather than on the question of whether internal or external staffing is to be used, that is at issue. Both approaches can provide high-quality information services. Both can provide poor service, and that becomes far more expensive in the long run, because in the absence of an adequate library only two scenarios are possible. Organizations either end up spending yet more compensating for the lack of library service, although that cost may be hidden. Alternatively, they make ignorant and uninformed decisions, and who knows what that ultimately costs?

AN APPEARANCE OF ECONOMY

Contracting may or may not be economical or, more importantly, cost effective. The answer will depend on many variables. In that search for effective information systems, slogans, or catchword commitments to "privatization" only serve to mislead us, because they point us toward conclusions before we have facts, and to an appearance of economy no matter what the real cost. Does contracting of government libraries provide a more cost-effective alternative? I can only respond with a dogmatic "sometimes."

Peter Drucker, in so many of his writings, points out the dangers we face. He notes that service organizations such as libraries tend to be measured by what they spend rather than by what they accomplish, and we must deal with that problem first of all. It is likely that good libraries, whether run by an in-house staff or by a competent and professionally monitored contractor, are more expensive than poor libraries. If dollars are all that we measure, then we almost inevitably drift toward lower quality, and this nation can't afford that sort of false economy. What price salami?

INDEX

A

Access to Library Materials, 270–80, 288–92, 309–10
Accreditation, 21–27
ACRL. *See* American Library Association of College and Research Libraries
Alaska Health Sciences Information Center, 257
American Library Association. American Association of School Librarians (AASL), 101–2
American Library Association. Association of College and Research Libraries, 44
American Library Association. Committee on Accreditation (COA), 21–29, 53, 93–94
American Society for Information Science (ASIS), 114
Anderla, Georges, 234, 307
Anderson, Arthur (A.J.), 224
Association for Library and Information Science Education (ALISE), 53
Association of Research Libraries (ARL), 34, 82, 126, 356
AT&T, 306
Auerbach Associates, 146, 305
Authority (of managers), 209

B

Baker, Dale, 234
Ballard, Thomas, 297
Basic Competencies, 31–42
Belker, Loren, 105, 218
Bell, Daniel, 124, 233, 304
Benefit. *See* Cost Effectiveness
Bernstein, Leonard, 154
Berry, John, 180
Bidlack, Russell, 21
Boorstin, Daniel, 302–3
Bowen, Otis, 49
Bradford, Samuel, 330
Brinberg, Herbert, 147, 285, 311
Buckland, Michael, 33
Budgeting, 141–42, 200, 272, 340–47, 358–66
Bundy, Mary Lee, 330
Burchinal, Lee, 234, 307

C

Callison, Daniel, 45
Canada Institute for Scientific and Technical Information, 140
Canadian Library Association, 123–44, 171
Carlyle, Thomas, 290
Carnegie Corporation, 51
Carpenter, Ray, 7
Cataloging, 184–88
Chemical Abstracts Service, 234
Clements, John, 211
COA. *See* American Library Association. Committee on Accreditation

Coca Cola Company, 201
Coleman, Earl, 193
Collins, Eliza, 226
Commission on New Technological Uses of Copyrighted Works (CONTU), 251, 277
Conant, Ralph, 51
Consultative Management, 159–64
Continuing Education, 43–50, 69–70, 79–80, 169–70
Contracting of Libraries, 372–76
Corporate Libraries. *See* Special Librarianship
Cost Effectiveness, 340–47
Council on Library Resources (CLR), 34, 82
Credentialing, 167 *See also* Library Education
Curriculum. *See* Library Education Curriculum

D

Dana, John C., 176
Day, Melvin, 373
De Gennaro, Richard, 277, 296
Debons, Anthony, 31
Decisions (making of), 217
Dewey, Melvil, 211
Drucker, Peter, xv, xvi, 89, 106, 150, 177–78, 194, 196–97, 200–201, 204, 216, 219, 311, 315, 359–60, 364

E

Education. *See* Library Education
Education, Department of. *See* US Department of Education
Effectiveness. *See* Cost Effectiveness
Entrepreneurship, 189–206

F

Finances. *See* Library Finances
Fry, Bernard, xiv, 320
Funding. *See* Budgeting

G

Galvin, Thomas, 107, 198, 271, 278

Garfield, Eugene, 193
General Electric Company, 284
Goodman, Ellen, 225
Gresham's Law, 23, 39, 88, 97, 180
Grohman, Robert, 194

H

Hannigan, Jane, 77
Hedberg, Bo, 198–99, 219, 363
Herner, Saul, 193
Hewlett Packard Corporation, 205
Hite, Shere, 225
Holley, Edward, 23
Holm, Bart, 121
Hughes, Howard, 189

I

IBM Corporation, 124, 190, 192, 200, 208, 306
Illiteracy. *See* Literacy Programs
Indiana University. School of Library and Information Science, 35, 47, 133, 235, 271, 319, 354, 367
Information Analysis Centers, 242
Information in Society, 304–12
Institute for Scientific Information (ISI), 291
Interlibrary Loan, 274–80, 283, 293–98
International Federation of Library Associations (IFLA), 123
Internships (in Library Education), 78
Intrapreneurship, 189–206
Iran. Pahlavi National Library, 274

J

Japanese Management Styles, 162–63
Jefferson, Thomas, 125
Jobs, Steven, 190
Journals, 247–69, 319–39, 354–57, 367–71

K

Kaser, David, 10, 126

Kent, Allen, 271, 278
King Research, Inc, 38, 52
Koenig, Michael, 36
Kramer, Joseph, 121

L

Ladd, Everett, 147, 229
Landau, Herbert, 373
Lane, Nancy, 8, 13
Leadership, 207–12
Levine, Kenneth, 174
Library Education, 34, 84–92
Library Education Curriculum, 51–83
Library Financing, 148–49, 315–39
Library Materials Budgets, 134
Library Networks and Consortia, 333–35
Library of Congress. See U.S. Library of Congress
Library Practice Work, 78
Library Research, 16–18
Library School Students, 72–73
Library Service to Children, 174
Library Service to the Aging, 174
Library User Studies, 281–87
Library Users, 134–48, 233–66, 288–92, 299–303
Literacy Programs, 174
Longfellow, Henry, 170

M

MacLeish, Archibald, 190
Management Justifications and Communications, 123–44
Management Styles. See Consultative Management, Participative Management
Marketing of Libraries, 141–42, 177–78
Marx, Karl, 294
Matarazzo, James, 150, 361
Medical Library Association, 48, 70, 80, 96
Miller, Wharton, xiii
Mooers, Calvin, 240, 286, 289, 306
Munn, Robert, 134

N

National Aeronautics and Space Administration (NASA). See U.S. National Aeronautics and Space Administration
National Commission on Libraries and Information Services. See U.S. National Commission on Libraries and Information Services
National Council for Accreditation of Teacher Education (NCATE), 101–2
National Federation of Abstracting and Indexing Services (NFAIS), 237
National Library of Medicine. See U.S. National Library of Medicine
National Library Week, 165, 179–83
National Science Foundation. See U.S. National Science Foundation
Newark Public Library, 176
Neyland, Robert, 85

O

OCLC, 186, 275, 336
Office of Personnel Management. See U.S. Office of Personnel Management
Organizational Placement, 117–22
Organizational Politics. See Political Process

P

Paris, Marion, 45–46, 97
Parkinson, C. Northcote, 177, 317
Participative Management, 159–64
Periodicals. See Journals
Perot, Ross, 190
Peter, Laurence, 210, 213–14
Pinchot, Gifford, 193, 205
Pittsburgh, University of, 243, 271
Political Processes, 145–53, 171–78, 299–303

Possum, Pogo, 351
Postmasters Studies (Library Education), 66
Practice Work. *See* Library Practice Work
Price, Derek, 305
Pricing. *See* Publishers
Proposition Thirteen, 172
Public Libraries, 171–78
Publishers, 247–69, 319–39, 354–57, 367–71

R

RAND Corporation, 146, 305
Research. *See* Library Research
Responsibility (of managers), 209
Rickover, Hyman, 195–96

S

Salaries, 89, 348–53
Scholarly Journals. *See* Journals
School Libraries, 100
Self-Respect, 165–70, 299–303
Service and Self-Service, 110, 126–27
Shapiro, George, 136, 240
Special Librarianship, 109–16, 145–53, 340–47, 358–67
Special Libraries Association, 45, 114–15, 176
Specialization Tracks (in Library Education), 76–77, 93–97
Strauch, Helena, 192
Supervision, 213–21

T

Taube, Mortimer, 193
Training (as opposed to education), 33
Trueswell, Richard, 229, 271, 278, 290
Turf (management of), 99–102, 154–58, 166, 299–303
Turner, Ted, 189

U

U. S. Department of Education, 41
U. S. Department of Education. Educational Resources Information Center (ERIC), 129
U. S. Library of Congress, 190
U. S. National Aeronautics and Space Administration (NASA), 31, 112–13, 239, 289, 291, 373–74
U. S. National Commission on Libraries and Information Services (NCLIS), 168
U. S. National Library of Medicine, 113, 239, 374
U. S. National Science Foundation, 247, 250–51, 271, 307, 319, 354–55, 367–68
U. S. Office of Management and Budget (OMB), 372
U. S. Office of Personnel Management (OPM), 32, 38–39, 85, 167
Undergraduate Library Education, 74–75, 86, 90
Users. *See* Library Users.

V

Van House, Nancy, 53
Veaner, Allen, 283, 293
Vickery, Brian, 135

W

Wall Street Journal, 292
Ward, Artemus, 145
Wasserman, Paul, 330
Watson, Thomas Jr., 190, 192–93, 200, 205
Webster, Daniel, 145
Weinberg, Alvin, 242
Westat Research, Inc., 294
White House Conference on Libraries and Information Service, 176, 302
Williams, Martha, 234, 307
Williamson, Charles (C.C.), 51
Wilson, Pauline, 15
Wilson, W. Randall, 175
Women in Librarianship, 222–26

Z

Zucker, William, 193

ABOUT THE AUTHOR

Herbert S. White received degrees in chemistry from the College of the City of New York and in library science from Syracuse University. After joining the Library of Congress as an intern and working in its technical information division, he assumed increasing management responsibility in library and technical information work for the Atomic Energy Commission and Chance Vought Aircraft. He served as program manager of the IBM Corporate Technical Information Center, executive director of the NASA Scientific and Technical Information Facility, vice president of Documentation Incorporated, senior vice president of the Institute for Scientific Information, and president of Stechert Macmillan. In 1975 he came to Indiana University library education as a professor and director of the Research Center for Library and Information Science, and became dean of the school in 1980.

Professionally active and visible, he has served as president of both the Special Libraries Association and the American Society for Information Science, treasurer of the International Federation for Documentation, as board member for both the American Federation of Information Processing Societies and the Society for Scholarly Publishing, and on the Council of the American Library Association. He has served on the Department of Education's Advisory Committee for Title II of the Higher Education Act, and the Department of Commerce Committee to advise on the management of the National Technical Information Service. He is the author of more than 150 articles ranging from scholarly research investigations to regular columns entitled "White Papers" in *Library Journal* and "Research and Reality" in *American Libraries,* and is the author or editor of five books.

Herbert White has been honored by the American Society for Information Science with its Award of Merit, Watson Davis Award, and by being named to the first group of Society Pioneers; by the Special Libraries Association through its Professional Award and election as an SLA Fellow; and by the American Library Association through presentation of the Melvil Dewey Medal. He is the first recipient of the Distinguished Alumni Award presented by the Syracuse University School of Information Studies.

He is the author of three other books published by G. K. Hall, including "Managing the Special Library," "Library Personnel Management," and "Education for Professional Librarians." His publication awards have included three Special Libraries Association Best Papers of the Year, two research paper awards from units of the American Library Association, and the American Society for Information Science Book of the Year selection.